Children and the Internet

Children and the Internet

Great Expectations, Challenging Realities

Sonia Livingstone

polity

First published in 2009 by Polity Press

Polity Press
65 Bridge Street
Cambridge CB2 1UR, UK

Polity Press
350 Main Street
Malden, MA 02148, USA

ISBN-13: 978-0-7456-3194-3
ISBN-13: 978-0-7456-3195-0 (pb)

A catalogue record for this book is available from the British Library.

Typeset in 10.5 on 12 pt Times
by SNP Best-set Typesetter Ltd, Hong Kong
Printed and bound in Great Britain by MPG Books Group

The publisher has used its best endeavours to ensure that the URLs for external websites referred to in this book are correct and active at the time of going to press. However, the publisher has no responsibility for the websites and can make no guarantee that a site will remain live or that the content is or will remain appropriate.

Every effort has been made to trace all copyright holders, but if any have been inadvertently overlooked the publishers will be pleased to include any necessary credits in any subsequent reprint or edition.

For further information on Polity, visit our website: www.politybooks.com

Contents

Preface

When I was a child growing up in the 1960s, the typical British family had one television with three channels, the phone was in a hallway or street corner, bedrooms were cold and forbidden in the day time, living rooms were formal and ruled by parental wishes, books came from the library, sums were calculated with a slide rule, and computers existed only in science fiction. Many will recognize this picture. For much of the world, it is already privileged. But for today's youth, it's a forgotten history.

Nowadays, at least in wealthy parts of the world, children live wholly surrounded by media of one kind and another. In the UK, four fifths (79%) of 7–16 year olds have internet access at home, and over half (53%) of even 5–6 year olds now go online; moreover, among 5–16 year olds, 37 percent have access in their own room (this including 26% of 5–10 year olds, rising to 57% of 15–16 year olds). Further, among 5–16 year olds, 77 per cent have a television in their bedroom (56% have multi-channel), 73 per cent have a mobile phone, 69 per cent have their own DVD player, MP3 player, radio and games console, while 55 per cent have their own PC or laptop (ChildWise, 2009; see also Ofcom 2008c).

The media landscape is far more commercialized than when I was a child, and now operates more on a transnational than a national scale. Indeed, 'mass' communication may seem almost an obsolete concept, transformed by the growth of interactive, personalized, mobile and social media. Convergence is making it harder even to distinguish different media and information forms as they intersect and hybridize, converging not only texts and technologies but also everyday social habits and practices and, further, the social institutions and governance structures that regulate the conditions of children's lives.

These are not just changes in technology, in the consumption of stuff – they are changes in the patterns of, and possibilities for, almost every aspect of our lives. When I went home from school, I re-entered a symbolic space defined by my parents' values, unable *easily* to stay in touch with my friends. But I could escape to my bedroom, and I could go out – the world was not a scary place.

In this book, I argue that changes in the media landscape – especially the advent of widespread internet use – have altered the opportunities and risks experienced by children and young people. And, even more importantly, I argue that changes in the social landscape alter the ways that children and young people use the media to connect and communicate with each other, with parents and other adults, and with the wider world. Also pertinent to our understanding of children and the internet are the historical and cultural shifts in youth culture, consumer culture and the growing children's market, and the domestication and privatization of leisure – consider the twentieth century transformation of the home into multiple personalized spaces of identity.

Society is positioning the internet as providing new routes not just to entertainment but also to education, workplace skills, civic participation, global connection and more. Children's uses of the internet have, therefore, wider implications than for any previous medium, even television, since the advent of the printed book and the rise of mass literacy. The commensurate rise of media and internet-related literacies will prove a major theme in my account of the opportunities afforded by the internet.

While academics and policymakers deliberate over the best way to maximize opportunities and minimize risk, children and young people are simply getting on with it – for them, these are welcome changes. The media are with them all the time – on their person, in their pockets and their ears, embedded – or part of the wallpaper – in most spaces they enter, whether public or private. And they are delighted that it is so – they could not imagine life without the media, turning on the television or internet the minute they wake up or come home, falling asleep with their iPod or mobile phone by their pillow. For the 'always on', 'constantly connected', 'digital' generation, it seems that few experiences now go unmediated, whether in the sphere of leisure or education, relations with peers or connection with their neighbourhood and beyond.

To ground my analysis, I hope to convey the enthusiasm, the richness and diversity, indeed the very texture of children and young people's experiences with the internet. For the past fifteen years, I have been researching – interviewing, observing, listening to, surveying – children and young people about their engagement with old and new media. Most of the empirical work included in this book draws on the ESRC-funded 'UK Children Go Online' (UKCGO)[1] project I directed, though I began working on children and the internet when British Telecom commissioned my in-depth study of thirty British families between 1999 and 2001. I next directed the 'EU Kids Online' project (2006–9), funded by the European Commission's Safer Internet *plus* programme.[2] And Knut Lundby's 'Mediatized Stories' project at the University of Oslo provided the opportunity for the social networking study – interviews and observations with teenagers in 2007.

Beyond listening closely to children's voices and experiences, a critical framework is also vital. One starting point is to observe the considerable anxieties associated with children's internet use which are widespread among social scientists, policymakers, the mass media and, of course, among the public. In the academic literature, such moral panics have been roundly critiqued for scapegoating new media so as to deflect public attention from the real problems in society and for attempting middle class control over working class pleasures, thus denying the agency, responsibility and general good sense of the public – including children.

It seems that when the debates over children's media get polarized and emotive, it is because 'the child' or 'childhood' has become a stand-in for something else – a means of articulating anxieties about Western capitalism. Often, these are debates about tradition, authority or respect for shared values, or about the balance between individualism and participation. In some circles, questions about children's protection and human dignity are 'heard' as elitist or moralizing or as an argument against adult freedom of expression and hence a covert move towards censorship, and given worldwide moves towards state control of the internet, of course one must recognize the force of this position.

But where does this leave children? What media and communication environment can and should be provided for them? Clearly, a critical rejection of both moral panics and the technological determinism they imply does not permit us to conclude, as some misguidedly do, that the media play no significant role in children's lives. But asking such questions demands engagement with a normative agenda, a direction not all researchers would follow, perhaps depending on the political climate in which they work. Recently, it seems that academic research has taken a normative turn, that evidence-based policy is expected and respected, and that academic collaboration with diverse stakeholders – including government, policymakers, industry, regulators and civil society actors – is cautiously welcome. In the UK, the wide-ranging deliberations that informed the UK Government's review of children and new technology (Byron, 2008) illustrate the point. Arguably, then, being 'expert' on children and the internet, it is incumbent on the research community to ensure that good research reaches those stakeholders who might act on it, especially if the outcome supports children's interests. Readers may judge whether the evidence I present justifies my conclusions, to which end I have sought to distinguish one from the other in writing this book.

My guiding principle, as signalled by the book's subtitle, is to understand why, so often, empirical findings suggest many children are not, or are not yet, enjoying the great expectations held out for them. I do not advocate that the internet represents the solution to all their problems – indeed, a theme running through this book is the identification of the many other factors shaping children's opportunities. But, to the extent that society appears willing to invest in online provision for children, whether through public investment or the market, it is surely worth thinking through how this provision could benefit children, bringing their actual experiences closer to the high hopes that many, rightly, have for them.

Every few years the newest trend attracts headlines, reshuffles expectations, wrong-foots adult observers and revives perennial anxieties. One constant is that it is children, young people and their families who tend to be in the vanguard of these new online activities, and so popular and policy interest in children and the internet remains intense, as does the need for rigorous empirical research. The result is an unfolding and fascinating interplay among technological innovators, ambivalent governments, big business, creative children and worried parents, as well as academic researchers seeking to track and interpret these unfolding trends.

Many of these trends, on close reflection, turn out to concern not only changes in technology but also, more fundamentally, changes in contemporary childhood. These, too, are now attracting widespread public attention. In the UK, the past year or so saw the Risk Commission's report on 'Risk and Childhood' (Madge and Barker, 2007) and 'The Good Childhood Enquiry' (Layard and Dunn, 2009), this latter following up on the huge international interest attracted by UNICEF's (2007) report, 'Child Poverty in Perspective: An overview of child well-being in rich countries', which placed the UK – closely followed by the USA – at the bottom of a league table of twenty-one wealthy countries. Concerns over children's wellbeing periodically reach the top of the agenda in many countries worldwide, bringing into focus another series of changes since the childhood of today's adults, those who are making the decisions about, worrying about, the lives of children today.

When I was a teenager, most teenagers in Britain left school aged 15 or 16 and began earning; few went to university. Now nearly all stay in school till 18, nearly half go to university, and they're still living at home through their twenties. In other words, it would appear that childhood is lasting longer. Further, as adults are fond of recalling, forty years ago, children packed their cheese sandwiches and headed off on their own for the day. Today, faced with anxieties about streets, parks, even the swimming pool, home seems safer. To occupy children at home, many parents – rich and poor – seek to fill their homes with media. To give children and parents some privacy, ever more media are located in children's bedrooms. To keep them in touch with friends, parents provide mobile phones and domestic internet access. If they are worried, guilty, rushed for time or flush with cash, the media – in one way or another – provide a ready answer, seemingly less the problem than the solution.

It is the conditions of childhood, and the ways they are changing, then, that demand critical attention before we can ask how the internet is fitting into children's lives, for these shape the meaning and consequences of internet use. This, therefore, is where chapter 1 begins. In the chapters that follow, I address key themes regarding children's relations to the internet, drawing on my recent writings and research findings. Thus I integrate and rework published and new material so as to offer a coherent and multifaceted analysis of children's engagement with the internet.[3] Since this book is empirically grounded, I acknowledge that it reflects the UK experience more than others, but the analysis is informed as far as possible by an international though still largely Western research literature.

Acknowledgements

It has been a pleasure, over the years, to work with some great colleagues – Magdalena Bober, Moira Bovill, David Brake, Leslie Haddon, Ellen Helsper, Andrea Millwood Hargrave, Uwe Hasebrink, Andrea Press, Panayiota Tsatsou and many wonderful colleagues from the EU Kids Online network, the Internet Watch Foundation and the Department of Media and Communications at LSE, as well as the committed international community of scholars concerned with children, young people and the internet: I have valued their conversation, their collaboration and their criticism.

I also thank Keri Facer, Sara Grimes, Dafna Lemish, Maggie Scammell and Elisabeth Staksrud for critiquing draft chapters during the writing process. And I thank my colleagues at LSE who allowed me the time off to work on this book, Yinhan Wang who assiduously tracked down my missing references, Todd Motto who tidied up my messy text, and John Thompson and Andrea Drugan at Polity Press who have been remarkably patient in waiting for its final appearance.

Many children, young people, parents, youth workers, content providers, regulators and teachers generously gave their time while I asked numerous questions, hung out in their homes and bedrooms and dropped into their classrooms and offices. I thank them all warmly. My parents have remained encouraging and engaged in my work long since my childhood in those days before the internet. My own children, expert and eloquent members of the digital generation, have had to answer more questions than any – Joe and Anna, I hope you think this was worth it! And for Peter, who offered constructive advice on my tangled arguments along with endless cups of tea, no amount of thanks can ever be enough.

1

Changing Childhood, Changing Media

In the past decade or so, almost every question long asked about society – about the nature of work, education, community, politics, family and identity – has been asked of the relation between society and the internet. Whether the internet is seen as the instigator or the consequence of social change, and whether it is seen as offering the potential for societal improvement or as introducing a new agenda of problems, the very breadth of questions asked and the multidisciplinary expertise already applied to answering them sets a daunting challenge to any attempt to review the present state of knowledge. The same may be said even for that subset of this emerging field of inquiry concerned with children and young people. For it is also the case that almost every question ever asked about children and young people – how they learn, play, interact, participate, encounter risks – has also been asked of the relation between childhood and the internet.

To focus on children may seem a specialized enterprise, even one that is somehow optional for the wider effort to understand the relation between society and the internet. Many pronouncements about 'the population' or 'society' and the internet turn out to refer to adults only, as if children constitute an exception. Yet not only do those younger than eighteen years old comprise one in five of 'the population' in developed countries (and nearly half of those in developing countries), but also every one of tomorrow's adults is a child today. Children's experiences, needs and concerns matter in their own right, requiring a critical analysis in the present. And, requiring an equally critical but also a more normative lens, they matter for the future. Since they are, with some justification, popularly dubbed the 'digital generation', it is also likely that understanding children's use of the internet can provide a richer insight into that future than could equivalent attention paid to adults.

At the same time, research on children and the internet is indeed a specialized enterprise. Children should not be 'lumped in' with the adult population, though nor should differences between children and adults be routinely presumed. Thus, research must attend carefully to questions of age and development; it requires methodological sensitivity if it is to explore children's experiences, and it should address some specialized questions regarding parenting, schooling, identity expression and risk-taking. Yet the same broad, multidisciplinary framework required to understand society and the internet is also required to understand children and the internet. In seeking to understand how children learn, laugh, interact, participate and encounter risks online, this book must draw on theories of learning, leisure, communication, participation and the risk society – just as is the case when investigating adults' use of the internet. The payoff is that one may then understand the continuities and differences between adult and child experiences, in empirical and theoretical terms, and one may identify the implications of the activities of this so-called digital generation both for children in particular and for society in general.

Also distinctive to the focus on children is the high degree of public attention, speculation and contestation that the particular combination of children, media and social change attracts. Children and young people are widely perceived, on the one hand, as the youthful experts or pioneers leading the way in using the internet and yet, on the other hand, as peculiarly vulnerable to the risks consequent on failing to use it wisely. This book draws on a range of original empirical sources to examine how young people are striking a balance between maximizing opportunities and minimizing risks as they explore the internet. As we shall see, despite considerable enthusiasm for going online and becoming 'youthful experts', children and young people (like many adults) are finding that access and motivation are necessary but insufficient for using the internet in a complex and ambitious manner. First, there is only qualified evidence that the internet is bringing about any of the changes anticipated; the great expectations are not always met. Second, the emerging picture stresses the variable and complex social conditions that influence how we fit the internet into our lives, these strongly mediating any consequences for work, education, community, politics, family and identity; the realities of internet use can be genuinely challenging.

The polarized public debate that surrounds questions of children and the internet – does the internet make for any change at all or not, does the internet make things better or worse, are children media-savvy experts or newly vulnerable and at risk – inevitably invites a plethora of empirically grounded qualifications of the 'it depends' or 'both/and' variety. The result is an explosion of empirical studies which are largely descriptive, charting first access to the internet and then use of the internet across countries and, within countries, by age, gender, class and so forth, in a wide variety of circumstances. Arguably, this initial agenda has run its course (Lievrouw, 2004; Livingstone, 1999, 2003; Wellman, 2004). Now the challenge is to theorize people's, including children's, engagement with the internet more thoroughly, asking, for example, not who lacks access to the internet but whether it really matters; not simply noting who participates in online forums but identifying whether and how this contributes to civic participation; not simply worrying about the risks children encounter online but asking what is meant by online risk and how it relates to offline risk; not simply asking whether children have the skills to engage with the internet but whether these enable them to engage with their society in all its manifestations – local and global, public and private, serious and playful, enchanting and dangerous.

But clearly, this emerging set of questions widens the focus considerably, encompassing not only children as internet users but also the internet as a mediator of children's participation in society. What do we hope for children in this regard? The following two contrasting quotations, the first from the UK's media and communications regulator, the second from an academic critic, pinpoint my starting point in this book:

> Through confident use of communications technologies people will gain a better understanding of the world around them and be better able to engage with it. (Ofcom, 2004b: para 3)

> Despite the growth in the numbers of internet users, a rather small minority of these users has the capability to use the internet in ways that are creative and that augment their ability to participate effectively in today's knowledge societies. (Mansell, 2004: 179)

As I shall argue, it is vital both to frame ambitious expectations for society and the internet, including for children and the internet but, also, it is vital to draw on rigorous empirical research to assess and critique claims that these ambitions are being realized. In other words, although as we shall see there is a considerable and growing body of evidence pointing to a substantial gap between the great expectations held out for the internet and the present realities of people's experiences, it is not my intention to use the latter simply to dampen the ambitions of the former. Of course, to the extent that the internet is mooted as a quick technological fix to solve endemic problems in society, such hopes can only be disappointed. But, after the first decade or so of theory and research investigating the social shaping and social consequences of the internet in the lives of children, families and communities, we can surely identify some lessons from the recent past and some guidance for the future regarding how best to reformulate society's ambitions for children and the internet and, thereby, better meet some of its present challenges.

To undertake this task, one could begin in either of two places. Many start with 'the internet'. Here, one may discern that research, especially that conducted in developed countries, is shifting its focus from questions of access and diffusion to questions about the nature and quality of internet use, recognizing the diverse ways in which people are struggling to come to terms with this complex and changing bundle of technologies that, supposedly, can deliver new opportunities for information, communication, entertainment or even, more grandly, 'empower' them in relation to identity, community, participation, creativity and democracy. This starting point has produced much valuable research that I shall review in the chapters that follow. But it also leads us into difficulties. 'The internet' tends to be positioned as the key agent of change, encouraging questions about its 'impact' on society as if it had recently landed from Mars, masking the crucial importance of other ongoing changes in society, including those that are shaping the internet itself. As society expects more and more of the internet, the notion of 'using' the internet has become so unclear as to be wholly unhelpful as a description of an everyday activity. Moreover, this approach tends to position children as 'users', a new category of person with little history or cultural meaning, to be understood for itself and thus inadvertently divorced from such rival categories as family member, school pupil, young citizen or new consumer.

Instead, I shall start with 'children', understood both socially – through their positioning within and engagement with societal structures of home, family, school and community – and historically, for childhood is itself changing, and these changes have a far longer provenance and more widespread implications than any changes associated with the recent mass adoption of the internet, notable though these may be. My purpose in this chapter to identify the key currents of thought and debate that can contextualize a critical analysis of children and the internet so as to overcome the limitations of a technologically determinist approach and to open up a richer account of how and why the internet has come to occupy so much of children's time and attention by understanding what else is going on in their lives.[1]

Change and crisis in the post-traditional family

In popular discourse, children are staying younger longer, yet getting older sooner. It seems to many that, in some ways, they leave the safety and privacy of the home and enter the public and commercial world 'too soon'; in other ways they delay taking on adult responsibilities for 'too long'. While the sense of golden-age nostalgia in these discourses, along with the moral criticism of young people thereby implied, may be questioned, it is the case that historians and sociologists of childhood report strong evidence for significant social changes in childhood over the twentieth century. Following an earlier shift away from children having a productive role in the household and the wider economy (Cunningham, 1995; Cunningham, 2006), in recent decades Western industrial societies have seen the extension of formal education from early to late teens and a commensurate rise in the average age of leaving home, this pushing back the start of employment and delaying the traditional markers of adulthood. In many countries over recent decades, post-16 education has expanded while the youth labour market has remained stagnant, altering the school-to-work transition (France, 2007). The result is an unprecedented period of 'extended youth' in which young people stay at home and remain financially dependent on their parents for longer.

These historical changes to childhood over the past century or more have themselves been shaped by a series of profound social changes in, notably but not only, the structures of employment, the education system, increased urbanization, relations between commerce and the state, the growth of affluent individualism, the transformation of gender relations, the ethnic diversification of national populations and the reconstruction of household and family. These structural changes are repositioning children within society and altering, even impeding, their passage to adulthood (Hill and Tisdall, 1997; James, Jenks and Prout, 1998). As Coontz observes:

> In some ways, childhood has actually been prolonged, if it is measured by dependence on parents and segregation from adult activities. What many young people have lost are clear paths for gaining experience doing responsible, socially necessary work, either in or out of the home, and for moving away from parental supervision without losing contact with adults. (1997: 13)

6   Changing Childhood, Changing Media

At the same time, these same structural changes have also enabled the world outside the home to make increasing incursions into what was once a private, largely non-commercial space defined by tradition and community norms. Ever younger children are now immersed in a consumer culture which emphasizes choice, taste and lifestyle as considerations not just for adults but also for children. The growth and scale of today's child and youth market is equally unprecedented, being not only highly lucrative but also creative in its specialized targeting of young people and, moreover, highly sexualized in its framing of identity and sociality (Kenway and Bullen, 2001). As shown in research by the UK's National Consumer Council (Nairn, Ormond and Bottomley, 2007), 34 per cent of 9–13 year olds would 'rather spend time buying things than doing almost anything else' and 46 per cent say, 'the only kind of job I want when I grow up is one that gets me a lot of money'.

As youth culture has come to fill the growing space between childhood and adulthood, the result is children and young people's growing autonomy in the realms of leisure, consumption, sexuality, appearance, identity, rights and participation (Osgerby, 1998).[2] Pressures towards independence and dependence are, in short, in tension with each other psychologically (hence the 'discovery' of adolescence and the teenager as fraught life-stages in conflict with adults; Abrams, 1959; Erikson, 1959/1980; France, 2007), socially (hence the notion of the 'generation gap' and its associated social conflicts) and historically (hence the sense that these are new problems and the adult nostalgia for the established traditions of hierarchy, authority and respect for one's 'elders and betters'). Further tensions also exist – the new youth market is largely funded by parents rather than by any growth in youth employment; efforts to increase youth participation now anticipate the voting age; protections for legal minors seem to constrain teenage rights (in relation to sexual experience, for example). In this new period of 'extended youth', children and young people are betwixt and between, caught in a series of cultural shifts whose effects are at times contradictory rather than complementary.

The economic and legal hiatus that opened up around teenagers over the past fifty years between dependent child and independent adult, exacerbating tensions between the discourses of needs and rights, is partly redressed by the new child-centred model of the family, for the task of tension resolution is transferred from society to parents. Parents must tread the difficult path between providing for their children economically for an extended period of time while simultaneously recognizing their independence in terms of sociality and culture. And it is mainly they who must oversee children's phased entry into the world rather than, as before, the workplace (e.g. via apprenticeships) or community organizations (church, union, clubs). Their task is hardly eased by the fact that, as Gadlin (1978) argues, it is historically distinctive that parents can no longer rely on their own childhood experiences to guide them in managing the spatial and temporal structures of their children's moral, domestic and family life.

These and other pressures together contribute to the process of de-traditionalization characteristic of late modernity. Giddens (1993: 184) argues that we are witnessing 'a democratization of the private sphere', a historical transformation of intimacy in which children, along with other participants in a relationship, are gaining the right to 'determine and regulate the conditions of their association' (p. 185) while parents gain the new duties: to ensure their children's involvement in key decisions, to be accountable to their children and to respect as well as expecting respect. Parent–child relations are thus being reformulated, Giddens argues, according to the emergent cultural ideal of the 'pure relationship', this being 'reflexively organized, in an open fashion, and on a continuous basis' (1991: 91). Thus, by contrast with the Victorian conception of the family, based on status hierarchies and the associated values of authority, duty, hard work and security, today's 'democratic family' (or 'negotiated family'; Beck and Beck-Gernsheim, 2002) prizes authenticity, intimacy, trust, reciprocity, recognition and role flexibility in support of a culture of self-fulfilment and individual rights.

In sum, contemporary families must negotiate a rapidly changing society without the traditional resources of established relations between the generations, with parents neither benefiting from the experience of their own childhood nor having the moral right to impose rules and sanctions without democratic consultation – no longer is a remote and authoritarian father expected to lay down the law and administer punishment on his return from work. Even what is referred to as 'family' has altered as the normative nuclear family is reconfigured (although in practice, it has always been more diverse than recognized by social norms). As Hill and Tisdall observe,

> the idea of family is to some degree a fluid one, with a mix of concepts at its core – direct biological relatedness, parental caring role, long-term cohabitation, permanent belonging. (1997: 66)

Children too face significant challenges in late modernity. Drawing on Giddens' notion of the 'project of the self', Buchner *et al.* (1995) argue that childhood increasingly includes the responsibility of constructing a 'leisure career' or 'biographical project', a responsibility that requires young people to anticipate future uncertainties and deal with risk and status insecurity in the context of a loss of traditional forms of family and community support. That loss is, as Coontz suggests above, a substantial one, though it is also liberating. Indeed, Qvortrup (1995) traces a series of paradoxical consequences for childhood as discourses and structures diverge. He argues that while society increasingly avows a positive view of children at the same time it systematically devalues, intrudes upon or excludes their needs and experiences; similarly, children are disenfranchised within the public sphere yet castigated for being apathetic or antisocial; they are subject to increasing surveillance yet seen as deceitful or subversive; their spontaneity and imagination is valued yet their lives are increasingly organized and controlled; society promotes child protection yet it allows many children to encounter serious risk; and so his list continues.

In explaining these paradoxes, Hill and Tisdall point to the strong forces resisting social change, observing that 'children's participation can threaten adult hegemony and established practice' (1997: 36). Indeed, 'despite the recognition of children as persons in their own right, public policy and practice is marked by an intensification of control, regulation and surveillance around children' (Prout, 2000: 304), this impeding rather than facilitating the ability of social institutions to encourage children's participation. Ambivalence is, perhaps, the dominant lens through which adult society regards children growing up – encompassing hopes that this generation will right the wrongs of the parent generation but also fears that today's youth exemplifies the loss of values, standards and traditions of which the parent generation has been guardian. Beck argues that today, 'the child is the source of the last *remaining, irrevocable, unexchangeable primary relationship'* (1986/2005: 118); he suggests that it is through our children that we seek the 're-enchantment' of our lives (see also Drotner, 1992, on childhood as 'paradise lost' for adults).

These paradoxes and ambivalences, tensions and challenges are not only debated by historians, sociologists and psychologists, but they also motivate the policy agenda. There are, it seems, increasing policy and legislative efforts to improve the conditions of childhood. In America, the *No Child Left Behind Act of 2001* seeks to 'close the achievement gap with accountability, flexibility, and choice, so that no child is left behind'.[3] In 2004 the UK Government passed the Children Act and published its paper *Every Child Matters: Change for Children* (HM Government, 2004), the aims of which include the right of a child, whatever their background or their circumstances, to have the support required to be healthy, stay safe, enjoy and achieve, make a positive contribution and achieve economic well-being. Unicef argues that 'the true measure of a nation's standing is how well it attends to its children' (UNICEF, 2007: 1). And the UN Convention on the Rights of the Child is internationally recognized and referred to, if not always implemented.

Concrete evidence of some of the difficulties faced by children and parents may stimulate the public policy agenda more than abstract concerns with tradition, respect, values and identity, though social scientists know these latter to underpin the former. In the UK, the Risk Commission (Madge and Barker, 2007) reported that each year, for every million children, six are abducted by a stranger (though less than one is murdered by a stranger), 24 are killed by a car and 2,400 are involved in a road accident, 40,000 are sexually abused by a parent, relative or carer, around 50,000 11–15 year olds have severe gambling difficulties, 140,000 2–10 year olds are obese, and 270,000 10–25 year olds say they have been the victim of crime in the previous year. Collishaw *et al.* (2004) report that children's mental health problems doubled from 1974 to 1999. The mental health charity, Mind, adds that 1 in 10 children aged 5 to 15 had a clinically diagnosed mental health problem in 2004; 'at least five per cent of teenagers are seriously depressed and at least twice that number show significant distress'; further, 'self-harm is becoming increasingly common among young people' and 'suicide is now the second most common cause of death amongst young people. The suicide rate for young males has risen by over 50 per cent over the past 20 years' (Darton, 2005; see also ONS, 2007). These are just some of the recent reports evidencing the difficulties of contemporary childhood, and they lead some to call the situation a 'crisis' (Palmer, 2007), though others demur (Buckingham, 2007a).

Given this complex and multifaceted picture of changing childhoods, my present purpose is to identify the wider social and cultural shifts which, in practical terms, lead children and young people to embrace the media as a specific and valued opportunity for freedom of expression and connection and, more ideologically, have also generated a public agenda of hopes and fears regarding childhood that are easily grafted onto cultural discourses surrounding the internet.

Individualization and the risk society

The reflexive project of the self … consists in the sustaining of coherent, yet continuously revised, biographical narratives. (Giddens, 1991: 5)

The goal of individual self-realisation overshadows community solidarity and stability. (Gadlin, 1978: 236)

Comparing the 1950s with the 1980s, Ziehe (1994: 2) argues that the new consumer opportunities of post-war Western societies, framed in terms of ambivalent desires for ever higher domestic and personal living standards, have generated 'an increasing orientation towards questions of life style' now evident in discourses of youth, cultural change and the generation gap. While Ziehe stresses the importance of music, for Osgerby (1998) television is also crucial as it has addressed young people distinctively in terms of their identity, lifestyle and attitudes, encouraging their construction of a leisure career that, being itself subject to pervasive market forces and peer pressures, is perceived by parents as making them 'grow up faster and earlier' while postponing adult responsibilities for longer. The diversity of niche connections afforded by the internet takes this separation of child and adult interests a step further, opening up a world of communication that the parent generation is barely aware of (Fornäs and Bolin, 1995).

As Meyrowitz (1985) and Postman (1983) observed, the mass media gave children unprecedented access to the adult world, blurring the adult/child boundary of knowledge. Yet the concomitant rise of youth culture suggests that children wish to know but not necessarily to engage with that new knowledge about adult society. Rather, they seem more motivated to seek out and experiment with identities and relationships within a peer-realm often inaccessible to the parental gaze. For Gergen (2002: 233), this shift in focus from vertical (cross-generational) to horizontal (peer) relationships is far from the democratic shift proposed by Giddens; rather it is resulting in 'a wholesale devaluation of depth in relationship' as youth becomes increasingly absorbed in sustaining multiple horizontal connections within their network rather than developing the rich commitments that characterize 'the vertical register' of close relationships with significant and co-present others. The loss of attention has costs in terms of commitment:

as the communal sources for an identifiable self are diminished, it becomes increasingly difficult to answer the questions of 'who am I?' We move then into a cultural condition in which our identities are increasingly situated, conditional and optional. (p. 234)

Yet Gergen's 'new floating world', dominated by image and spectacle (Debord, 1995) is, for others, a new opportunity to escape the constraints of convention and tradition. In pursing the reflexive 'project of the self', children and young people are seen to relish particularly the internet as a valued new place for social exploration and self-expression (Holloway and Valentine, 2003). More generally, the combination of young people, positioned betwixt and between public and private spheres, and the media, with their unique power to penetrate private spaces and to construct new publics, is resulting in some ambiguous, exciting yet explosive renegotiations of self and other, private and public (Livingstone, 2005b). The media more than many other cultural resources in their lives, offer the raw materials for a flexible, creative exploration of oneself and others. It is hardly surprising, then, that the media also provide the focus for inter-generational tensions.

Drotner (2000) proposes three distinct ways in which young people may specifically be said to be 'cultural pioneers' in their use of new media technologies, centring on innovation, interaction and integration. Under 'innovation', she notes how young people combine multiple media, multitask, blur production and reception and so make creative use of the opportunities available (see also Bruns, 2008; Ito, 2008). By 'interaction', she points to how young people engage with each other within and through different media and media contents, opening up opportunities for intertextuality and connectivity (see also Fornäs, 2002). And by 'integration', she points to the transformation of the distinction between primary (or face-to-face) and secondary (mass mediated) socialization, resulting in diverse forms of mediated communication (see Thompson, 1995):

> for the young, the media are part of a range of cultural signs available for processes of interpretation that are situated in time and space and dependent on constraints of production, distribution and resources for reception. (Drotner, 2000: 59)

However, the case for this flexibility should not be overstated. The media also seek to position children and young people subtly but firmly according to commercial and other interests. Recognizing that this new opportunity brings its own pressures and constraints, Buchner observes that:

> every child is increasingly expected to behave in an 'individualized way'... children must somehow orient themselves to an *anticipated* life course. The more childhood in the family is eclipsed by influences and orientation patterns from outside the family (...) the more independent the opportunity (and drive) to making up one's own mind, making one's own choice ... described here as the *biographization* of the life course. (1990: 77–8)

In seeking to construct a biographical project, and in resolving the series of developmental tasks along the way – entering work, sexual maturity, political enfranchisement and financial independence – communication plays a key role at all stages for young people. On a simple level, the media are available to fill the ever-growing leisure of extended youth. However, the media are far from neutral observers on the sidelines of change. Importantly, the media have remade themselves in recent decades – through youth television, pop music, globalized children's culture, the expanding magazine market and video games – precisely to serve, or exploit, children's needs in 'growing up' (Brown, Halpern and L'Engle, 2005; Buckingham and Bragg, 2004; Kinder, 1999; Kline, 1993). Through their contents, the media directly address the concerns, interests and experiences of young people. Through their forms, the media provide the personalized, mobile, stylized, casualized media goods that today mark out the spaces and timetable of young people's lives.

Since not only the conditions of childhood but also communicative environments are changing in late modernity, so too are the contexts for the development of identity. Identities are increasingly defined through the often transient markers of lifestyle and media practices rather than the traditional, typically stable markers of age, gender, ethnicity and place. And increasingly, identities are performed under conditions of uncertainty, compared with the rich multimodal dynamic information typical of face-to-face interaction (Merchant, 2006). Such changes are productively theorized as part of a long-term historical trend towards individualization discernable even by the end of the seventeenth century, when one could already identify 'the privatization of families from each other, and the individualization of members within families' (Luke, 1989: 39). Defining individualization as the process by which traditional social distinctions – especially social class – are declining in importance as the factors shaping people's lives, this disembedding from tradition is resulting in a fragmentation or undermining of the norms and values which have, hitherto, defined how people live their lives (Beck and Beck-Gernsheim, 2002).

Life choices are increasingly 'governed by a dialectic of disintegration and reinvention' (Elliott, 2002: 298), this on the one hand arousing popular fears of the selfish, 'me-generation' but, on the other, suggesting new freedoms through self-actualization and intensified reflexivity. Ambivalence regarding individualization is perhaps inevitable. Beck may read as if he celebrates individualization as a form of 'empowerment', but in repudiating this reading he comes close to the Foucauldian notion of rationalities of the self (or governance of the soul; Rose, 1990). He argues, first, that in late modernity social stratification is far from erased: 'these detraditionalizations happen in a *social surge of individualization*. At the same time the *relations* of inequality remain stable' (Beck, 1986/2005: 87) – an apparent contradiction made possible by what Beck terms the advent of 'capitalism *without* classes' (p. 88). Second, he argues that:

> individualism does not signify the beginning of the self-creation of the world by the resurrected individual. Instead it accompanies tendencies toward the *institutionalization* and *standardization* of ways of life . . . All of this points to the special forms of control which are being established here. (Beck, 1986/2005: 90)

And, a third reason not to celebrate, we can only identify opportunities for 'novel personal experimentation and cultural innovation against a social backdrop of risks, dangers, hazards, reflexivity, globalization' (Elliot, 2002: 298). Indeed, individualization is fraught with risk because the biography must be constructed in a context of loss of traditional certainties, growing inequalities and insecurities, and a tendency to blame the individual when things go wrong. Choices involve weighing risks, and more choice means more risk (Giddens, 1995). Or as Beck put it, modernity 'has become the threat *and* the promise of emancipation from the threat that it creates itself' (Beck, 1986/2005: 183). Thus:

> we are eye-witnesses – as subjects and objects – of a break within modernity, which is freeing itself from the contours of the classical industrial society and forging a new form – the (industrial) 'risk society'. This requires a delicate balancing between the contradictions of continuity and rupture within modernity. (p. 9)

He identifies three historical steps towards the risk society: the disembedding (i.e. the removal of, or perhaps liberation from) tradition; the loss of traditional security (loss of faith, undermining of practical knowledge or societal norms, in short, a growth of disenchantment) and last, the re-embedding (reintegration through new forms of social commitment – to expertise, to new social movements, to community and peer groups). Although neither Giddens nor Beck devote much attention to the changing conditions of childhood in particular, others have developed their thinking so as to provide a framework for understanding the position of children and youth in a wider context. Jackson and Scott observe that:

taken together, these two processes – individualization and de-traditionalization – create a context in which greater parental invest-ment in children occurs within what seems to be a less predictable and less safe world. In addition, colonization of the future has made space for specific anxieties in relation to children. (1999: 89)

Perhaps the dominant source of perceived risk posed to children, again marking a notable change from just a few decades ago, concerns that associated with public space. Over the second half of the twen-tieth century, many Western societies have witnessed a gradual shift away from children's leisure time spent outside (in the streets, woods or countryside) and towards that spent primarily at home, this both reflecting and shaping cultural conceptions of childhood over the past half century.[4] Interviews with parents about their own childhoods reveal a pervasive image of a carefree childhood spent out of doors (Livingstone, 2002). Nostalgic though this may be, historians of child-hood confirm the:

> shift from a life focused on the street to one focused on the home [and] this was accompanied by a change in the social organization of the home. Parents, and in particular fathers, became less remote and authoritarian, less the centre of attention when they were present. (Cunningham, 1995: 179)

This transformation has been significantly led by a growing culture of risk. For example, in 1971, 80 per cent of British 7–8 year olds walked to school on their own; by 1990 this had dropped to 9 per cent (Hillman, Adams and Whitelegg, 1990). In 2007, the Children's Society reported that 43 per cent of UK adults say children should not be allowed out with friends until they are 14 (The Children's Society, 2007). As the outside is increasingly construed as 'unsafe' for children and as opportunities for outside play are commensurately reduced (Gill, 2007), the home becomes a sanctuary for children's safe explora-tion and leisure, this resulting in pressure on the family to embrace a media-rich home in compensation (Burdette and Whitaker, 2005; Karsten and van Vliet, 2006; Livingstone, 2002).

Growing up in late modernity

Thus far I have treated the category 'children and young people' as homogenous though this is far from the case in reality. Yet attending to the differences among children is troublesome. In presenting empirical findings, all claims must be qualified according to gender, socioeconomic status and many further subdivisions. Further, in terms of theory, there is particular contestation over how to address the main factor that divides children, that of age.

For the new sociologists of childhood, 'childhood is socially constructed rather than being intrinsic to the state of being a child' (Jackson and Scott, 1999: 91). For developmental psychologists, childhood is precisely defined in large part by the state of being a child, this focusing attention on the complex process of individual development. One might say, in conciliation, that the former are interested in cultural, historical and discursive factors shaping childhood while, separately, the latter are interested in the biological, cognitive and social factors that shape the development of each child. Yet it remains the case that little rapprochement has been achieved between these two persistently polarized approaches to researching 'children and young people'. Each persistently misunderstands the other – sociologists accuse psychologists of asserting a universalistic, invariant, decontextualized approach; psychologists consider that sociologists are unable to conceive that development has any basis other than that constructed *ad hoc* by a particular culture. Although neither is in reality so simplistic in its theorization, each offers a strongly contrasting conception of children and, therefore, a competing approach to analysis.

Piaget's developmental psychology has provided one dominant research paradigm (Piaget and Inhelder, 1969), with the focus on the individual child's cognitive development in 'ages and stages' through an active and curious exploration of the environment, including the media environment (Dorr, 1986; Valkenburg, 2004). Its strength is a careful account of children's interests and abilities at different ages, including a theory of developmental transitions from one age to the next. Its weakness is a relative neglect of the ways in which the process of development towards adulthood is shaped by the activities, expectations and resources of a host of socializing agencies and institutions – parents, teachers, technology and content providers, marketers, welfare bodies, politicians, governments. The importance of these in mediating social relations, including providing a social 'scaffolding' for learning, is now being articulated by those following Vygotsky (1978) as noted below.

The new sociology of childhood emerged in the 1990s as a reaction against Piagetian individualism and universalism (James, Jenks and Prout, 1998). Qvortrup (1994) characterizes this approach as stressing, first, the structural aspects of childhood, with its dynamics and determinants, rather than a naturalistic conception of the individual child and its development; second, the relational – neither 'the child' in isolation from others, nor 'the household' as sufficiently descriptive of its members, and these relationships are worthy of study in and of themselves; and third, the present – children as people now, their relationships and cultures considered worthy of study in their own right, rather than forward looking – children as merely persons-to-be and so as indicative of the adults they will become. Thus Corsaro (1997) observes that through their daily actions, often invisible to adult eyes, children construct their social worlds as real places where real meanings (rather than fantasy or imitation) are generated, and thus they contribute to social structures which have consequences for both children and adults. This involves, too, a politicization of childhood: childhood is seen as not only a demographic but also as a moral classification which is central to the project of making children count and so addressing their needs and rights when apportioning the resources of society (Qvortrup, 1994).

These two approaches result in polarized approaches to children and the internet. On one view, children are seen as vulnerable, undergoing a crucial but fragile process of cognitive and social development to which the internet tends to pose a risk by introducing potential harms into the social conditions for development, justifying in turn a protectionist regulatory environment. On the contrary view, children are seen as competent and creative agents in their own right whose 'media-savvy' skills tend to be underestimated by the adults around them, the consequence being that society may fail to provide a sufficiently rich environment for them. As both approaches generate hopes and fears, four distinct positionings for children may be discerned:

	Active	Passive
Hopes	Agent	Beneficiary
Fears	Villain	Victim

In understanding children and the internet, each is useful in moderation but problematic when framed in a strong form. To be sure, children cannot be fitted into just one of these boxes; rather the challenge is to keep all four possibilities in mind when asking questions in research.

But this classification does not advance our analysis of the problematics of age and development. Moving child psychology away from Piaget's stage theory of cognitive development, Goswami reported to the UK's Byron Review as follows:

It is now recognized that children think and reason in the *same* ways as adults from early in childhood. Children are less efficient reasoners than adults because they are more easily misled in their logic by interfering variables such as contextual variables, and because they are worse at inhibiting irrelevant information ... The major developmental change during the primary years is the development of self-regulatory skills ... Cognitive development is experience-dependent, and older children have had more experiences than younger children. (Goswami, 2008: 1–2)

To understand how experiences – framed as social and contextual – underpin learning and development, psychologists increasingly turn to Vygotsy's intersubjectivist approach that recognizes the social, symbolic and material mediations that underpin development, itself now reconceived as a life-long process rather than one that reaches a state of adult completion by the end of adolescence (see Bruner, 1996; Erstad and Wertsch, 2008; Wertsch, 1985). Crook characterizes this socio-cultural perspective as a means of re-connecting cognition with social interaction through Vygotsky's radical proposal that:

all hidden mental actions were first experienced within the external plane of joint activity. So, at first, attending, remembering and reasoning are things done between people. Most powerfully, they are done between experts and novices, teachers and learners. (Crook, 2008: 32)

Starting, then, not with the individual child but rather with the community of practice in which they are embedded, and asking not how they externalize what they know but rather how they internalize (via the notion of inner speech) what they and others are doing (and discussing), the traditional problem dividing psychologists and sociologists can be transcended, perhaps rendered obsolete. An exciting challenge for media research, then, is to explore how far the media, especially the internet, play a role in reconfiguring the communities of practice within which children experience themselves and the world, potentially supporting particular peer-based or networked structures of intersubjective communication and scaffolding learning through appropriately (or inappropriately) designed representations with which children interact.

Another psychologist, also one who wrote many years ago but, ironically perhaps, finds renewed relevance for the contemporary analysis of youth in late modernity is helpful in understanding the passage from childhood through to adolescence and adulthood. Erikson (1959/1980) foregrounds as central to development the process by which adolescents and young adults construct an emotionally satisfying, culturally meaningful, materially feasible, socially connected 'self'. Writing in the psychoanalytic tradition, he argued that actions commonly construed as risk-taking or even delinquent are, rather, part of the struggle of identity development, a struggle in which the adolescent must develop and gain confidence in an ego identity that is simultaneously autonomous and socially valued, and that reflexively balances inner unity with societal expectations. Critical of a society that construes identity in terms of an abundance of choice, while allowing its youth so little power to make meaningful choices, insisting instead on standardization of norms and roles, Erikson observes a painful oscillation between conformity and rebellion. At times,

> Youth after youth, bewildered by some assumed role, a role forced on him by the inexorable standardization of American adolescence, runs away in one form or another. (Erikson, 1959/1980: 97)

At other times,

> to keep themselves together they temporarily overidentify, to the point of apparent complete loss of identity, with the heroes of cliques and crowds. On the other hand, they become remarkable clannish, intolerant, and cruel in their exclusion of others who are 'different'. (p. 97)

Problematically for adult society, the extended youth characteristic of late modernity seems to stretch too far the 'psychosocial moratorium' which has traditionally permitted adolescents to experiment with identities or delay life decisions. On the one hand, they are subject to persistent critique from adults who deplore the various forms of youth culture; on the other hand, the psychological task of constructing the self is increasingly left to adolescents to manage for themselves, without the structures established in traditional societies (strong age-related norms for behaviour, acknowledged public rites of passage; Douglas, 1966). Interestingly, as we shall see in this book, the media and especially the internet seem to compensate, constructively or otherwise, by providing many of the resources for explorations of identity, emotion and sexuality, for experimentation with self-disclosure, trust and reciprocity, for negotiating the balance between conformity and rebellion, and for reinventing rites of passage (now taking the form of acquiring a mobile phone, seeing a porn movie, getting a MySpace profile).

The 'arrival' of the internet

Where does the internet fit into this picture? Although it has only recently reached mass adoption in households with children in developed countries, the internet has a history stretching over nearly half a century – back to ARPANET's first decentralized communications network in 1969, if not still further back (Castells, 2001; Winston, 1996). Each step in its development has attracted considerable hopes and fears, initially among its elite developers, funders and users, more latterly also among the wider public. Email was introduced in 1975, followed by usenet and bulletin board services, a series of interim innovations born of interactions between scientists and hackers in the 1970s, then Unix users' tradition of the 'open source movement' during the 1980s. It took the development of hypertext language by Tim Berners-Lee in 1989, the first client browser software in 1991 leading to the World Wide Web, to bring the internet widespread recognition beyond the technological elite. At the end of that year, US Senator (later, Vice-President) Al Gore (1991) attracted world-wide attention to 'the information superhighway' when announcing the huge public and private investment to be concentrated in the 'national information infrastructure', and this was soon followed by Microsoft's introduction of the Windows browser Microsoft Internet Explorer in 1995.

By the mid to late 1990s, the internet was fast becoming an every-day technology, reaching sizable proportions of homes, schools and workplaces in the developed world. Internet diffusion in the USA took just seven years to reach 30 per cent of households, a level of penetration which took 17 years for television and 38 years for the telephone (Rice and Haythornthwaite, 2006). This rapidity is in itself distinctive. I recall a girl asking me in 1997, 'Isn't it [the internet] something you plug into the back of the TV?' In a survey of British 6–17 year olds I conducted that year, only one in five had used the internet – with only 7 per cent having home access, and one in five had not even heard of it (Livingstone, 2002). In short, the arrival of the internet in people's lives has required some fast footwork to figure out what it is, how to use it and what to do when difficulties arise. Just a decade or so on, many children – and adults – say they could not live without it.

Today, 86 per cent of Norwegians, 74 per cent of Japanese, 73 per cent of Americans, 71 per cent of Britons and 67 per cent of Germans are online, although there remain many parts of the world where access is low or absent, according to the usage website, world-internetstats.com (see also Pew Internet and American Life Project, 2008, which concurs that three quarters of American adults are online, and Oxis, 2007, for evidence that 66 per cent of households had an internet connection, and 56 per cent had broadband, in the UK in 2007). Despite the rapidity of the diffusion process, there remain considerable cross-national differences (Norris, 2001; World Internet Project, 2009) and, notwithstanding the turn to broadband and a continual upgrading of speed and connectivity, a notable levelling-off in the proportion of households gaining access.

Although everybody is affected, in one way or another, by the very ubiquity of new online technologies, children and young people are usually among the earliest and most enthusiastic users of information and communication technologies. Households with children are significantly more likely to have access than others (Ofcom, 2007b)[5] and ever younger children are now going online, often 'ahead' of their parents.

- By the time the UK Children Go Online survey was conducted, 98 per cent of children aged 9–19 had used the internet – 92 per cent at school, 75 per cent at home, and 64 per cent elsewhere (Livingstone and Bober, 2004b). By 2009, 79 per cent of 7–16 year olds had gained internet access at home, one third having access in their own room (ChildWise, 2009).
- The World Internet Project (2009) found similarly that among 12–14 year olds internet use was 95 per cent or over in the UK, Canada, the Czech Republic and Israel.
- In Europe, internet use is rising even for younger children – among 6–10 year olds, use reached 77 per cent in Sweden, 88 per cent in Finland, 57 per cent in Romania, 56 per cent in Germany and 34 per cent in Italy. The overall average for 6–17 year olds in the EU27 now stands at 75 per cent (Eurobarometer, 2008).
- In the USA, 99 per cent of 12–18 year olds use the internet (Cole, 2007). Further, 78 per cent of those aged 2–17 have internet access at home and 13 per cent have access in their bedroom (Rideout, 2007).

The ways in which the internet is becoming embedded in everyday life raises questions about access and inequalities, about the nature and quality of use, about the implications for young people's social and educational development and, ultimately, about the balance between the risks and opportunities posed by the internet for children and their families. As is often argued, children appear to be more flexible, creative users than adults, having fewer established routines or habits and being oriented towards development, innovation, and change (Ito, 2008). As they make the transition from their family of origin towards a wider peer culture, young people find that the media, especially mobile media and the internet, offer a valued resource for constructing their identity and for mediating social relationships (Peter, Valkenbury and Fluckiger, in press). And in so doing, they are developing online competencies and literacies that exceed those of their parents, proudly labelling themselves 'the internet generation' (Livingstone and Bober, 2003), this mirroring popular rhetoric regarding youthful 'cyberkids', 'digital natives' or 'the digital generation' (Prensky, 2001).[6]

But the internet is not just a new appliance in the household akin to getting a washing machine or a new car. Crucially, the communication environment is diversifying, specializing, globalizing and becoming more interactive. The internet encompasses not simply one-to-many communication (also characteristic of the mass media and, in turn, of mass society) and one-to-one communication (as in telephony and in face-to-face communication, and characteristic of the yet longer history of oral culture), but also the communication from many to many distinctively characteristic of a network society (Castells, 2001). This resulting expansion of communicative possibilities extends further into our lives than could be said for any other recently arrived screen entertainment technologies. But, like the telegraph and telephone (Carey, 1992) as well as the book, the internet permeates all spheres of life, connecting public and private in significantly altered ways – arguably more even than was the case for television (Dayan, 2001; Ellis, 2002) – and so contributing to the reconfiguration of opportunities and risks in children's lives in relation to social, cultural, educational, civic, health and, still important, leisure activities.

The internet is not, however, being introduced into otherwise unchanging households. Historians of media consumption show that, in a market fuelled by the continual innovation and multiplication of media goods, as each new medium enters the home, it undergoes a gradual transition from pride of place at the centre of family life to a variable status pitched somewhere between focal and casual, communal and individualized uses, where these are spread spatially throughout the household and temporally round-the-clock (Flichy, 1995; Livingstone, 2002; Mackay, 1997; Spigel, 1992; Silverstone and Hirsch, 1992). Each new medium remediates previous media, with the latter moving gradually into the background to make way for the newest arrival, possibly becoming more specialized in its use, although its taken-for-granted presence continues to permeate our lives (Bolter and Grusin, 1999). Consider the shift from 'family television' (Morley, 1986) to a screen-rich 'bedroom culture' (Livingstone, 2007c; see also Lincoln, 2004) with its own television installed for the majority of children (and adults) in Western homes – and a similar story has been told for radio, telephone, hi-fi, video recorders and computers. Each has begun its domestic career in the main collective family space of the living room but, as prices fall and multiplication and mobility of goods becomes feasible, each has moved into more individualized, personalized and, for children, unsupervised spaces, resulting in what Flichy (1995) termed 'living together separately' and what van Rompaey and Roe (2001) termed the 'compartmentalization of family life'.

While the internet has often entered homes intended for communal use in the living room, it too is migrating to more specialized and personalized locations around the home. In terms of space, the decision for many households is no longer whether to have the internet but rather how many connections to have and where to locate them in the home, facilitated by a continual process upgrading and recycling existing technologies through the household. As desktops give way to laptops, mobile and other platforms, even these decisions become unnecessary as access becomes ever more flexible. Similarly in terms of time, we no longer divide our time between media and other activities but rather we use media as a way of structuring many of our activities, both commonplace and special (Bryce, 1987; Scannell, 1988). These altered time–space conditions for everyday life reshape social relations, and here the trends are towards individualization, privatization, personalization. In understanding these processes, we should not only focus on media as objects of consumption. As with other media, the internet is not only a material resource that occupies space and time in the household; it is more significantly a symbolic force that renegotiates the boundary between home and outside, also altering the relations of audiences (or users) and producers from the established institutional separation that long characterized mass broadcasting.

Online, content creation is easier than ever: one and the same technology can be used for sending and receiving, with desktop publishing software, easy-to-use web creation software, digital cameras and webcams putting professional expertise into the hands of everyone (Bruns, 2008). Many are already content producers, developing complex literacy skills through the use of email, chat or games and the social consequences of these activities – participation, social capital, civic culture – serve to network (or exclude) in ways that matter. On the other hand, a consequence of this network society is the increasing mediation of relations that were hitherto conducted face-to-face, exacerbating problems of credibility, expertise, reciprocity, alienation, trust. What does this mean for relations between individuals and institutions? For critical literacy as a means of 'reading the world' (Freire and Macedo, 1987)? Ironically, overwhelmed with complex and uncertain information, many seek powerful intermediaries, old and new, to manage these difficult judgements for them, and thus established institutions – often those already powerful in the mass media – regain any lost power, now no longer acting quietly in the background but, on the contrary, highly visible and trusted brands from both public and private sector.

But these are grand claims. To defend or, better, examine them, we must first rethink their framing so as firmly to avoid naive claims about the impact of the internet, instead contextualizing the internet within the society that has produced it.

From impacts to affordances

> We know the computer, we're the generation of computers. (Focus group with 14–16 year olds, London, 2003)

> Technology is an essential and inescapable part of 21st Century living and learning. All aspects of school life are enhanced and enabled with technology. Technology is crucial to making sure that each individual maximizes their potential through the personalization of their learning and development. (Department for Education and Skills, 2006: 5)

For the general public, including children, and for policymakers, the very salience of the internet in society supports the popular positioning of the technology itself as the self-evident agent of change – whether this is evaluated as for better or for worse. Discursively, if the term 'internet' (or its equivalents – digital, cyber, technological) is put at the start of the sentence (as in, 'What's the impact of the internet on . . . ?') or used as a strong qualifier (digital childhood, cyberkids, technological literacy), this masks the social arrangements of institutions (education, family, commerce, state) and the shaping role of everyday activities and practices. Yet it is these activities and practices that, for example, led educators to turn to technology over print, governments to promote domestic internet adoption, universities to develop the internet as a decentralized network, and families to encourage their children to become internet users.

In short, a focus on the impacts of the internet leads the argument astray in several ways. First, it is theoretically incoherent, as the many scholars who have critiqued technological determinism have forcefully argued. Rejecting the assumption that 'new technologies are invented as it were in an independent sphere, and then create new societies or new human conditions' (Williams, 1974: 13), studies of the social shaping of technology stress that 'the technological, instead of being a sphere separate from social life, is part of what makes society possible' (MacKenzie and Wajcman, 1999: 23; Selwyn, 2008). MacKenzie and Wajcman further distinguish between technological determinism as a theory of technology and as a theory of society. As the former, technological determinism fails: technological innovation is a thoroughly social process, from conception, design, production, marketing, diffusion, appropriation, use and consequences (Mansell and Silverstone, 1996). But as a theory of society and social change, MacKenzie and Wajcman (1999: 3) argue that technological determinism contains 'a partial truth'. Provided it is understood that technologies are social products which embed human relations in their very constitution, we may as a matter of convenience cast them in the role of actors, along with other kinds of actor, when explaining social processes (although see Latour, 1993). Crucially,

> precisely because technological determinism is partly right as a theory of society (technology matters not just physically and biologically, but also to our human relations to each other), its deficiency as a theory of technology impoverishes the political life of our societies. (MacKenzie and Wajcman, 1999: 5)

Second, it is empirically unsatisfactory, for it leads us to miss the many social processes of everyday life by which people themselves shape the significance and consequences of internet use. As statisticians chart the rise in internet access across and within countries, and as governments rely on the public to gain access at home, evidence for the gradual diffusion of the internet from the 'innovators' and 'early adopters' through the mass market until eventually reaching the 'laggards' is readily obtained (Rogers, 1995). But this neat account of the spread of a more-or-less stable technology through the market – which invites questions about technology's impacts and consequences – is quickly complicated and qualified once one explores the nature of use, for the internet itself means different things to different users and at different points in the passage through design, production, marketing, consumption and use (Silverstone, 2006). Beyond the obvious practical and financial barriers that face ordinary users, ethnographic studies of technology use and domestic consumption practices draw attention to the symbolic struggles involved in going online, struggles that reshape the very meaning of the technology through contingent processes of use (to be explored in chapter 2).

Third, it misleads policy, for it positions technology *per se*, rather than the institutions that design, fund and shape the technology and its implementation in children's lives, as the solution to social problems. Indeed, the very multifunctionality of the internet increases the range of problems to which it is seen to provide a solution. So, when politicians worry that youth is becoming politically apathetic, they hope online forums can revise youthful participation. When educationalists want to move on from traditional notions of learning, they seize upon the idea that e-learning offers an exciting answer. When health educators wish to advise teenagers about health, sex or drugs, they hope an anonymous advice site will circumvent the embarrassments of face-to-face guidance. These are not necessarily misplaced hopes, but they are ill-framed, for they underestimate the social and contextual factors surrounding the problem, especially the roles to be played by social actors in using the technology, content or service to address the problem (the teacher training requirements associated with introducing information and communication technologies into the classroom, for example) as well as the unintended consequences of relying on a technological solution (the difficulty of ensuring the comprehension or effectiveness of health advice provided for unknown users, for example).

How, then, shall we understand the internet in social terms? Beyond an account of the internet as a technology – a material bundle of hardware and software that is designed and sold, installed and used – the internet is also, indeed is more significant in terms of communication. All forms of media, from print to the internet, mediate between speaker and hearer, producer and audience, or among interacting parties. In contrast, with face-to-face communication, characterized by co-presence, they enable the considerable advantages of communication on any scale, even the global, as well as those of asynchronicity, anonymity and more. The contemporary conceptual toolkit centres on the prefix 're-'; remixing, reconfiguring, remediating, reappropriating, recombining (Bolter and Grusin, 1999; Dutton and Shepherd, 2004; Lievrouw and Livingstone, 2006). This recognizes the activities by which innovations are rendered both continuous with and distinct from that which has gone before, simultaneously remediating the familiar; a focus on mediation also adopts a frame of enabling and constraining rather than of determining or causing, focusing on the interpretative potential of technology as text (Woolgar, 1996) and the interpretative activities of designers and users (Bakardjieva, 2005; Bijker, Hughes and Pinch, 1987).

Convergent media culture is characterized by personalization, hypersociality, networking and ubiquity, all of which engages the collective imagination and affords new 'genres of participation' (Ito, 2008; Jenkins, 2006a; Jensen and Helles, 2005). At the same time, this move away from a reliance on the face-to-face situation introduces a radical degree of uncertainty regarding the effectiveness of the communication – both from the point of view of the intentions or ambitions of the speaker and the responsiveness of the hearer. Speakers may lose authority and authenticity, and so find it difficult to establish trust. Hearers become unpredictable, from the speakers' viewpoint, and may more easily disrupt, resist or simply ignore the message. Both parties lose the flexibility of a face-to-face situation. And the effects of the medium itself, as well as the institution behind it, often act to stabilize, standardize or commodify the message. Even though, in practice, face-to-face communication can, of course, be angry, negligent, resistant, deceitful or inflexible, somehow it remains the ideal against which mediated communication is judged as flawed.

In support of this rethinking of the way in which both people and technologies mediate communication, Hutchby draws on Gibson's ecological psychology to replace technological determinist claims with an analysis of technological affordances, suggesting that:

> affordances are functional and relational aspects which frame, while not determining, the possibilities for agentic action in relation to an object. In this way, technologies can be understood as artefacts which may be both shaped by and shaping of the practices humans use in interaction with, around and through them. (2001: 44)[7]

Even the very infelicity of reframing questions of 'impacts' with questions of 'affordances' insists upon inclusion of both processes of social shaping ('shaping by and shaping of') in any social inquiry about technology. As Oudshoorn and Pinch (2003: 1–2) observe:

> There may be one dominant use of a technology, or a prescribed use, or a use that confirms the manufacturer's warranty, but there is no one essential use that can be deduced from the artifact itself.

Hence the importance of studying technologies in use (Bakardjieva, 2005; du Gay, Hall, Janes and Mackay, 1997; Selwyn, 2003; Silverstone and Hirsch, 1992). A simple example is that of the Sim Series software designed to promote public values – supposedly teaching children 'about pollution, city planning, and the creation of healthy environments' (Calvert, 1999: 186). Yet as any parent of a pre-teen knows, such software is gleefully played 'against the grain' – destroying the city, encouraging urban destruction, experimenting with the means of killing the inhabitants – in other words, precisely subverting such public values (Reid-Walsh, 2008).

A further, albeit equally infelicitous semantic distinction adds to the analysis by distinguishing individual acts of communication from the institutional structures that systematically shape communication in particular ways and in furtherance of particular powerful interests.

Distinguishing 'mediation' from 'mediatization', Hjarvard proposes that:

> mediation refers to the communication through one or more media through which the message and the relation between sender and receiver are influenced by the affordances and constraints of the specific media and genres involved . . . Mediatization is the process of social change that to some extent subsumes other social or cultural fields to the logic of the media. (Hjarvard, 2008: 5)

Although, in my view, 'mediation' can encompass both meanings (Livingstone, 2009), this quotation stresses two useful points. First, all communication is mediated, necessarily, for it inevitably occurs through one or another channel or medium (including language and bodily or nonverbal face-to-face interaction) which has its own influence (Silverstone, 2005). This demands an empirical account of the specific forms and practices associated with a communication medium – whether social networking sites or fanzines, telephones or the printed book. Second, the specific affordances and constraints of specific media may be shaped by a distinctive logic whose character is established historically and culturally through the development not only of practices and technologies but also of institutions of power and whose sphere of influence extends far beyond the specific mode of communication they control.

To illustrate, both the book and the social networking site have their own characteristics that afford certain activities on the part of their readers or users. But print culture – associated with institutions of learning, the accreditation of knowledge, standards of expertise, and so forth – has a 'logic' (or logics) whose influence is far-reaching, 'mediatizing' the spheres of education and work (Luke, 1989; Thompson, 1995). Online communication forms also mediate specific activities, shaping them in certain ways, affording some opportunities over others; but whether they also constitute something as grand as a new digital culture or network society, thereby mediatizing other spheres of social life remains to be established. As Lundby puts it,

> mediatization implies that the media influence social institutions in ways that exceed the simple fact that all institutions rely increasingly on mediated information and communication. (2008: 363)

This requires a social and cultural analysis that contextualizes the changing array of communicative modes in relation to the variously complementary or contradictory processes of social change underway in late modernity.

From great expectations to challenging realities

In contrast to many public fears and some policy claims, the consensus among academic researchers is that the internet, being socially shaped by the diverse political, economic and cultural contexts of its development, distribution and use, is implicated in multiple and concurrent evolutionary rather than revolutionary processes of social change, variously affording the recombination, reconfiguration and remediation of everyday social practices, forms of knowledge and institutional structures (Haddon, 2004).

As was also argued in relation to television – recall Hall's (1980) analysis of the disjunctions between the contexts of encoding and the contexts of decoding – information and communication mediated by the internet cannot be reduced to a model of linear, one-way effects in which messages as intended reach users as anticipated. Hence the persistent sense of uncertainty, newness and anxiety associated with the internet. When inquiring into the internet's significance for society, simple answers and straightforward predictions should not be expected, because although new media:

> are usually created with particular purposes or uses in mind, they are commonly adopted and used in unanticipated ways – reinvented, reconfigured, sabotaged, adapted, hacked, ignored. (Lievrouw and Livingstone, 2006: 5)

Great expectations abound regarding children and the internet. Optimists relish new opportunities for self-expression, sociability, community engagement, creativity and new literacies. For children, it is hoped that the internet can support new forms of learning, new ways of thinking even, and that it can overcome political apathy among the young. Pessimists foresee the expanded scope for state surveillance, commercial exploitation and harmful or criminal activities. For children, it is feared that the internet is introducing new risks and harms into their lives – commercial, sexual, ideological, abusive. The fears may dominate the newspaper headlines, and they are readily expressed by parents, teachers and children themselves. But it is the great expectations that are driving internet adoption and use at the level of government policy, commercial enterprise, community provision and domestic consumption.

Popular discourses tend to float freely above the everyday realities of children's internet experiences, occasionally acknowledging puzzled dismay that young people live in such a different world from the (nostalgically remembered) youth of today's adults. Too often they 'essentialize the child category, denying children's diversity and their status as social actors, and because they rest on technologically determinist understandings of ICT' (Holloway and Valentine, 2003: 72; see also Buckingham, 2007a). As this chapter has suggested, in theoretical terms, the new sociology of childhood offers a way forward for the former problem, while the sociology of technology and consumption promises to resolve the latter. But theory tends not to capture the public imagination and without strong empirical findings moral panics readily take hold, as they have done many times before, catalyzing society's perennial anxieties about childhood and triggering media headlines, public anxieties and official inquiries. Throughout the twentieth century,

> each new media technology brought with it great promise for social and educational benefits, and great concern for children's exposure to inappropriate and harmful content. (Wartella and Jennings, 2000: 31)

With the shift from mass media to a mixed media ecology, including both mass and also interactive or peer-to-peer media, these promised benefits and moral concerns are exacerbated by new risks – of contact with strangers and of conduct among peers, in addition to new forms of content risks. Bettelheim (1999) traces moral panics about new media back via Goethe's 'Sorrows of Young Werther', blamed for a wave of suicides in eighteenth-century Germany, to Plato's ideal state that banned imaginative literature for corrupting the young. Since even the waltz appeared dissolute when first introduced, it is hardly surprising that public concerns accompanied the arrival of comics, cinema, television, computer games, internet:

> The indecent foreign dance called the *Waltz* was introduced . . . at the English Court on Friday last . . . It is quite sufficient to cast one's eyes on the voluptuous intertwining of the limbs, and close compressure of the bodies . . . to see that it is far indeed removed from the modest reserve which has hitherto been considered distinctive of English females . . . we feel it a duty to warn every parent against exposing his daughter to so fatal a contagion. (*The Times of London*, 1816)

How then to connect the theoretical and empirical frameworks so as to counter moral panics surrounding children and the internet? First, it must be recognized that the research agenda is already hugely broad: as observed from the outset, almost every question asked of children is now being asked of children and the internet. Adopting the overarching lens of opportunities and risks, and setting aside for the moment the crucial issue of the relations and overlaps between them (though this will be a theme threaded throughout this book), we may scope the agenda thus:

Online opportunities	**Online risks**
Access to global information	Illegal content
Educational resources	Paedophiles, grooming, strangers
Social networking among friends	Extreme or sexual violence
Entertainment, games and fun	Other harmful offensive content
User-generated content creation	Racist/hate material and activities
Civic or political participation	Advertising and stealth marketing
Privacy for identity expression	Biased or misinformation
Community involvement/activism	Abuse of personal information
Technological expertise and literacy	Cyber-bullying/harassment
Career advancement/employment	Gambling, phishing, financial scams
Personal/health/sexual advice	Self-harm (suicide, anorexia)
Specialist groups/fan forums	Invasions/abuse of privacy
Shared experiences with distant others	Illegal activities (hacking, copyright abuse)

Doubtless these lists can be extended further, but already they require research expertise not only in relation to children and the internet but also from the fields of education, information science, criminology, psychology, health, and many more. Each of these fields has dominant theories, its defining debates and its preferred methodologies. In the chapters that follow, we shall see what each has to offer and where further work is needed.

As argued in this introductory chapter, my approach is child-centred more than internet-centred, asking how children's lives afford (or not) the opportunities for certain kinds of activities, including internet-related activities, depending on social arrangements of time, space, cultural norms and values, and personal preferences and lifestyle. This invites recognition of the degree to which children and young people construct their own local contexts, rendering media use meaningful in specific ways, and so not only respond to but also influence their immediate environment, including their mediated environment (Livingstone, 1998b). As I hope to show, this child-centred, contextualized approach also allows us to recognize what is, perhaps, one of the key contributions of the internet, namely the ways in which it is used to blur the relations among hitherto distinct social spheres, altering the relations between and meanings of long-established oppositions such as public/private, local/global, masculine/feminine, learning/fun, work/leisure, adult/child.

Of course, no one sets out to blur boundaries – that is, rather, a fascinating and important if unintended consequence of other deliberate activities. Children and young people's activities are primarily exploratory, seeking freedoms online that may be constrained offline, negotiating the social expressions of identity, developing new forms of valued expertise, taking risks with social norms and personal experiences and, ultimately, integrating online and offline in developing the 'project of the self' so characteristic of late modernity (Giddens, 1991). The consequences, albeit always complex and contingent, are the youthful cultures of sociality, consumption, sexuality and creativity that do, precisely, mix and remix elements of once-distinct spheres, undermining established oppositions and generating hybrid spaces, activities and modes of expression (Drotner, 2005; Fornäs, 2003; Ito, 2008; Jenkins, 2006b).

As we shall see in the final chapter, these trends towards risky opportunities and youthful expertise, together with the tension between independence and dependence, and the democratization of the family, complicate society's attempts to guide and regulate children's use of the internet. This matters since, although children and young people benefit from the early take-up of new opportunities afforded by the internet and other online or mobile technologies, notwithstanding significant and persistent inequalities in access, use and skill (see chapter 2), the evidence also points to the risk of harm to children's safety and social development (chapter 6). These risks, it seems, are expanding in range, intensity and scope as online contents and services themselves expand and grow, including risk of bullying, sexual harassment, pornography, privacy invasion, race hate, self-harm, physical or symbolic abuse, and so forth (Hasebrink, Livingstone and Haddon, 2009; Internet Satety Technical Task Force, 2008). Here too, children and young people are often in the vanguard, exploring new activities, especially peer networking, in advance of adult scrutiny and regulatory intervention and, perhaps too often, encountering negative experiences that are unanticipated, for which they may be unprepared, and which may challenge their capacity to cope.

In balancing the opportunities and the risks, a critical perspective is vital. This book will persistently question the prioritization, implicit in the currently dominant, celebratory discourse of youthful experts or digital natives, of one side in each of these theoretical polarities – agency over structure (Giddens, 1984), tactics over strategy (de Certeau, 1984), resistance over conformity (Hall and Jefferson, 1976) lifeworld over system world (Habermas, 1981/7). To be sure, we shall explore how children exert agency online, but this will also show that they do so in the context of structures set by others – usually powerful adults, notably parents, teachers, politicians, youth workers, information providers, broadcasters. Children creatively resist some adult pressures but at the same time they succumb to others – commercial pressures that entice and entertain, normative pressures that reward certain kinds of behaviour (e.g. exam revision) over others (e.g. file sharing). Children develop and express new interests but the institutions they address may be unresponsive – politicians who invite youthful feedback but don't act on it, teachers who invite creative expression but can't evaluate it, parents who encourage online exploration but then anxiously constrain it.

In short, while this book will review the many grounds for optimism when observing children and young people as they engage with the internet for learning, communication, participation, creativity and literacy, it will also show that children alone cannot meet society's grand expectations. The everyday realities of children's internet use pose the challenge for us – adults – of drawing out from these realities the lessons that may enable society to meet some of its grand expectations. Two cautions: first, this is not, primarily, a challenge for children but rather for the society in which children live; second, these are not, at heart, great expectations held out for the internet – they are, rather, great expectations held out for children. Herein lie many uncertainties. What world do we imagine children living in, now and in the future? What skills and competences will they need? What kind of people will they be? It is such uncertainties that fuel society's inflated aspirations for children's activities and achievements online. Hence the grand claims – that the internet facilitates a whole new way of thinking, one that is flexible, collaborative, creative, or that learning is now freed from the classroom and children can learn anywhere, anytime, or that community can now encompass the globe and children transcend physical boundaries to reach out to others with shared interests. Understanding the extent to which these are being, and could yet be, realized is the task of this book.

2

Youthful Experts

Great expectations

> It's just like life, you can do anything really. (Lorie, 17)[1]

> I think from the children's point of view they are so incredibly lucky to be able to have the information in their dining room . . . and I think they are at an incredible advantage to other children. (Mother of Anna, 10)

Especially in industrialized countries, a story is emerging of 'great expectations' among both parents and children, strongly fostered by governments and business. Are these being realized? What are the real benefits? Despite having acquired a home computer and internet access precisely to improve their child's educational opportunities, parents are both confident and vague as to how this may help, quickly falling back on a faith in authorities ('the school encouraged us'), on a generalized optimism ('computers are the future') or, signifying some considerable anxiety, on peer pressure ('everyone else has got it') or competitive individualism ('I want my child to keep up/get ahead').

This chapter charts the efforts of families to go online at home, while the next chapter focuses on use of the internet in schools. It reveals the range of ways in which children are using the internet and some of the pleasures they derive from it. It also reveals, however, the difficulties of 'going online', as ordinary families navigate the many, sometimes unexpected, often confusing or contested decisions involved. Hence, this chapter questions the popular notion of the 'digital native', expert in maximizing the opportunities afforded by the internet. Getting the best from the internet turns out to be highly resource-intensive, demanding time, money, effort and skill from those variably equipped to provide them. Some children are, however, enjoying new forms of creative engagement and other opportunities online and, though these are often unevenly taken up at present, due to familiar socio-demographic inequalities, these activities may nonetheless point the way ahead for children's internet use.

To begin the UK Children Go Online project (Livingstone and Bober, 2003), we invited the younger children to talk about the internet by telling them a story:

> An Alien from another world has been watching people here on the planet Earth very carefully. It has been able to see everything, but meeting you is the first opportunity it has had to ask questions about things it has seen. It wants to know what the internet is, and you have to explain . . .

We then placed a large sheet of paper on the table and gave each child a coloured pen. In the middle was a picture of a little green alien with speech bubbles around it, and the children were asked to fill out the speech bubbles in answer to questions like, what is the internet, where do you use it, what is the best or worst thing about the internet, what is fun or boring about it? Metaphors from familiar domains help make the unfamiliar more comprehensible: the metaphor most commonly used for the internet was that of a reference book – a 'directory', 'giant book about everything', 'encyclopaedia', 'dictionary'. Beyond this, many revealed extravagant expectations – it is 'a world of opportunities', even 'the future'. Younger children especially described the internet as a 'place', while older children more often regarded it as 'a link' or 'a system'. The sense that the internet is all-encompassing was pervasive.

Often centred on potential education and information benefits, one must wonder whether these grand expectations of the internet are satisfactorily met, despite being widely promoted by marketing activities. Notwithstanding children's excitement about the potential of the internet for opening up a new 'world of opportunities', families' expectations are easily frustrated by the limitations of hardware or software design and, further, by the everyday realities of domestic life. Once bought and brought home, the computer and internet begin their domestic 'career', gathering and changing meanings as they find their place in the life of the household, both materially and symbolically (Silverstone and Hirsch, 1992). The outcome, always provisional and shifting, is strongly shaped both by the institutions that produce and distribute technologies and services and, also, by families' often-aspirational narratives, by their internal dynamics of gender, class and generation, and by the fit (or otherwise) between online and offline activities in the home and outside. As Silverstone and Mansell put it:

> When the veil of technological inevitability is challenged ... we begin to see that information and communication technologies are being employed by producers and users in ways that depend on and alter highly culturally specific understandings about how communication relationships and the production and exchange of information are integrated within social, political, and economic life. (1996: 3)

Generally, parents welcome the transformation of the home into a personalized learning environment even though this brings with it 'the curricularization of everyday life' (Buckingham, Scanlon and Sefton-Green, 2001) in which free time is transformed into work, play is evaluated in terms of benefits or targets, and computers are sold as vital to 'good parenting' through marketing materials in which 'the distinction between promotion and consumer advice is often some-what blurred' (p. 33). This marketing, they contend, promotes 'the notion of gaining competitive advantage for your children and the relationship between learning and 'fun'' (p. 36), subtly exploiting parental anxieties about the quality of public education when offering, in effect, an alternative, digital curriculum:

> Technology is frequently presented both to teachers and to parents as the solution to a whole range of social and educational problems; and yet it is a solution that, under present circumstances, is provided largely by the commercial market ... What counts as a valid educational use of technology is, it would seem, inextricable from what sells. (pp. 38–9)

The blurring of education and leisure reverses the previously dominant enthusiasm for turning the home into an escape from the demands of the outside world, in effect a screen-entertainment leisure centre. That story began with radio (the original 'wireless') and peaked just a few years ago with homes packed with multichannel televisions, games machines and other leisure devices (Livingstone, 2002; Spigel, 1992). But now that computers and, especially, the internet have become standard features of most Western households, the notion of home is again re-imagined, now less as a haven from the outside world of work and education and more as a node in an ever-widening network of formal and informal connections that crosses boundaries of work, learning, commerce and leisure. Consequently, the child, too, is repositioned – no longer the fortunate beneficiary of screen-entertainment pleasures, he or she is now the household 'expert' with a valued role to play in sustaining the family's place in the wider network.

How does this changing domestic context, with its distinct household arrangements and resources and its family values and generational dynamics, shape the ways in which children go online? Let us begin with an ethnographic exploration of three children's lives in order to situate internet use in context, seeing this from the child's perspective and, importantly, showing how highly interconnected are the practices that – as also in this book – are typically separated analytically under the headings of education, communication, participation, and so on.

Meet three children

I first visited Megan when she was eight years old. A bright girl from a working-class family, Megan lived in a media-rich but small house with her parents and older brother. She loved writing stories and animals, especially her pet hamster. She also loved playing on the computer, and her parents proudly termed her 'an information junkie', having high educational aspirations for her. At the same time, they kept an eye on her internet use from the living room, being cautious about her online activities and encouraging visiting trusted sites rather than bold exploration, gently restricting her to information rather than communication applications. When I sat with Megan while she showed me her online activities, my observations suggested that her skills were somewhat exaggerated by her parents, her internet use being narrowly concentrated on three sites – AskJeeves for searching, Nickelodeon for games (linked to her favourite children's television series *Rugrats*), and a few sites about pets (e.g. Petstore. com). Her use of these sites often proved frustrating and inefficient.

I returned to the family when Megan was 12. Though various aspects of family life had now changed – her father had a new job, her mother had returned to full-time work, her brother had taken over from her father as the 'computer buff', the computer had been upgraded, and Megan had begun secondary school – it is the constancies that were more striking in this close, quiet family. Lively and chatty as ever, grungy if not quite a teenager yet, Megan still reads and writes stories – now on the computer, using the AOL story-writing option on the kids' page. She still searches for homework or leisure-related interests, now using Google. As before, she follows her interest in animals onto the internet – for example, using Neopets to name and care for a virtual pet (Grimes and Shade, 2005).

Other things have changed. She's become a fan of *The Sims*, visiting the Sims website and sites with game cheats and, having gained a taste for horror, she enjoys playing 'against the grain' by murdering her Sims (Reid-Walsh, 2008) and writing gothic tales of murder and destruction. Yet, as before, her online skills seem more limited than her confident talk suggests. She had lost the password for her Neopet, and could not manage to get the webmaster to email it to her. She has an email account but rarely uses it, and there is nothing in her inbox when she looks. She ignores invitations on sites to chat, vote or email. When I ask what is bookmarked under 'Favorites', she says she does not know, having never looked, and when something goes wrong, she skims over the problem rather than stopping to figure out what happened. So though her online style is quick and competent, getting where she wants efficiently, her range is narrow, with little exploration. And there seems little need to worry about online risks, for Megan has internalized the caution once explicitly impressed on her by her parents.

Megan's parents gladly position her as the internet expert, even though her actual skills are less than they suppose and even though this engenders some ambivalence in them regarding her competence to manage online risks. Also typical of many, her internet use reveals a strong continuity between her offline and online interests (e.g. pets, stories) or, to put it another way, she herself creates and reproduces the connection between virtual and material practices. She is also less malleable than some might imagine, showing a continuity over time in individual learning style (and family mediation practices) even though the specific practices change as she, and the technology, develops. But not all young people are as cautious as Megan, as my next example illustrates.

Fifteen-year-old Anisah is from a Ghanaian family and lives on a once-very troubled housing estate. We first visited Anisah, a middle child, lively and confident, when she was 12. The family lived in a small two-bedroom flat, the computer squeezed into the living room along with most other family activities. Her educated parents had not found work in the UK which matched their qualifications, leading them to place huge educational expectations on their three children – evident in their many encyclopaedias and educational CD-ROMs, the emphasis placed on homework and computer access, and the parental support for children's offline and online learning.

At 12, Anisah was active and outgoing – she danced, played netball, shopped, and socialized through the church – but as she lived far from her school friends and was often alone, she also used the internet on most days, enjoying making friends in chat rooms, liking to feel ahead of her classmates (most of her peers didn't have home access). Though she benefited from using the internet to research school projects (using Yahoo, Excite or BBC Online), her skills were imperfect: she told us about doing a project on China (the country) for which she needed an illustration; she searched, downloaded and inserted into her work a picture of china (porcelain) from a website in Maine, USA, not realizing the problem.

By 15, Anisah had become a charming, strong-minded, articulate teenager, doing well at school and hoping to become a designer. Having moved to a new house, she and her sister now have a bedroom to themselves, which, to her delight, also houses the computer. Interestingly, the family's serious, moral attitude has become even stronger in Anisah. Unusually for her age group, Anisah reads the news on the homepage of her internet service provider. She also revises for exams online using the BBC's curriculum revision site, Bitesize. We discuss how – unlike her peers – she refuses to download music, it being both illegal and wrong. She claims to have seen no pornography, though her mother worries about this, checking up on Anisah and so invading her privacy, as Anisah sees it.

The interview with her mother pinpoints an ambivalence between saying 'children are children' who require guidance and seeing Anisah as part of the 'guru generation' who know about the internet. Though she uses email and instant messenger, often chatting to her friends late into the night (a practice of which her mother is unaware), Anisah is now scathing about chat rooms because of the risk from dangerous contacts and because chatting to strangers seems pointless (this reflecting a widespread campaign in the UK about the risks of chat rooms; Internet Crime Forum, 2000). Much of her internet use is purposeful – to research artwork for a project, to follow her interest in design, to find a cheap flight, and so forth.

From Anisah's experience, we can add to the picture gleaned from observing Megan. Being both older and more experienced, Anisah has bypassed some of the struggles Megan has with accessing online content. But this means she faces the next level of challenge – what exactly did Anisah need to know about the porcelain pictures to avoid her mistake? And did the mistake result from her poor searching skills (using an ambiguous search term, 'china') or her assessment of the website's content and reliability (finding a commercial site on the wrong topic) or, even, a problem occasioned by poor website design or search engine algorithms? One also wonders what complementary knowledge would be required by the teacher, if s/he is to detect such a mistake and, in school, how the teacher could have better advised Anisah. The Internet literacy surely is not simply a feature of the individual but rather emerges (or fails to emerge) from the interrelation between individual skill, education and interface design, a point I shall develop in the next chapter.

Anisah's case also shows the importance of family background in shaping internet use – her parents' cultural capital compensates for their lack of economic capital (Bourdieu, 1984) in helping Anisah 'get ahead', a motivation held, but not always achieved, by many parents for their children (Facer, Furlong, Furlong and Sutherland, 2003). Less typically, though characteristic of religious families (Hoover, Clark and Alters, 2004), Anisah's parents' strong moral values guide and restrict the nature of her online activities in a manner that, for the most part, she accepts. Where Anisah diverges from her parents – in seeking covert opportunities for peer-to-peer communication – she reminds us that literacy encompasses all skills, both those approved of and those disapproved of by adults.

My third case adds further dimensions to our growing account of youthful internet use: Ted was 14 when we first visited. More affluent than either Megan or Anisah, Ted was privately educated and lives in a white, middle-class family. Perhaps because he is an only child and dyslexic, Ted was rather over-protected at home; he watched a lot of television, though he also spent time playing sports and out with friends. Education seemed less emphasized in this household except as a means to gain a comfortable lifestyle. Like many children, Ted could not remember a time before the family had a computer, though the internet was recent at the time. Unlike many others, he did not profess much expertise about these technologies. 'I haven't got a clue', he said, when things went wrong.

Indeed, being a computer consultant, his mother was the expert at home, guiding Ted in his use of the internet. She bookmarked the BBC's Bitesize for him, though he did not use it, and also checked the history file to see what he had done online. Indeed, internet use in this family was fairly social, with a parent often in the study while Ted researched his homework online or played games, and he also went online with Mark, his friend and internet 'guru' (Bakardjieva, 2005). They checked on their favourite stars, television programmes, sports stuff, sent jokey emails to their mates, and visited Yahoo Chat – pretending to be older, to be other people, to meet girls. For Ted, the internet was mainly 'fun and funny, it's good, frustrating some-times' – especially in relation to effective searching.

We revisited Ted when he was 18, about to go to university. Family life had changed, with fewer family activities and Ted spending a lot of time in his room. Yet Ted still says his mother is better at using the internet than he is, particularly for searching (this seems likely, when we observe his rather poor searching skills). And when we ask, he has little idea why sites exist or what purposes they may serve. Like many teenagers, though unlike Anisah who considers it wrong, Ted now spends a lot of time downloading music via the peer-to-peer file sharing system Kazaa while, multitasking, he exchanges instant messaging with friends. Again unlike Anisah, Ted hardly searches the web at all now – only checking out university sites for possible courses when he needs to. The internet has become for him a medium of communication and music, not of information or education.

Regarding the discrepancy between economic and cultural capital, Ted's is the contrary case to Anisah's. Where Anisah illustrates the hopes of those who provide internet access for the otherwise disadvantaged, Ted shows that simply having the resources (financial, educational and parental) does not necessarily get you ahead if a genuine interest in learning and exploration is not cultivated effectively. Second, Ted's use of the internet is more social than either Megan or Anisah – where Megan takes turns with her brother on the internet, and Anisah uses it alone or to guide her little sister, Ted goes online with his friend or his mother and so gains from their greater expertise: literacy is, for Ted, part of a social practice, not just a cognitive skill, a point I return to in chapter 7. Last, one should note that although Ted, like the other two, would appear to a superficial observer to multitask effectively, the benefits he gains from the internet are curtailed, first, by his lack of interest in information, education or exploration and, second, by his poor skills in searching and evaluating websites.

We can compare their take-up of the interactive potential of the internet as follows. Megan mainly uses the internet to search websites and play games – what McMillan (2006) terms user-documents and user-system interactivity respectively. For Ted, user-user interactivity (chat, email) is more important. Anisah makes perhaps the broadest use of online options, treating the internet as a more flexible and diverse tool. These three rather different young people also share some common experiences. Each, for reasons of gender, class, ethnicity or special educational needs, is partly on the 'wrong' side of the digital divide (Warschauer, 2003), challenged to use their skills and resources to overcome this and get what they want from and through the internet. Each is treading a careful line between parentally approved and child-favoured activities, raising issues of domestic regulation (and its dependence on national regulation) which balance freedom, safety and privacy. And each is developing valued expertise

– 'internet literacy', though they seem more focused on making the interface work rather than on developing the broader and more ambitious critical and creative literacies that internet use affords.

I make no claim that these three children are typical of all others, though they are not exceptional.[2] My point is that examining internet use even in relation to just three children's lives raises a host of complex and fascinating questions. Before proceeding, however, we must ask how far these experiences are typical of children and young people. And what of their frustrations – are these typical even of this so-called digital generation? The next two sections consider these issues in detail, before addressing two central debates regarding children and the internet. First, are children really the experts online, especially compared with adults? And, if so, does this mean the so-called 'digital divide' does not apply among children and young people?

Appropriating the internet

> The children, well, Kathy really, said you must get on the internet . . . Well, we have looked up quite numerous things on the Internet but I think it was everybody else saying how good it is. (Father of Kathy, 15)

As statisticians chart the rise in internet access across and within countries, and as governments rely on the public to gain access at home, it is easy to forget the private struggles involved in going online. But the internet, as with many other media and consumer goods, challenges the assumption of trickle-down or diffusion theories (Rogers, 1995) that its use follows neatly from the spread of a more-or-less stable technology from the privileged early adopters to the mass market. Further, once they have passed the front door, once they have made the transition from marketing to purchase and then to use, the continually shifting significance of new media technologies as they become embedded in everyday life is hard to track.

The struggles implicated in going online are partly practical, albeit generating considerable frustration, as Kiesler *et al.*'s (2000: 327) report of calls made to technical help services makes plain: in their field trial of new internet users in the HomeNet project, 89 per cent of the 93 families needed helpdesk support in the first year for a range of problems from 'I can't log in' (because the Caps Lock was on and so the password typed didn't work) to 'I can't send this email' (because the domain suffix was wrong) to 'I can't get my MPEG videos to play' (because the settings needed to be configured). These struggles are also financial, for the hidden costs that follow the initial computer purchase decision are rarely highlighted: Caron and Caronia (2001) describe the cascade of further, often unanticipated demands – for a printer, a scanner, a faster modem, a webcam, updated software, new virus checking services, filtering software, and all the various leads and connections that many cannot even name.

In short, the simple question, 'have you got the internet at home?', belies the fact that access is a dynamic and social process, not a one-off act of hardware provision (Selwyn, 2004). Use depends on the answer to many questions about the ongoing quality of provision – does the internet connection work, can you afford it, is your operating system updated, have you got broadband, have you acquired so much adware and spyware that the service has slowed down, is the hard disc full, is the scanner working, can you afford more colour toner, do you know how to update software, download programms, install a filter, uninstall old software, connect a new printer? Use may also depend on whether you know someone who can help you, this being a social resource which is unequally distributed across the population. Unlike other domestic decisions (changing electricity supplier, buying a washing machine, learning to drive), 'going online' stands out as a substantial and often expensive leap in the dark. Even well-off homes contain broken or faulty equipment. And even skilled users under-use the capabilities of the technology they purchase. Ten-year-old Eve's father observes,

> It is odd about computers because you buy a computer and there's no instructions really. There's how to plug it together and now you get on with it. I mean we bought the book *Windows for Dummies*, so sort of ploughed through that bit by bit. The children use a lot of paint box . . . but I'm still not sure how to print it properly, it still comes out as a little tiny block as opposed to the whole sheet.

Fifteen-year-old Jane's father agrees:

> I didn't have a clue what was going on. You know, how to install stuff really, and it was, because the storage space, there's a C drive and D drive, we all tried to install it in the wrong place and I didn't have a clue what I was doing.

Given these various struggles, it would seem that, although the internet is, undoubtedly, becoming part of the taken-for-granted infrastructure of our daily lives, it has not fully achieved this status yet (Star and Bowker, 2006). For many families, the internet remains a fragile and opaque medium, being experienced as unfamiliar, confusing, easier to get wrong than right.

Adding to this account of practical and financial barriers, ethnographic studies of technology use and domestic consumption practices draw attention to the symbolic struggles involved in going online (Miller and Slater, 2000; Silverstone and Hirsch, 1992). For example, mothers have traditionally regulated their children's media use, and fathers have traditionally been relied on to fix household appliances, but the internet may challenge their competence and, therefore, their social standing in the family. Living rooms have long been places of leisure, but now they contain an object from the office – grey and ugly, undermining the care with which other furnishings have been chosen, squeezed uncomfortably onto the end of the dining table and making mealtimes difficult. Living rooms have also been places for shared activities – eating, watching television, talking – but now they contain an object that monopolizes one person's attention and excludes the others. Other solutions exist, but many are awkward.

Computers are being located in hallways and under staircases, or in cubby holes once filled with hanging washing or old toys. Increasingly, they find their way into children's bedrooms, supporting an individualized 'bedroom culture' (Livingstone, 2007c) which counters official advice to keep the computer in a public place for safety reasons. Fifteen-year-old Nell's father describes how the smallest room in the house has become a valued shared space:

This box room, what we call the study, is a communal room . . . so everybody can use it . . . Two years ago Gill was at home, she spent a lot of time doing homework, project work, on the computer, and now Nell is doing the same, and occasionally Chris uses the computer, and in the evening, the weekend, I use the computer as well. So everyone can have their own privacy in their own little room, and yet we've got this little box room that everyone can go to.

Through many such processes of appropriation, local practices of use develop around a new object or medium once in the home, anchoring it within particular temporal, spatial and social relations and thereby rendering it meaningful. As Bakardjieva (2005: 14) observes, 'The internet is a paradigmatic case of an open and ubiquitous technology' – unlike, say, the vacuum cleaner, it has 'a high degree of openness to interpretation', one consequence being that it affords an active interpretative role for the user. Silverstone and Hirsch term this interpretative process the 'domestication' of a new technology, a process which not only gives a meaning to the new arrival which likely differs from that anticipated by those who produced and marketed it but which also reiterates the 'classificatory principles that inform a household's sense of itself and its place in the world' (1992: 22).

Close observation of family dynamics suggests that the everyday practices required to fit the internet into domestic spaces, timetables and social routines serve both to blur and yet also to reinforce traditional social distinctions (Berker, Hartmann, Punie and Ward, 2006; Silverstone, 2006; Van-Rompaey, Roe and Struys, 2002). For example, the blurring of the spheres of education and entertainment marks a difference between the parent generation and that of their children, seen to inhabit a new and freer world that delivers valued competence through motivated but non-instrumental activities. Thus parents, along with educators and the educational technology sector, work to promote opportunities for learning through fun, in the hope that the child will meet parental ambitions by doing what they want to do anyway. They have been willing to reshape their homes, bringing educational and information technologies into leisure spaces, ready to learn alongside their children. Children's tactics of micromanagement within the household also blur the learning/fun boundary as they seek control over their own activities – by multitasking homework and instant messaging, for example, or by claiming an educational value for their favourite game.

However, this blurring of boundaries gives rise to some doubts among parents, for they recognize that the learning-through-fun thesis remains unproven and, after all, what looks like children simply playing and, by implication, wasting time, might really be the case. Thus we may also witness activities that reinstate and reinforce traditional social distinctions. Consider, for example, the deals parents and children strike up as part of the 'moral economy' of the household (Silverstone, 2006) – no games till you've done your homework; only use the printer for school work; priority on the internet goes to whoever is using it for something 'serious' and, in middle-class homes with more space, this may become a spatial economy also, as the home is divided into work and leisure spaces in which the computer is put in a dedicated study as merits its expensive and serious nature while keeping the living room for entertainment. This reassertion of the boundary is also evident in parental attempts to develop lay theories about what exactly is 'educational' about the internet (e.g. stressing keyboard skills, technical competence, internet literacy). Children's classification of internet sites and activities as either boring (i.e. educational) or cool (i.e. entertaining) also reinforces the learning/fun boundary, and their parents and teachers may well share their classification, albeit reversing the value judgement.

Thus boundaries are both undermined and reconstituted through internet use, resulting in the 'uncertain pedagogy of the computer' (Buckingham, 2002; see also Clark, 2003; Seiter, 2005). This applies more at home than in the more tightly controlled culture of the school, with evidence that children are freer to explore and experiment with the internet at home, using it for a wider range of activities, with less supervision and so, many argue, gaining more in competence (Kerawalla and Crook, 2002; Livingstone, 2002; Loveless and Ellis, 2001).

Enthusiastic take-up of (some) online opportunities

What do we know of emerging practices of internet use? How much are children and young people taking up online opportunities? By 2004 half of all UK 9–19 year olds had been online for over four years, using the internet frequently though for moderate amounts of time. Most go online for less than an hour, meaning that time online is similar to that spent doing homework or playing computer games and greater than time spent on the phone or reading; it is still less than spending time with the family and, at least for younger children, watching television (Livingstone and Bober, 2005; Ofcom, 2008a). So, what are they doing with this time?

Even a simple tally of online activities reveals that young people are, indeed, using the internet to explore, create, learn, share, network and even subvert. Consider this list of activities, here asked by the UK Children Go Online survey of the 9–19yr olds in the UK who use the internet at least weekly (84% of the population):

- 94% search for information
- 90% do school work
- 72% send/receive email
- 70% play games
- 55% instant messaging

- 55% (12+) visit civic/site

- 46% download music
- 44% (12+) seek careers info
- 44% completed a quiz
- 40% (12+) search goods/ shop

- 40% visit sites for hobbies
- 34% made a website
- 28% visit sports sites
- 26% (12+) read the news
- 25% (12+) seek personal advice
- 23% seek info about computers
- 22% voted for something
- 21% visit chat rooms

- 17% post pictures or stories
- 10% visit a porn site

These figures chime with parallel surveys conducted elsewhere. In a survey of five Northern European countries, 66 per cent of 9–16-year-old boys used the internet to play games and 49 per cent to download music, while the most popular activities for girls were email (58%) and using the internet for homework (43%) (Larsson, 2003). In the USA in 2003, 84 per cent of 12–19-year-old internet users went online to send/receive emails, 69 per cent for instant messaging, and 51 per cent for games (USC, 2004; see also Roberts, Foehr and Rideout, 2005). A time–use study of 8–18 year olds in the USA found that, of the 62 minutes they spent on computers daily outside work or homework uses, 19 minutes were spent gaming, 17 minutes were spent on instant messaging and 14 minutes were spent visiting websites – in addition, many young people play with consoles or handheld games (Roberts, 2005). Thus across countries, we see a fairly constant and familiar picture, with children mixing multiple activities so as to tailor internet use to suit their interests, potentially blurring the boundaries between education and entertainment, information and leisure, public and private, local and global.

For many internet users, the move is well underway from being primarily an information receiver (typically of mass-produced content on a one-to-many model of communication, albeit often an actively interpretative receiver) to also being a content creator (typically of peer-produced content, on a one-to-one or some-to-some model of communication). A Pew Internet survey in the USA found more than 64 per cent of online teens are creating content in one way or another (Lenhart and Madden, 2007). Among 12–17-year-old internet users, 39 per cent share their own creations online (e.g. artwork, photos, stories, videos), 33 per cent have created or worked on webpages or blogs for others, 27 per cent maintain a personal webpage, 28 per cent have created their own blog and 26 per cent have remixed online content to make their own artistic creation.[3] The Digital Youth Project similarly identified significant amounts of online creative activity among American teenagers (Ito, Horst, Bittanti, boyd, Herr-Stephenson, Lange et al., 2008). The rise of social networking (see chapter 4) is rapidly advancing these and other forms of user-generated content creation and sharing, opening up possibilities for participation well beyond a few media-savvy aficionados.

Notwithstanding the widespread incidence of diverse online activities, looking across the teenage population as a whole, the European Mediappro project is typical in warning of relatively low levels of creativity:

Creating their own content is much less widely practised than forms of communication: for instance, 18 per cent of young people say that they have a personal site, and 18 per cent a blog ... while in some cases, young people seemed uncertain what a blog was ... [T]he evidence here was that creative work was limited, with a minority of young people developing their own websites or blogs, and some evidence that these products could easily become inert. (2006: 12–13, 16)

The sense of disappointment implicit in the above account is echoed in other research. So, while popular activities centre on homework, games, communication and information-seeking of various kinds, it is also the case that civic activities are rather less practised, that education activities are often narrowly curriculum-focused, and that much of the 'information' sought online is superficial, if useful – weather reports, celebrity news, games cheats, jokes and product information are all popular.

Websites invite their users to interact with them in a range of ways, each of which asks the user to contribute something and, often, promises a response. Among 9–19-year-old internet users, the UK Children Go Online survey found that 44 per cent have completed a quiz online (more girls than boys), 25 per cent have sent an email or text message to a website (more older teenagers), 22 per cent have voted online (more middle-class and older teenagers), 17 per cent have sent in pictures or stories (more younger children), 17 per cent have contributed to a message board (more middle-class and older), 9 per cent have offered advice to others (more older), 8 per cent have filled in a form (more older) and 8 per cent have signed a petition online (more middle-class and older). Overall, 70 per cent report at least one form of interactive engagement with a website, suggesting a high level of interest and motivation. Yet, on average, young people claimed to have responded to just one or two out of a list of eight activities, suggesting that despite the many invitations to interact – to 'tell us what you think', 'email us your views', 'join our community', 'have your say' – take-up remains relatively low among this supposedly pioneering 'internet generation'.

A similar picture lies behind the finding that one third has made his or her own website (Livingstone and Bober, 2004b). When the UK Children Go Online survey asked those young people if their site was online, responses were as follows: 34 per cent never got it online, 17 per cent said it had been online but not any more, 17 per cent said yes but they hadn't updated for a long time, 21 per cent were not sure if it was still online and only 32 per cent said yes, it was online and updated regularly. Interestingly too, when asked why they made the website, 45 per cent said the school had required them to make the site for a school project, though 34 per cent (the next most common answer) said, 'I like doing creative things', thus revealing the balance between choice and constraints, or agency and structure in directing young people's activities. Last, when the two thirds who have not tried to make a website were asked why not, the most common answer was, 'I don't know how to do it' (54%), closely followed by 'it doesn't interest me' (41%).

Even as children and young people move beyond the initial hiccups of acquisition and early exploration, it seems that many make the unfamiliar familiar by establishing a fairly conservative pattern of use primarily defined by pre-existing interests and preferences, notwithstanding the huge diversity of possible activities and contents. These familiar use practices tend to be mass media-related (particularly, through preferences for certain television programmes, popular music groups or football teams) or strongly branded – with entertainment, game playing and educational uses for young children especially managed through the provision of 'walled gardens'. This suggests that youth consumer cultures, often expressed through specific fandoms, frame young people's engagement with online contents.

For example, the twenty most visited websites among British 4–15 year olds in May 2007 (Ofcom, 2007a: 194)[4] were, in order of popularity, Bebo (a youth-oriented social networking site), BBC Children, MiniClip (games), Nickelodeon Kids, BBC Learning, Piczo (social networking), Disney Online, RuneScape (a multiplayer game), GameSpot, VideoEgg (video sharing and advertising), Freeonline-games.com; RockYou! (social networking and photo sharing), Club Penguin (online community and games), Cartoon Network, Funny Games, Disney International, Stardoll (celebrity dressing up games), Adventure Quest (multiplayer game), BBC Teens and Everything-Girl.com (e.g. Barbie, Polly Pocket). While in many ways, these are much enjoyed by children, it is notable that they are all commercially produced sites, driven by advertising and sponsorship or marketing opportunities, except for the three BBC sites (itself a major brand).[5] There is little here that is civic in orientation, alternative in values or boundary pushing in terms of creativity or learning, though the BBC sites do offer curriculum and health-related information of value and, no doubt, the opportunities to play multiplayer games can be stimulating and absorbing for those who become involved (Gee, 2008).

Digital natives?

> I think in comparison to my parents and loads of the older generation I know, I do know more. But I think there are a lot of people that know a lot more than me ... A lot of my friends know a lot ... And I learn from them. (Lorie, aged 17)

Doing research, it's easier with books than on the internet – but maybe it's quicker because there's so much on the internet. What you want to find is really hard to find. With books it's a lot easier. I can't really use the internet for studying. (Abdul, aged 17)

Part of the challenge of making the most of the internet is the degree of expertise required. It is not hard to find teenagers confessing to difficulties in using the internet, notwithstanding popular rhetoric regarding youthful 'cyberkids' (Facer and Furlong, 2001) or 'the digital generation' (critiqued for its technological determinism by Buckingham, 2006). Digital media contrast with previously new media – books, comics, cinema, radio and television – since for these, even if parents weren't familiar with the particular contents their children engaged with, at least they could access and understand the medium and, if they wished, share the activity with their children. The demands of the computer or web interface render many parents 'digital immigrants' in the information-age inhabited by their 'digital native' children (Prensky, 2001). As the mother of 10-year-old Anna says,

> I'll have to come up to a level because otherwise I will be a dinosaur, and ... when children laugh at you and sort of say 'Blimey, mum, don't you even know that?' ... Already now I might do something and I say 'Anna, Anna, what is it I've got to do here?' and she'll go 'Oh mum, you've just got to click the ...' and she'll be whizzing, whizzing, dreadfully.

Unsurprisingly, children and young people themselves, conscious of being the first generation to grow up with the internet, concur with this popular celebration of their status. Amir (aged 15) says confidently, 'I don't find it hard to use a computer because I got into it quickly. You learn quick because it's a very fun thing to do'. Nina (aged 17) adds scathingly, 'My Dad hasn't even got a clue. Can't even work the mouse ... So I have to go on the internet for him.'

While these claims contain a sizeable grain of truth, we must also recognize their social value for children. Only in rare instances in history have children gained greater expertise than parents in skills highly valued by society (one instance is the significance of diasporic children's learning of the host language and culture in advance of, and for the benefit of, their parents). More usually, youthful expertise – in music, games or imaginative play – is accorded little serious value by adults, even if regarded with nostalgia.

However, although young people's newfound online skills are justifiably trumpeted by both generations, it would be unfortunate if this blinds us to the real challenge of using digital media to realize their potential for engagement with information and education content and for participation in online activities, networks and communities. At a more reflective point in the interview, Amir both supports the claim of a reverse generation gap (Holloway and Valentine, 2003; Ribak, 2001) but also revises the notion that it is easy to learn to use a computer:

> Well, my mum doesn't use the computer, she doesn't even log on. But my dad – he doesn't know how to use the computer as well – but he always asks me 'how do you do –?' It doesn't take a day to learn how to use a computer, it's very difficult to use it. But when you get used to it, you're able to use it.

Indeed, the very difficulty of accessing and using the internet beguiles many adults into believing that if only they could master 'clicking' on links with the mouse, then they – like their children – would be inter-net 'experts'. This is not a belief that we hold for the pen, else we'd stop teaching pupils 'English' once they had learned to read and write; but the child who 'whizzes' around the screen seems so skilled that, we conclude comfortably, they know all they need to know already.

Even for the task of finding information online, a task in which the UK Children Go Online project found most young people (87%) to be confident, not all is plain sailing. Heather (aged 17) complains that,

> Every time I try to look for something, I can never find it. It keeps coming up with things that are completely irrelevant . . . and a load of old rubbish really.

In the survey, only 22 per cent of 9–19 year olds who go online at least weekly say they always find what they are looking for, although 68 per cent 'usually' find the information they need. Further, only two in five claimed to know how to send an instant message (44%), and fewer could fix a problem on their computer (40%) or set up an email account (39%), while just one in three knew how to download music (34%), and less than a fifth could set up a filter (18%) or remove a virus from their computer (18%).

How should we conceptualize the practical skills and subtle com-petencies which facilitate confident internet use, the lack of which limits the use of new and inexpert users if not excluding them alto-gether? Empirical investigation of online expertise is only now getting underway, either measuring 'self-efficacy', a self-reported global assessment of one's skill level, strongly influenced by self-confidence (Eastin and LaRose, 2000), or measuring claimed specific online skills which, though also self-reported measures, may be more accurate about concrete skills, as in the findings above, or, finally, directly observing skills in use, arguably the most objective method but expensive to measure among large samples (Hargittai and Shafer, 2006). Generally speaking, these measures are highly correlated; thus, while skills matter, it is noteworthy that the perception of oneself as more or less expert online matters too. Also important is the finding that both self-efficacy and online skills measures are correlated with the take up of a range of online opportunities: in other words, the more skilled one is in using the internet, the greater the range of activities one undertakes online, and vice versa (Livingstone and Helsper, in press).

Using the global self-efficacy measure, the UK Children Go Online survey found that over half (56%) of the children and young people who use the internet at least weekly consider themselves 'average' in terms of their online skills. Indeed, neither children nor parents who used the internet claimed great expertise, though children and young people claim greater online self-efficacy than do their parents: 37 per cent consider themselves 'advanced' or 'expert' vs. 15 per cent of parents (Livingstone and Bober, 2004b). Age differences were strongly marked, with judgements of self-efficacy rising sharply with age. Consistent with long-term concerns regarding gender differences (Hargittai and Shafer, 2006), slightly more boys (35%) than girls (28%) considered themselves 'advanced', suggesting greater levels of confidence and, perhaps, skill among boys.

These skill levels translate into some genuine struggles to make the internet work effectively. Pursuing children and young people's search skills, for instance, the survey found that the majority (41%) look only at the first ten search results, though 37 per cent compare information across several sites to make sure it is reliable, and one in five (19%) checks when a site was last updated. Further, one in five (18%) asks for help when they can't find something, and one in three (32%) bookmarks or adds a good site to their 'Favorites'. Significantly, older children, those from a middle-class background and those who judge themselves more expert tend to have better searching skills (looking beyond the first ten sites, using bookmarks, checking information across sites); girls, younger children and the less expert are, by contrast, more likely to ask for help (Livingstone, Bober and Helsper, 2005).

It seems that learning to search can be a hit or miss affair. Young people (and, indeed, adults; Machill, Beiler and Zenker, 2008) may not grasp the principles of how to search or the different options open to them. They are sometimes caught out by their inability to spell, or replicate the address correctly. Many of the youngest users have fairly simple interests in pop stars or television sites and know only a few key website addresses, perhaps four or five which they remember off by heart. Some only ever visit one site. The commercial websites that they commonly visit have little incentive to provide links outside their own site and browsing from such 'sticky sites' is unlikely to widen their horizons. Even at 18 and at a private school with great IT facilities, Ted struggled to search effectively, typing in key words inappropriately, confused about bookmarking and so always retyping addresses, and not understanding why you can't always go 'back' (itself a good question; Isaacs and Walendowski, 2002). Similarly, Megan, at 8, kept forgetting her Neopets password, couldn't work out how to get the site to remind her of it, so her pet died. Since her teachers say she is an intelligent girl, perhaps the problem lies with the site design? Certainly, when I observed her attempts, the lack of any site feedback on her repeated mistakes seemed a striking failure to provide the 'just in time' information supposedly characteristic of the internet (Smith and Curtin, 1998).

One observational session in 13-year-old Candy's middle-class household clearly illustrates the problems of information access. Candy was trying to find a German website on food and drink to help her school work. First, she checks with her father that 'du' is the German url suffix. He suggests 'dr' but this doesn't work, so she tries www.esse. com.du. This doesn't work, so she tries .de, with no more success. The researcher suggests www.essenundtrinken.com.de but this doesn't work either, because mistakenly Candy typed 'trinke' without the 'n'. Even with the 'n' added, the url doesn't work (because the .com is a mistake). Candy's father then suggests .dr for Deutsche Republik or 'just to leave the last bit off and see if it finds it'. Neither works. Her brother, Bob, comes across to try to help, but he can't remember any German sites. Now Candy is trying www.yahoo.co.du. Bob suggests capital 'D'. Her mother suggests .uk to see if 'the whole thing is working'. Her mother clicks on 'refresh' but Candy warns, 'Don't do that! It goes on to a porn page!' (She knows this means someone in the family had previously accessed this). Finally, her mother tries www. yahoo.co.uk, which works, so the family concludes that the problem lies with the name of the German site not with their skills. Candy gives up. As this example illustrates, not only can it be hard to obtain the simplest information but also trial and error learning is not always effective, social support can make things worse not better, and fears of online risks can make even normal internet functions taboo.

In this section, my intention has not been to criticize young people – they are undoubtedly enthusiastic, creative and motivated in their exploration of online opportunities – but rather to raise questions about whose responsibility it is to support their internet use, whether through interface design, parenting or education. In this connection, it is pertinent that parents are more modest about their own online skills (Livingstone and Bober, 2004b). Among those who use the internet, 28 per cent of parents describe themselves as beginners compared with only 7 per cent of children. Half (52%) of parents consider their skills average, and only 12 per cent consider themselves advanced compared with 32 per cent of children. Even though parents agree that children are more advanced than they are and that fewer of them are beginners, they still consider more children to be beginners and fewer to be advanced than do the children themselves. This generational skills gap between less-expert parents and more-expert children poses an interesting challenge to parents' ability to guide their children's internet use.

Familiar inequalities

> Some people can't afford it, which is just a sad truth. (Steve, aged 17)

The resources, expertise and difficulties discussed thus far are unequally distributed through the population. The UK Children Go Online survey found that children in 88 per cent of households classed as middle class (ABC1) versus 61 per cent of working-class (C2DE) households had access to the internet at home. Yet the prominent academic and policy debate over the digital divide is almost exclusively focused on adults, considering children only insofar as they live in differentially resourced households (Rice and Haythornthwaite, 2006; Selwyn, 2004; Warschauer, 2003). Some even assume that, since the 'digital generation' is mostly online and appears so competent, that the digital divide will disappear once today's children become adults (e.g. Compaine, 2001; see Wyatt, 2005, for a critique). But for children as for adults, matters of inequality are both subtle and persistent.

> A lack of meaningful use ... is not necessarily due to technological factors ... or even psychological factors ... engagement with ICTs is based around a complex mixture of social, psychological, economic and, above all, pragmatic reasons. (Selwyn, 2004: 349)

In recent years, and in recognition of the complexity of inequality, academic debate has reframed the 'digital divide' in terms of the social inclusion agenda, refocusing attention on 'digital inclusion' or 'digital differentiation' (Van Dijk, 2005):

> A framework of technology for social inclusion allows us to re-orient the focus from that of gaps to be overcome by provision of equipment to that of social development to be enhanced through the effective integration of ICT into communities and institutions. This kind of integration can only be achieved by attention to the wide range of physical, digital, human, and social resources that meaningful access to ICT entails. (Warschauer, 2003: 14)

Insofar as people continue to approach learning, careers, advice, participation or any other social benefit through both online and offline means, with the balance of resources still greatly favouring offline routes to inclusion, inequalities in digital inclusion may matter little. But if and when this balance alters – as it surely has already for young people in relation to education and communication especially – then online routes to inclusion will become more important, and the costs of digital exclusion will become more apparent. The UK Government frames an equivalent policy shift in terms of a refocusing from 'basic' access to 'advanced' use thus:

> Encouraging remaining non-users onto the first rung of the internet ladder will remain an important challenge to guide policy in the next few years. However, for individuals to fully realize the benefits of the internet we must help them move up the ladder – to move from basic activities such as e-mail and browsing to more advanced uses such as e-learning and transactional activities like buying, banking and accessing government services. (Office of the e-Envoy, 2004: 11)

Although few children and young people in the UK are wholly excluded, there are many ways of charting differences among them (Livingstone and Helsper, 2007a). The UK Children Go Online survey found that most 9–19 year olds are either daily (41%) or weekly (43%) users; a few used it less often (13%) and, although one in four lacked access at home, just 3 per cent counted as non-users (as most had access at school) compared with 22 per cent of their parents. In short, a binary divide between haves and have-nots, or users and non-users, no longer applies in a simple fashion to children and young people.[6]

This does not mean we should forget the minority who make little or no use of the internet, nor the larger proportion whose use is less than optimal (however and by whomsoever defined). Although little research has asked why some children don't use the internet, there is a growing body of research examining reasons given by adults. The Office of Communications (Ofcom, 2004a) lists lack of interest and costs among the main explanations for non-use. The Oxford Internet Survey found that, besides access and interest, a lack of skills was an important reason as well as a certain fear of technology (Dutton and Helsper, 2007; see also Selwyn, 2003; Wyatt, 2005). Similarly, the main reasons for adult non-use in the USA include lack of access, followed by a lack of interest and not knowing how to use the internet (USC, 2004). Parallel questions in the UK Children Go Online survey suggested that, as for adults, and across all ages, limited access is the most important reason that prevents children and young people from using the internet at all or, for low users, from using it more, followed by lack of interest; lack of skills seemed less a barrier for children than for adults (Livingstone and Helsper, 2007a). Lack of interest may seem puzzling, given the enthusiastic reception of the internet by the majority, and it is noteworthy that, when asked, nonusers do not grasp the attraction of those uses to which their peers put the internet – as Dutton and Helsper argue, the internet is an 'experience technology', you have to use it to understand its potential.

One factor that clearly differentiates households is that of 'cultural capital' (Bourdieu, 1984). Strongly but not entirely related to social class, cultural capital encompasses the ways in which variation in parental education and knowledge mediates their children's ability to use the internet constructively. Well-educated parents are more likely to actively support educational values in the home, to use computers at work and be knowledgeable about them, to have high educational aspirations for their children and to be able to send them to well-resourced schools. The middle-class child is often also advantaged in terms of 'social capital' or social support – a knowledgeable family member ready to fix problems or guide you in getting started, friends who know how to update the software or where to get help. For example, Ted's middle-class mum takes the computer to work to receive new software and asks a colleague at work for help when the family computer crashes. Ted himself has a school friend who has taught him almost everything he knows about the internet. Others have to find such things out for themselves and the chances of their lacking confidence, competence or simply lapsing from use is far higher. Although one might hope such children would catch up with Ted, it is instead the case that middle-class households actively seek to maintain their position of advantage, continually improving their quality of access and use so as to stay ahead (Golding and Murdock, 2001; Hargittai and Walejko, 2008; Kiesler, Zdaniuk, Lundmark and Kraut, 2000).

Even among the majority – those 84 per cent in the UK Children Go Online survey who use the internet at least weekly – inequalities persist. Gender, age and socioeconomic status (SES) all matter to where and how young people gain internet access. Boys have access to the internet in more places, and are more likely to have it in their bedroom, compared with girls (41% vs. 34% in 2008, according to ChildWise, 2009). Further, boys use the internet more often than girls, have been online for longer, and spend longer online. Unsurprisingly, then, boys claim more skills than girls: while girls are more likely to know how to send instant/text messages, boys are more equipped for almost all other activities, the biggest differences being in knowing how to download music (42% vs. 25%), get rid of a virus (22% vs. 13%) and solve a problem on the computer (44% vs. 35%). On the other hand, there are signs that gender inequalities are gradually disappearing (McQuillan and d'Haenens, in press).

Interestingly, regarding age, the oldest and youngest groups have less home access than the younger and middle teenagers, while older teen-agers have more points of access, and more private access in their bed-rooms. The number of skills increases with age, although the oldest group (18–19 years old) claims fewer skills than the 16–17 year olds. Regarding socio-economic status, middle-class children have more access points, and the most affluent are considerably more likely than the poorest group to have home access, broadband and bedroom access. Doubtless, as a result, working-class children make less use of the internet and interact with websites less than do middle-class children, and they judge their expertise as lower, this suggesting the persistence of a digital divide not (only) in terms of access but in the quality and depth of use.

Note that there is a danger of misinterpretation if one simply com-pares usage across unequal groups without first taking account of dif-ferences in access. For this reason, we also analysed usage patterns only for those with home access (Livingstone and Helsper, 2007a). This showed that, even when all have access to the internet at home, there are still differences in use by age and gender: boys and older teenagers use the internet more frequently than girls and younger children. Interestingly though, the socioeconomic status difference all but disappears if we compare only those with home access. In other words, children from working-class homes who have home internet access use it just as much as those from middle-class homes. This sug-gests that providing home internet access in low SES households may help to close the gap in use, potentially reducing disadvantage – a finding that justifies policy efforts to overcome inequalities in provi-sion, as in the HomeNet initiative in the USA (Jackson *et al.*, 2006b), the Home Access initiative (BBC News Online, 2007) in the UK, and similar initiatives elsewhere. However, it is also the case that, since middle-class children tend to have better quality access and support at home, they make a broader and more interactive use of the internet than do working-class children (see also Hargittai and Walejko, 2008).

We can account for gradations in children's internet use, resulting from differential access, together with stratified economic, social and cultural resources, as follows (Livingstone and Helsper, 2007a):

- Non-users are more likely to be from working-class households and from the 9–11 or 18–19-year-old groups. Only half of the non-users have access to the internet at school and very few have home access or access elsewhere. A fair proportion claims to have little interest in using the internet, though, unlike adult non-users, they seem not to feel they lack the skills to use it; however, they may lack a sound appreciation of what users are doing online.
- Occasional users are again more likely to be working class, though over half have home access, and most have access at school. Their quality of access is poorer than for more frequent users (in terms of broadband, and bedroom access). Not only do they not go online very often, they also spend less time online and, like the non-users, they explain their low use in terms of difficulties of access and lack of interest.
- Those who go online at least weekly are spread across the socio-economic status categories. Most have access at home, school and elsewhere, and they spend longer online than the occasional users. They consider themselves 'average' in their skills, and they take up about five of the online opportunities we asked about, mostly using the internet for school work, information, games and email. In the previous week, they claimed to have visited between one and four different websites.
- A little older than the weekly users, the daily users come from more middle-class homes and benefit from better quality internet access. One in three has access in their bedroom, and nearly half have broadband. They have been online for longer than the other groups, and spend longer online each day. They also consider themselves more skilled (self-labelling themselves 'advanced' users), and they take up on average seven of the opportunities we asked about. This makes their internet use less predictable: for example, they claimed to have visited five to ten different websites in the previous week. Over half use it for school work, information, email, instant messaging, games, downloading music and looking for cinema/theatre/concerts.

Thus, children and young people are divided in terms of their take up of online opportunities. For some, the internet is an increasingly rich, diverse, engaging and stimulating resource of growing importance in their lives; for others, it remains a narrow and relatively unengaging if occasionally useful resource.

Creative engagement

Although as we have seen, only some children and young people are sustained content producers, the democratizing potential of the new multimedia landscape occasions considerable optimism among commentators and scholars. Kress, for one, relishes the liberation from linear, authoritative, elitist texts long favoured by established institutions (education, government, church), arguing that:

> The work of reading, and the demands made of readers, will, in this new landscape, be different and greater. The anxieties of cultural pessimists about the 'decline in cultures of reading' . . . are premature. The opposite will very much be the case. (2003: 166)

Illustrating just this point, Jenkins makes much of the case of home-schooled *Harry Potter* fan Heather Lawver who, in her early teens, launched 'The Daily Prophet', an online newspaper for Hogwarts.[7] *Harry Potter*, he argues, is what Eco (1979) terms an open text, for it 'allows many points of entry'. Thus,

> A girl who hadn't been in school since first grade was leading a world-wide staff of student writers with no adult supervision to publish a school newspaper for a school that existed only in their imaginations. (2006a: 172)

Another example is provided by 14-year-old Lucas Cruikshank, who is reaching millions with his own channel on YouTube, the hugely popular user-generated content site.[8] Presenting himself as a manic, weird six year old called Fred with an alcoholic mum and an occasional girlfriend, he speaks rapidly straight to camera in a high-pitched voice to reveal, apparently naively, the crazy world inhabited by adults as seen from a child's perspective. These short episodes demand a witty, cynically, reflexive reader of no little sophistication (Livingstone and Thumim, 2008).

Albeit with more ambivalence, given the commercial provenance of their object of study, Buckingham and Sefton-Green (2003: 396) argue similarly that Pokémon 'both invites and positively requires activity on the part of audiences', thus representing 'a new emphasis in children's culture'. Such texts, as Jenkins shows in relation to *Harry Potter* fan fiction, lead children spontaneously to read widely, to develop their writing skills by experimenting with diverse literacy forms and genres and to sustain a committed community of peer contribution and constructive critique.

Reflecting on the activities of 13 year olds Sophia and Brian, Leander and Frank (2006) conclude that the creative possibilities afforded by convergence culture are indeed empowering, enabling the construction and performance of a unique and expert self embedded in an affirming community of peers. Sophia spends many hours selecting, organizing, editing and remixing images of her favourite band, creating icons, collages and wallpaper according to a personal aesthetic which, interestingly, contrasts with the mainstream popular culture images that decorate her bedroom. In this way, Leander and Frank suggest, she has created 'new meaning from fragments collected from the flow of circulating images in which she inserted herself' (p. 193) and then distributed this as a public resource – as theorized by Jenkins (2006a), Corsaro (1997) and de Certeau (1984) in media studies, childhood studies and sociology respectively. Sophia's continuous activity of revising, adapting and improving her collection is one way of undertaking precisely the continuous construction, revision and updating of the self required in late modernity (Giddens, 1991).

Brian conducts similarly creative identity work through a literate engagement with the online game, 'Star Wars Galaxies', shaping and adjusting the virtual body of his online character in the game, although in this instance, the decisions to be made were set by the parameters of the software rather than conjured up entirely from his imagination, as in Sophia's case. So, where Sophia found that the biographies of the band were nowhere to be found on the web, leading her to construct and disseminate these anew, Brian had to make his selections from the palette of options provided by the producers. Testimony to children's creativity, over a year later the researchers observed that Brian had become involved in developing a new game with his online friends, generating collective expertise and aesthetics in the process. Both children, argue Leander and Frank, have entered 'a hybrid of the producer and consumer roles of cultural production' (p. 204), marking a significant break from the forms of engagement available with traditional mass media, especially for young people.

Through empirical accounts such as these, we can begin to ground Kress' largely semiotic 'reader' as also a social actor, realized through both a literate engagement with multimodal resources and also contextualized within particular socio-cultural life circumstances.

However, the shift in focus from semiotic readers and writers to social actors also reminds us that children's life circumstances are pressured, constrained, stratified. As we saw earlier, only a minority have tried to set up their own webpage and commonly these sites are neither currently online or updated regularly – it seems likely that their online engagement is constrained both by their literacy skills and by the limited affordances of the sites they use.

Rather more common than the activities of Sophia and Brian is the highly formatted, often commercialized, forms of interaction that, also, are labelled 'creative', assessed as indications of media literacy. For example, Willett (2008) observes young teenage girls visiting websites in which they are invited to dress a figure, change its looks or select its clothes. Restrictive though the options available to them are, and even though playing the online game is strongly shaped by normative peer culture, including highly evaluative attitudes to their bodies (see also Thomas, 2000), Willett argues that these games permit girls a space to fantasize about their own changing identity in a manner that can be empowering and agentic.

Recall Megan, who when aged twelve showed me how the AOL kids' home page offered a story writing option. The site contained a standard story with gaps – you insert your own name, that of a friend, your favourite colour and so on – and the result was a personalized story to print out. Megan enjoyed this, but it did not detain her long. Our discussion then turned to story writing in general, and Megan switched to Microsoft Works to show me a story she was in the middle of writing. This turned out to be a lengthy, closely written thriller, heavy on dialogue and drama, containing tragedy, murder, and centring on a mysterious beautiful foreign woman saying dramatic and intriguing things as she rushes about solving mysteries. In telling her story, Megan had employed elaborate forms of expression, a complex vocabulary, and an exciting and witty writing style, if rather breathless and melodramatic.

What can we learn here? The same girl writes two stories, one minimally literate and even impeded by some 'creative' software, the other highly literate yet enabled merely by the blank page. I suggest that, while 'the internet' provides the resources for some children to be creative, perhaps indeed extending creative possibilities to those who, in previous times, did not feel comfortable with pen and paper, for the most part children's online creativity – including Heather, Lucas/'Fred', Sophia, Brian and Megan – reveals creativity they would have engaged in anyway, with or without the internet. It is another question whether, as a result, they gain skills online that transfer to other forms of learning (see chapter 3).

New opportunities?

Media are articulated simultaneously as both technologies and as texts (Silverstone, 1994). Hence the internet can be considered both in terms of the diffusion and appropriation of technological goods or consumer durables (computer, broadband access, printer, scanner, webcam) and also in terms of the particular symbolic forms whose construction and circulation increasingly mediates information, communication and learning (websites, interactive services, search engines, multiplayer games, social software). While examination of the former tends to dominate public policy and business circles, academic research increasingly argues that access is only the beginning of the story of 'going online', and that questions of symbolic use must now come to the fore.

This chapter has observed families' significant investment in resources (time, money, space, effort), as invited of them by government and industry, to keep up with the 'moving target' of quality internet access and use. They are buying expensive equipment and squeezing it into whatever space is available, with the hope of enhancing their children's educational prospects, thereby transforming their homes from a screen-rich 'leisure centre' into an 'informal learning environment'. The internet-mediated links among children's different activities – as learning becomes fun, as play may (or may not) be educational or as online chat serves (perhaps) to sustain networks – raises new challenges for parents, educators and others concerned with children's welfare.

Families' various struggles to sustain and manage the place of the internet within the home matter because the home is, increasingly, a node in a broader network that connects children's lives to a range of opportunities to learn, communicate, know, participate, and so forth. Inequalities across and within households continue to matter also. Boys, older children and middle-class children all benefit more from greater and better quality access to the internet than girls, younger and working-class children, and while access does not wholly determine use, it certainly sets the conditions within which children explore, gain confidence and skills, and so take up more or fewer online opportunities. Further, setting aside the extraordinary news headlines of young hackers breaking national security codes or teenage entrepreneurs making a fortune on eBay, not to mention the youthful origins of such recent successes as Google and YouTube, this chapter has argued that, for most children and young people, their digital or internet-related expertise is productive but limited, and we should be cautious regarding hyperbolic claims regarding the 'digital generation'.

What are the consequences of this newfound expertise? Although it certainly seems that the internet makes many activities easier, altering the patterning of young people's social and leisure activities, radical change is less in evidence than often supposed. Yes, they love Google and can find any information anywhere, but is this really expanding their horizons? Yes, the internet is their first port of call for homework, but are current uses transforming processes of learning and thinking? Yes, they can email grandparents and holiday friends in far away countries, but is this reshaping global connections in a new cosmopolitanism? When this 'internet generation' was asked which medium they would most miss if it disappeared tomorrow, only 10 per cent named the internet in 2004 (Livingstone and Bober, 2004b), though by 2007 this had risen to 24 per cent of 12–15 year olds (almost as high as television at 29%; Ofcom, 2008a). As Marie (aged 16) put it:

> If we didn't have the internet, we'd get everything we have on the internet somewhere else. And I don't think the internet is the solution to anything. And especially not education because there are too many distractions ... I just think the internet can be an easy way of doing things.

Even assuming this view will change, with the internet rising up young people's 'must have' list, the question of transformative change remains. When Linda (aged 13), says, 'I use it for like homework, emailing my cousin in Australia and keeping in touch with my friend in Cornwall', one wonders whether this is what was meant by empowering young people or democratizing participation? Do such uses reflect a growing breadth and sophistication of use? Do they justify the investment made by governments, teachers and parents? What do we hope Linda will use the internet for next? And will it be worth running the attendant risks for?

Between the large hopes for social progress and the mundane realities of email, surfing and game play are two mediating steps – first, the online resources; contents and services which enable new opportunities, and second, the desires and motives, and the interpretative and critical competences, of children as they engage with these resources. While the latter are much celebrated in public discourse, the former easily slip from critical view. In this book, I try to keep both in focus simultaneously when exploring, in turn, children and young people's engagement with the internet for learning, communicating, participating and dealing with risk.

3

Learning and Education

ICT can improve the quality of teaching, learning and management in schools and so help raise standards. That's why ICT is at the heart of the DCSF's commitment to improving learning for all children.' (ICT in Schools)[1]

Increasing use and reliance on the internet means that for a growing percentage of students the quality of online services and self-support options can directly affect their learning. (Lankes, 2008: 102)

There is little doubt that society's main ambition for children's use of the internet centres on learning – informally at home and through formal education in school. Today in Britain, nearly every child uses the internet and other online technologies, most of them at home and school, some only at school, some elsewhere also. Not just computers on desks, information and communication technologies (ICTs) are becoming embedded in the fabric of every activity, part of the infrastructure that supports learning, communication, and participation. In schools, lesson plans and classroom arrangements are being redesigned. At home, the perceived educational benefits of domestic internet access have fuelled its rapid diffusion – indeed, in our aspirational culture, little else could have so effectively driven the domestic ICT market than the expectation that internet access gets one's child 'ahead' or at least stops them 'falling behind'.

The educational expectations held out for the internet are not entirely instrumental. The notion of 'having the whole world at your finger tips' is regarded with enthusiasm and delight by children and adults discussing the internet – many can hardly imagine finding information without it. Academics agree, with many now conducting sometimes pragmatic but often idealistically motivated research on the possible pedagogic benefits of educational technology. Governments are putting huge resources into equipping schools with information and communication technologies of all sorts, not only hardware but also connectivity, software and electronic curriculum materials. In the UK, the British Educational Communications and Technology Agency (Becta) claims that it

> leads the national drive to inspire and lead the effective and innovative use of technology throughout learning. It's our ambition to create a more exciting, rewarding and successful experience for learners of all ages and abilities enabling them to achieve their potential.[2]

As this quotation illustrates, the hope is not only to improve traditional educational outcomes but also to enhance learning more widely, as part of the move to support informal and lifelong learning.[3] Yet while governments can determine policies for schools – envisioning, planning for and resourcing the incorporation of educational technologies at will – determining policies for private homes is a different matter. National policies for enhancing informal learning 'anywhere, anytime', supporting 'the home-school link', building 'a whole school community', and so forth depend, crucially, on the active participation of individual parents. Two hurdles exist: one is attitudinal, for parents must share this educational and technological vision for their child; the other is material, for parents must possess the resources (time, space, knowledge and money) to implement this vision. We saw in chapter 2 that the attitudinal change is well underway, with many parents committed to providing computer and internet access at home for their children. But the material hurdle poses a different challenge, and as we also saw, parents may be struggling to pay for it, to fit it into crowded homes and daily timetables, and to maintain and update it. In early 2008, the UK Schools Minister argued that,

> We have to find a way to make access universal, or else it's not fair. More than a million children – and their families – have no access to a computer in the home. I want a home computer to be as important as having a calculator or pencil case is … The so-called 'digital divide' cannot be allowed to reinforce social and academic divisions.[4]

This speech announced a policy of supporting home access among disadvantaged children, the principle being that:

Universal Home Access (UHA) [is] the next stage in realising the transformational benefits of ICT to learners through anytime access . . . We intend to extend learning outside the classroom so every learner has the same opportunities to learn and access the digital benefits that virtual learning can provide.[5]

Over the past decade, the notion of 'ICT skills as a third skill for life alongside literacy and numeracy' (Office of the e-Envoy, 2004), once an outlandish idea, has moved to centre stage. This is not because ICT skills are important in and of themselves but because, like print literacy, they constitute the means by which people can access information of all kinds, learn in a multimedia environment, communicate in a global context, participate in civic activities, express themselves creatively and, not least, obtain employment in a competitive knowledge society. As the Office of the e-Envoy (2004: 11) continues, the purpose is 'to enable all adults to have the ICT skills they need to learn effectively online, become active citizens in the information age and . . . contribute productively to the economy.' It seems that digital technologies are set to be as important in the twenty-first century as was the book – and the mass literacy movement – in the nineteenth (Luke, 1989). And the social changes they stimulate may be as radical.

With government policies being formulated to provide ICT to support all children learning to their full potential, with industry behind the diverse initiatives designed to make this happen, and with households with children gaining and sustaining internet access at home, one might think there was little left to discuss. But, are these exciting ambitions being realized? Do internet access and use at home and school really deliver benefits in educational terms? Are today's children learning more or, perhaps, differently, compared with earlier generations?

Accompanying every step of these policy developments, critical commentators have expressed doubts that more/better ICT means more/better education.[6] These suggest that the use of computers in educational settings undermines creativity, isolates children from face-to-face communication, increases social inequalities, and distracts educators' attention from children's needs by focusing instead on technology. Expecting ICT *per se* to transform education surely smacks of technological determinism, even though it is, indeed, a popular hope. Parents may judge a school's computer facilities even before they meet their child's teacher. Home access initiatives give more thought to the provision of connected computers in homes than to the purposes to which those computers could and should be put. Public discourse focuses more on the introduction of technology than on the introduction of new teaching practices in the hope of benefiting pupils.

Setting aside arguments that are simply anti-technology, setting up an ideal of 'innocent childhood', two significant issues demand attention. The first issue is empirical: does the evidence really support the claim that ICT enhances learning? The second issue is conceptual: what do we mean by learning and is our very conception of learning changing? Addressing these two issues forms the substance of this chapter. As shall be seen, the former can be addressed relatively straightforwardly, though the need for further research is unremitting. However, while the second must be considered seriously, consensus may never be reached for, as Scribner and Cole (1973: 553) noted, 'every theory of education clearly requires a theory of society as a whole and of how social processes shape education'. Several decades later, a theory of society is hardly consensual, not least because society itself continues to change.

The promise of the transformed classroom

Interviewer   What about at school? Do they encourage you to use the
             PC, or did they teach you a lot about it?
Angie (9)   Yeah, it's IT, that's what it's called, and you go, you have
             about 10 computers in a big computer room and you work
             in groups to do like stuff on the computer. They let you go
             on the internet but it has to be educational stuff you look
             up and all that. That's boring but we don't listen to that and
             we look up what we want when the teacher's not looking.

In the wake of Al Gore's (1991) famous 'information superhighway' speech, the UK Government announced its plan for the National Grid for Learning in 1997. By analogy with the electricity grid and other cornerstones of national infrastructure, the plan was to introduce the internet into all schools by 2002 (DfEE, 2007). A period of considerable investment and rapid expansion followed, with £102 million spent on learning technologies in schools in 1998–9, the first year of the National Grid for Learning programme, rising year on year to £860 million in 2007–8 (DCSF, 2007). In 2007–08, this translated into an average ICT spend (hardware and software) of £17,800 per UK primary school and £76,380 per UK secondary school (BESA, 2008).

In 1998, only 17 per cent of UK schools were connected to the internet, quickly rising to 86 per cent by 2000, with an average of 60 computers connected to the internet per secondary school (DfEE,

2000). In March 2005, the e-strategy, 'Harnessing Technology: Transforming learning and children's services', shifted the emphasis from access to use, and particularly drew on the potential 'of digital and interactive technologies to achieve a more personalized approach within all areas of education and children's services' (DfES, 2005). This included a £60 million 'Computers for Pupils' scheme targeted on 1,000 schools in the most deprived parts of the country, followed in 2008 by the £30 million 'Home Access' initiative' to support the acquisition of internet access in the poorest homes (BBC News Online, 2007). In 2006, virtually all schools were online, with an average of 231 connected computers per secondary school (BESA, 2006). A similar story can be told in many developed countries worldwide. In the majority of EU countries, schools now provide at least one computer for every ten pupils, and one for every five pupils in many countries (Eurydice, 2005). Data from the Programme for International Student Assessment (PISA) survey reveal that on average at least 60 per cent of schools in Europe have computers connected to the internet (Eurydice, 2005).

Has this investment transformed teaching and learning? There is certainly evidence that ICT is being widely used. In 2001, 54 per cent of UK 11–18 year olds used the internet for school work, rising to 83 per cent in 2002, and by 2004, almost all teenagers had used the internet for school work (Hayward, Alty, Pearson and Martin, 2002; OfSTED, 2004). The UK Children Go Online survey reported that among 9–19 year olds who go online at least once a week, 90 per cent use the internet to do work for school or college; further, 1 in 5 uses it daily, and nearly three quarters use it at least once a week (Livingstone and Bober, 2004a). Digital resources are used by 4 in 10 UK primary teachers and 3 in 10 secondary teachers for lesson planning: although ICT in schools is mostly used for whole class activities, arguably perpetuating the traditional learning model of the teacher at the front of the class by using display technologies such as the interactive whiteboard, a substantial minority of teachers (2 in 5 primary and 1 in 5 secondary schools) have used ICT for small group work, often using subject-specific software (Kitchen, Finch and Sinclair, 2007).

Is all this sufficient to judge that educational technologies have, indeed, become as much part of the national infrastructure as the electricity grid? It is hard to answer such a question when it remains unclear what character this infrastructure should have. Is ICT, for example, intended to replace the book? Or should it be integrated with books in some way? Is the crucial technology the interactive whiteboard at the front of the whole class or the laptop on the desk of each child? Over and again, notwithstanding the grand expectations of technological determinists, the history of new technologies shows that these tend to supplement rather than radically displace previous technologies (Adoni and Nossek, 2001; Kayany and Yelsme, 2000; Livingstone, 2002; Neuman, 1988). The generation gap is evident from the finding that, for many pupils, the internet has rapidly become their first port of call: the survey found that 60 per cent of 9–19 year olds in full-time education regard the internet as the most useful tool for getting information for homework; only 21 per cent named books (Livingstone and Bober, 2004a). By comparison, parents still think that books are most likely to help their child do better at school (82%), albeit closely followed by the internet (73%), the computer (40%), and television or video (22%).[7]

However, as Bolter and Grusin (1999) have convincingly argued, although new media rarely displace older media entirely, they do 'remediate' them, altering their potential or encouraging their further specialization because of the altered array of communicative possibilities. In other words, following the advent of the internet, the book itself is not what it once was. On the one hand, the linear format of traditional print media is still regarded by many children as inaccessible, exhausting or simply 'boring' (Livingstone, 2002). But on the other hand, there has been a transformation in textbooks and other printed educational resources in recent decades: 'the contemporary science textbook is no longer a book in that [traditional] sense at all; it functions as a packaged resource kit' (Kress, 1998: 65). Thus today's textbooks require of their readers precisely the visual literacy that screen-based technologies also emphasize (Kress, 2003).

Intriguingly, it is not only adults who retain some doubts as to whether the internet could and should replace books. Yes, the internet is widely seen to provide access to almost all forms of information and knowledge, while simultaneously affording self-paced content delivery, as-needed testing, just-in-time advice, shared learning resources and specialist networking, and much more. Still, consider this focus group discussion among 14–16-year-old boys from London:

Interviewer	So it's said the internet helps you with your school work?
Elkan	Not really …
Interviewer	Yeah, I'm just wondering how true that is. What do you think Faruq?
Faruq	That isn't really true. Mostly we use it, mostly for what you want to know. Say, it does help you with school with

subjects, depending on what the information you want, some subjects like geography and things that you can look around the world. Geography's a good example of the internet. You can do some research about other cultures and other communities ... And mostly like things like English, Maths, it's not ...

Interviewer   It's not so useful. OK.

Prince   To really understand for people of our age group, we don't really use the internet to do like research most of the time. You're just on the internet to look for football news and things like that.

Star and Bowker (2006) define infrastructure as that which is so thoroughly embedded in the social structures of everyday life that it is rendered 'transparent', its shaping role having become invisible and taken for granted. Infrastructure, they further suggest, is linked into the conventions of a community of practice, embodying particular standards, expectations and values. As political and policy struggles continue regarding the introduction of ICT-related changes in teacher training, classroom practice, curriculum redesign and practices of educational assessment, it seems that getting the hardware into schools is, as with equivalent struggles in the home, only the beginning of a lengthy process of transforming educational infrastructure. Undoubtedly, government targets are being set, pupils' and parents' expectations are changing, and so are teaching practices. But little of this is yet taken for granted and, far from invisible, the very prominence of these changes on the public and policy agenda points to the efforts still required if ICT is to become genuinely part of the learning infrastructure.

Learning to use the internet

We do have internet at school and we do have IT lessons but they don't really help us. I don't quite know where I've learnt it ... I think it's just been fiddling around with it basically. (Nell, 15)

Before children can learn by using the internet, they must learn to use the internet – just as learning to read and write has long been a prerequisite for learning of all kinds. Learning to read is, of course, a major task for education in the early years. But acquiring print literacy extends throughout the school career, as pupils are taught to use dictionaries and encyclopaedias, to search for specialist resources in libraries, to evaluate alternative sources, determine authorial authority and critique complex texts. A parallel trajectory for acquiring 'internet literacy' is not yet well-developed, although in key ways, the underlying requirements of critical literacy are equivalent (Kellner, 2002; Snyder, 2007).

Although many children, it seems, learn to read by just 'picking it up' informally at home, the efforts of parents to support (or 'scaffold') their children's literacy skills have long quietly complemented the formal curriculum. For internet literacy, equivalent parental skills may be lacking yet, perhaps for similar reasons, teachers also seem to leave learning to informal processes. In their study of young children's use of computer and videogame technology, Smith and Curtin (1998) confirm Turkle's (1995) influential observation that children 'just do it', figuring it out how to use the internet intuitively through trial and error, testing out hunches, 'just mucking around', and by drawing where needed on informal 'teachers' (relatives, friends) rather than beginning with the rules in the manual and then implementing them.

Children are not unhappy with this, enjoying the image of the internet as 'their domain', but as we shall see, the absence of formal teaching of web search and evaluation, for instance, may not optimize the educational potential of the internet. Kim (aged 15) explains, with some gratification, 'I think it's better to do like trial and error because you can like learn from the mistakes from it, and you can find new places and stuff, for different sorts of things.' Claire, also 15, agrees: 'I don't think you can teach anyone how to use it. You sort of just have to try yourself.' Stuart (aged 17) sees more of a role for the school, saying that pupils do 'learn about search engines and all them and the actual internet as a whole.'

However, this informality has some serious implications for the role and authority of teachers, as Smith and Curtin point out:

> With all these teachers the relationship is informal and the instruction experiential and 'just-in-time' (provided as required). This 'learning-by-doing' model contrasts with the teaching approach that attempts to provide a store of knowledge and skills before practice' (1998: 219).

It also has consequences for pupils if their informally acquired expertise turns out to be more claimed than actual, part of the widespread 'myth of the cyberkid' (Facer and Furlong, 2001). While teachers struggle visibly with changing models of learning and children struggle more quietly, perhaps, with having fewer skills than are popularly attributed to them, the social consequence is a challenge to the long-established hierarchy between teachers and pupils, potentially undermining teachers' authority as sources of knowledge – certainly compared with their greater competence regarding reading, books and libraries. Partly as a result, children claim to learn more from friends than teachers, and they often do so out of the classroom as well as in it. As Lorie (aged 17) says, 'I think I picked it up – well, my old secondary school didn't really have internet access. So I was never really taught much about it there. But I mainly picked it up from friends.' Often an older sibling is helpful. As Claire (aged 15) says:

> If I get stuck on it, I always go and ask my brother because he's like started a job in computers like that. Or I ask my dad because he's worked with computers for years, basically his whole life. So if I don't know stuff, I go and ask them. I never ask my mum' cause she, like, she doesn't know that much about them really.

But this is not to say that teachers play no role. In the UK Children Go Online survey, we asked 9–19 year olds who go online at least once a week who had helped them use the internet.[8] Two thirds (66%) said a teacher helped them; for almost half of them (44%) it was a parent; for a third (33%) it was friends and for 17 per cent it was siblings. A further 4 per cent claimed to be self-taught, 3 per cent learned from a website or an online course, and 1 per cent mentioned guidance from another relative. Perhaps if we had asked who helped them learn to read a book, more would have mentioned parents as well as teachers. What is different, then, is first the role of peers (friends, siblings) in supporting learning and, second, the positive discourse of informal, trial-and-error learning that predominates over that of formal education. Both make learning to use the internet appear fun, certainly compared with learning to read, bringing it under children's control and allowing them to learn at their own pace. But it also has some disadvantages – children's competence in using the internet can be patchy and unequal.

The survey also revealed considerable variation in the formal teaching of internet literacy. Of those in full time education, the majority had received lessons on how to use the internet; 23 per cent report they have received 'a lot', 28 per cent 'some' and 19 per cent 'just one or two' lessons. However, nearly one third (30%) report having received no lessons at all on using the internet. It might be expected that these children may have lessons yet to come in the curriculum; however, it is teenagers who are less likely than younger children to have been taught how to use the internet at school.[9] Not surprisingly, 69 per cent of non-users claim to have received no lessons, yet 36 per cent of daily users also report receiving no lessons in internet use. The lack of lessons matters to both groups, for while the former group risks digital exclusion from educational and other online opportunities, the latter group risks the dangers of ill-informed or inappropriate uses.

In public policy terms, the school has the potential to equalize the social inequalities that exist at home. While one would hardly claim that all children receive the same quality of education, schools represent a public policy tool to equalize provision or compensate for disadvantage. In support of this, the survey found that children reported similar levels of teacher guidance irrespective of their socio-demographic background, although middle-class pupils claimed to have received a little more guidance on searching than did the poorest group – 74 per cent of those from upper middle class (AB) households vs. 62 per cent of those from lower working-class (DE) households. By contrast, parental support is more stratified: while on average, 44 per cent have been helped by parents in learning how to use the internet, twice as many middle-class than working-class children claimed this (59% AB vs. 28% DE). Perhaps in consequence, working-class children were more likely to identify a teacher as helpful (74% DE vs. 59% AB; 66% overall), thus pointing up the relatively greater importance of formal educational support for poorer children in helping to overcome disadvantage. Schools clearly have an important part to play.

A reliable learning tool?

Using the internet as a learning tool requires a different, arguably greater degree of critical understanding than was needed for books. Twenty years ago, a library of books may have been difficult to use, off-putting especially for underprivileged children and relatively unsupportive of informal or sociable models of learning. But they did not generally contain unreliable or biased information; for print media, quality thresholds, gate-keeping checks and editorial standards are customary. Since editorial standards are much more variably applied to online texts, this places much greater demands on children to evaluate their quality and reliability. This is by no means easy, as Faruq (aged 15) told us:

> It's like you don't know who's doing what, whose website it is, who wants what, who wants you to learn what. So you don't know who's put what information there, but . . . it's reliable – but you don't know who's put it, who wants you to gain what from that information.

In other words, while accessing the internet feels 'easy', the intellectual demands are much harder. Critical literacy is no simple skill, for it rests on an understanding of the social, cultural, economic, political and historical contexts in which online content is produced and distributed. Audiovisual media literacy programs have long been concerned to disabuse their students of the myth of technology's neutrality, a favourite exam question being, 'television is a window on the world: discuss'. Yet popular discourse implies that the world of information and learning made available by the World Wide Web is, indeed, a window on the world, with, implicitly, no constraints or biases and no interests at stake (Burbules, 2006).

The UK Children Go Online survey also found that four in ten (38%) pupils aged 9–19 say that they trust most of the information on the internet, half (49%) think that some of the information can be trusted, and one in ten (10%) are sceptical about much of the information online. Of course, much depends on the sites that they access – shall we regard the trusting or the sceptical as more literate? A hint can be gained from the further finding that those who judge themselves beginners in using the internet are more distrustful towards internet content than expert users. It is not, then, that the beginners are more naive and therefore more trusting. Rather, it seems that experienced users have gained the skills to locate material they can trust, for example, by checking information across several sites; they are also more likely to say that they have been taught how to decide if information is reliable. Beginners, on the other hand, lack searching and critical skills and so are more distrustful of online content.

However, only 33 per cent of 9–19 year olds who go online at least once a week say that they have been told how to judge the reliability of online information, according to the survey, leaving two thirds of young internet users with no advice or explicit instruction on evaluating online information. They are learning, however: an audit of UK children's media literacy found that only 31 per cent of 12–15 year olds make some kind of check (e.g. of the date or source) when visiting a new website (Ofcom, 2006a) though by 2008 this had risen to 56 per cent (Ofcom, 2008a). Given the enormous variation in nature and quality of information available online, a crucial skill that all users must acquire is that of determining the quality and worth of the information they find. As Hazel (aged 17) reports with some frustration,

I don't really find the internet that helpful really. When I'm looking for things I can never find them. And it's always so vague when you do find them, and never pinpoint something down.

Even a sceptical attitude may not be enough to identify reliable online sources, as the skills required are subtle, lacking also among many adults (Henry, 2005; Walton and Archer, 2004). Sixteen-year-old Jim's suggestion that 'if it's got a long name, it's probably like a home website and it's not likely to be that really accurate is it?' is indicative of the myths that grow up when sound guidance is lacking. Meola (2004) recommends 'chucking the checklist model' (i.e. checks on authority, accuracy, objectivity, currency and coverage) in favour of three contextual techniques of evaluation based on peer- and editorially reviewed resources, making comparisons and seeking corroboration to ensure reasoned judgements of information quality (see also Lankes, 2008). Fifteen-year-old Jane has more-or-less worked this out for herself, for she observes,

> I have found before you're researching a person and you find different things on different sites and you don't know which to believe kind of thing. Em 'coz I guess it's like not all official kind of thing.

But, like Jim, Jane solves this problem not by contextual judgements but rather by going to well-established, branded sites – 'I'll try the BBC because they're quite good at having stuff.' While a brand like the BBC may provide a shortcut to editorially reviewed resources, trust in brands may also limit search judgements, especially when brand preferences are made on stylistic grounds. Anisah, aged 12, claims:

> I like colour, I'm a colourful person. I just don't like dull things. Whenever I go on to it, it's like dull, there's no big bubble writing, big letters, just ordinary typing, black and white, and if there's a really important word they're just blue, and that's just boring for me.

Similarly, asked to define a good website, Jim focused first on ease of navigation, second on the variety of interactive options and third on visual presentation; only fourth did he mention content as a criterion. In view of young people's preference for pictures and interactivity, it is unsurprising that their judgements of quality refer to the visual aspects of website design and opportunities for interactivity. Moreover, their reluctance to read lengthy printed text on websites means they may also not realize just where a search has taken them and what kind of information they are receiving in consequence (for parallel judgements of trust in the domain of online health, see Sillence, Briggs, Harris and Fiskwick, 2004). Some have learned to cross-check sources for corroboration. Ted, 14, says:

I looked at stuff on the internet and I've looked up Encarta and it's been different – and then you don't know which one's right and which one's wrong. So you sometimes decide to check the second time on the internet and see if it's the same as on Encarta.

His friend Mark adds, with some sophistication,

they could both be right but they're just using different sources of information ... it's good, 'coz then you get different point of views.

Not all viewpoints are equivalent, however. Jane, 15, recalls learning the difference between Holocaust information sites and Holocaust denial sites:

When we did the 2nd World War there was quite a lot of stuff ... We found a lot of like people who were like, what's the word, Nazi supporters ... And we were told not to look at those sites, because, well, that was not what we were looking for but they came up anyway because that was with the 2nd World War ... when you search for them it gives you a description of what it is and what's it about, so we'd read that and then not look at that site.

But other distinctions are less straightforward. Who offers the 'best' account of environmental hazards – the Ministry for Agriculture or Greenpeace? Is a good website one that provides the facts objectively or one that questions 'the facts'? Should critical literacy include a knowledge of, even a critique of, the commercial basis of the web – of branding, walled gardens or the commercial interests that structure search directories?

Critical literacy is not simply a skill to be acquired by the user – it can also be aided or impeded by site design. Eastin, Yang and Nathanson (2006) examined how young children (on average, nine years old) in the USA determined the credibility of online information. They found that most had trouble recalling online information when the text including advertising pop-ups in addition to plain text and that they tended to believe sites that included advertising and lacked a clear source compared with those that provided a source or that lacked advertising.

Evaluating the reliability of sources is also difficult because children lack an understanding of the political economy of online content production – something that has long been argued as crucial to media education, even though it is often omitted (Buckingham, 2005). Asked who makes the games websites he had been looking at, John, a bright, middle-class 8 year old, said he does not know and has never thought about it. Prompted further he revealed a very altruistic idea of the producers' motivations. Ted and Mark, middle-class 14 year olds, showed a similar lack of interest. Asked about the site they were playing on (www.hoddle.com, a commercial site with simple but up-to-date, jokey games combined with the advertising of football-related items), they first said they have never really thought about why such sites are made. Pressed for an answer, they suggest that the producer did it to amuse himself, or that he perhaps had something against the players. Even Steve, aged 17, considered that sites exist because 'somebody's just thought this is my interest, and I'm going to share it with the world'.

Indeed, most children and young people we interviewed in the focus groups appeared to be naive about the motives behind the websites they were using (Livingstone and Bober, 2003) and only a few were aware of the commercial interests or strategies at stake (see also Montgomery and Pasnik, 1996; Turow, 2001). The task of judging, and discriminating among, the plethora of websites turned up by any online search does, it seems, represent a serious challenge for educators in the digital environment.

Enhancing traditional learning outcomes

> The outcomes of the initiatives are more evident in improvements in pupils' achievements in ICT capability than in their application of this learning in other subjects. (OfSTED, 2004: 4)

ICT provision is resulting in pupils gaining internet literacy. But the considerable financial investment in ICT hardware and software in schools has not been directed to this end. Rather, three distinct claims regarding the educational benefits of ICT have been advocated – that ICT aids traditional learning outcomes, that ICT helps compensate for specific forms of disadvantage, and that ICT enables new, even radically transformed, learning outcomes. The three sections that follow address these in turn.

As the above quotation suggests, evidence for the claim that ICT aids traditional learning outcomes is, perhaps surprisingly, lacking. A recent report to Congress in the USA found that test scores in classrooms using reading and mathematics software for a full year were no different from those using traditional teaching methods (Dynarski et al., 2007). This study found some indication that more use could improve results for reading, but not mathematics, among 9 year olds and that, among 5 year olds, results were greater when class sizes were smaller. Since, for the most part, ICT investment uses resources that might otherwise be used to reduce class sizes, this latter finding – indeed, all the study's results – is not encouraging.

A similar study, conducted from 1999–2002 for the British government to evaluate the ICT in Schools Programme (following implementation of the National Grid for Learning), obtained similarly mixed findings regarding improvements in national test scores (Harrison *et al.*, 2003). Its conclusion appears encouraging:

> ImpaCT2 is one of the most comprehensive investigations into the impact of information and communications technology (ICT) on educational attainment so far conducted in the UK ... In every case except one the study found evidence of a positive relationship between ICT use and educational attainment. (p. 1)

Yet the report adds that, 'in some subjects the effects were not statistically significant and they were not spread evenly across all subjects' (p. 1). Specifically, comparing those in 'high ICT' or 'low ICT' groups (according to their usage in particular subjects) over an 18-month period, examination of test score results for pupils aged 11, 14 and 16 years old produced a rather haphazard set of findings. ICT use was associated with improved performance in English but not science or mathematics for Key Stage 2 pupils (aged 10–11 years); it was associated with improved science but not maths or English scores for Key Stage 3 pupils (13–14 years), and it was associated with improved science and design/technology scores for Key Stage 4 pupils (aged 15–16 years).

As with the American study, explaining so particular a pattern of significant and insignificant findings is difficult, inviting *ad hoc* explanations. In neither of these studies were the researchers able to offer a clear account of why some learning outcomes were improved for some children and not others; indeed, neither really attempts this, though the researchers' disappointment in the gap between expectations and realities is evident. In a second strand of the ImpacCT2 research, focusing on the nature of ICT use in the classroom, along with the views of parents and teachers, it became clear that pupils experience computers and the internet far more positively at home than at school – in terms of their autonomy, flexibility and length of time online (Somekh *et al.*, 2002). ICT use at school appears constrained in terms of pupils' freedom, and contained within specialist ICT lessons rather than thoroughly integrated into the everyday classroom experience. The researchers recommend that teachers:

> need to consider how to build on their pupils' experience, developing
> skills and enthusiasm in relation to networked ICT ... [and] schools
> and teachers need continuing support ... [if] they are able to achieve
> the necessary changes in school culture and teaching practices to reap
> the benefits of the Government's investment. (p. 3)

Five years on, Sheard and Ahmed (2007) found from their detailed
examination of five secondary schools, that use of the internet is now
more embedded in classroom practice, especially for 14–16 year olds.
The main technologies in use were interactive whiteboards, a virtual
learning environment, educational computer games, email, and
e-learning for independent study. They observed that,

> situations where engagement in learning was evident due to the use of
> technology showed that pupils used the technology as a cognitive tool,
> an organizing tool, and, to a lesser extent, as a social tool for learning.
> (p. 1)

These findings are broadly positive, especially as regards motivation
and personalized learning opportunities. However, they are tempered
by commonplace observations of restrictions on access, difficulties in
the effective use of discussion boards and other collaborative learning technologies, and continued challenges for teachers and teacher
training in integrating e-learning and face-to-face learning. As Seiter
documents, the more educational software is ambitious in its learning
outcomes, the more it poses real difficulties for teachers in managing
the class:

> The hours of trial-and-error that many digital skills require and the
> freedom to develop a deep understanding of software that includes
> programming are nearly impossible to practice in a public school com-
> puter lab. (2008: 36)

More conventional uses of ICT in school are beginning to reveal
modest benefits. Thiessen and Looker (2007) examined whether
learning to complete a range of computer and educational software
tasks transfers positively to reading, finding that for Canadian 15 year
olds, more ICT use on educational tasks was associated with improved
reading achievement scores up to a certain point, but beyond that,
more ICT use was associated with lower scores. This curvilinear relationship may account for the often contradictory or inconclusive
findings obtained by those seeking wider educational benefits of ICT
use in the classroom or home. As Thomas and Ludger add, from the
international student survey, PISA:

bivariate analyses show a positive correlation between student achievement and the availability of computers both at home and at schools. However, once we control extensively for family background and school characteristics, the relationship gets negative for home computers and insignificant for school computers. Thus, the mere availability of computers at home seems to distract students from effective learning. (2004: 1)

They report a similar curvilinear relationship: those who sometimes use computers or the internet at school perform better than those who never use them; but those who often use computers/internet perform even worse. It is hard to disentangle the degree to which prior ability or socioeconomic background may account for this finding, but what is clear is that a simple increase in ICT provision is not straightforwardly associated with enhanced educational performance. Intriguingly, exactly the same conclusion was reached about educational television some years ago (Huston and Wright, 1998).

Not only is the amount of use crucial, so too is the quality of use, as Lei and Zhao (2007) found when examining the student learning outcomes for 12–13 year olds in an American middle school. Improvements in grade point averages were associated with subject-related technology uses – dedicated software resources or games produced to support particular curricula elements of science, maths or history; but, unfortunately, these tended to be among the least popular activities. This contradicts the easy assumption that because children like using technology, this in and of itself gives them the confidence and motivation that enhances learning. It also contradicts the hope for a positive transfer from entertainment and communication uses to those that specifically facilitate school grades. And it brings into question the teaching in ICT lessons of what are, essentially, clerical skills (using databases, PowerPoint presentations, word processing) – while useful for future employment, these may be neither motivating nor supportive of knowledge that can transfer to new subject domains. But it does show that specialist uses of ICT, when designed to support particular curriculum goals, can be beneficial.

Although many commentators concur with Twining *et al.* that 'there is a lack of robust evidence on the impact of ICT on learning' (2006: 21), Condie and Munro are more optimistic:

the evidence seems to point to an impact on attainment where ICT is an integral part of the day-to-day learning experiences of pupils, although the weight of evidence is insufficient to draw firm conclusions. (2007: 24)

This conclusion stresses the importance of adopting a wider lens so as to include the teacher/pupil relation and the classroom culture. Without this, or if the focus is placed on access rather than use, if the conditions for high-quality use (including teacher training, curriculum redesign, supporting collaborative learning practices) are neglected, if children remain unclear regarding searching, navigating and evaluating online content or, worst, if ICT provision is permitted to substitute for good teaching in the classroom, then children's education will not benefit. Put positively, all this does suggest the conditions under which ICT could be effectively employed in the classroom to improve traditional learning outcomes. While certainly not as easy as putting a computer in the classroom, it may be that ICT can support education if these relatively demanding conditions are met.

Compensating for disadvantage

One strand of policy and research has focused on the specific 'catch-up' potential of ICT for disadvantaged pupils (Bradbrook et al., 2008). In the HomeNet Too study in the USA, low-income, mainly ethnic minority children were provided with a home computer and internet connection, as well as sufficient technical backup to ensure the technology worked. 'Mere connection' was found to improve these children's school achievement as a direct function of their frequency of use (Jackson et al., 2006b). Conducted as a longitudinal study over a period of 16 months, this intervention was particularly successful in reducing the digital divide. As Jackson et al. conclude:

> Children who used the internet more had subsequently higher GPAs and higher scores on standardized reading achievement tests than did children who used the internet less. The reverse was not true. Children who had higher GPAs and standardized test scores did not subsequently use the internet more than did children with lower GPAs and test scores. (2006a: 158)

In other words, it is not that already high-achieving children get more from gaining access to the internet than low-achieving children. Rather, the findings showed that, for all these children, increased internet use raised achievement in reading, though not in mathematics. Ironically perhaps, the benefits of internet use appeared to lie in the reading of printed text on the screen, this especially benefiting children who otherwise read little. While such findings augur well for initiatives such as the UK's Home Access programme, there remains some doubt as to whether these findings can be scaled up as connectivity grows. In the HomeNet Too intervention, the researchers suggested that these disadvantaged children may only have benefited from the internet because their friends could not afford access; hence though they read and searched for information, they did not chat or play online (unlike better-off children).

Also problematic is the likelihood that, far from schools compensating for inequalities, inequalities may grow as schools become more effective over time in building on skills gained at home. McPake, Plowman, Stephen, Sime and Downey (2005) suggest that the reason why evidence is lacking that disadvantaged children without home access really miss out is not because ICT use confers no benefits but rather because schools are (as yet) unable to respond flexibly to the new literacies being acquired by media-rich children at home and so these latter do not, in practice, capitalize on their skills to pull ahead.

There are, in short, few grounds here for complacency – simply letting the educational technology market expand may not serve pupils' interests, especially those from disadvantaged backgrounds. Furthermore, now that inequality is generally defined in relative not absolute terms, even as disadvantaged children gain more internet access they may remain relatively disadvantaged both in terms of the quality of internet access they enjoy (e.g. functioning technology, updated software, broadband speed, and so on) and because one form of disadvantage is generally correlated with others (e.g. parents' disposable time, parental education and expertise, educational values at home, calm places for study, and so forth).

The risk is that of a vicious circle in which ICT provision, whether at home or school, further advantages the already advantaged, these tending to act so as to maintain social distinctions by taking up new resources disproportionately (Bonfadelli, 2002; Bourdieu, 1984; Seiter, 2008; Valentine, Marsh and Pattie, 2005). Thus, introducing internet access into a class of children from mixed backgrounds may exacerbate rather than reduce pre-existing differences in resources, motivation and confidence – even though internet access is often mooted precisely as a means of reducing inequality by aiding those children who are most turned off by traditional, print-based teaching methods. Empirical findings already point in this direction. Snyder *et al.* (2004) showed that gaining ICT at home was not enough to ensure that disadvantaged families used the internet as richly as the advantaged family. Peter and Valkenburg (2006a) found similarly that more affluent and more educated parents supported their children's use of the internet for information and social activities, while those from lower status backgrounds were more likely to use it for entertainment.

More positively, some findings suggest that the introduction of ICT into schools can improve the motivation of disaffected pupils (Cook, 2005), as well as the learning outcomes of pupils with special educational needs (Passey, Rogers, Machell and McHugh, 2004). The next step for policy and research might be to widen the frame when identifying and evaluating learning outcomes for disadvantaged pupils, especially insofar as they might benefit from the use of ICT to support new pedagogies (Johnson and Dyer, 2005) and alternative learning styles (Morgan and Kennewell, 2005). Just such arguments are, moreover, now being advanced not just for disadvantaged pupils but for all learners, young and old, as examined below.

Broadening expectations – enhancing soft skills

Is education best assessed through increases in grade point averages, reading ages or exam results? Surely the potential of the internet is greater than this – as, more importantly, is the potential of a child to learn. While government departments call for ICT to improve test scores, reduce disadvantage and ensure delivery of the basic skills of reading, writing, maths and science, critics reject the lack of imagination in this agenda, seeing it as wedded to a twentieth, even a nineteenth century conception of drill-and-skill education, with scholastic aptitude testing the only legitimate outcome measure (e.g. Smith and Curtin, 1998).

An alternative proposition, attracting considerable interest and enthusiasm, is that ICT enables the development in or, better, outside the classroom of precisely the soft skills vital for meeting the new demands of the global service and information economy of the twenty-first century (Gee, 2008; Jenkins, 2006b; Merchant, 2007; Shaffer, Squire, Halverson and Gee, 2005; Squire, 2005). This conception of learning capitalizes on the evident enthusiasm with which children use the internet for exploration, creativity and fun when at home (Livingstone and Bober, 2004b). Thus it encompasses not just ICT-mediated formal educational and information resources but also, indeed especially, the use of instant messaging, online gaming and social networking. These, it is held, foster constructive learning practices and encourage learner motivation. If one argues that the relative failure to demonstrate clear benefits of ICT use in the classroom is due less to the limited potential of ICT than to the limited expectations of educationalists, there are, clearly, far-reaching consequences for teacher training, classroom management and curriculum design. This too might prove welcome for those disillusioned with present arrangements.

Marsh *et al.* quote a teacher describing the beneficial effect for one little boy of engaging in a media/ICT-based project at school:

> Shafeeq, who doesn't particularly talk a lot unless it's, 'I'm gonna shoot you', that kind of thing, he really got into it and he wanted to tell us a story. His story came alive and it was alive for him and everyone was listening to his story. Well usually it's, 'Come on, don't talk about guns, don't talk about that.' So he really found a vessel to tell his story and to ... I think he's got more friends now through it. (2005: 69)

This does not simply illustrate how ICT can motivate a previously disaffected child, but it also points to the potential of ICT to help children formulate their ideas, find a voice and communicate effectively. Jenkins calls these the 'soft skills' or new literacies required by 'convergence culture', each of which, he argues, could be positively supported by engaging with ICT if only schools could move beyond the individualistic skill-and-drill model of learning, with its hierarchical teacher-pupil relation and its narrowly instrumental specification of educational outcomes. He identifies these soft skills as follows:

- Play – the capacity to experiment with one's surroundings as a form of problem-solving
- Performance – the ability to adopt alternative identities for the purpose of improvisation and discovery
- Simulation – the ability to interpret and construct dynamic models of real-world processes
- Appropriation – the ability to meaningfully sample and remix media content
- Multitasking – the ability to scan one's environment and shift focus as needed to salient details
- Distributed cognition – the ability to interact meaningfully with tools that expand mental capacities
- Collective intelligence – the ability to pool knowledge and compare notes with others towards a common goal
- Judgement – the ability to evaluate the reliability and credibility of different information sources
- Transmedia navigation – the ability to follow the flow of stories and information across multiple modalities
- Networking – the ability to search for, synthesize, and disseminate information
- Negotiation – the ability to travel across diverse communities, discerning and respective multiple perspectives, and grasping and following alternative norms (2006b: 4).

This list is refreshing for its celebration of children's creativity, thoughtfulness and desire to learn anywhere, anytime. And its conception of the learner contrasts with traditional models of the transfer of knowledge from authorities to pupils which require pupils to compete with each other and to meet a nationally set pace of learning. Disappointingly, then, one must observe that, having already noted the lack of evidence that ICT supports traditional educational outcomes, so too is the jury out regarding the claim that ICT can be used to enable new and creative forms of learning. one reason may lie in uncertainties over how to assess the acquisition of soft/alternative learning skills within educational settings. So, although educational software and other electronic resources materials are often marketed as the 'fun way to learn',[10] it is not yet clear how these can intersect with educational practices so as to support new digital literacies and deliver the exciting outcomes their advocates hope for. Some case studies may point the way forward.

Nyboe and Drotner (2008) describe a school-based Danish animation project that deliberately broke with school routine and teacher-pupil hierarchies in order to enable pupils to co-design a digital animation over a two-week period. The researchers observed how pupils' decision-making, design, construction and implementation all emerged from lively and often playful peer interaction – showing how learning itself is social rather than purely individual, being enabled by discussion, negotiation, imagination and conflict resolution. Significantly, as often argued but too rarely demonstrated, the project proved effective in terms of pupils' learning not only about software, media production and team working but also in terms of their gaining the media literacy required to analyse and critique the multiplicity of representational forms and knowledge claims that constitute and surround them in daily life. In short, peer culture was harnessed to deliver learning outcomes valued by teachers, children and, most likely, future employers.

In another project, after noting the success of one specific learning technology termed 'the story listening system', Cassell also emphasized how technology supports collaborative learning processes (see also Goldman, Booker and McDermott, 2008; Sefton-Green, 2004). These, she concludes, 'demonstrate the importance of the social context of peer collaboration, its playful, spontaneous, personally meaningful dimensions, and its ability to evoke a desire to make oneself understood' (2004: 101). Nocon and Cole are equally optimistic, observing that 'flexible sites of informal education, after-school programs have allowed low-income and immigrant children access to safe places and flexible responsive programming as well as contact with diverse perspectives' (2006: 117–18).

Some, however, sound a note of caution. Willett's (2005) observational study of ten boys aged 9–13 years old in a Saturday morning workshop on computer game production (learning to use Photoshop and Flash animation) revealed some of the difficulties, rather than the successes, encountered in attempts to use ICT to support education when informal and creative learning is stressed. As she notes, it can be difficult in practice to ensure all children learn in the sequenced steps that the task may require, particularly if learning to use complex professional software. It is also difficult to ensure that teacher support is available just when the child is ready to advance his or her understanding – 'just in time learning', much mooted by radical educationalists, is not easy to provide. Further, these boys' knowledge of professional games made them quickly dissatisfied with the level of production they themselves could achieve, threatening to disempower more than to empower them. After reading her account, one has some sympathy for the traditional vision of an orderly classroom, attentive children and an authoritative teacher.

Do such accounts undermine the demand for change? We may note that the optimistic signs observed in the work of Marsh, Drotner and Cassell derive from the ways that technology affords intrinsically motivating opportunities for peer collaboration and social learning. The more pessimistic signs, as in the work of Willett and that reviewed earlier regarding traditional test scores, are associated with uses of technology to support what Cassell calls the pedagogic relation between 'an expert and a novice' (p.19) – in other words, teaching led by teachers. In short, technology may enhance children's learning more in a heterarchical than in a hierarchical context. What matters is less the technology than how it is used.

Learning in a convergent environment

> Printed texts are by nature selective and exclusive ... hypertexts on the Web are by nature inclusive. (Burbules, 1998: 103)

In *Young People and New Media* (Livingstone, 2002), I argued that the internet could play a transformative rather than a merely supportive role in education. The decision to replace, or complement, linear media (print and audiovisual) with hypertext challenges traditional knowledge authorities (teachers, books, curricula, qualification bodies), liberating children from 'the single, exclusive, intensive focus on written language [which] has dampened the full development of all kinds of human potentials' (Kress, 1998: 75). While 'the conventions of print have already been socially negotiated ... the single most attractive feature of hypertext is that it has none' (Douglas, 1998: 160). Moreover, in an age of information abundance, an alternative to the traditional reliance on clear authoritative sources and long-established learning practices is, surely, required. As Smith and Curtin (1998: 212) note, children are 'the first generations to live in an all-encompassing electronic habitat ... to deal with this complex habitat, children develop forms of cognitive and attitudinal organization that enable them to interpret the world and perform it'.

The declining authority of the written word is paralleled by the rise of a creative remix culture of image and multimodal texts, such that 'writing is no longer the vehicle for conveying all the information ... some things are best done by using writing, and others are best done by using images' (Kress, 1998: 63). This mobilizes multiple activities as mediators of learning – not only reading and writing but also creating, designing, performing, searching and playing, and it renders the role of the learner more flexible, more negotiable, precisely because what there is to be known is more fluid, open to interpretation. Turkle describes this shift as profound, from a culture of calculation, where 'the modernist computational aesthetic promised to explain and unpack, to reduce and clarify' (1995: 19) to a culture of simulation, where what is valued is tinkering and experimentation with the interface – 'getting the lay of the land rather than figuring out the hierarchy of underlying structure and rules' (p. 35).

All this requires a pedagogic shift from a rule-based model of education to an immersive model of 'learning-through-doing' (Green, Reid and Bigum, 1998) that, for example, extrapolates from children's preferred orientation to and facility with computer games – where manuals are rarely read or rules learned, but rather the player just pitches into the game, learning through trial and error what they need and when they need it – to the kinds of educational benefits that the internet may afford (Gee, 2008). Although we should take care not to romanticize games – for in practice, 'flexibility and original ideas are generally not rewarded' (Lafrance, 1996: 308) – computer games can value 'the ability to process multiple streams of information simultaneously, and the propensity to experiment in free-form, ill-defined problem domains' (Johnson-Eilola, 1998: 191). Observing his 8-year-old daughter's play, Johnson-Eilola comments:

To someone raised in an historical worldview – one valuing linearity, genealogies, tradition, *rules* – Carolyn's explanations of the game sound haphazard, unplanned and immature. But to someone familiar with global information spaces such as the World Wide Web, games such as these provide environments for learning postmodernist approaches to communication and knowledge: navigation, constructive problem-solving, dynamic goal construction. (p.188)

For Carolyn and her generation, 'conventional school curricula and pedagogical procedures are out of step' (Smith and Curtin, 1998: 212). This leads Buckingham, for instance, to propose that creative work with digital media:

> should substantially replace the compulsory specialist subject of ICT in schools and also be much more centrally integrated within the core subject of English (or language arts). (2007a: 173)

At present, the great expectations associated with non-traditional approaches to education have been neither supported nor disproved by evidence; nor, however, has the huge investment sunk into injecting ICT into the traditional model yet proved its worth. I am therefore more agnostic than when I concluded *Young People and New Media*, though there is, as yet, no need to let go of the potential for transformation. But whether society can harness the internet to deliver the more radical and ambitious vision, whether it even really desires an alternative pedagogy, and whether education can resist the commercializing pressures to co-opt, constrain and commodify the routes to knowledge opened up by this vision all remains to be seen. For there is, undoubtedly, both money and power at stake here – 'vying for position . . . are not only educators but also publishers, commercial hardware and software producers, parents, governments, and the telecommunications players of the corporate world' (Hawisher and Selfe, 1998: 3). Or, as Buckingham *et al.* put it,

> Technology is frequently presented both to teachers and to parents as the solution to a whole range of social and educational problems; and yet it is a solution that, under present circumstances, is provided largely by the commercial market. . . . What counts as a valid educational use of technology is, it would seem, inextricable from what sells. (2001: 38–9)

Let me illustrate. I once spent an afternoon at a project design meeting for a major public sector organization, contributing to an expert discussion on the creation of a new educational online game for children. To my dismay, questions of presentation, branding and promotion were discussed with far greater vigour, focus and commitment than the difficult but pressing questions in my mind – what exactly do we want children to learn from this, how will it complement what they already know, what use will such knowledge be to them and is this what children themselves want to learn? I was assured that all this would be sorted out in the research and evaluation stages that fed into, and followed up on, the production of the new resource. But these stages are often contracted out to external agencies which, though professionally competent, tend to evaluate whether children (or parents and teachers) liked the product or thought they had learned something, rather than asking the hard questions about what they had actually learned and what value it would have for them in the future. On this occasion, the final outcome, while in many ways interesting and, undoubtedly, good to look at, essentially disseminated chunks of adult-determined information in a fun way and then tested children's retention immediately afterwards. The opportunity to do something original, to rethink what might really benefit children, was passed up.

At issue, then, are not simply the changing learning practices of children, teachers and parents but a shift in the entire educational establishment, together with its relation to the home, the state and the private sector (Buckingham, 2007a; Rudd, Morrison, Facer and Gifford, 2006; Livingstone, 2005c). Clark (2003) queries the presumed 'social good' which computer and internet access represents, following her ethnographic observations in a local American community centre which revealed the everyday ways in which the adults in charge judge and even exclude those activities not deemed 'valuable' or worthy of the expensive equipment and investment involved. Seiter (2005) observed similar normative assumptions delimiting children's creativity in a nursery setting, even though radical educationalists argue that it is precisely in informal, playful or learner-led contexts that soft skills are best facilitated (Papert, 1980).

The everyday normative judgements shaping (and limiting) the potential of a new technology exemplify a broader principle, namely that familiar social practices are conservatively reproduced in relation to the internet much more readily than is the internet used to challenge or reconfigure offline practices (Woolgar, 2002). Thus the optimistic hopes that the internet would herald new ways of learning – more open, heterarchical, informal, flexible, dialogic, playful (see, for example, Stead, Sharpe, Anderson, Cych and Philpott, 2006) are, as yet, little in evidence, significantly because of the influential but conservative factors still dictating the design of curriculum materials, teacher training, assessment procedures, employer expectations and financial resources.

Conclusions

We are, it seems, at a particular juncture in the introduction of the internet into education and, by implication, at a particular juncture also in the research enterprise designed to guide and evaluate this process. This chapter has critically reviewed arguments and evidence for a claim held to be obvious by many, namely that internet use benefits children's learning. It has revealed that, notwithstanding the apparently unlimited capacity of the internet in relation to information and educational resources, it is far from proven that internet use brings children greater pedagogic benefits than they would have gained without it. Partly, I have suggested, a fundamental lack of clarity over purposes undermines these many and well-meaning initiatives – essentially, do educationalists expect the internet to enhance the efficient delivery of a pre-defined curriculum or do they wish it to enable alternative, student-centred, creative forms of knowing?

What's the best that could be said for the role of ICT in the traditional classroom? Its defenders could reasonably argue that, even if ICT is unimaginatively used only to further traditional outcomes, and even if it produces only moderate improvements in basic literacy and science, while also enhancing pupil motivation and compensating for some forms of disadvantage, this would still be a valid enterprise. Of course, this must be well implemented and also carefully evaluated against alternative interventions (e.g. if compared with the likely benefits of spending an equivalent amount of public money on reducing class sizes). There is some merit to this argument: technology, especially the internet, can very effectively permit the widespread sharing of valuable resources in both traditional and interactive forms, and it affords the means of collaborative learning, distributed over time and place as needed. If used well, it is also popular with children. And there are some signs, albeit tentative as yet, that some uses, under some conditions, are associated with improved test scores measuring standard educational outcomes.

Why can we not produce stronger evidence in favour of alternative, more creative pedagogic uses of ICT in response to imaginative developments in both academia and policy circles (see, for example, Futurelab's 2006 re-imagining of learning spaces and the potential of technology within these)? One difficulty is that, contrary to the demands of policy evaluations, 'soft skills have yet to be adequately defined and their importance, relative to formal qualifications, for different groups of people and at different stages in the life cycle is unknown' (Sparkes, 1999: 7). Partly, there is a lack of empirical research in this relatively new field. And partly, last, we might ask what kind of evidence is expected? No one doubts the value of print media, though they both provided new routes to advancement for poorer children and, more often, they represented a new means of excluding the working class. No one demanded comparisons of results obtained from classrooms in which books were or were not introduced. And no one has sought to define the main contribution of books to learning, for clearly they can be used – and this is the key – for narrow or broad, traditional or alternative, creative or rote learning purposes.

Notwithstanding the rather downbeat conclusions drawn in this chapter, it does seem that we are witnessing the reconfiguration of pre-existing learning activities and opportunities for the majority of children and young people. While once children went to the library to get a book for their homework, now they also search online. While once they asked for advice from a parent, now they also 'ask an expert'. While once they painted with paint and paper, now they do so also with a paint program, posting their pictures online to share with others. It also seems that we are witnessing – albeit only for a minority of young people – some genuinely new learning opportunities, centring on possibilities of child-oriented digital creativity and on collaborative communication with those who share similarly specialist or niche forms of interest and expertise. It is the successful embedding of these and related opportunities within the formal structures of the school and the curriculum, for the benefit of all children, that remains uncertain.

4

Communication and Identity

Why communicate online?

Adults may wish children to go online for educational reasons. Children's motivation centres on the new opportunities for communication – to express their identity, to create and sustain social relationships, for fun. Despite the apparently mundane nature of much online conversation, they value the protracted, playful, sometimes tricky negotiations with their peers over 'everything from appropriate attire to appropriate academic and career aspirations' (Clark, 2005: 206). This extends life offline to the online domain with, arguably, more freedom to experiment away from the adult gaze. Being 'in touch' and 'always on' allows children to be physically present in the home or school yet psychologically absent, engaged in the dynamic interplay of their social networks rather than family dynamics (Gergen, 2002). In their daily lives, teenagers especially are engrossed in managing the social psychological transition from being anchored in the family home to (also) participating in the wider world. On the internet, Pew Internet found two thirds of US teenagers thought the internet keeps them from spending time with their family while half said they use it to improve relationships with friends, suggesting a generational shift away from familial (hierarchical) to peer (egalitarian) relations (Lenhart, Rainie and Lewis, 2001). Taylor and Harper (2002) provide a telling illustration, noting how teenagers text each other 'goodnight' from their bedrooms, this perhaps even replacing the face-to-face greeting to their parents.

Beyond this extended opportunity to engage with friends even when away from them physically, what does the internet afford children's communication and identity? Hall observes that, because identities are constructed within, not outside, discourse, we need to understand them as produced in specific historical and institutional sites within specific discursive formations and practices, by specific enunciative strategies [and] within the play of specific modalities of power. (1996: 4)

Online as offline, this analysis sets some demanding and subtle requirements for the understanding of identity construction. While Hall, Giddens (1991), Poster (2001) and others have developed an anti-essentialist, discursive notion of identities as enacted, performed and, in consequence, as plural and contextually contingent, albeit mediated by gender and class positions (Walkerdine, Lucey and Melody, 2001), media researchers have explored how this plays out in a digital environment (Buckingham, 2008; Fornäs, Klein, Ladendorf, Sunden and Svenigsson, 2002; Slater, 2002; Turkle, 1995). This distinctively foregrounds multimodal writing practices that include written text, photos, videos, music and visual design and that encourage the textual borrowing, re-embedding, re-mixing and re-configuring central to convergence culture and relished by youth culture (Jenkins, 2006a). As boyd and Heer put it, 'mediated conversations require individuals to write themselves into being' (2006: 1; drawing on Sundén, 2003).

Intriguingly, this spontaneous and enthusiastic adoption by children and young people of online opportunities for self-presentation and relationship construction is not technology driven – the successive adoption of email, chatrooms, text messaging and social networking was hardly anticipated by their producers, though each was keenly co-opted by them in developing new markets. Rather, what drives online and mobile communication is young people's strong desire to connect with peers anywhere, anytime. It is not only technology producers who are taken by surprise as the next innovation unexpectedly takes off. The mass media remind us that, on each occasion, wrong-footed adults from parents to governments panic about youthful enthusiasms. The recent explosion in social networking sites illustrates the point. The 'MySpace generation', headlines shrieked, has no sense of privacy or shame. One attention-getting headline read, 'Generation shock finds liberty online: the children of the internet age are ready to bare their bodies and souls in a way their parents never could.'[1] And another claimed: 'Kids today. They have no sense of shame. They have no sense of privacy' (Nussbaum, 2007). Moreover, social networkers are supposedly wholly narcissistic: says one technology producer of today's youth, 'MySpace is about me, me, me, and look at me and look at me.'[2]

However, the rapidly expanding research literature examining how people create online profiles and participate in various forms of online community largely eschews pathologizing those engaged in online communication, for this perpetuates public anxieties which have little empirical support (boyd, 2006; boyd and Ellison, 2007; Hinduja and Patchin, 2008; Lenhart and Madden, 2007a). Researchers have also learned not to draw so sharp a line between online and offline, for users move flexibly between these realms, mixing diverse forms of mediated and face-to-face communication (Ling and Haddon, 2008; Orgad, 2007; Slater, 2002). This frequent passage between the online and offline may blur the distinction – it is now hard to say when or for how long a user is 'really' online, just as it is hard to tell, when a child says they 'talked to' a friend, whether they are referring to face-to-face, telephone or online modes . of communication. But it would be a mistake to conclude that these distinctions no longer matter, for connected spaces are not identical spaces.

Researchers have also learned that, contrary to popular myth, children cannot be usefully divided into sociable kids who meet face-to-face and isolated loners who chat to strangers online. The latter, a minority, do exist, meriting attention insofar as their internet use may exacerbate their problems (Wolak, Mitchell and Finkelhor, 2003). But Gross (2004) and others challenge early assumptions that teenagers interact with strangers for reasons of lonely curiosity, despite the early findings of the HomeNet project from the days before a critical mass of peers was online (Kraut *et al.*, 1998). In other words, for all but the already isolated, it appears that the internet fosters rather than undermines existing social contacts (Kraut *et al.*, 2002; Mesch, 2001). In today's media-rich environment, the sociable teenager who does not communicate online as well as offline is a rarity, and online, they communicate mainly with already established, often local friends, the strongest ties being centred on pre-existing local or study contexts (Boneva, Quinn, Kraut, Kiesler and Shklovski, 2006; Hampton and Wellman, 2003; Mesch and Talmud, 2007). As Valkenburg and Peter (2007) show, the 'rich get richer' hypothesis works especially for instant messaging (rather than for chat rooms) as the self-disclosure afforded by one-to-one online communication encourages intimacy and thus strengthens relationships.

The UK Children Go Online survey found that, among those who use the internet at least weekly, email, chat and instant messaging are all popular forms of social media, though social class, gender and age all make a difference: middle-class, older girls tend to take part the most, and younger children the least (Livingstone and Bober, 2004b).

In the USA, 55 per cent of online 12–17 year olds have a social networking profile (Lenhart and Madden, 2007a). In the UK, 77 per cent of 7–16 year olds have visited a social networking site, 59 per cent have their own profile and 51 per cent currently use a social networking site (ChildWise, 2009). Although most social networking sites attempt to bar those under 13, 27 per cent of UK 8–12 year olds have a profile on one or more sites (Ofcom, 2008b). Across Europe, 32 per cent of online 16–24 year olds use social networking sites at least monthly (EIAA, 2006). These figures continue to grow worldwide, though they may have peaked in the USA and UK (comScore, 2008). Other online activities such as game-playing also connect peers, resulting overall in a complex mix of communicative forms.

This chapter explores the nature of these networks and forms of self expression.[3] What are children and young people communicating about themselves online, and under what conditions of intimacy or privacy? The online environment is no neutral context: as we shall see, it affords certain forms of expression more easily than others, reconfiguring norms of privacy and intimacy and placing distinctive demands on both media literacy and the management of risk to the self.

'Constant connection'

Children use the opportunity of private spaces online to experiment with new identities, to seek confidential advice on personal matters, to eavesdrop on the interactions of others, to meet people from far-off places or from the next street, and, most of all, to engage in uninterrupted, unobserved immersion in peer communication. Indeed, although online talk can appear vacuous to the adult observer, for participants it is a highly valued social activity – after all, this is 'the constant contact generation' (Clark, 2005).

To bewail the mundane and trivial nature of many online exchanges – asking how people are, what they're doing on Saturday, how their day went – is to miss the point. Online conversations are largely phatic, meaningful more for sustaining contact than communicating content (Drotner, 2005). Should there be news, one is in the right place to hear it, but in the meantime, it's an opportunity to hang out, pass the time, to know you're not forgotten or ignored. As Kim, aged 15, put it: 'even if you've just seen them at school like, it'll be like you're texting them or talking to them on the phone or on MSN'. Offline, friends may be occupied elsewhere, but the multiple contacts on instant messaging or social networking generally means someone will be online and, if not, the asynchronous exchanges permit conversation even if participants are online at different times. As Jenny says of her use of MySpace,

> you look through other people's profiles and look through their pictures, different pictures of their mates and that . . . if someone gives me a comment I'll comment them back . . . you get like addicted to it.

Billy, similarly, leaves about twenty comments per day: he told me, 'I go from one [profile] to another, like with my friends, I say hi, how are you?' Nicki notes that, by sending a quick comment, 'it feels like I've kind of kept in touch'. While such interactions may involve few dramatic disclosures or risky encounters, they are as much a means of positioning oneself within the peer network as are the many acts of recognition and affirmation constitutive of social relations offline.

As the integration of on and offline communication implies, contacts are generally local rather than distant (or 'virtual'), with friends rather than strangers. Access to new communication technologies need not result in a larger or geographically wider social circle. Particularly, there is – perhaps disappointingly – little evidence for the 'global village' hyped in early discussions of the internet. Getting to know new people on the other side of the world seems as effortful as writing letters to a pen pal was several decades ago. However, the internet does permit some broadening of everyday networks, strengthening already existing relationships which are otherwise hard to maintain – friends from abroad, distant relatives, staying in touch with people who have moved. Lorie (aged 17) says:

> I think mobile phones and the internet are a good way of keeping in contact with friends. For example, I have friends in other countries who use MSN. I can send them an email everyday rather than phoning them up and running up a huge phone bill, or sending them a text message. And it's just a good way of keeping in contact with people.

The question of making new friends is the subject of debate among young people themselves. Most are little interested in talking to people they do not know on the internet, preferring to communicate with friends. Indeed, children who have chatted to strangers online describe it as 'weird' or 'dodgy', they don't see the point. Older teenagers tend to prefer instant messaging to chat rooms because 'you know who you're talking to' – a phrase used over and over in the UK Children Go Online focus groups; they are clearly aware of media reports warning children of online dangers (Livingstone and Bober, 2007). Risks from stranger contact online remain unclear. Ybarra and Mitchell (2008) found more unwanted sexual solicitations were experienced by teenagers via instant messaging (43%) or chat rooms (32%) than through social networking (27%). Peter, Valkenburg and Schouten (2006) found that chatting to strangers itself is the risk factor that predicts inappropriate contact, especially as part of the playful interactions favoured by younger teenagers.

For example, it being common practice for several friends to gather in front of the screen, Ted – whom we met in chapter 2 – describes a lively scene when his friend Mark and his brothers come to visit. They all shout out, ' "No, don't write that, write this." That's what we do when all his brothers are there . . . taking different turns to type in stuff.' On one of our visits, we watch while these 14-year-old friends try to disrupt an adult Yahoo chat room for police and fire officers, pretending to be a blind orphan in a home with abusive carers. They type in lines like 'Help!' 'They're coming to get me!' Someone replies and asks if they are blind how come they can type? Mark replies 'Braille keyboard' and gets the retort, 'And braille screen?' They are disappointed that their cover is blown.

In another household, I listen as Manu, also 14 years old, talks with enthusiasm about how rude he and his friends get, trading insults with each other or with other people. Particularly, they like to pretend to be other people when chatting online with friends they know from school, insulting them and then teasing at school the next day until the friends catch on as to the identity of those unknown others. One game is for the participant to be so annoying to people in chat rooms that he (or she) forces them to leave. As Manu says proudly,

> I drive people out all the time, it's my speciality. When the room is empty, I feel really content with myself. . . . I just sit there and wallow in my glory and then I leave. I might go to another room.

Across the range of online activities, teenagers' playful, occasionally resistant, approach to peer networking (online as offline) is evident. This is also characteristic of their representation of the self online. For example, when we interviewed her, Beccy, aged 14, was a fan of the pop group, S Club7, and on her personal homepage she had married herself off to two of the lead singers. Similarly, in their social networking profiles, although most include a personal photograph some instead post an image of their dog or a band or a cartoon image. And although many post their real age, a fair proportion add a year or two: Billy is typical in describing himself as 16 rather than 14 because the friend who set up his profile thought 16 the minimum age permitted; and some use joke ages – Ryan says he's 98.

This is not only fun, it is also an evasion of site design. Questions asked as standard by social networking sites (e.g. what is your income?) are equally resisted as standard by teenagers (a favourite response being £250,000). In consequence, the norms of use deviate from the norms built into site design. Yet in their own terms, these responses are meaningful – wishing to appear a little older (or richer) is a desire of many young teenagers; similarly, Manu's disruptive approach to chat rooms, hardly intended by the providers, is a meaningful response to the anonymity afforded by the design as well as consistent with youthful 'horseplay' offline.

Making communicative choices

Most online communication is neither deliberately deceitful nor scrupulously honest. It is, rather, carefully judged to reveal something but not too much, to sustain connection without losing face, to open the way for a deeper engagement while providing a safety route if misunderstood. In analysing the nature of what they call 'technologically mediated sociability', Licoppe and Smoreda extend Barthes' notion of the conditions for satisfactory 'living together' in late modernity as resembling a school of fish:

> Living together is an adjusted form of collective life that rests on an ethic of distance. Its dynamic equilibrium and its maintenance presuppose that the investment of individuals takes a suitable form, particularly with regard to efforts made to articulate the time of absence and meeting; the time of being present together and coexisting. If the whole holds together too loosely, there is a strong risk that individuals will become too distant from each other . . . If the tensions of living together weigh too heavily on individuals who are subject to other exigencies, there will be friction. (2006: 301)

Those engaged in technologically mediated sociability find their own rhythms and cadences, their own flows of contact and distance. Licoppe and Smoreda explain that this 'play between absence and copresence' is, in terms of social relations, 'a play between lack of attention and absorption, between safety and interactional vulnerability' (p. 311). In social networking, the activities of visiting friends' profiles, checking what's new and adding the occasional comment represent a way of managing and maintaining this ethic of distance, reasserting connection, establishing presence, somewhat at arm's length. Replies are delayed, responses are not obligatory, short absences need not be explained, multitasking is expected. Other forms of online communication afford other forms of technologically mediated sociability.

Rather than seeing face-to-face communication as automatically superior, a position assumed by many adults, young people evaluate the available forms of communication according to their distinct communicative needs, making careful choices among face-to-face, writing, email, instant message, chat rooms, telephone, social networking, text messaging and so forth, and treating face-to-face conversation as one form among many. One of the liveliest conversations to have with a group of children – especially early teenagers – is to ask them when they use which form of communication for what. Immediately, the affordances of the particular communicative forms come into focus, each being judged in terms of its implications for privacy, intimacy, controllability, message complexity, efficiency, urgency, reciprocality and – the advantage of asynchronous communication for many teenagers – the management of 'face' (avoiding embarrassment, misinterpretation, anonymity, allusion and innuendo).

Stuart (aged 17) prefers texting, saying – 'Text message – if you want to speak to them immediately.' Cause email, they've got to be on the internet, they've got to see it. For emergencies. And for convenience.' Beatrice (aged 13) says it depends:

> Emailing, I just do it like if it's not a long bit to say and not a short bit to say ... But text messaging I just ask questions – it's just short questions. And phoning, I just have a long conversation with people, about nothing really.

She adds, reflecting the difficulties of managing face-to-face conversations, 'when you're like talking to them face-to-face, you're like – you've got other people around you, and they can't tell you what they really think. So like instant messaging, you can.' This leads some to say most unwelcome things: Cameron (aged 13) confessed, 'I once dumped my old girlfriend by email ... Well, it was cowardly really. I couldn't say it face-to-face.'

This does not, however, mean that face-to-face communication is being displaced. Indeed, while social networking is to some degree displacing other forms of online communication (email, chatrooms, website creation), it incorporates others (instant messaging, blogging, music downloading) and remediates yet more (most notably, face-to-face and telephone communication) (Bolter and Grusin, 1999). At present, it seems that talking online is (still) often seen as less satisfying than face-to-face conversation, for it raises serious questions of trust. Mark (aged 17) asks:

> If you're talking to someone on the internet who's a friend, you actually talk to them saying stuff, but feelings and everything are real ... but if you're talking to someone you haven't met, how do you know if what they're telling you is the truth?

Ryan (aged 15) explains the necessary steps to judging trustworthiness on social networking sites:

> you look at their pictures, see if they are authentic or not, so if they ain't got any comments and they're just adding people, then I can't believe them.

The face-to-face situation remains valued for its trustworthiness and reciprocity. On the other hand, its potential for embarrassment is also high. Thus half of email, instant message and chat room users think that talking to people on the internet can be as much or more satisfying as talking to them in real life and a quarter identify significant advantages to online communication in terms of privacy, confidence and intimacy (Livingstone and Bober, 2004b). Pew Internet found that 37 per cent of US teenagers had used instant messaging to say something they wouldn't have said in person, and 18 per cent had looked for sensitive information and advice online (Lenhart, Rainie and Lewis, 2001). In the UK Children Go Online project, a quarter of 12–19 year olds who use the internet at least weekly say they go online to get advice, more among older teenagers and, interestingly, boys; again, though, some worry about the reliability and privacy of online advice-seeking.

On the internet, young people feel themselves to be in control, and when they feel themselves to be losing control, they can simply leave. Gus, age 13 years, compared chat room conversation with the telephone:

> On the telephone like you can be speaking but then if you don't know what to say you'll be just standing there not doing anything but with that [chat room] em it's like OK to be a bit late not be saying anything because it's not like you're waiting for them to ... on the other end of a telephone ... it's not so much of a rush. ... You're not like confronted to someone. 'Coz if you say something they might not agree with they can't like hit you or say something back to you that's going to make you do something that – if they'll stand in front of you.

Feeling 'in control' is often mentioned as vital to the selection of communicative forms, enabling not only truth-telling but also confident identity play. Customizing their conversations by drawing on the language of street talk and the style features of youth culture, unlike the 'chore' of writing letters, is great fun, and the emergent linguistic codes are valued precisely because they effectively express identity through connection with others. In an interview with 11-year-old Susie, observed in front of her computer screen, we watched her write in one code to her grandparents ('To Gran and Grandad, We arrived home safe and well. Helen is really pleased with her necklace and sends her thanks. Thank You for having us we really enjoyed ourselves. Thanks again for having us, love from Susie ××××') and in quite another to her friend ('howd the move go? i cant wate 2 c yor new howse come round when you can!! from Devilduck').

Representing the self

> Your identity on the computer is the sum of your distributed presence.
> (Turkle, 1995: 13)

Identities are performed and experimented with across a range of places, and the boundaries between those spaces matter: we all act differently with different people, in different situations, and children are no exception. On our first visit, 12-year-old Neil and his younger brother Euan, aged 10 years, had just started sending emails, using the family email address. Their mother would open the email account and call them if there was anything for them. By our second visit a few weeks later, both boys had set up new, private email accounts for themselves, using different providers. Neil explains they are sending more emails now that they have privacy. Both brothers are anxious to hide their pin numbers from each other, and there is a lot of teasing over this as they try to peek over each other's shoulders. Neil now checks his mail every time he goes on the Internet, sending and receiving about three messages a week among his circle of 5–10 correspondents, all school friends.

The language of online communication both facilitates communication among peers and impedes the parental gaze. As Greenfield *et al.* (2006) note, adults are frequently floored in their attempt to follow the conversational flow in online interactions, the point being that children maintain their privacy not only by keeping their conversation away from physical scrutiny but also by rendering it symbolically inaccessible. As identity becomes more complex for older teenagers, so too do their online strategies for identity construction. Some we talked to have as many as eight email addresses, keeping several in play at once. Others have lost count of how many they have or have lost track of the names they have used, and others are more systematic. As Mark (aged 14), says, 'I normally give my own personal email address out and not just – not – we've got a family one like Ted's got and I've got my own personal one so I just give that one to my friends, not the family one.' Jane keeps one email address for her correspondence with friends, and the other, which she uses much less often, is the one she uses when asked to provide such information on a website to protect herself against unwelcome junk mail or 'spam', it all being directed to one site, where she deletes it when she has time.

Something as simple as an online name can say a lot. Adopted names in chat rooms, even more than email addresses, allow the trying-out of new roles as sexual beings or otherwise desirable, dynamic personalities. Consider, for example, the names of an American/English e-mail circle of 12–13 year olds: Littlelover, pixel_117, applesauce128, fireball318, actingurl, and fuel_chick. Some sites encourage anonymity through fun pseudonyms. Candy, aged 13, chose Kissmequick, saying,

> it's quite fun having a jokey name but it's privacy as well. I don't like my mum and dad reading all the e-mails I send because I write quite dodgy stuff. And when he writes back mum and dad usually read 'em and some of the things he writes are quite rude.

Similarly, Manu and his older brother share seven chat room identities (the maximum allowed on their system) and alternate among them or modify them as the mood takes them. Having shown the researcher all his profiles and how to edit them, Manu explains that the people in the chat room 'won't know who I am because I keep on changing my name . . . It depends who I'm talking to. Say if I want to annoy someone, then I want to remain anonymous, then I'll change my name and they won't realize who it is. It's quite good.' Although the manner is light-hearted, these identity practices can be serious. The online rules of the game (where experimenting and fooling around is expected) license the trying out of new roles, permitting young people, without compromising their everyday identity, to play around with the crucial boundaries between truth and fantasy, information and imagination, the real and the unreal. In all these and other ways, creating and networking online content is becoming, for many, an integral means of managing one's identity, lifestyle and social relations.

Yet young people have always devoted attention to the presentation of self. Friendships have always been made, displayed and broken. Strangers – unknown, weird or frightening – have always hovered on the edge of the group. And adult onlookers have often been puzzled by youthful peer practices. The recent explosion in online social networking sites such as MySpace, Facebook, Bebo, Piczo and others has particularly attracted the popular claim that something new is occurring. Social networking sites enable communication among ever-widening circles of contacts, and they invite convergence among the hitherto separate activities of email, messaging, website creation, diaries, photo albums, and music/video uploading and downloading. From the user's viewpoint, more than ever before, using media means creating as well as receiving, with user-control extending far beyond selecting ready-made, mass-produced content. The very language of social relationships is being reframed; today, people construct their 'profile', make it 'public' or 'private', they 'comment' or 'message' their 'top friends' on their 'wall', they 'block' or 'add' people to their network, and so forth.

Compared with instant messaging or email, far more personal information is captured by social networking sites. Hinduja and Patchin's (2008) content analysis of a random sample of several thousand public MySpace profiles produced by under 18s showed multiple forms of identity management, including design customization (45%) and personal photos (57%), though only 9 per cent posted their full name, 8 per cent showed evidence of age inflation and 5 per cent had a picture of themselves in swimsuit/underwear. Vazire and Gosling (2004) add that, regarding adults' personal websites, the self-expressive content is broadly accurate. Pew Internet concludes that, among the 55 per cent of online American 12–17 year olds who use social networking sites, most are successfully balancing the sharing of personal information with trusted friends while also revealing enough about themselves to make new friends online (Lenhart and Madden, 2007b).

When studying social network users, I found the strategies for representing the self to vary considerably, combining personal information, style features and multimodal text in creative ways (Livingstone, 2008c). For example, Danielle's Piczo profile has a big welcome in sparkly pink, with music, photos, a love tester, guestbook and dedication pages all customized down to the scroll bars and cursor with pink candy stripes, glitter, angels, flowers, butterflies, hearts and more, thereby drawing on what Perkel (2008) calls 'cut and paste literacy' (copying segments of html code from informal sites created, initially by teenagers, to tailor the appearance or features of their profile). As

Danielle told me, what she enjoys is that 'you can just change it all the time [and so] you can show different sides of yourself'. By contrast, Danny has not completed the basic Facebook options of noting his politics, religion or even his network ('I haven't bothered to write about myself.')

Most profiles are designed, in one way or another, to provide 'a way of expressing who you are to other people', as Nina put it. Elena, 14, spends several hours each day updating and altering her MySpace, Facebook and Piczo profiles. She says:

> I think layouts really show like who you are. So look at the rainbow in that. I think that would make you sound very like bubbly . . . I like to have different ones . . . it's different likes, different fashion, different feelings on that day.

In response to this continual activity of re-presenting the self, Elena's friends have peppered her profile with nice comments – 'I'm always here for you', 'you're gorgeous' – as part of a reciprocal exchange of mutual support, an ethic of care (Gilligan, 1993) which she appreciates:

> It's nice like if you've got a nice picture of you and people are, 'oh, you look nice'. It's like quite nice, I think when people say you're pretty . . . I like it when they comment me because like it shows that they care.

One striking feature of a social networking profile is its representation of the self as unified and organized. Joshua, like others, appreciates everything about him being in one place ('it tells me all my information, it has my profile'). Although, as Marwick (2005) argues, this reflects the commercial logic of the social networking businesses model, and although it seems to undermine the experimental and dispersed notion of identity that the internet is noted for (Poster, 2001), it may also support the adolescent's struggle to sustain a unified self in the face of uncertain emotions, shifting identifications and conflicting social demands (Coleman and Hendry, 1999; Erikson, 1959/1980). Commonplace activities include 'repairing' (Goffman, 1959) or updating their profile as required – changing photos, deleting unpleasant comments, altering listings of friends, asking people to change their representation of you, and even starting all over again. As Leo says of his MySpace profile,

> the one I made before I thought I didn't really like it, so I thought I'd start again, I'd start a new one . . . it was just, . . . people I didn't like had the address, so I thought I should start fresh.

Not only can identities be more easily rewritten online than offline, but they instantiate a looser relation between self-representation and personal identity (Thumim, 2008). Profiles are not simply to be read as information about an individual. Jenny, like others, is well aware that people's profiles can be 'just a front'. Or, they may be simply more of a placeholder, a location in a peer network, rather than a self-portrait presenting genuine and personal information. Initially, I misunderstood this. For example, on Leo's site there was a comment from his friend 'Blondie' saying that she's pregnant: when I asked, he observed that, of course, 'she's joking' – the point being to share (and display) their humorous relationship not a personal self-disclosure. Sixteen-year-old Simon confused me even further, for – unusually – he shared a profile with his best friend Matt. Although they had started the profile together, and often go online together, all the content on the profile referred to Matt (as MySpace assumes, in its layout, a single user) rather than Simon – the name, the birthday, the photos – except that some comments left by their friends included Simon as well as Matt.

A more commonplace instance of the gap between user and profile is illustrated by Paul, aged 13. A confident and sociable boy who 'got pulled into the world of Bebo' because 'everybody was talking about it', he has constructed his profile as a joke. With a funny photo of him, it announces him to be 36, married, living in Africa, a person who likes to humiliate people and to get unconscious. Yet in the interview, Paul takes little notice of this, since his brothers and friends (with whom he, like some others, has shared his password) have often changed his profile for fun. His profile is thus meaningful to him not as a means of displaying personal information about him to the world, as often supposed, but precisely because the joking content is evidence of his lively and trusting relations with his brothers and friends.

Pointing up the lack of a one-to-one match between users and profiles, a point also evident in the way some users maintain several profiles on different sites, Paul explains how the profile may display the peer group more than the individual:

> When we go out together, like they take photos on their phones and stuff and then they upload them on there . . . so everybody else can see what we've done and like see all of our friends and when we're together and it's just like remembering the time when we did it.

Indeed, designing a profile is not solely a matter of individual choice. It is geared towards others through the choice of site as one must select that already used by one's friends, through mode of address as most say they put on their profile the content they consider their friends would enjoy and, practically, by the moment of setting up a profile – this is commonly achieved with the help of a friend who already uses the site, one result of which is that age information is often inaccurate, following the peer group belief (not necessarily accurate) that they are too young to be allowed on the site; correcting misleading information later is not something they can do, several teenagers told me.

Thus, although it indeed appears that, for many young people, social networking is 'all about me, me, me', as quoted earlier, this need not imply a narcissistic self-absorption. Rather, following Mead's (1934) fundamental distinction between the 'I' and the 'me' as twin aspects of the self, social networking is about 'me' in the sense that it reveals the self embedded in the peer group, as known to and represented by others, rather than the private 'I' known best to oneself.

Transitions in identity development

Identity is something we *do*, rather than simply something we *are*. (Buckingham, 2008: 8)

Online communication jumps sharply in popularity when children graduate from primary to secondary school, with email, instant messenger, chat and so forth being relatively little practised among those under 11 years old (Livingstone and Bober, 2004b). Even for teenagers, however, age matters. In the UK Children Go Online focus groups, older teenagers tended to prefer to hold private conversations face-to-face, considering this more secure, more private than online communication. As 17-year-old Hazel points out,

If you wanted to have a private conversation, then I'm sure you'd talk to them face-to-face rather than using the internet, because if you know they can be listened to, or someone else can see what you're doing, then I wouldn't have thought that you'd want that to happen. So you'd therefore talk to them, meet up and talk to them face-to-face.

Contrast this with some of the younger teenagers quoted earlier, for whom mediated communication offers some safeguards against embarrassment, a greater concern for them even than privacy. The project found that, compared with face-to-face conversation, 15–16 year olds consider talking online less satisfying, less confidence boosting than do younger teenagers. However, when the older teenagers do talk online, they are more inclined to disclose accurate personal information, and less inclined to pretend than are the younger teenagers.[4]

Why this shift over the teenage years? From my interviews with 13–16 year olds about their social networking practices, it emerged that, collectively, my interviewees had a story to tell about developing identities, one that they expressed in terms of decisions regarding the style or choice of site (Livingstone, 2008c).[5] Nina, 15, described the move from MySpace to Facebook thus:

> With profiles, everything [on MySpace] was all about having coloured backgrounds . . . whereas I just suppose like Facebook I prefer to have, like older people, and it was more sophisticated, can I use that word? . . . I found when I was 14 I always wanted to be like someone that was older than me . . . When I first got MySpace, I thought it was a really cool thing because all older people had it, and they were all having their templates and things like that . . . but I'm sort of past that stage now, and I'm more into the plain things.

Ellie, 15, points to a similar distinction when comparing her Facebook profile with her 12-year-old sister's use of MySpace:

> The reason they [younger girls] like MySpace seems to be because you can decorate your page with flowers and hearts and have glitter on it, whereas on this [Facebook] it's sort of a white background with not so much, it's just a photo and a name, which is pretty much the same for everyone. [Talking of herself] I can't really see the point. This isn't to show off about my personality. I'm not trying to say, oh, I love purple or I love hearts . . . It's more just like talking to three friends and, seeing as my friends know me, there's no real need for me to advertise my personality . . . On MySpace, everyone's got these things like, I love this, I hate this, and trying to show off who they are and I just don't think that's necessary if these actually are your friends.

Once sensitized to this stylistic shift, it became apparent to me that some teenagers preferred elaborately customized profiles while others favoured a plain aesthetic. Daphne, Danielle and Ryan enjoy changing the backgrounds and layouts of their profile every day, typically adopting a highly gender-stereotyped style of, for example, pink hearts and sparkly lettering for girls and black backgrounds with shiny expensive cars for boys. Nicki observes,

> it's funny how on MySpace you kind of go through phases where everyone might have a really busy . . . background, and then everyone will have a kind of plain background.

To everyone, the flexibility of social networking sites in affording revisions of one's identity is welcome. But to teenagers, whose identities are developing and changing fast, this is particularly valued (Peter *et al.*, in press). What might this particular shift, whether managed by changing one's social networking site or just one's profile, signify for younger and older teenagers? Ziehe argues that lifestyles should be recognized as:

> collective ways of life ... [which] point to common orientations of taste and interpretations; they demonstrate a certain group-specific succinctness of usage of signs. (1994: 2)

In a manner evocative of social networking practices, he argues that lifestyles are characterized by, first, self-attention, a subjective disposition which 'raises the question ... of a successful life as an everyday expectation', second, stylization, in which 'objects, situations and actions are placed into a coherent sign arrangement and "presented"', and third, reflexivity, whereby 'lifestyles are an expression of an orientation pressure which has turned inwards. The new questions are 'what do I actually want?' and 'what matters to me?' [resulting in] an everyday semantic of self-observation and self-assessment' (pp. 11–12).

Thus Ziehe suggests that the project of the self is represented according to highly coded cultural conventions (here including technological interfaces) and social preferences (here embedded in the norms of consumer culture). With this in mind, Ellie, Nina and others seem to suggest that, for younger teenagers, self-attention is enacted through constructing an elaborate, highly stylized statement of identity as display. Thus a visually ambitious, 'pick and mix' profile, that frequently remixes borrowed images and other content to express continually shifting tastes offers for some a satisfactorily 'successful' self, liked and admired by peers. But this notion of identity as display is gradually replaced by the notion of identity as connection. Here elements of display are excised from the profile and replaced by the visual privileging of one's contacts, primarily through links to others' profiles and by posting photos of the peer group socializing offline. Now we may see that Danny's omission of personal information on his profile, noted earlier, is less a curious neglect of the self than the prioritization of a self embedded in social connections. It is not that Danny cannot be bothered to display his personal information but that instead his identity is expressed through connections – for he sustains links with 299 friends and checks every day to see 'if I've got any, like, messages, new friend requests or anything like that, like, new comments'.

In this way, social networking sites enable people 'to codify, map and view the relational ties between themselves and others' (Marwick, 2005: 3), a codification that undergoes continual revision. As Leo says, 'I'll always be adding new friends.'

Users may elaborate their self-presentation as a node of information and/or by elaborating the links to others. The former approach prioritizes a stylized display of identity as lifestyle, but it risks invasions of privacy since the backstage self is on view (Goffman, 1959), potentially occasioning critical or abusive responses from others. With the latter approach, the node may remain relatively unembellished but still be resonant with meaning through its connections with selected others; here the project of the self is more at risk in terms of one's standing in the network – how many friends do you have, do people visit your profile and leave comments, are you listed as anyone's top friend?

Intimacy and privacy

Intimacy is the other face of privacy. (Giddens, 1995: 94)

Instead of speaking of a single public/private boundary, it may be more accurate to speak of a more complex re-structuring in a series of zones of privacy, not all of which fit easily with our standard images of what the public/private boundary is. (Fahey, 1995: 688)

Identity is primarily constructed within intimate relationships, requiring the communication to some people of that which is kept private from others. In sustaining multiple interaction contexts online, distinct aspects of identity are variously performed for particular rather than indiscriminate anticipated audiences, including oneself. For children and young people especially, it seems that some of the fun stems not only from controlling but also from playing with the possibilities of who knows what, exploiting the ambiguous thrills of forwarding on and blind copying of messages, shifting from public to private chat or using anonymity to construct witty, cheeky or even rude online identities for oneself and others.

Offline spaces for intimacy are marked in many ways including the front door, marking the distinction between life in the community and family privacy, and the bedroom door, marking the distinction between family life and the private life of the child (Livingstone, 2002). Online spaces of intimacy continue to change with the proliferation of mobile and interactive devices, blurring the offline and online in flexible and complex ways. While there is no door to cyberspace to parallel the front door and bedroom door so significant to children, the transition is still marked with logins, passwords and so forth controlling just who may enter. Consider the significance of getting one's own front door key, visualize the symbolism of the 'keep out' or 'private' or 'My room' labels on the bedroom door – and then recall Neil and Euan's teasing over sharing pin numbers and passwords.

Steele and Brown (1994) describe teenage 'room culture' as the place where media and identities intersect through the bricolage of identity work objects on display; bedrooms represent 'mediating devices' by which young people experiment with who they are and who they want to be (see also Frith, 1978; Lincoln, 2004). The media-rich bedroom in the 'juxtaposed home allows teenagers to remove themselves from adult supervision while still living with their parents' (Flichy, 1995: 165). A parallel analysis holds for 'online culture'. A social networking site, for example, constitutes a social situation with its own rules and conventions, contributing to the 'situational geography' of everyday life (Meyrowitz, 1985) by mediating the relations among participants.

When setting up a profile on a social networking site, the affordances of the site become especially salient, posing the new user with key decisions about intimacy and privacy. What do you post? What do you keep for face-to-face or other communication? What should only your friends see? Who, indeed, are your friends online? Social networking sites are far from neutral regarding these decisions. Participants are invited to represent themselves through photo albums, bulletins, folders, music, blogs, events, messages, forums, groups, comments, videos, sending gifts, recording your mood, personality quizzes and surveys, chain messages, guest book, birthday greetings, and more. The site classifies contacts ('friends') in, typically, a binary manner: for MySpace, information is displayed to all your contacts or to all users, for Facebook, it is displayed to your friends, your network, or everyone. On setting up a profile, one is invited to answer a standard set of questions that display to others precisely the types of personal information that previous generations have regarded as private. As Ellie observes,

> I don't have any too personal things on it, like, I'm very happy to say I'm Jewish or [have] conservative political views and I'm happy to say my birthday or I'm from London. There's nothing too detailed that will give anyone too big a picture of me.

Partly, she means that no one can trace her or her address from the personal information displayed, but for the adult generation, taught never to tell, or ask others, about religion, political views, sexuality or income, Facebook's questions can seem intrusive. Yet even Danny who, as we saw, omits this information, does so not because it is private but because 'I just don't have political views at the moment . . . [and] I'm not sure of my religion.' Most, similarly, have few qualms in describing everyone they've added as 'friends'. Yet Ryan, Daphne and some of the others are not unusual in telling me that they do not remember who all their 'friends' are.

The new user must also decide whether to set their profile to 'public' or 'private'. The UK's Office of Communications (Ofcom, 2007b) reports that 58 per cent of UK children aged 8–17 make their profile visible only to friends, while similarly, Pew Internet's survey of American 12–17 year olds found that most (66%) keep their profile wholly or partially private. It also found that, of the information that is public, most is either non-revealing or false, and that only half (49%) claim to make new friends through social networking, most preferring instead to use social networking to contact those who are already friends; further, boys and younger teenagers are more likely to post false information, while older teenagers, especially girls, are more likely to reveal detailed personal information (Lenhart and Madden, 2007b).

Though it is surely the search for intimacy that motivates much online (and offline) communication, it is the consequences for privacy that attract public and policy attention. Privacy has been defined in many ways (Sheehan, 2002). Often instantiated in legal frameworks as rights, definitions include privacy as the right to be left alone, to be able to keep one's personal information out of the public domain, to be protected from control by others, to decide what personal information to share with others, to know what personal information is being collected by others, and to access one's personal data held by others. Underlying these varying definitions lies a division between those centred on keeping information out of the public domain and those centred on determining (or controlling, or knowing) what personal information is available to whom.

Young people – indeed all users – rarely wish their information to be kept entirely private. Rather, they wish to control who knows what about them. As Samarajiva put it, 'privacy is designed here as the capability to implicitly or explicitly negotiate boundary conditions of social relations' (1996: 134). But they seek to exercise this capability in spaces that are privately owned, thus encountering what Six, Lasky and Fletcher describe as:

> a central fault line around which societies in the developed world are shaped. This is the continuing, and perhaps growing, tension between

the impulses of economic liberalization, with its commitments to removing constraints upon trade and exchange, and of political liberalism, with its impulse to construct and then protect a conception of individual or family life from unfettered openness to trade or governance. (1998: 9)

Thus safeguarding children's privacy rights on the internet may be seen as a constraint upon trade and exchange. Increasingly, it seems, 'the ability of computers to collect, search and exchange data feeds a growing market for personal information and harbors the potential to erode personal privacy' (Stein and Sinha, 2006). Or, as Six, Lasky and Fletcher (1998: 23) argue, 'what is distinctive about informational capitalism is that *personal information* has become the basic fuel on which modern business and government run.' Hence, across industrial societies, governments are consulting, debating and attempting to regulate the shifting boundaries of who can and should know what about whom and for what purpose. Cross-national differences are already apparent, for example, with the United States placing relatively more stress on economic liberalization, though COPPA (the Children's Online Privacy Protection Act[6]) provides specific legal protections for children under 13 years old; the European Union gives comparatively more weight to cultural rights and protection (Fernback and Papacharissi, 2007). For children, these issues are especially fraught, both because as minors they are too young to enter into consumer contracts and because age verification online is lacking.

Much of this debate has centred on external threats to privacy – indeed, mainly on state and commercial threats to individual privacy (Montgomery and Pasnik, 1996), as well as the rare but dangerous threat posed by paedophile activity online (Arnaldo, 2001; Finkelhor, 2008; see chapter 6). Yet, consistent with the definition of privacy as managing rather than preventing access to personal information, children themselves are most concerned with maintaining their privacy in relation to others within rather than outside their social network, whether peers or adults. Since the number of contacts is considerable – a 2006 US survey, of 1,487 8–18 year olds found that among 13–18 year olds, the average number of social networking 'friends' is 75 (Harris Interactive, 2006), with many having several hundred contacts – the potential benefits and risks are equally sizable (Rosen, 2006).

The UK Children Go Online survey found that, for 9–19-year-old frequent users, nearly half (46%) said that they have given out personal information to someone that they met on the internet, including their hobbies (27%), email address (24%), full name (17%), age (17%), name of their school (9%) phone number (7%) or sent a photograph (7%). In part, this is playful, though no less risky for it: 40 per cent say that they have pretended about themselves online – using, for example, a different name (27%), changing their age (22%), appearance (10%) or gender (5%). And though they often know the rules, a minority (7%) admits to forgetting about safety guidelines online while 17 per cent enjoy being rude or silly on the internet (Livingstone and Bober, 2004b). For parents, this provokes anxiety: as Candy's mother said, 'she's very happy to give her address or telephone number to any Tom, Dick, or Harry and you just think "Oh no! Don't do that darling." . . . She's a bit too trusting.'

Although teenagers may disclose personal information to up to several hundred people known only casually, it would be a mistake to conclude that they are unconcerned about their privacy (Barnes, 2006; Dwyer, 2007). As Sophie says to those accusing her generation, 'I don't give stuff away that I'm not willing to share.' The question of what you show to others and what you keep private was often the liveliest part of the interviews, suggesting an intense interest in privacy. Perhaps the Japanese opposition between *Uchi* (roughly, inside, us) and *Soto* (outside, them) captures their motivations better than the Western 'public' and 'private', since 'private' is often taken to mean not revealing information to anyone at all. As analysed by Takahashi (2008), the concept of 'uchi' – akin to one's intimate circle – recognizes the importance of belonging to a social group (typically school friends, for children and young people) held together by close, committed interpersonal relationships. As she observes, where once the *uchi* depended on 'the constant sharing of the locale and constant face-to-face interaction', today 'the *uchi* has emerged, not just through face-to-face interaction in spatial localities, but also through constant mediated interaction via the internet in non-spatial localities' (p. 420).

Restrictive affordances

Teenagers describe thoughtful decisions about what, how, and to whom they reveal personal information – drawing their own boundaries about what information to post, making deliberate choices about modes of communication. Online as offline, they must and do disclose personal information both to sustain intimacy but also to refresh or expand their intimate circle. But in so doing they risk undermining their own privacy. Two difficulties undermine teenagers' control over personal disclosure: one derives from the affordances of social networking sites, for these may be poorly designed from the users' point of view; the second derives from limits on young people's developing media or internet literacy. Clearly these are mutually dependent – the more problematic the site design, the greater the demand on teenagers' skills to manage their communication.

One key restriction imposed by social networking sites is the binary classification of contacts, for being required to decide whether personal information should be disclosed to 'friends' or to 'anyone' fails to capture the subtleties of privacy that teenagers wish to sustain. Like many teenagers, Jason, 16, wishes his private space online to be 'public' (i.e. visible) to his friends but private from his parents:

> You don't mind [other] people reading it, but it's your parents, you don't really want your parents seeing it, because I don't really like my parents sort of looking through my room and stuff, because that's like my private space.

To achieve this, he must set his privacy settings to 'private' not 'public' and, further, refuse his parents as 'friends'. In short, the very language of the privacy settings is itself confusing. Simon says, 'people that know us, it is probably going to be on like public for them' – by which he means that he has set his profile to 'private' so that only people who know him can see it. Similarly, when Nina complains about Facebook that 'they should do something about making it more like private, because you can't really set your profile to private', she does not mean that she has not set her profile to 'private'; rather, she is frustrated that this is insufficient to allow her to discriminate who knows what about her within her 300 or so 'friends'.

Teenagers classify their friends in a range of ways. When asked about her 554 friends on Facebook, Ellie describes friends from school, friends from a holiday in Manchester, friends from the London Network, and so on. Though some reject this trend towards an ever-expanding social circle (Jason, for example, has only 39 friends because those are, he says, his real friends, and having hundreds of friends is 'pointless'), this does not mean those with many friends make no distinction among them. Nina's classification is graded in terms of intimacy:

> Well, I have my best friends, and then I have friends that I'm good friends with, and then I have friends that I see every so often, and they're normally out of school friends . . . And then I have just people that I don't really talk to, but I know who they are, and maybe it's hi and bye in the corridor at school sort of friends.

It is unclear to these teenagers how they can reflect such gradations of intimacy in using the privacy settings provided. The relation between internet literacy and the interface design of social networking sites and settings is also problematic. A fair proportion of those interviewed hesitated when asked to show me how to change their privacy settings, often clicking on the wrong options before managing this task, and showing some nervousness about the unintended consequences of changing settings (both the risk of 'stranger danger' and parental approbation were referred to here, though they also told stories of viruses, crashed computers, unwanted advertising and unpleasant chain messages). For example, having set his profile to private, Billy tells me it can't be changed to public. Leo wanted his profile to be public, since it advertises his band, yet still says uncertainly, 'I might have ticked the box, but I'm not 100 per cent sure if I did'; sitting in front of the computer with him, I observe that he is unsure how to check this. Or again, Ellie signed up for the London network instead of that for her school when she first joined Facebook and now can't change this, saying 'I probably can, but I'm not quite, I'm not so great that, I haven't learned all the tricks to it yet.' The result is that she sees the private information for over one million Londoners but not that of her schoolmates; moreover, Londoners she does not know can see her information. Unsurprisingly, then, when asked whether they would like to change anything about social networking, the operation of the privacy settings and the provision of private messaging on the sites are among teenagers' top priorities.[7]

Last, it is worth noting that, rather than compromise their privacy too far, many choose to express their more personal experiences using other modes of communication. For example, Ellie shifts to instant messaging for private conversations with her best friends and, like many others, for flirting. Nina, Daphne and most others talk to their best friends face-to-face or, again, by instant messaging. If upset, Joshua turns to neither phone, internet nor even a friend, but rather listens to loud rock music in his room. As Sophie explains,

> when you're moody, MySpace isn't really the best thing to go on . . . you can't really get across emotions on there because you're writing. It's good for making arrangements and stuff, but it's not good if you want a proper chat.

In other words, although to exist online, one must write oneself and one's friendships and community into being, this does not mean one must thereby include every aspect of oneself. Deciding what not to say about oneself online is for many teenagers, an agentic act to protect their identity, intimacy and privacy.

Creative affordances

> In today's game simulations, people experience themselves in a new,
> often exotic setting. The minds they meet are their own. (Turkle,
> 1995: 31)

Social networking enables as well as restricts. boyd (2008) argues that
online communication affords new kinds of 'networked publics'
insofar as it is distinctively characterized by persistence (being
recorded and thus permitting asynchronous communication), search-
ability (permitting the easy construction of new, extended or niche
relationships), replicability (enabling multiple versions with no
distinction between the original and the copy) and, last invisible
audiences (a radical uncertainty regarding who is attending to the
communication – and, one might add, who is speaking – being built
into the architecture of online spaces, exacerbated by conditions of
anonymity). All of these features serve to disembed communication
from its traditional anchoring in the face-to-face situation of physical
co-location, reembedding them in other, more flexible and, notably,
more peer-oriented relations of sociability (Heverly, 2008; Thompson,
1995). As Giddens argues,

> Disembedding mechanisms depend on two conditions: the evacuation
> of the traditional or customary content of local contexts of action, and
> the reorganizing of social relations across broad time–space bands.
> (1995: 85)

Thus, while 'tradition placed in stasis some core aspects of social
life – not least the family and sexual identity' (ibid, p. 56), in 'post-
traditional' society, relations of gender, class, culture and generation
are being rewritten. Much of the content on social networking
sites, instant messenger services and the World Wide Web is, as noted
earlier, strikingly familiar, conforming to commercialized peer-group
norms shared by many. This may be critically read as evidence
of individualization (as discussed in chapter 1; see Beck and Beck-
Gernsheim, 2002), with the development of 'taste' and lifestyle
content significantly shaped by powerful commercial interests in
the fashion and music industries (as was also argued for 'bedroom
culture' by McRobbie and Garber, 1976). Not only are advertisements commonly placed at the top or centre of homepages, blogs,
chat rooms and social networking sites, but also the user is encouraged to define their identity through consumer preferences (music,
movies, fandom).

However, the distinctive affordances of online communication also enable the proliferation of niche peer groups or communities of interest, from hobbyists or fans of a particular Indie band or cult TV programme to those interested in self-harm, racism and much else. A good example of the way in which an online, converged media environment affords distinctive forms of social identity is the popularity of witchcraft and 'wiccan' subcultures (sometimes based on television programmes or films such as *Buffy the Vampire Slayer, Sabrina the Teenage Witch, Charmed, Bewitched*). This testifies to the fascination of many, especially girls and young women, with the themes of female power, spirituality and adventure, these providing a cultural repertoire with which to resist disempowering norms of femininity (precisely without, typically, embracing the term 'feminism'). Clark (2002) argues that the wiccan subculture affords powerful identities, mediated and online, that contrasts with the relatively powerless position of teenagers in everyday life and, further, allows for an exploration of morality and, indeed, an identification with 'goodness' (for these are typically good, not evil, witches) which sidesteps acceptance of dominant adult morality (as often expressed, especially in the USA, through organized religion).

Creative and 'self-authoring practices' may be especially significant when the participants are those 'whose lives are often storied by others,' as Vasudevan (2006: 207) observes when examining the online identity practices of African American adolescent boys. Again because their lives are often represented more powerfully by others than themselves, the exuberance and diversity of a girls' subculture online seems especially compelling. Mazzarella and Pecora (2007) argue that this affords a means of affirming the experiences of those who otherwise, being on the edge of adolescence, stand to lose their 'voice' in the face of a mainstream public culture in which commercializing, pathologizing or marginalizing messages predominate. So, extending the critical work of McRobbie and Garber (1976) on girls' magazines, and that of others on teenage bedrooms as a site of identity construction and display (Kearney, 2007; Livingstone, 2007c), Stern (2008) argues that web content created by, rather than for, girls enables the construction of a self-presentation by which girls can speak to each other in what Gilligan (1993) called 'a different voice'. As Kearney observes with some optimism, when noting how online creation is located in girls' bedrooms,

contemporary female youth are not retreating to private spaces; they *reconfiguring* such sites to create new publics that can better serve their needs, interests, and goals. (2007: 138)

Illustrating the point, Guzzetti (2006) discusses two girls aged 17–18, Saundra and Corgan, who had co-created a zine (online magazine) integrating activist themes of social justice and feminism with punk rock and entertainment content. Following the social literacies tradition (Street, 1995; see also chapter 7), Guzzetti argues that the development of digital literacies required to sustain the zine is not only embedded in social practices via the online community activities surrounding zines, rather than simply reflecting individual skill, but also enables identity work that affirms these young women as authentic members of the punk community, a world in which their expertise is essential, their performances valued and in which they could escape stereotyped notions of gender. Offline, such benefits were observed to influence Saundra's offline writing, stimulating a satirical and witty writing style with ultimate consequences for her social and cultural capital.

Conclusions

> Our lives are lived as *representations to ourselves* ... our biographies are, partly, intertextual'. (Tomlinson, 1991: 61)

This chapter has argued that identity is constituted through interaction with others. While most people with access to the internet greatly enjoy the opportunities it affords for communication, today's teenagers are particularly absorbed in constructing online identities and relationships. Although the notion of a fixed, essential identity remains discursively popular (as in the ready claim that one's homepage or social networking profile represents the 'real me'), in practice this need not imply a long-term commitment to, or consistency in, online (or offline) representations of the self. Indeed, it seems characteristic of youthful online identity practices that they are both in earnest and yet playful, they seek consistency yet tolerate contradiction and although they are intensively and intensely performed they may be suddenly overturned ('deleted'). Such ambiguity and ambivalence is undoubtedly afforded by the communicative interfaces of instant messaging, social networking and chat rooms, fitting well with the changing and fluid nature of young people's social relationships.

Within this discursive context of negotiation and experimentation, identities are expressed online not as a free-floating, individual activity but as embedded in and shaped by specific social and technological conditions. Self-actualization (Erikson, 1959/1980) demands the careful negotiation between the opportunities (for identity, intimacy, sociability) and the risks (regarding privacy, misunderstanding, hostility) afforded by internet-mediated communication. On social networking sites, for example, younger teenagers relish the opportunities to play and display, continuously recreating a highly decorated, stylistically elaborate identity (Livingstone, 2008c). Having experienced this phase, older teenagers tend to favour a plain aesthetic that foregrounds their links to others, expressing a notion of identity lived through more authentic relationships with others. In expressing their identities online, children and teenagers are constrained by the expectations of their peer group, the affordances of internet sites and their own skills and literacies.

This engenders risks as well as opportunities. For those focused on identity as display, online risks may arise from their willing, sometimes naive self-display of personal information to a wide circle of contacts, not all of whom are close friends or, sometimes, are even remembered. For those focused on identity as connection, online risks may arise from their very confidence that they can know, judge and trust the people with whom they are intimate, as well as from the possibility of being neglected or excluded from the peer group. Last, risks may also arise from the teenagers' limited internet literacy combined with confusing or poorly designed site settings, leaving them unclear regarding their control over who can see what about them. Each of these risks may only adversely affect a minority, but they render public policy measures (such as improved site design, internet literacy efforts or parental guidance) appropriate, as discussed in chapters 6 and 7.

In closing, we might ask what children and young people do with these new freedoms to reorganize their social relations in new and changing time–space contexts. Positively, children and young people embrace online communication to enable peer communication, prioritized over parental relations, at any time and any place. In addition to having fun, valid in its own right, this permits a flexible and creative construction of identity (or identities) in a manner that fits the demands of the changing, experimental, uncertain and easily embarrassed yet highly sociable adolescent. Teenagers use these networks to extend practices of personal support and advice, and to establish and sustain an often strong ethic of care among peers. In so doing, they are reshaping the possibilities for identity, privacy and intimacy.

However, although teenagers are not so superficial as to construe their identity in terms of colours, layout and style features, much online communication remains repetitive, few social networking profiles reveal evidence of great creativity, and those who join niche subcultures or create their own fanzines appear to be in the minority. Further, insofar as young people primarily communicate with local friends, few of them take up the global pen pal idealistically promoted in the early days of the internet, and they show relatively little interest in global political movements, at least, with a large 'P'. This is the issue I develop in the next chapter.

5

Participation and Civic Engagement

High hopes for young citizens online

> The emergence of the internet presents . . . the possibility of a qualitative shift in the practice of political communication, as significant for the pre-millennial 1990s as TV was for the 1960s . . . [with] hitherto unprecedented possibilities for citizens' deliberation and public input to decision-making processes. (Coleman, 1999: 69)

> Our MPs are desperately trying to appear cool in a bid to win over young, internet-savvy voters. They've all set up their own websites but it's a fine line between being able to relate to the younger generation . . . and coming over like a 'square' father letting what's left of his hair down. (Smith and Fletcher, 2007)

In recent decades, political scientists have been charting, with mounting concern, the steady decline in political participation across many countries, as measured by such indicators as voter turn-out, party loyalty and representation in decision-making bodies (Bennett, 2008; Norris, 2001; Pattie, Seyd and Whiteley, 2004; Pharr and Putnam, 2000). Since this decline has coincided with the spread of mass media into daily life, critics have scrutinized every dimension of the media's relations with political institutions and the public sphere. While the mass media, especially television, are often held responsible, not entirely fairly (Couldry, Livingstone and Markham, 2007), for the public's apparent distraction or withdrawal from civil society (Putnam, 2000), for the new, interactive media it is, research suggests, a different story.

Online, people are discovering common interests with a potentially huge network of like-minded peers, developing new critical skills and building alternative deliberative spaces – all activities that raise the possibility of a virtual public sphere (Dahlgren, 2005). Indeed, many argue that the internet is inherently 'democratic'. Even though its features (interactivity, global scale, fast connectivity, unlimited capacity) are not themselves radically new, taken in combination the internet is held to afford a qualitative shift in the potential for democratic communication (Bentivegna, 2002), one that particularly suits direct communication among citizens on a local, national and global scale, while undermining or disintermediating traditional gatekeepers, both political elites and global media corporations.

Intriguingly, there appears to be a promising match between the style of deliberation afforded by the internet and that preferred by the very population segment – young people – who seem the most disengaged from traditional forms of political activity. The very architecture of the internet, with its flexible, hypertextual, networked structure, its dialogic mode of address, and its alternative, even anarchic feel, appeals to young people, fitting their informal, peer-oriented, anti-authority approach. In the online environment, it may be that young people feel more expert and empowered, especially by contrast with the traditional, linear, hierarchical, logical, rule-governed conventions often used in official communications with youth.

It does seem, therefore, a viable proposition to encourage youthful participation through this means, and many are working hard to make this proposition a reality. Online, we are witnessing the flourishing of life-political and single issue networks, campaigns and new social movements, many of which may be expected to – and are often specifically designed to – appeal to young people (Bennett, 2008; Kann, Berry, Gant and Zager, 2007). This 'abundance of civic and political activity by and for youth' uses the internet to 'invite young people to participate in a wide range of issues, including voting, voluntarism, racism and tolerance, social activism and, most recently, patriotism, terrorism and military conflict' (Montgomery, Gottlieb-Robles and Larson, 2004: 2).[1] The result is new formations, new groupings that are often idealistic in their hopes but pragmatic in the low-level of obligation expected of members (Coleman, 2003). Their communicative conventions are characterized by openness and spontaneity, generating ad hoc, low-commitment, self-reflexive and strategic communications within a flexibly defined, peer-based network.

So, can we learn from these initiatives to identify ways in which the internet may facilitate youthful civic participation? Can the internet play a role in engaging children and reversing youthful apathy? These questions will be addressed both through a critical exploration of recent empirical findings and also, as will become necessary, through theoretical consideration of the nature of participation itself. In this chapter, I deliberately widen the traditional political focus to include children as well as young people in relation to citizenship online; in a later section, it will prove necessary to distinguish children (below the voting age) and young adults. First, however, let us identify the problem for which online participation is proffered as the solution.

'Politics is boring'

Interviewer	And what about politics? Are any of you interested in politics?
Sean	No!
Ryan	Don't be silly!
	(focus group with 14–15-year-old boys)

Focus groups with young people, conducted as part of the UK Children Go Online project (Livingstone, 2007d) readily suggest a generation bored with politics, attracted instead by commercial offerings, absorbed by celebrity and keen to conform to peer norms. Fifteen-year-old Faseeha is dismissive of politics: 'I don't want to know ... I don't really like politics ... it's too hard.' And Steve (aged 17) asks, 'Why care about something going on miles away when you've got something going on in a hundred metres?'[2] If these are typical reactions from mid-teenagers, will they be ready and keen to vote at 18?

Undoubtedly, there are grounds for concern in the evidence of a significant decline in young adults' voting since the 2001 general election in the UK (Hansard Society, 2001). In the 2005 UK general election, only 37 per cent of 18–24 year olds and 48 per cent of 25–34 year olds voted (The Electoral Commission, 2005). When asked for their likelihood of voting at the next general election, only 24 per cent of 18–24 year olds were certain they would vote, compared with an adult average of 55 per cent (The Electoral Commission, 2007). Below 50 per cent turnout among the under 24s is not unique to the UK – voting was below 50 per cent for this age group in the USA from 1976 to 2004 (Lopez *et al.*, 2006) although it rose to 52 per cent for the 2008 election (CIRCLE, 2008) and similar declines are found in Japan and elsewhere (The Electoral Commission, 2004). Yet the creative use of the internet to revitalize the youth vote in the US

2008 election campaign may mark a turning point in reversing this decline.

Young people's apparent disaffection with politics has become a focus of widespread attention in academic, policy and public debate. Understanding and explaining this lack of interest is less easy. Is young people's political participation low because they lack motivation, or political knowledge, a sense of political efficacy? Among teenagers, research finds that a knowledge of politics and understanding of political processes is positively associated with civic participation (Coleman and Hendry, 1999); indeed, the same holds true for adults too, and both political interest and political self-efficacy are also predictors of voting (Pattie, Seyd and Whiteley, 2004).

This suggests that part of the problem is not specific to youth. The Public Connection project found that, among adults of all ages, there is a notable gap between access to information (with 81 per cent saying they know where to get the information they need) and political efficacy: only 39 per cent say they can influence decisions in their area, and as many as 55 per cent feel that 'people like us' have no say in what the government does, while 73 per cent sometimes feel strongly about something but do not know what to do about it (Couldry, Livingstone and Markham, 2007; see also Pharr and Putnam, 2000). But for young people learning to become citizens, discovering that civic action has low efficacy can be a powerful and disheartening lesson. Mumtaz (aged 15), interviewed by the UK Children Go Online project, readily recounted prominent news stories in which people expressed their views without effect:

> Like the war in Iraq, there are some people protesting and same as for the fox hunting – some people are protesting but the government just ignores them.

Arguably, the failure of the worldwide protest against the Iraq war in 2003 deeply impressed a whole generation with the futility of 'having their say'. Mumtaz was also influenced by the 'Fathers for Justice' protester who climbed Buckingham Palace dressed as Superman,[3] this illustrating how far the public must go to get attention; 'you have to break the law to do something', he concluded.

Although disentangling the links between a low interest in 'politics' and low political efficacy is complex, many would argue that the latter is more crucial than the former. In other words, we should not criticize a generation for its relative lack of interest or, especially, its apparent apathy, but rather we should inquire into the conditions that sustain (or undermine) the vital perception that participation is effective. I shall return to this point later, as the very interactivity of the internet is what has persuaded its supporters that this medium, more than any other, has the potential to enhance efficacy even if – as we shall also see below – it may not manage to stimulate new political interest in those who are not already engaged. But first, the narrow definition of politics employed thus far must be addressed.

Widening the definition of the 'political'

Voting does not necessarily capture the essence of politics or, certainly, citizenship, for participation is broader than the act of voting every few years. Indeed, a groundswell of critical opinion holds that the claim of youthful disaffection with politics is overstated because of its limited definitions and simplistic measures (Bennett, 2008; Lister, Smith, Middleton and Cox, 2003). The exact words matter here. Only 54 per cent of the UK public say they are interested in 'politics', and only 46 per cent of 18–34 year olds; but over two thirds do claim an interest in 'political issues' at the local (79%), national (75%) and international (70%) levels (The Electoral Commission, 2007). As the quotation that opened this section illustrates, young people react particularly negatively to the word 'politics', and the fact that this quotation occurred during a focus group discussion is not irrelevant. Political interest is partly a matter of peer group norms, and young people seem particularly unlikely to discuss party politics with a capital P in each other's presence. Discussing 'politics or political news with someone else' in the last two or three years was also notably lower for 18–24 year olds (at 27%) than the population overall (40%), according to the Electoral Commission (ibid.).

Once politics is defined more widely, many researchers and policymakers find encouragement in measures that reveal 'a high level of idealism and engagement in single-issue politics among adolescents' (Coleman and Hendry, 1999: 201), notwithstanding – or perhaps even because of – their disenchantment from the formal political system (MORI, 2004; Morris, John and Halpern, 2003). One survey asked 14–16 year olds in the UK whether they had undertaken any of a standard list of forms of participation over the past year: it found rather high levels of participation – 70 per cent had signed a petition, 66 per cent had helped at a charity event, 64 per cent had gone on a march or rally and 59 per cent had boycotted something (Roker, Player and Coleman, 1997).

Yet the evidence is contested. Notably, the Electoral Commission (2007) found for 18–24 year olds (admittedly, an older group than

Roker *et al.*'s teenagers) that 'the youngest age group scored lowest on every measure of political activism', including signing a petition, boycotting products, participating in a demonstration, joining a campaign, and so forth. This is not especially, they suggest, because their political efficacy (e.g. their sense that they have a say in how the country is run) is low – for though it is low, so too is that of most adults. Rather, the Electoral Commission points to a problem of motivation, since 18–24 year olds also have the lowest scores on political interest and political knowledge. But this may reflect the use of precisely that narrow conception of the 'political' that others challenge.

If we can 'see beyond the formal political system' (Dahlgren, 2003: 164), so as to include not just matters of party politics, ideological belief systems and voting but also civic and community issues, life politics and new social movements, then the view of young people as apathetic and ignorant about politics is challenged by evidence of a more lively, contested, and actively interested citizenry. Indeed, this wider definition of participation permits recognition of diverse forms of activism also practised by adults (Bromley, Curtice and Seyd, 2004). Bennett persuasively argues that:

> what is changing about politics is not a decline in citizen engagement, but a shift away from old forms that is complemented by the emergence of new forms of political interest and engagement ... civic culture is not dead; it has merely taken new identities, and can be found living in other communities. (1998: 745)

Construing participation more widely also permits us to reject a simple critique of all media as undermining political interest and participation, for not only other forms of civic engagement but also other forms of media engagement can come into view. Putnam's 'bowling alone' argument – that the growth in time spent with television over the past half century is not only correlated with the decline in community participation but is actually the cause of this decline – has been challenged by empirical evidence (e.g. McLean, Schultz and Steger, 2002; Norris, 1996). And as Livingstone and Markham (2008) found for the adult population, being engaged with the news in particular is positively related to voting, even controlling for demographic factors and levels of political interest, although time spent watching television in general makes little difference to either voting or political interest (though it is associated with lower levels of civic activism).

Endorsing this wider conception of both the political sphere and the media, Barnhurst asks how young people can become citizens when their main resources for decoding the world come from the mass media (see also Buckingham, 2000). Interviews with young people lead him to reverse the commonplace critique of the media's role, noting that:

> They discuss their emerging selves, in reference to the media, with peers. They find more sources and expose themselves more widely to alternative media because of teachers. They are what can be described as active citizens in the interstices of power/knowledge, even if not in the modes and regions prescribed by democratic theory ... understanding an issue comes scattershot ... from pop songs, TV commercials, documentary films and – most importantly – personal discussions more than from journalists. ... Far from being dummies, [they] are deeply committed to finding the truth about the political worlds they inhabit. (1998: 215–16)

Written before widespread adoption of the internet, it is now timely to ask whether and how the internet complements or intensifies this picture.

Can the internet make a difference?

Putting together the declining vote and political interest among young adults with the distinctively youthful profile of internet users, one might suppose that the internet is part of the problem more than of the solution, updating Putnam's (2000) *Bowling Alone* thesis to hypothesize that it is now the internet that fragments and distracts the public from a common sense of civic purpose.

A growing body of research and, especially, policy hopes to invert this pessimistic conclusion, instead capitalizing on young people's interest in the internet so as to encourage them into a greater engagement with politics. In the USA, for example, 'digital software and technology were a central part of many of the orchestrated efforts to promote youth voting during the 2004 presidential election' (Montgomery, 2008: 29) – this seems even more the case for the Obama/McCain election 2008 (Schifferes, 2008; Smith and Rainie, 2008). There is some evidence that the internet can enable a degree of civic engagement, both for young people in particular and for adults more generally (e.g. Lusoli, Ward and Gibson, 2006; Newman, Barnes, Sullivan and Knops, 2004). For example, nearly one in five of those aged 18–35 years in the UK have contributed to an online discussion about a public issue of importance to them, while for those over 35 the figure falls to 5 per cent (Couldry, Livingstone and Markham, 2007). Another

UK survey found that while only 10 per cent of 15–24 year olds took part in any form of political activity offline, three times that many did something political on the internet (Gibson, Lusoli and Ward, 2002). Indeed, in the US, 38 per cent of 12–17 year olds said they go online to express their opinion (Lenhart, Rainie and Lewis, 2001).

Thus it is hoped that, since young people relish using the internet to sustain and extend their communication networks and since they also commit to these networks a considerable investment in time, motivation, sociability and identity, then surely this energy can be harnessed to civic ends. Such an extension – from communication to participation – seems a small step perhaps, often requiring a moderate effort compared, say, with attending face-to-face meetings or other offline activities. As Poppy (aged 16), reported,

> There's a Greenpeace website which had a petition about like global warming and stuff and we should do something about it. And I signed that just because it's easy and you might as well put your name down.

Several examples of young people taking this 'small step' also emerged from the Social Networking Study discussed in the previous chapter. Ellie, 15, an active Facebook user, had joined 163 groups, including the appreciation society for her local bus, one for a favourite television programme and one for a charity she supports. Her profile includes a 'cause' (breast cancer) where she invites others to donate to breast cancer research. Ryan, also 15, included on his elaborate Piczo profile (a black background, with moving computer code, as in *The Matrix*, in light blue running down the screen in constant motion) a tribute page to 9/11, explaining, 'I just felt like making a tribute to them ... to let people know that I care.'

This is encouraging evidence of a youthful ethic of care – an emotional and political identification with distant others (Couldry, Livingstone and Markham, 2007; Gilligan, 1993). Yet some may wonder how much further we can stretch the notion of 'participation'. The UK Children Go Online survey of UK 9–19 year olds asked users about several activities that might be counted as 'participation' and these were practised to widely varying degrees. Information and communication uses of the internet are near-universal, suggesting that the internet facilitates peer-to-peer networking and makes all kinds of information highly accessible. Is this to stretch 'participation' too far? The same survey found that only 22 per cent of 9–19 year olds who go online at least weekly have voted online (and this could include voting for favourite pop stars), 17 per cent have contributed to a message board and just 8 per cent have signed a petition online.

Further, among 12–19 year olds weekly users, 26 per cent said they read the news online, although one may judge this figure to be fairly high, especially as all of these figures show a steep rise across the age range (Livingstone, 2007d).

What about visiting these websites designed to appeal to their public or civic interests? Avoiding the tricky term 'politics', we asked 12–19 year olds who go online at least weekly about their use of specific types of civic websites (e.g. about charities, the environment, government, human rights, conditions at school/work). Over half (54%) had visited at least one, though often not more than one, using them mainly for information (i.e. as a form of one-way communication) and interacting with them rather little. When we asked those who use the internet for communication if they discuss political or civic issues peer-to-peer on the internet, more than half (56%) said they never talk about these issues with anyone by email, IM or chat, though 14 per cent have done so once or twice, 24 per cent sometimes and 4 per cent often.

In a multiple regression analysis seeking to predict which young people discuss these issues on the internet, age and internet-related self-efficacy were found to be significant predictors: older teenagers and those more confident of their online expertise are more likely to have discussed civic issues with others on the internet. Conversely, looking at the reasons why many (42%) teenagers never visit civic/ political sites, low levels of online political participation appeared to be due to a general lack of interest rather than to more specific problems, such as website design, trust or searching skills (Livingstone, Bober and Helsper, 2005). This suggests that those who are interested in civic or political issues will be motivated to seek out relevant websites (and that those who are not will not) but that interacting with these sites is not itself a matter of political interest but rather of age (perhaps, peer-group acceptability) and online expertise. Further, there is little evidence that those whose motivation is, instead, to explore the internet creatively or interactively for its own sake find themselves drawn into greater civic or political engagement than expected – although there are positive if weak correlations between most online activities, suggesting at least some transfer of skills and interests from one online activity to another.

Indeed, for 12–17-year-old users, the UKGCO project found that interactive and creative uses of the internet are encouraged by the very experience of using the internet – these permitting growing levels of interest, skills and confidence, especially among boys. But this is not the case for visiting civic websites, which, instead, depends primarily on demographic factors (with older and more middle-class girls being most likely to visit civic sites, irrespective of variation in amount of time spent or level of expertise online). This suggests that those with already established civic or political interests find the internet a useful resource for pursuing these interests, pointing to the importance of understanding processes of political socialization more than internet-related experience and expertise. It also undermines the straightforward hope that interaction and civic engagement represent sequenced 'steps' on a 'ladder' of participation from minimal to more ambitious modes of participation (Hill and Tisdall, 1997). Lorie (aged 17) puts it succinctly:

> At the end of the day, you're going to look at what you're interested in. And if you haven't got an interest in politics, you're not going to get one from having the internet.

In this context, it is unsurprising that an American survey of 15–25 year olds found the internet to be an even less effective means of engaging disaffected young people than traditional routes, though undoubtedly very effective at mobilizing the already interested (Levine and Lopez, 2004). And perhaps it begins to explain why evaluations of online civic initiatives are often disappointing, notwithstanding the exciting promise of revived political enthusiasm that has motivated so many politicians and youth organizations (Phipps, 2000).

Varieties of online youth

It is clear, and unsurprising, that young people are far from homogenous in their civic practices online. Using the statistical technique of cluster analysis, the UK Children Go Online project grouped 12–19 year olds who use the internet at least weekly into three distinct groups (Livingstone, Bober and Helsper, 2005):

- The 'interactors' were the most likely to interact with and even make their own websites. More often boys, and middle class, they are the most privileged in terms of home access and they use the internet the most. Consequently, they have developed considerable online skills, permitting them to discover many advantages of the internet and so using it in a wide range of ways, apparently ready to take up new opportunities as offered. Yet interestingly, this range and depth of online engagement does not lead them especially to pursue civic interests online.

- The 'civic-minded', by contrast, were not especially likely to interact with websites generally or to make their own site, but they do visit a range of civic websites, especially charity and human rights-based sites. More often girls and middle class, these young people have adequate access to the internet and they make average use of it. Consistent with their civic interests, they also visit websites for clubs they belong to and are least likely to chat or download music. It seems unlikely that new online opportunities on the internet are drawing these young people into civic participation. Rather, having developed civic interests offline, they see the internet as one way of pursuing them, even though they do not consider themselves especially skilled online.
- Third, the 'disengaged' were the least active in online participation, however measured – being much less likely to interact with sites, visit civic sites or make their own website. A little younger than the other groups, and from lower socio-economic status backgrounds, they are less likely to have home access or a broadband connection. The result is a less experienced, less expert group of internet users who make average use of the internet for information and music, visit few websites and communicate less online. Being disengaged in terms of both access and use, these young people, it seems, are on the wrong side of the digital divide.

For those seeking to engage children and young people via the internet, these three target groups require rather different modes of address and different forms of provision. In what follows, I note, first, that even engaging the already engaged (labelled the 'civic-minded' above) is not a straightforward business. Then I turn to the tougher challenge, that of drawing in the interactors and, possibly, the disengaged, for all of these are, at least, already active online, if not especially interested in civic matters.

Engaging the already engaged

Mobilizing the already interested in new ways is itself a valuable aim, albeit different from that of encouraging new interest among the disengaged. Thus, even if political interest originates in socialization rather than in online activity, the online environment can surely facilitate and promote youthful interests, as illustrated by this group of 15 year olds:

Interviewer	OK. One thing I was thinking about . . . when they had stop-the-war protests, and they said lots of young people got involved, and when they did, they organized their protest through the internet.
Milly	You find out, like if you searched it, you would find out stuff in your area.
Kim	Also like when you send emails to people, you can also do it on MSN when the war was going on, there was like a, hmm, tribute to people in the war. There was like a little, what was it?
Claire	A ribbon?
Kim	And if you, you've just got to send it to as many people as you can, it sort of like goes round all your friends and their friends and . . . loads of people sign up.
Milly	I can't remember exactly what it was, but it was like you know, to show respect to people who died.

It seems likely that, for the already committed, specific affordances of the internet may enhance their activities. Milly, we learn later from her contribution to the UK Children Go Online message board, comes from a political household: 'my Dad like teaches politics at University, so I get interested in it.' This seems to enable her to use the internet expressively to communicate both her lively political interest and her frustration with her peers:

Message no. ##
Posted by MILLY
Subject: Re: Email Tony Blair
I really don't understand how people could have said that they aren't interested in politics! What about the 'Don't attack Iraq' rallies and marches. There was a massive under-18 turn out. What about the banning of live music without licensing! What about the massive probability that everyone in the UK will have ID cards within the next 5 years! What about national curfews for under 18s!

Milly makes her argument on the basis of what she sees as the self-evident importance and relevance of these issues to young people. But the likely role of her parents in discussing politics at home, getting engaged in various forms of action, and encouraging her developing interest, should not be underestimated. In Roker *et al.*'s (1997) study, whose findings were noted earlier, when the most active subgroup of this sample were asked why they became involved, one quarter said it was because of parents or siblings, 17 per cent said a friend encouraged them, and a fifth said it was because of their membership of a local organization (such as church or youth club). Identity issues (e.g. being teased for taking part) and proximity (reducing travel difficulties) also mattered. Online, by contrast, one can participate anonymously (reducing identity/impression management problems) and there are no costs in time and travel. On the other hand, nor is there likely to be much local involvement or family encouragement.

Dahlgren and Olsson's (2008) study of civically active youth found that use of the internet facilitated their existing activities but could not replace the importance of face-to-face interaction for sustaining motivation, deepening bonds and aiding decision-making. An interesting illustration is provided by Joshua, 14, one of the few teenagers in the Social Networking Study whose political interests – stimulated by his orthodox Jewish family in North London – were supported by the internet. As he explained, on the bus going to school familiar debates over Israel's stance to the Palestinians could easily turn into conflictual, even hostile arguments with Muslim teenagers sharing the bus journey. But on Facebook, he has joined a group committed to peace in the Middle East, where young Jews and Muslims could talk to each other constructively, seeking a mutual understanding, and this proved to be an activity he learned from and valued.

Designing opportunities to 'have your say'

For those not already engaged, even though there is little evidence as yet that the internet is successfully drawing in young citizens into new forms of civic engagement, many remain optimistic that this could work. As we saw in chapter 2, children and young people's internet use suggests that they are, at least initially, interested and willing to try out the online invitation to participate – they search for a wide range of information, attempt to create content, and respond to online invitations to interact. But as we have also seen, they often don't follow through – they visit only one or two civic sites, they tend not to interact with them much, and if they can't get their website online, they do something else.

The gap between opportunities to participate online and young people's everyday responses is not only a matter of political engagement; it is also a matter of communication. In terms of online engagement, political roles of government and citizen can only be realized in terms of the communicative roles of producer and receiver. Young citizens draw on their media and internet literacy as well as their political knowledge when decoding civic websites. Listen to these 14–15 year olds:

Interviewer	Do you ever go to any [name of their city] websites, any sites that are about what's happening in [city]?
Ryan	They're so boring!
Jim	Yeah, they're hyper-boring. You can tell they're so cheaply made as well.
Sean	Yeah.
Jim	Yeah, it's like the italic links with the boxes round them on cheap websites. It has things like that, it's just unbelievable.
Sean	Yeah, there's no effort into the backgrounds. It's plain white! [...] They won't even spring for a picture, they'll just write Leisure World in the most plain black text!

In this discussion, it appears that teenagers' expectations are formed through experience with commercial sites, leading them to judge online content first and foremost in terms of glossy production values rather than civic opportunities. This mismatch in expectations points to a more significant problem, however.

In a case study of civic websites, centring on Epal (www.epal.tv),[4] a Government-sponsored pilot website for the Greater Manchester area, I analysed the relations among producer, text, reader and context, in order to understand the communication gap between providers and young citizens, based on interviews with both sides (Livingstone, 2007a). Unremarkable in itself, this site was selected as typical of many low budget, public sector sites developed to appeal to young people by using 'new technology to innovate to deliver public services to young people differently', because 'technology adds value', the site's producers explained.

I inquired, first, into what was being communicated. Here, Epal's producers claimed that following 'very serious market research', they had developed a strategy to 'join up' services for youth by facilitating a 'partnership' among 'stakeholders' (service providers, civic bodies, youth organizations, employers), each of whom could 'pour content into it'. When I asked teenagers, however, they found the aim of 'joining up' services puzzling, for it blurred familiar content distinctions between leisure/school, home/work, political/social and fun/useful. Joining up provision across the age range from 13–19 year olds (a category that may be narrow for adults but is seen as very broad by teenagers) also puzzled them, for it seemed to offer information that is too old for them or too young or too general. Kanita (aged 15) worried that the site would contain what 'the adults think the teenagers are gonna want to look at'. Meanwhile, teenagers have their own agendas which may or more often may not fit that of the civic youth websites. Luke and Mumtaz, working-class 15 year olds, were cogent in what information they wanted – about education, what to do after leaving school, getting a job, unemployment and global warming and how it could affect London. They also wanted to say things back to politicians: Luke wanted to explain to politicians that the link between youth and crime is 'because we ain't got nowhere to play football and we're messing around 'coz of this'.

The second line of inquiry asked how the subject matter was being communicated. The 'look and feel' of the homepage was, according to the producers, 'funky' and 'cool'. The formal composition resembled a youth magazine, with a brightly coloured mix of text, image and interactive opportunities, a youthful cartoon-style avatar ('Asha') to help the user navigate the site, and three primary routes into the site labelled 'Create' ('Be a creative champion' – for user content creation, including contributions from 'young journalists'), 'Issues' (for 'all the important information you may need', these ranging from global warming and volunteering to young people's rights at work), and 'Interact' (where teenagers are invited to 'check out our lively forum' and 'have your say on the site!'). Initially, the teenagers were appreciative, though they did not call the site 'funky' or 'cool' – Ethan called it 'cheesy' and 'dull'. Mia and Natasha wanted 'more girly' colours and 'wiggly lines'. But behind the homepage, the expensive design features disappeared and the one click took the user to a simple list of options coloured a dull plum. It provided a striking array of information (where else would teenagers go to discover their rights at work, or get the address of a local gay support group?) but in a far from striking manner. Tabia complained, 'this hasn't got a picture, just chunks and chunks and chunks of writing'. Nor had it any personal stories or photos, games or interactivity, not even any advertisements, 'just facts'. The teenagers also encountered problems of navigation. For example, Ethan gave up on trying to find any careers information, partly because he selected 'Create' rather than 'Issues'.[5]

Third, I inquired into who is communicating with whom and with what effect – which proved surprisingly difficult questions to answer. The producers explained that Epal's branding tries to avoid something that 'looks like another government site' – they wanted it to be 'something that young people would look at anyway'. Though their concern is understandable, their decision obscures the provenance and authority of the information – for example, the url selected was 'epal.tv' rather than 'epal.gov' because the market research showed that young people prefer media-based sites. Nor is there an 'about us' link to clarify the identity of the 'we' addressing the user, and the editorial policy is also unclear – are all user postings included, or are they selected or edited? The 'youth' thereby represented are also hard to evaluate for their reliability or representativeness. As Bailey said, 'there isn't anything that says it's from Connexions . . . [it] looks if like some other people had made it' He later speculated about another civic site, 'they've done it so that no one is to know about where they are . . . they kind of keep it secret'.

What is the effect of such communication? The producers of Epal claimed it is 'about participation in the broadest sense', because services for young people 'need to engage with young people in a participatory way'. Yet when pressed, they could not state what kind of participation they aimed for. Tellingly, they said, 'we're putting lots of bits of fun' in the 'hope that young people will throw lots of stuff at it' so that they can 'check they are hitting the mark'. Anticipating such a haphazard process of engagement sits curiously with the considerable planning that has gone into other aspects of the project such as fundraising and design. Moreover, in well-meaning statements such as, young people 'need to know about a lot more these days to make the right choices', a monologic, one-to-many view of the communicative process emerged, in which authorities seek to ensure young people to know certain things so as to make what adults consider 'the right choices'. Teenagers, not surprisingly, are inclined to resist such an approach. Ethan – both internet literate and politicized – complained that Epal is 'so stereotypical' for it assumes that all young people like David Beckham. Those informed about a particular issue found the treatment of that issue superficial. Others seemed briefly attracted but equally easily confused or distracted.[6] Samantha – who has made several websites herself – explicitly rejected the generic 'youth' category, for 'you can't really get one [a site] that would please everyone'.

Indeed, the producers had little indication about whether the site was successful, partly because budgets are generally tight, permitting little systematic market research. Typically, public sector sites rely on what Montgomery *et al.* call 'glimpses' or online traces of the activities of real users – the children who send in web material, those who visit on open days, phone calls from parents, hits to websites or queries to advisors. This leaves unresolved the crucial question of whether these are a self-selected and privileged minority of the already engaged or whether new audiences are being drawn into civic engagement as hoped. As Montgomery *et al.* (2004: 13) say,

> Youth civic websites open doors to access and participation in civic projects, but which young people utilize these opportunities, how, and with what effects over time, are topics that call for more systematic research.

Who's listening?

> I think the problem is how formal they are because they probably have a secretary typing it for them, if they're Prime Minister or something like that. With the email, they won't read it anyway. (Mitch, aged 17)

The children and young people we interviewed in the UK Children Go Online focus groups expressed considerable disillusion regarding the prospect of online participation. Over and again, the conversation flagged when we switched topic from communicating with friends to the idea of connecting with a wider public world. While 'politics' is indeed an issue, so too is the nature of the communication on offer. Young people may be invited to have their say but, they asked repeatedly, who is listening to them? Indeed, they were full of stories of being ignored, and these everyday 'lessons in life' seemed to generate a high level of scepticism. When I asked whether 'the internet makes things more democratic, 'because now you could email your MP, or go on a political chat room . . .?', Hazel, 17, agreed with Mitch, saying cynically, 'Yeah, you can email him, but is he going to listen?'

As Bennett (2008: 15) observes, 'politicians often appear to be faking it in the eyes of young citizens, who are finely tuned to media performances' (see also Coleman, 2003). Celebrities may well be seen as more responsive than politicians, as one 15-year-old girl explained:

Padma	Yeah. I get like a – sometimes, like, two weeks, every two weeks, I get personal mails from celebrities. My favourite celebrities. That's ok!
[. . . . .]	
Interviewer	Ok, ok. But you don't get in touch with politicians, or . . .
[Laughter]	
Padma	I'm not really interested in . . . They all chat crap, so . . .

When Oliver, a middle-class 17 year old, commented on the project message board, 'I'm not in the least bit interested in politics, and think it extremely boring, no amount of games can disguise the content,' we had a chance to explore his reasons further, focusing on the much publicized case of youthful protests over the Iraq War in early 2003:

> *Interviewer*   One of the things we were interested in was how kids got involved in the stop-the-war [anti-Iraq war, 2003] protest . . .
>
> *Oliver*   Kids don't see that they have a choice in the matter, it's a 'Grown up' thing . . . Ask almost any child and they will tell you 'War is bad' . . . The net just gives them a way to tell everyone and to share their ideas with each other.

In other words, he believes teenagers do hold political (anti-war) views, and that the internet offers them a voice, but since no one but other teenagers are listening to them, such expression is pointless. A BBC report observed that the public (aged 18–44) finds it difficult to relate 'politics' to their everyday lives precisely because they can see no means of two-way dialogue with politicians. We might add, not only is it the case that 'news and political broadcasting lacks a tier of entry points to engage or re-engage people' (BBC, 2002: 4) but, more importantly, so too do politics and politicians.

A detailed comment posted on our message board from 15-year-old Anne drives home the point that the routine instances of marginalization of young people by adult society undermines any expression of civic interest:

Message no. ##
Posted by ANNE
Subject: Re: Email Tony Blair
Politics causes me to become frustrated because the Government has too much control over your lives, e.g. euthanasia being illegal. Anyway, I don't think young people are interested in politics due to the example set by the adults we are surrounded by, i.e. the poor turn out of voters and one of our teachers telling us they don't see the point in voting etc.

I have never written to, or emailed my local MP, or the PM [Prime Minister] because I do not think my letter/email will even be looked at. I am also put off by society's ageist attitude towards people of our age. An example would be a local cafe in town kicked my friends and I out because 2 out of the group of 5 of us had failed to purchase more than a drink. On another occasion my family and I went there, and only my mother ordered something, but no hostility was shown by the management. The behaviour of both groups were not at all dissimilar. Anyway, sorry to digress, but to sum up, young people's opinions are not at all valued, especially not by politicians.

Like many, it is not that Anne is uninterested in politics – she has strong views on euthanasia and on the regulation of ordinary lives. But she is unimpressed by the adult apathy she is surrounded by and she is disillusioned by what she sees as the injustice with which young people are treated. Recognizing this as a widespread yet ignored social phenomenon, Goldman *et al.* refer to this as 'adultism', thereby placing on a par with sexism and racism 'the practice of adults' systematic discrimination against young people' (2008: 187).

This devaluing of youthful views can be internalized by young people themselves, leaving them confused in enacting peer group norms regarding the political: politics is 'uncool'. In one focus group with 14–15 year olds, when we asked about the stop-the-war protests, Jim initially jumped in with enthusiasm but quickly backtracked when Ryan expressed cynicism:

Interviewer	One of the things I was thinking about was when they had the stop-the-war protests about six months ago before the war, and they said all these school kids went on strike.
Jim	Yeah, I went on strike! It was great! I was in the paper!
Interviewer	Did you?
Jim	Yeah.
Ryan	Thing is, the only reason you go on strike is so you can miss school.
Interviewer	That's what they said about you.
Jim	We didn't actually go there, we were like 'yeah, we're going to go!' and then, 'nahh, we're not going to go, are we'. I just went on Saturdays. It was great fun.

Indeed, Ryan's cynical view was widely expressed by the popular press at the time, publicly downgrading the youthful protesters' motivations to the selfish desire to miss school. To save face in the group, Jim hastily agreed that they did not in fact join the strike, that they just sought fun instead. But when Ryan changed course and advocated a political opinion that was positively hostile to the anti-war protesters, Jim became muddled, saying that he had supported the war initially (in order to agree with Ryan) but was now rethinking his position (so as to be consistent with his claimed support for the protest):

Interviewer	So you were protesting. You felt strongly against the war?
Jim	I just wanted a bit of fun.
Ryan	I think they should have gone to war.
Jim	Yeah, I did agree with it, but it's getting a bit much now because they're still out there.

Feeling perhaps that the popular press would now agree with his change of opinion, Jim (below) pushed the point more clearly. Sean then joined in, agreeing with Jim by noting the then failure to capture Saddam Hussein. But he then reminded the group of the futility of young people's political action. Interestingly, Jim became defiant, stating his view more clearly, though simultaneously subordinating his political views to the desire for fun asserted by his critics:

Jim	Why are they still out there? There's no point them actually being there.
Sean	Well, they haven't actually caught anyone yet.
Jim	There's no reason for them to be actually out there now.
Sean	There wasn't any point in protesting anyway because they weren't going to bring back 250,000 troops because some school kids weren't going to school.
Jim	I did support it, I just thought it would be a bit of fun, walk around with some strange hobos!

The interviewer tried to bring the discussion back to the internet, much discussed in the press as a mediator of anti-war protest planning, but in their case at least it seemed to play little part – phones, posters and face-to-face communication appeared more influential here in coordinating the action:

Interviewer	Was it organized through the internet? Did you keep in touch – how did you all know you were going to be in a certain place at a certain time?
Sean	Phones.
Jim	And mad like stickers all over town and stuff.
Sean	Yeah.
Jim	Posters and things.

Not only is being listened to already difficult for young people, whether the audience is their peers or influential adults, it is far from clear that the internet improves matters except for an already engaged minority. For the most part, the cacophony of voices mediated by the internet seems to raise expectations of an audience while simultaneously increasing disappointment. Following a review of political websites directly targeted at younger voters, Xenos and Bennett identified:

> a reluctance of many mainstream political actors to speak directly to young people through the web, and a surprising underdevelopment of linkages between youth politics websites and the wider web of political information online. (2007: 443)

Citizens now or citizens-in-the-making?

> Well, we might think they should listen to us but from their point of view, we can't vote so there's no point in listening to us . . . we can say one thing, but they don't have to do it. (Luke, aged 15)

Several persistent confusions mar attempts to engage children and young people through the internet: first, the question of their status as citizens, especially for those too young to vote; second, the question of exactly what it is that they could or should be participating in; and third, the broader question of societal opportunity structures for young people's participation. I address these three points before concluding the chapter.

In most countries, those under 18 years old are traditionally construed as 'citizens-in-the-making'; only once voting age is attained does a young person become truly a citizen, it is held, and so it is only for these youth that the headline panics about political apathy apply. Yet much online civic media are targeted at 'children and young people', a public policy phrase that obscures their status as citizens. And of this, some is really concerned with those 'citizens-in-waiting' (Marshall, 1950) who must be prepared for their future adult responsibilities. This repositions the potential of the internet more as a means of civic education than of participation, providing 'opportunities to hone a variety of civic skills as part of their political socialization,' including the chance to 'develop and articulate their thinking on issues of public concern'; 'share ideas with youth from different backgrounds, who may hold contrasting opinions'; 'build the habits of initiative, analysis, and independent thinking'; and 'develop their own sense of being invested in civic issues and actively involved in the civic arena' (Montgomery, Gottlieb-Robles and Larson, 2004: 14).

While this approach has its merits, it suffers two limitations. The first is communicative – whatever the producers' intent, if youth believe they are being invited to participate in order to bring about actual change in their lives, they will become disillusioned if this is not forthcoming, as Luke suggests above (see also Thumim, 2008). The second is political – if youth have, in the present, rights and responsibilities they wish to and/or should exercise, then these sites will let them down. The political status of children's rights before they reach 18 is seriously contested. Smith, Lister, Middleton and Cox (2005) criticize as a 'deficit model of citizenship' any approach which assumes that young people lack knowledge and interest regarding citizenship issues and so require citizenship education or other initiatives before becoming the citizens at 18. How, if citizenship only begins at 18, can we recognize the activities of Asta, aged 16, who Dahlgren and Olsson (2007) assure us, is far from rare in using local and national email lists, message boards and networks, newsletters and more to mobilize support for her political organization, 'Green Globalization'?

The historically radical alternative positions children and young people as citizens now. This extension of the twentieth-century movement for civil rights, women's rights and human rights to encompass also children's rights is formalized in the UN Convention on the Rights of the Child (1989). While most often implemented (to the extent that states do, indeed, observe the Convention) in relation to welfare matters (such as youth offenders, custody in family breakown, ill or disabled children or child poverty), there is a growing move to include children's voices – defined in the Convention as those under the age of 18 years – in all matters that affect them, from educational policy to local environmental consultations. For example:

> By involving young people we empower them to help us build stronger and more cohesive communities in which they have a real stake. This is good for our services, our communities and for the future health of our democracy (John Denham, Minister for Children and Young People, 2002).

This quotation accords with the spirit of Article 12 of the UN Convention on the Rights of the Child, which seeks to promote participation, consultation and democratic opportunities for young people to learn about getting heard, having a voice and becoming active citizens. This is being taken forward in different ways in different countries.[7] For example, the European Youth Forum 'represents and advocates for the needs and interests of all young people in Europe, through their positive and active participation,'[8] aiming to:

> be the voice of young people in Europe, where young people are considered as equal citizens, and are supported and encouraged to achieve their fullest potential as citizens of the World.

Participation in what?

But what exactly does it mean that children are to participate in society? Without denying the dedicated enthusiasm of the adults working to improve opportunities for children and young people, it is problematic that the concept of 'participation' can mean different things to different people. The Merriam-Webster dictionary defines 'participation' as 'the state of being related to a larger whole'. The Oxford English Dictionary states, similarly, that participation is:

> The process or fact of sharing in an action, sentiment, etc.; (now *esp.*) active involvement in a matter or event, esp. one in which the outcome directly affects those taking part.

The process of sharing in an action can, surely, be effectively mediated by the internet, provided greater efforts are made to build interest, trust and reciprocity through more thoughtfully and ambitiously designed websites. But the notion of active involvement in something – an issue, event or decision, shared with certain others, whose outcome affects one directly – points to a continuing challenge that has little to do with the internet. Nominalizing the verb 'to participate' as 'participation' (as in the goal of 'enabling participation', or 'increasing participation') masks the issue, permitting participation to be defined as an end in itself and so seemingly positioning the internet as a sufficient solution. But the internet is a means not an end, in this context. As the *Carnegie Young People Initiative* noted with concern about many of the projects they reviewed, 'the benefits and impacts of children and young people's participation are not clearly identified' (Cutler and Taylor, 2003: 11). Online as offline, such lack of clarity can provoke confusing or unrealistic expectations among youth which may then be, unsurprisingly, disappointed.

Some civic websites invite users to participate in the website itself while some present the website as a route to participate in wider society. Some seek to stimulate the alienated, while others assume their audience is already motivated but lacks structured opportunities to participate. Some aim to enable youth to realize their present rights and responsibilities while others focus on preparing them for the future. Some, primarily concerned to disseminate information or educational materials, add on a participatory section ('have your say') to appear accountable and interactive, but may be insufficiently resourced to respond to youthful contributions in a timely, constructive and sustained manner. Some are free-standing initiatives while some represent the online interface of a pre-established organization where relations are already established among stakeholders and citizens. Some, last, seem to promise to deliver resources to youth but actually, reversing this, seem designed to deliver youth to organizations (hence Jensen and Helles, 2005, call for 'a politics of interactivity'). Discerning which kind of website is which, what to expect of it, and how to respond requires a high level of digital literacy, not least because the sites may not communicate effectively what form of participation they offer.

To some extent, such diversity is desirable, provided this is communicated to young people through good design and a clear mode of address. But partly, this diversity reflects underlying confusion regarding the very purposes of youth participation. Do we want young people to participate in the internet for its own sake, or do we want them to participate in society by means of the internet? Presumably the latter, though the former can appear to be the case from certain public policy pronouncements – those that invite youth to 'have your say' on a civic website with no obvious consequences, for example, or those that evaluate their 'success' by measuring numbers of site visitors rather than consequences for young people's lives (Raynes-Goldie and Walker, 2008). Is any form of participation in society acceptable or is the hope that enticing youth through green or life politics, for example, will draw them next into more traditional forms of political participation? Is the purpose really to engage them in a deliberative decisionmaking processes or, less ambitiously, merely to sustain the informed consent required by a representative, rather than participatory, democracy? Can we really expect young people to 'get political' when so few adults show the way?

Opportunity structures for civic engagement

Contrary to the popular discourses that blame young people for their apathy, lack of motivation or interest, I have argued instead that children and young people learn early that they are not listened to. Hopes that the internet can enable young people to 'have their say' will miss the point if no one listens. Who should listen includes peers for sure, but also adults – those with the power to make decisions that affect young people's lives; both peer and adult audiences are crucial, both are difficult to obtain (Levine, 2008). Online dialogue must be situated within an institutionally supported framework firmly connected to what Meyer and Staggenbord (1996) term the 'opportunity structures' that facilitate, shape and develop young people's participation. In other words, what matters:

> is not whether new media are capable of capturing, moderating and summarizing the voice of the public, but whether political institutions are able and willing to enter into a dialogical relationship with the public (Coleman, 2007: 375)

Sociologists of childhood and youth claim that over recent decades, society has offered young people ever fewer, rather than more, ways of participating in their neighbourhoods and, so, of gaining serious civic responsibilities (Kimberlee, 2002). As outlined in chapter 1, with years in education extended, the entry to work delayed, and many forms of local community organizations reduced or absent (whether scouting groups, church groups, youth clubs, sports teams or trade unions), the path to political engagement has become eroded (Hill and Tisdall, 1997; James, Jenks and Prout, 1998). Bennett argues similarly that shifts in the post-war labour market have produced growing economic insecurity and career uncertainty on the one hand, and changing group structure, loss of tradition, growth in risk and altered sense of belonging or loyalty on the other, so that what is:

> replacing traditional civil society is a less conformist social world . . . characterized by the rise of networks, issue associations, and lifestyle coalitions facilitated by the revolution in personalized, point-to-point communication (1998: 745)

Notwithstanding this trend towards greater individualization, research demonstrates significant benefits to the individual who does get involved, not to mention to benefits to society. Civic engagement facilitates a sense of agency, decisionmaking and social skills, while reducing isolation and, possibly, risky and anti-social behaviours (Coleman and Hendry, 1999). In short, not only do engaged young people feel more confident and competent but they also feel more respected – a virtuous circle of civic engagement (Norris, 2000).

Although community and work may provide fewer opportunities for youthful engagement than previously, the school remains a primary institution shaping children's lives. Moreover, unlike home influences, the role of the school is potentially more inclusive and equal, leading Levine to advocate the 'difficult but promising ... [strategy] which is to turn adolescents' offline communities – especially high schools – into more genuine communities' (2008: 119). In a discussion among inner-city 14–16-year-old boys, the school rather than the internet appears to have played a key role in instigating their involvement in the anti-Iraq war protests:[9]

Interviewer	Because when they had all those stop-the-war protests, and lots of kids were involved weren't they? I don't know if there was anything here in school, or people protested or ...
Elkan	All done in a non-uniform day.
Amir	We paid one pound.
Elkan	We all paid one pound, send money for ...
Prince	For the children of Iraq. So we paid a pound to ...
Elkan	Non-uniform.
Interviewer	And did the school organize that?
Prince	Yeah, the school did.

In another example, Chloe (aged 15) enthused about their recently introduced school council, 'which I think is a really good idea 'coz it's our school mostly'. Pupils' proposals, from decorating a Christmas tree to acquiring lockers for students had, it seems, produced results. In this context, it is unsurprising that Roker *et al.*'s (1997) study found teenagers were much more likely to have campaigned for something at school (60%) than to have written to an MP or councillor (16%). Chloe's account of the school council included an enthusiastic description of how the council is constructed, what mechanisms link pupils to the forum, and what action (new lockers) had resulted. These and other policymaking procedures, which Goldman *et al.* (2008) describe as 'the cultural technologies' vital to effective structures of participation, are too rarely apparent on online forums where, by contrast, contributions appear decontextualized, editorial decisions are unstated, and action consequences are unclear.

So this pinpoints three problems: first, how to encourage young people whose civic interests have been stimulated at home or school to engage more widely; second, how to encourage young people who remain disengaged; and third, how to transfer interests developed in diverse civic spheres to traditional party politics and, especially, voting. A significant part of the solution in each case must lie in the nature of those wider opportunity structures that connect young people and their political representatives in a dynamic and effective communicative relationship. But these problems are surely made worse by inviting children into these relationships and then failing to follow through – not listening, not translating talk into action, not feeding back consequences. For then the message will be one of an apathetic society, and an apathetic youth will surely result.

Conclusions

Democracy requires 'channels of communication providing for a free flow of information both amongst citizens and between representatives and voters' (Coleman, 1999: 67). In crucial ways, these channels are increasingly online – more convenient and accessible than, say, visiting one's politician or hearing parliament debate one hundred or even twenty years ago, yet also more technologically demanding and unequally distributed. Opportunities to participate are thus being reconfigured, increased for some people and for some forms of communication, reduced for others. To the extent that 'internet access has become a basic entitlement of citizenship in the digital age' (Murdock, 2002: 386), inequalities in use threaten what Hargittai and Walejko (2008: 239) call 'the participation divide' and what Norris (2001: 12) terms a 'democratic divide' between 'those who do and do not use the multiple political resources available on the internet for civic engagement', those who are heard or are not heard (Bessant, 2004; Cammaerts and Van Audenhove, 2005).

In this chapter, I have largely focused on the civic interests and potential of the majority of children and young people, rather than focusing on the notable, often exciting exceptions – instigators of new social movements and the like – that attract popular acclaim or notoriety (see, for example, Kahn and Kellner, 2004; Poster, 1997; Tsagarousianou, Tambini and Bryan, 1998). I have argued that, insofar as participation is or could be mediated by the internet, both providers and users – politicians, youth organizations, citizens – face a series of conceptual, technical, political and communicative challenges. This includes determining whether children and young people under the age of 18 'count' as citizens, as well as determining exactly what they could participate in. Ironically perhaps, a narrower definition of

citizen (i.e. only those of voting age) permits a more satisfactory definition of participation, for the societal structures are better established for adult participation and, thus, less disappointing, than is the
case for those who are younger. Here we may observe, with some
optimism, the many youth organizations and civic websites seeking
to engage young adults in political participation (Livingstone, 2008d;
Montgomery, 2008; CivicWeb, 2008).

But much of the enthusiasm regarding the potential of the internet
to engage youth is precisely directed at younger children and, especially teenagers, raising many questions of purpose and delivery, as
discussed in this chapter. Depending on which measure of participation one adopts, anything between a small minority and a bare majority of children can be said to respond positively to the invitation to
participate on the internet. The rest, by implication, do not, claiming a
lack of interest and a lack of knowledge; although, as we have seen,
demographic factors of gender, age and social class all play a role in
shaping political interest. Overall, children and young people appear
neither so passive and accepting as supposed by those who call them
apathetic nor so motivated and effective as to meet the high standards
some hold out for them. Rather, they sustain a somewhat variable,
sometimes enthusiastic, sometimes critical gaze on the complex civic
world that is partially presented to them but partially closed to them.

Efforts to increase youthful participation must tackle not only the
democratic deficit but also what we might term the communicative
deficit – the gap that exists between the user as imagined by the producers and the actual users who use the internet in their real world
contexts. One key mismatch is that, while producers hope young
people will 'have their say', young people want to know, who is listening? Without an answer, many will continue to 'check out' the sites and
then leave, neither interacting nor returning. Political and youth organizations have, belatedly, come to recognize the vital importance of
listening to young people, especially when they have invited them to
participate in the first place. A second mismatch, as we have seen,
occurs between the alternative, perhaps even radical interests of some
young activists and the 'official' vision of youth engagement held by
some producers, this tending to accord more with a model of top-
down information delivery than one of open dialogue. A third is that
the producers – in the attempt to appear 'youthful' or 'fun' rather than
adult or official – may lack plausibility or transparency regarding their
own identity, something not to be compensated for by supportive
statements from self-selected middle-class children.

To leave behind the non-interactive use of the internet just to
provide information or to 'collect views' will demand the commit-

ment of considerable resources, more human than technical. If forthcoming, this could communicate sufficient respect for youth to overcome the widespread resentment of 'adultism' (Goldman, Booker and McDermott, 2008) that, read superficially, results in the misguided judgement of youthful apathy. It could also build rather than undermine internet literacy, by setting high standards regarding the classic markers of trustworthiness – up-to-date sites, speedy responsiveness, attention to safety considerations, well-designed interfaces and more (Livingstone, 2007a). Addressing these communicative challenges in the digital age additionally poses some specifically technological demands. Montgomery summarizes these in calling for:

> equitable access to technology, open architecture and nondiscrimination for both consumers and procedures of digital content, flexible and fair copyright rules that allow for creativity and sharing of cultural content, and open-source applications that will encourage collaboration and innovation. (2008: 42)

If all these efforts are made, what could be achieved? Instead of expanding the notion of citizenship so as to expect all children to become politically engaged or, equally problematically, expanding the notion of politics to encompass all dimensions of everyday life, we must perhaps recognize that these are grey areas, matters of degree and, to some extent also, questions of choice. In other words, society could seek to enable and welcome diverse forms of participation from a wider constituency of young people without castigating those who do not take up this offer, at least when still children. By recommending this half-way position, I do not mean to argue conceptually against the vital, mutually sustaining connections between everyday life and the political or public sphere (see Dayan, 2001; Livingstone, 2005b). Rather, I mean to suggest that these connections need not become simple public policy targets or, worse, the focus of media panics about 'apathetic' youth.

In theorizing the connections between the lifeworld and the public sphere in a deliberately open and inclusive manner, Dahlgren reframes the notion of the 'civic' as an in-between concept, to recognize the diverse knowledge, commitments and actions that lay the ground for, intersect with, and so sustain political participation:

> 'civic' should . . . be understood as a prerequisite for the (democratically) political, a reservoir of the pre- or non-political that becomes actualized at particular moments when politics arises . . . The key here is to underscore the processual and contextual dimension; the political

and politics are not simply given, but are constructed via word and deed. (2003: 155)

This is not to revive the deficit model of citizens-in-waiting, for Dahlgren means this to apply to the whole population, not particularly to children, in order to recognize that everyone is simultaneously engaged yet ambivalent, committed yet disengaged, active yet distrustful (as revealed by Couldry, Livingstone and Markham, 2007). Participation must, on this view, be continually performed, in one way or another, by all actors – citizens and elites – if it is to be sustained. These various ways include, for Dahlgren, reinforcing and enacting the relations among (1) values, anchored in the everyday, formally articulated as the basis of democratic principles; (2) affinity, the minimal sense of commonality and trust required for collective or community action; (3) knowledge, the literacy required to make sense of the world so as to select among competing directions; (4) practices, the traditions, habits and performances that mobilize meanings and bring about democratic society; (5) identities, the reflexive sense of social belonging and subjective efficacy required to mobilize people as a public or citizenry; and (6) discussion, the means of communicative interaction that embodies principles of inclusiveness, visibility and problem-resolution.

Helpfully, this conception of the underpinning of civic culture provides a classification of the various possible purposes of civic websites for, we can say, they may articulate values, build trust, enhance knowledge, mobilize practices, support identities and/or encourage discussion, and clarity regarding these various purposes would represent an advance on current confusions and miscommunications. But the key point – for Dahlgren and also, as we have seen, for young people – is that these dimensions of participation must be mutually reinforcing rather than disconnected or incomplete, also linking the online and offline so that participation becomes embedded in young people's lifeworlds and, conversely, so that it embeds their activities in the wider opportunity structures of society.

In conclusion, if judged according to Habermas' (1962/1989) ideals for the public sphere, it seems that 'the virtual political sphere clearly fails the test' (Murdock, 2002: 389), being insufficiently inclusive, interactive or consequential, and this is especially the case for children and young people. At the worst, 'individualization, unequal access, and disenfranchisement may be the outcome of net politics' (Golding, 2000: 176). The optimists, however, argue that it is too early to judge, but that the embryonic signs provide grounds for hope (Hampton and Wellman, 2003; Papacharissi, 2004), for 'politics in cyberspace is attempting to redefine itself in the light of the profound changes affecting the social system in the past decades by exploiting the internet's intrinsic potential' (Bentivegna, 2002: 51).

Norris (2001) also concludes on a note of cautious optimism, not because a ringing endorsement of e-democracy is (yet) possible, but of the encouraging if tentative evidence that the internet permits a more open space for debate among a wider diversity of political actors, thereby amplifying voices that might otherwise not be heard, facilitating rapid, flexible responses to events, some degree of critical challenge to the establishment and, most of all, the easy sharing of information locally and globally. For today's children and young people, this could yet provide some exciting opportunities to come.

6

Risk and Harm

Beyond moral panics

> It is not only children who are perceived as being 'at risk' but the institution of childhood itself... [thus] risk anxiety helps construct childhood and maintain its boundaries. (Jackson and Scott, 1999: 86)

With headlines full of paedophiles, 'internet sex beasts',[1] cyber-bullies and online suicide pacts easily predominating over positive stories of the educational, civic or expressive dimensions of internet use, it is perhaps unsurprising that public anxiety regarding risk in relation to children and the internet is considerable, at times resulting in disproportionate reactions to perceived threats. This is exacerbated by the coincidence of three factors: first, the extraordinary rapidity of the internet's development and diffusion, outpacing adults' ability to adjust; second, an endemic cultural fear of the new, encouraged by media panics framing the internet as an unmanageable source of threat to children's safety; and third, the novelty of a reverse generation gap whereby parental expertise and authority is exceeded by children's ability to use the technology and to evade adult management.

Anxieties about childhood have long focused on matters of sexuality, morality and aggression, often expressed through a discourse of children's 'special' status as innocents who, if kept separate from the ills of adult society, might bring better prospects for the future. Visual screen media attract particular concern, for images are widely held to be powerful insofar as they bypass two forms of cultural protection: individual literacy (reading ability, rational thought, critical judgement) and the mediating practices of parents or teachers

(Drotner, 1992; Katz, 2003). Yet similar public anxieties regarding the 'child in danger' (and the 'dangerous child'; Oswell, 1998) have accompanied the introduction of each new medium from the nineteenth-century comic through cinema, television and computer games up until and including the internet and mobile media of the twenty-first century. As Critcher says:

> The pattern is standard. A new medium, product of a new technology or a new application of an old one, emerges and finds a mass market. Its content is seen as criminal or violent or horrific. It constitutes a danger to children who cannot distinguish between reality and fantasy. (2008: 100)

Moral panics construct their own supposedly natural categories of people (Douglas, 1966; Willett and Burn, 2005) – on the internet, these include the 'groomer', 'cyberbully', 'lurker' and so on – all constructions which, Douglas argues, may serve a positive function in sustaining community loyalty. But as Lupton (1999: 44) observes, paedophiles 'are seen as wicked both because they have transgressed cultural norms or taboos and because they place others in danger by their actions'. Problematically, academic research on children and the internet has tended to shy away from trying to disentangle the discursive constructions from the genuine threats, preferring to focus on 'the positives' and examine online opportunities such as education, participation and expression. This is partly because of the historically suspect relation between public anxieties and media research (Barker and Petley, 2001; Rowland, 1983) and partly because risk anxiety has its own pernicious consequences, including the call for censorship of adult speech or the curtailing of children's rights.

In all, four lines of critique warn against academic engagement with the media/risk/child agenda. First, moral panics encourage a scapegoating of the media, distracting public and policy attention from more significant causes of crime or social ills (Pearson, 1983). Second, they imply a middle-class critique of working-class pleasures, in which the working class are construed as irrational masses, undisciplined media consumers and so blamed for social disorder (Cohen, 1972). Third, they deny the agency, choice and wisdom of ordinary people (including children) who, if asked, have more nuanced, subtle and complex judgements to offer about media content, who do not react in simple and unthinking ways to media content, and whose critical media literacy should be recognized and valued (Buckingham, 1998). Last, moral panics tend to justify a normative reinforcement of the status quo by supporting conservative values and the public expression (and mobilization) of diverse views and critical voices, at times resulting in repressive and censorious but popular regulation (Akdeniz, 2001; Winston, 1996). In short, that which purports to act in the interest of children may mask a more fundamental motivation to shore up the interests of the establishment.

Yet though the arguments against engaging with the risk agenda seem compelling, engage with it we must if we wish to recognize children's own experiences and give them voice, for their experiences with the internet are not all positive. Moreover, as social scientists we have the capacity to conduct rigorous empirical research on risk, and the independence to evaluate findings critically; thus it is surely incumbent on us to ensure that the knowledge gained from our research is used carefully to inform the evidence base for policy development. Several forms of possible harm are already on the research and policy agenda, each of which may be exacerbated by those same features of the online environment that enable identity expression, social networking and participation – persistence, search-ability, replicability and invisible/anonymous audiences (as discussed in chapter 4; cf. boyd, 2008). For example, 'cyberbulling' differs from offline bullying insofar as it offers a degree of anonymity to the bully plus a degree of publicity to the victim that is in itself distressing; it affords the use of visual images as well as hurtful text and words; the bullying message can be quickly spread among a peer group; and the messages may be read in the victim's private and supposedly safe places (their bedroom, on their phone, at home) (Patchin and Hinduja, 2006). The resultant disembedding of communication has the effect of removing users from their traditional anchoring in the norms of society (or, for Habermas, 1981/7, from the lifeworld) and reembedding them in alternative, niche peer cultures distanced from the values and demands of everyday life (Giddens, 1995).

Before reviewing the evidence for online risk in childhood, it is important to recognize the wider context. As will be shown below, in order to disentangle moral panics from genuine threats to children's well-being, we must complicate the polarities of both opportunity versus risk and victim versus villain before reaching a balanced assessment.

Going online in the risk society

> Risk may be defined as a systematic way of dealing with the hazards and insecurities induced and introduced by modernization itself. (Beck, 1986/2005: 21)

In his account of 'the risk society', Beck (1986/2005: 15) argues that as a result of contemporary social changes, 'a new twilight of opportunities and hazards comes into existence – the contours of the risk society', contours that we are only now beginning to glimpse. These social changes are such that society is,

> ... concerned no longer exclusively with making nature useful, or with releasing mankind from traditional constraints, but also and essentially with problems resulting from techno-economic development itself ... Questions of the development and employment of technologies (in the realms of nature, society and the personality) are being eclipsed by questions of the political and economic 'management' of the risks of actually or potentially utilized technologies. (p. 19)

The notion of 'risk' has shifted historically from the uncertain and uncontrollable possibility of a natural threat, excluding the implication of human fault or responsibility, to the statistically calculable and manageable possibility of a human-made threat (Lupton, 1999). For Beck, risks are co-determined by natural hazards and the social environment by which they are shaped, expressed and addressed. They are, in short, an unintended consequence of modernity, modernity having brought with it not only industrialization and capitalism but also the institutions of surveillance, the science of probability and statistics, and an expectation of human progress through rational action. Today, the very complexity of knowledge regarding contemporary risks results in ambivalence – the nature of risk is contestable and contested, undermining expert authority and paralysing action (Lupton, 1999).

The same factors that now shape risk and the new institutions that assess, manage and communicate it also exacerbate public concern, especially when their findings are amplified by the mass media (Kitzinger, 2004). The result is a widespread perception that people are faced with risks on all sides. As modernity enters its later, reflexive stage, for the individual,

> these changes are associated with an intensifying sense of uncertainty, complexity, ambivalence and disorder, a growing distrust of social institutions and traditional authorities and an increasing awareness of the threats inherent in everyday life. (Lupton, 1999: 11–12)

Nowhere is this more evident than in Western thinking about childhood and, for parents especially, risk anxiety has become 'a constant and pervasive feature of everyday consciousness' (Jackson and Scott, 1999: 88; see also Ferguson, 1997). For adults, accounts of online bullying, grooming or hatred activate long-standing anxieties regarding, first, the protection of childhood innocence from adult harm and, second, the dangers of harm from children themselves (James, Jenks and Prout, 1998). For children, their potential to be either victims or villains is fascinating as well as frightening. They hold lively conversations among themselves about paedophiles – whether the 'dirty old man' in the park or the 'weirdo in the chat room' – in their attempt to work out for themselves what adults consider 'normal' or 'dangerous' and to find a rationale for themselves for adult-imposed constraints on their freedoms (Willett and Burn, 2005). Bullying, similarly, is much discussed as children work out not only what to expect and accept from others but also how to intervene – for in this domain it is children themselves, rather than parents or teachers, who manage and constrain peer behaviour.

This points up some of the specific demands of adolescence in the risk society. Without in any way wishing to minimize the distress or harm experienced by some children as a consequence of their and others' online activities, an issue I give serious attention to below, we must also acknowledge, with Beck, that risk is endemic, ordinary and, at times, even pleasurable. If our analytic lens dictates that risk is only and inevitably a problem, then some of young people's activities online will seem puzzling – rash, irresponsible or even wicked. For psychological and social reasons, teenagers engage in what Hope (2007) calls 'boundary performance' – risk-taking is often publicly performed as part of the process of identity construction in a peer group context. Hence teenagers test adult authority, challenge adult-imposed rules and boundaries and evade parental scrutiny. In other words, whatever we as adults worry about, whatever social norms we seek to defend, children will be motivated to transgress precisely those norms that society has constructed as vital to the preservation of childhood innocence. Thus teenagers may take risks with 'friends of friends' or even recognized 'weirdos' at the edge of their online social networks. Rosie (aged 13) says,

> I've got about five buddies on my thing, but you can't really say, oh, this is a young girl, she's got brown hair, blue eyes, 'cause she could be an old – she could be a he and it's an old man but I suppose it's quite nice to just say, oh, I've met someone on the internet.

This seems to be the online equivalent of Green, Mitchell and Bunton's (2000) account of offline risk taking in which young teenage girls tell their parents they are staying at a friend's house but then dare each other to sleep in the street or park instead. It would be to miss the point to suppose, simply, that once teenagers know the dangers they will cease to take risks. Rather, learning to take calculated risks, and to cope with the consequences, is central to adolescence. Indeed:

young people are constantly engaged in risk assessment, actively creating and defining hierarchies premised upon different discourses of risk as 'normal' and acceptable or 'dangerous' and out of control. (Green et al., 2000: 123–4)

Furthermore, as Lupton (1999) observes, 'living dangerously' as a lifestyle choice is on the increase – witness the growing popularity of 'extreme sports', surely flying in the face of attempts to control, to ensure safety and take precautions. The valorization of risk-taking – of daring, transgression and the skilful circumvention of danger – is consistent with the theorization of late modernity, for it affords ways of performing the self as an individual agent by flouting norms in order to achieve both excitement and individuation. Dominant discourses, Lupton argues, generate their own counter-discourses: 'risk-taking may be regarded as the flipside of modernity, a response to the ever-intensifying focus on control and predictability of modernity' (1999: 156). This counter-discourse is gathering public, even official support. Attempts to minimize risks to children – led by a culture of risk assessment, litigation, public inquiries following accidents, and the growth of the insurance industry – are attracting growing disquiet from teachers, child welfare workers, play leaders and parents (Gill, 2007; Madge and Barker, 2007).

Children, it is argued, must not be wrapped in cotton-wool; they must take risks to grow – intellectually, emotionally, socially. Parents too regard their child's learning to cope with a risk as a positive development, as do children themselves. Theories of child development and adolescence concur: risk-taking is part of self-actualization, necessary for psychological development. As Coleman and Hagell put it, 'resilience can only develop through exposure to risk or to stress' (2007: 15). This is not to advocate risks of any and all kinds, but rather to recognize the value of those that fall within the child's 'zone of proximal development', as Vygosky (1978) expressed it – in other words, those experiences that stretch the child's capacity, thus enabling learning, without exceeding this capacity and so resulting in harm. Or as teenagers themselves might express it, they want to experience life 'on the edge' but to retain control, to pass the test.

What risks do face children online?

Some online risks to children, notwithstanding the above arguments about both society in general and adolescents in particular, go beyond what is acceptable to the general public – and, even more importantly, contravene the rights of children to be protected from harm. Two kinds of online risk give rise to considerable concern – the paedophile and the bully. Both these risks position the child as vulnerable victim against the feared sexual or violent aggressor. The 'paedophile' represents the threat to children from unknown adults, the bully represents the threat from other known children. While the former represents a very rare though dangerous risk to children, the latter is much more common and of varying severity; it is also fast rising up the public policy agenda. Offline, conduct between people, whether strangers or acquaintances, is socially regulated by norms of behaviour, with sanctions for their transgression which do not apply so clearly online. While not claiming that online behaviour goes ungoverned by social convention, online conventions appear more flexible and they may be circumvented without sanction under various circumstances. New forms of bullying and harassment arise from socially transgressive conduct of various kinds, and these are distinct from the content and contact risks already noted insofar as children are positioned in these not only as victim but also as perpetrator, raising new challenges for the informal and formal regulation of conduct online.[2]

Online grooming and paedophile activity are phenomena for which society holds little or no tolerance and which are increasing addressed by the criminal law (Arnaldo, 2001; Finkelhor, 2008; Goode, 2008; Palmer and Stacey, 2004; Quayle and Taylor, 2005). The UK's hotline for child abuse images (IWF, 2008) reports that some 80 per cent of internet sites hosting child abuse images are commercial operations, and that 10 per cent of the child victims being sexually abused – this including scenes of rape, in photographs or videos on these sites – appear to be under two years old, 33 per cent appear between three and six years old, and 80 per cent appear to be under 10. Their data show a trend towards increasing severity of the abuse portrayed, supporting the IWF's claim that 'behind every statistic is a child who has been sexually abused and exploited and, whilst images of the abuse are in circulation on the internet, that abuse is perpetuated' (p. 8). In 2007–8, the UK's Child Exploitation and Online Protection Centre (CEOP, 2008), which addresses the relation between online activities and child victims, reported that it had rescued 131 children from sexual abuse, made 297 arrests, and dismantled six organized paedophile rings.

Content-related risks are more controversial. Notably, online and offline, pornography represents a phenomenon widely tolerated by most societies and so regarded with considerable ambivalence in policy debates. Partly, this tolerance reflects liberal, even libertarian, views regarding freedom of expression; partly it is sustained by established cultural conventions that keep such content apart and, especially, separating it from places to which children have access. The absence of such conventions online (see chapter 8) is resulting in users' commonplace, generally accidental encounters with such content which, in turn, has revived public attention to difficult questions of community standards and cultural values (Millwood Hargrave and Livingstone, 2009). Explicit images of heterosexual, teenage, gay, anal, violent, bestial or other forms of sexual act are, for instance, readily accessible via a simple Google search (Waskul, 2004). Although research cannot always establish exactly what children have been exposed to, in a parallel study of film, an Australian survey reported that 73 per cent of 16–17-year-old boys (and 11% of girls) report having seen at least one X-rated film (i.e. containing real depictions of actual sexual intercourse), with a small minority watching regularly (Flood and Hamilton, 2003).[3] Problematically, the lack of an accepted language for describing the explicitness of pornographic images, particularly a language that can be used when interviewing children, means that it is generally unclear whether children reporting exposure to pornography have seen mild nudity or obscene images (although see Peter and Valkenburg, 2006b).

Other content-related risks are barely researched at all, though there are growing concerns about their potential to harm particularly 'vulnerable' or 'at risk' groups (Millwood Hargrave and Livingstone, 2009). Rajagopal (2004) and Biddle et al. (2008) identify an increasing number of websites providing graphic details of suicide methods. Willard (2003) examines 'harmful' online speech produced by school pupils – including defamation, bullying, harassment, discrimination, and so forth. Several groups catalogue the proliferation of hate sites on the internet (e.g. The Simon Wiesenthal Center and HateWatch). Some of this content is child-perpetrated, and some is hard to judge in terms of harm: some find that viewing pro-anorexia websites reduces young women's self-esteem (Bardone-Cone and Cass, 2007), though Whitlock et al. capture the ambivalence of many in noting that self-harm content may provide 'essential social support for otherwise isolated adolescents, but they may also normalize and encourage self-injurious behaviour' (2006: 413).[4]

After reviewing much of the available evidence, the EU Kids Online network produced a classification to impose some order on the array of risks on the public agenda. First, it distinguished content risks, in which the child is a recipient of unwelcome or inappropriate mass communication, from contact risks, in which the child is a participant of risky peer or personal communication (Hasebrink, Livingstone and Haddon, 2009). The former risks arise because regulation restricting the distribution of certain contents is barely in evidence on the internet (compared with television, film or even print). The latter arises because little or no regulation restricts who can be in touch with anyone else, particularly when age can be disguised online. With the explosion of user-generated content, some hosted on commercial (i.e. professional) websites (e.g. social networking, gaming or blogging sites) and some circulated peer-to-peer (e.g. via email or instant messaging), the distinction between content and contact is breaking down. Thus a third category of risk is proposed, that of conduct, risks in which the child is positioned as an actor, contributing to or producing risky content or contact.

The variety of risks can be further categorized in terms of the motivations of online producers – notably commercial, aggressive, sexual and values-related motivations – resulting in the classification shown below. This usefully organize the available research evidence on the incidence of online risk experiences into the following twelve cells, although as we shall see later, there is really only a substantial body of evidence relating to four of these cells, pornographic and violent content, bullying and meeting online contacts offline.

A classification of online risks to children

	Commercial	**Aggressive**	**Sexual**	**Values**
Content – *child as* *recipient*	Advertising, spam, sponsorship	Violent/ hateful content	Pornographic or unwelcome sexual content	Racism, biased or misleading info/advice (e.g. drugs)
Contact – *child as* *participant*	Tracking/ harvesting personal info	Being bullied, stalked or harassed	Meeting strangers, being groomed	Self-harm, unwelcome persuasion
Conduct – *child as* *actor*	Gambling, hacking, illegal downloads	Bullying or harassing another	Creating and uploading pornography	Providing advice e.g. suicide/ pro-anorexic chat

(Source: EU Kids Online; Hasebrink, Livingstone and Haddon, 2009)

While concerns about these risks is widespread, including among children themselves (Eurobarometer, 2007), only a very small minority of children encounters the worst of these. But more encounter some degree of risk, with European studies suggesting that overall,

15–20 per cent of online teenagers have felt distressed or threatened on the internet (Hasebrink, Livingstone and Haddon, 2009). Consequently, this chapter seeks to go beyond the moral panics so as to provide an empirical account of children's online risk experiences, within a critical framework of risk phenomena that neither colludes with nor evades the public agenda but which, instead, aims to inform it.

Online risk – how much of what kind?

Before reviewing evidence for online risks, one must note several practical difficulties. First, the online environment is itself fast-changing, and so too are children's practices; second, the very conception of risk is contested – among researchers and policymakers, adults and children, protectionists and libertarians, industry representatives and public policy or parenting groups, as well as varying across cultures. Third, there is no agreed language for describing or evaluating 'problematic' content. The range of violence, hate content and pornography available online varies enormously, from the equivalent of top-shelf magazine images to content that is otherwise highly restricted or illegal. It is difficult to ask children exactly what they have seen, though as noted earlier, Peter and Valkenburg (2006b) make a good attempt. Fourth, ethical considerations leave little scope for empirical research that deliberately exposes children to such material in order to assess the consequences (Helsper, 2005). This in turn generates difficulties of research design – research that assesses what follows after exposure under ordinary circumstances cannot eliminate the possibility that children so exposed are distinct in some way (i.e. that it is something about the child, rather than the online content, that accounts for any observed consequences).[5]

Consider the example of 10-year-old Anna, who confesses to have seen some 'pretty rude pictures' when she inadvertently opened an email of her father's, resists any suggestion that she may have been shocked: 'I'm quite grown up, I know all about everything, sex life and stuff…Sometimes I read stories that some people my age wouldn't be like, would be like [deep intake of breath], and I'm just like cool.' Ethically, one cannot easily pursue with her exactly what she saw, and clinically, one cannot be sure that her ideas of sexuality were unaffected. A very indirect indication of harm can be obtained from the UK Children Go Online survey which found that, when asked to reflect, 45 per cent of 18–19 year olds who had seen pornography (on any medium) considered they were too young to have seen it when they first did (Livingstone and Bober, 2004b). However, such methodological limitations result, typically, in qualified conclusions regarding media effects generally.[6]

Across Europe, 18 per cent of parents/carers state that they believe their child has encountered harmful or illegal content on the internet (Eurobarometer, 2006). For some, this may be very serious indeed. For others, this may be frightening or upsetting but, arguably, relatively temporary, a bad moment easily forgotten. For yet others, it may receive a laugh or merely be ignored. Again, interpreting even this simple statistic poses difficulties. Is one in five high or low, worrying or reassuring? What do they mean by harmful or illegal? Are parents the right people to ask or should we instead ask children? Like most averages, this one masks considerable cross-national variation, whether different cultural interpretations of 'harmful' or genuine differences in risk – for example, 45 per cent of Swedish and 33 per cent of Dutch parents said 'yes', compared with only 11 per cent of German and 9 per cent of Portuguese parents.

In the UK, 15 per cent of parents said 'yes', which is comparable to Ofcom's (2006a) finding that 16 per cent of 8–15 year olds claim to have come across something 'nasty, worrying or frightening' online. Higher figures were found in the UK Children Go Online project (Livingstone and Bober, 2004b). Children and young people aged 9–19 years old who go online daily or weekly reported that:

- 57 per cent had seen online pornography of some sort, 31 per cent had seen violent and 11 per cent racist content.
- One third had received unwanted sexual (31%) or bullying comments (33%) online or by text message.
- 8 per cent had gone to a meeting with someone first met online.

The importance of asking children is immediately evident when one compares these figures with the systematically lower estimates provided by their parents. Among parents of 9–17 year olds, the survey found that only 16 per cent thought their child had encountered online pornography, and just 7 per cent and 4 per cent thought they had seen violent or racist content respectively. Equally low figures held for estimates that their child had received unwanted sexual comments (9%), bullying comments (4%) or had gone to a meeting with an online contact (3%). While one cannot determine whether children overestimate or parents underestimate, and while one would hardly expect parents and children to give identical accounts, this gap between children's and parents' recognition of online risk is both interesting and problematic (Livingstone and Bober, 2006).[7]

National surveys in Norway, Sweden, Ireland, Denmark and Iceland found similarly that a quarter to a third of 9–16-year-old internet users had accidentally seen violent, offensive, sexual or pornographic content online (Larsson, 2003; Staksrud, 2005; note that in these surveys also, parental estimates of risk were lower than children's). A 2006 update in Ireland found that 35 per cent had visited pornographic sites, 26 per cent had visited hateful sites (mostly boys) and 23 per cent had received unwanted sexual comments online (again more boys). One in 5 chatters was upset/threatened/embarrassed online, and 7 per cent had met an online contact offline; of these, 24 per cent turned out not to be a child but an adult, and 11 per cent said the person tried to physically hurt them (Webwise, 2006).

And again, similar figures are obtained in the USA (see the Internet Safety Technical Task Force, 2008, for a recent review). A national survey of 1,500 10–17 year olds in 2006 found that,

- Compared with their earlier survey in 2000, online exposure to sexual material had increased (34% vs. 25% of young internet users), as had online harassment (9% vs. 6%), though unwanted sexual solicitations – often from acquaintances rather than strangers – had reduced (13% vs. 19%).
- In 2006, 4 per cent had been asked for nude/sexually explicit photos of themselves, and the proportion who had been distressed by such experiences increased (9% vs. 6%) (Janis Wolak, Mitchell and Finkelhor, 2006).

In their survey on teenagers' experiences of bullying, Pew Internet found that 32 per cent of 12–17 year olds online had been the target of some form of annoying/menacing activities – 15 per cent had had a private message forwarded on or posted publicly, 13 per cent had been the target of online rumours, 13 per cent had received a threatening or aggressive message, 6 per cent had had an embarrassing picture posted without permission (Lenhart, 2007).

According to an online survey in 2006, over one fifth of social networking teenagers in the Netherlands have had cybersexual experiences and 40 per cent of boys and 57 per cent of girls had been asked to undress on webcam, of whom 1 in 3 boys and 1 in 10 girls did. Nearly half of the girls had received an unwanted request to do a sexual act on webcam, though nearly all refused. In all, 35 per cent of girls and 12 per cent of boys claimed a negative experience, including 9 per cent of girls and 3 per cent of boys who had posted sexual photos and then regretted it. Although these figures are higher than for other surveys, possibly because the method used was a voluntary online survey rather than a nationally representative sample, this study points to the importance of recognizing that threats come from peers more than from strangers, and it is noteworthy that here the teenagers were particularly unclear about the negotiation of personal boundaries (De Rutgers Nisso Groep, 2006).

In countries where internet diffusion is more recent, risk figures are rather higher, presumably because here especially, youth encounter online risk in advance of regulators and policymakers. In Bulgaria, a national survey of 800 5th–11th grade children offline, plus a survey of 1,688 12–17 year olds online, found that 1 in 3 internet users have met in person somebody they got to know online, that 1 in 3 have experienced insistent and persistent attempts to communicate with them (often about sex) against their will, and that 4 in 10 are unaware of the risks of meeting online contacts offline (Mancheva, 2006). In Poland, a survey of 1,779 teenagers aged 12–17, conducted in 2006, found that 2 in 3 internet users make friends online, and almost 1 in 2 had gone to a meeting with someone met online, half of them going alone and one in four of those describing the behaviour of the other person as 'suspicious' (CANEE, 2006).[8]

Having reviewed some 400 studies across 21 countries, the EU Kids Online network (Hasebrink, Livingstone and Haddon, 2009) concluded that among online teenagers, giving out personal information, while not strictly speaking a risk, is very common and, it may be surmised, provides a precondition for many of the risks shown in the table earlier. Content-related risks appear the next most common – especially exposure to unwelcome or inappropriate sexual or aggressive content (though commercial and value-based content risks have been little researched). Contact risks vary in incidence, with bullying being fairly commonplace, sexual harassment rather less common and, the most risky category of all, meeting online contacts ('strangers') offline being the most rare. In rank order of frequency, and bearing in mind cross-national differences in methodology for data collection, the findings were as follows:

- Giving out personal information: around half of online teenagers (with national variations spanning 13%–91%);
- Seeing pornography: around 4 in 10 across Europe (ranging from 25%–80%, no doubt depending in part on matters of definition);
- Seeing violent or hateful content: around 1 in 3 (fairly consistent cross-nationally);
- Being bullied/harassed/stalked: around 1 in 5 or 6 (higher in few countries);

- Receiving unwanted sexual comments: around 1 in 10 teenagers in Germany, Ireland, Portugal; around 1 in 3 or 4 in Iceland, Norway, Sweden and the UK; rising to 1 in 2 in Poland;
- Meeting an online contact offline: around 9 per cent (1 in 11) online teenagers in most countries, rising to 1 in 5 in the Czech Republic, Poland and Sweden;

To those who doubted that the internet poses a risk to its young users, the evidence surely contradicts this convenient assumption. To those who fear that the internet is dangerous to children, some of these figures may be reassuring. There is, however, no consensus on where to draw the line between tolerable risk and danger. Much hinges on questions of definition (e.g. 'pornography'), of scale (e.g. 'distress'), of interpretation (e.g. 'unwanted') and of benchmarking (i.e. what risks did children face before the internet?). Qualitative research gives us a better feel for some of the experiences captured by these surveys (Livingstone, 2006).

In the 'Families and the Internet' project, we observed an 11-year-old girl who, trying to find pictures of Adolf Hitler for a school project during one of our visits, innocently accessed a site labelled 'Adolf Hitler pictures'. She failed to note the rubric 'gaysexfreepics' and found herself face-to-face with a porn site. As is common with such sites, it was very difficult to shut down, with the first few attempts merely producing other similar sites. We also watched 13-year-old Candy flirt in a teen chat room, asking, 'Hi r there any fit guys on here??? pm me if interested.' Though she hoped for a private message, instead she gets rude talk ('giz uz a snog' and, perhaps directed at someone else, '**** OFF BITCH').

In another family, 10- and 12-year-old brothers told us what happened when,

> we once looked up the band Boyzone, but it came up with something else ... Men doing stuff with other men ... On a beach, like one was like that, and one was like that – it was a bit sick. [he demonstrates rectal penetration with humping movements]

A 16-year-old boy told us how,

> I went onto one, it was on a search engine one and it came up with, I don't know, how to make bombs and things like that ... I mean I got off it straight away because I don't want to know how to make bombs to be honest, and there was, oh yeah, there was one how to cook humans as well which was ooaarghh.

These and other experiences do seem to go beyond what society expects for children and young people as they pursue their studies or leisure at home and school, though perhaps not beyond what society has long silently tolerated. Nonetheless, the translation from risk to harm remains difficult to ascertain, partly because harm is not easy to define. The European Commission's Safer Internet programme offers a very open definition, noting that 'Harmful content is content which parents, teachers or other adults responsible for children consider harmful to them.' But definitions vary from one culture and even one person to the next.[9] The Council of Europe addresses the problem of definition by listing types of risk,[10] and it also works with the positive concept of well-being (O'Connell and Bryce, 2006). In researching 'Harm and Offence in Media Content', we found the dictionary definition the clearest – 'physical or mental damage' (Merriam-Webster) or 'material damage, actual or potential ill effect' (Oxford Dictionary of English). What empirical research addresses, by and large, is the incidence and demography of risky experiences – activities and encounters which are associated, or likely to be associated, with the possibility of harm. This leaves for future research both the question of the likelihood of harm and the severity of harm, two factors normally part of scientific risk assessment but largely lacking in this field.

Let's pursue the finding from the UK Children Go Online survey that 57 per cent of 9–19 year olds who go online at least weekly have come into contact with pornography online. First, note that age makes a sizable difference – overall contact with pornography jumping from 21 per cent among 9–11 year olds to 58 per cent among 12–15 year olds, 76 per cent among 16–17 year olds and 80 per cent among 18–19 year olds. So, the risk to the youngest group is the smallest although, it must be acknowledged, they may be the least able to cope. Second, note that children's responses vary. Asked in a private self-completion section of the questionnaire, the respondents reported mixed reactions to online pornography: of those who have come into contact with online pornography, 54 per cent claim not to be bothered by it, 20 per cent were disgusted, 14 per cent disliked what they saw, 8 per cent wished they had never seen it, 7 per cent thought it was interesting and 7 per cent enjoyed it.[11] In short, half of those who see pornography online claim not to be bothered by it, while a significant minority were unhappy at seeing it – especially girls and younger children: 35 per cent of girls but only 10 per cent of boys thought it was disgusting, and around one in four 9–15 year olds thought it was disgusting compared with one in seven of the 16–19 year olds. There might be reasons why children falsely claim not to be bothered by pornography – wanting to be 'cool', for example. There might also be reasons why children claim to be bothered when they are not. Yet there seems more reason to be sceptical that as many as 54 per cent don't think too much about seeing online pornography than to think that a fifth would claim to be disgusted when they were not – though maybe this seemed to some a funny survey response.

In addition to noting demographic and individual differences in risk experiences and responses, we should also consider the contexts in which children encounter pornography. For most children, such encounters were unintentional contact – through pop-ups (38%), junk mail (25%) or email from someone they know (9%), rendering the experience both surprising and, for some, shocking. However, 10 per cent had visited pornographic websites on purpose, this being only one per cent of the 9–11 year olds but 26 per cent of the 18–19 year olds, and only 3 per cent of girls but 17 per cent of boys aged 9–19. A substantial minority of the older teenagers circulate pornography among themselves or those they meet online – more boys than girls (14% of 9–19-year-old boys have been sent pornography from someone they know but only 3% of girls), suggesting that for teenage boys, pornography plays a role in their shared culture (Staksrud and Livingstone, in press).

Mapping online risk

Are all children and young people equally 'at risk'? Although Beck stresses that today's risks, unlike the hazards of pre-modern times, are 'democratic' – because they affect everyone now and into the future (he is thinking here particularly of environmental risks), at other points he observes that, since people are differentially resourced to deal with these hazards and insecurities, an account of risk should include a mapping of 'social risk positions'.[12] How are risks distributed across society, and with which other sources of social inequality are they associated? Further, how do different risk factors intersect so as to produce a more satisfactory account of complex social phenomena?

Millwood Hargrave and Livingstone (2009) argue that the search for simple and direct causal effects of the media – including the nascent investigation of 'the impact of the internet on ...' – is no longer appropriate. Rather, we should seek to identify the complex array of factors that directly, and indirectly, through interactions with each other, combine to explain particular social phenomena (e.g. aggression, prejudice, bullying) so as to contextualize the role of particular media within that broader array (see Kline, 2003). An analysis of cyberbullying, then, would first identify the problem to be bullying, however mediated, rather than cyberbullying in particular. It would then identify the set of possible factors that might result in bullying (such as the child's self-esteem, social circumstances, appearance, relations with parents, friendships). And, then, it would examine the specific contribution of the child's practices of online/mobile communication (and those of their peers) within that larger set. The result will be a more complex explanation of what are, undoubtedly, complex social problems. At present, the research literature merely provides some indications of what the likely factors might be.

Looking across the available studies in Europe, the EU Kids Online network found that older teenagers encounter more online risks than younger teenagers (unfortunately, there is little evidence on risks encountered by younger children) (Hasebrink, Livingstone and Haddon, 2009). It is also the case, however, that teenagers gain in online skills with age, suggesting that even though younger teenagers may encounter fewer risks, they may also lack the skills to cope with them. The picture for gender is less straightforward. While overall, gender differences in internet use appear less strong than did earlier findings on computer use, girls and boys do prefer rather different activities online and this, it seems, leads them to encounter different types of risk. As Hasebrink *et al.* conclude,

> Boys are more likely to seek out offensive or violent content, to access pornographic content or be sent links to pornographic websites, to meet somebody offline that they have met online and to give out personal information. Girls are more likely to be upset by offensive, violent and pornographic material, to chat online with strangers, to receive unwanted sexual comments and to be asked for personal information but to be wary of providing it to strangers. Both boys and girls are at risk of online harassment and bullying. (2008: 69)[13]

Most research on youthful risk behaviour notes a strong association with measures of deprivation – poverty, family difficulties, educational failure, marginal status, and so forth (Coleman and Hendry, 1999; Hill and Tisdall, 1997). However, risky experiences online are a little different. Since access to the internet has diffused from the privileged to the less privileged, with the privileged retaining their advantage in terms of the quality of access and speed of connectivity long after the lowest socioeconomic groups have gained some measure of access to the internet, a simple correlation between socioeconomic status and online risk shows that it is the more middle class, not the more working class, teenagers who encounter more risks (Livingstone and Helsper, in press). The correlation is strong if one includes those without home access (for of course these both experience less risk and are lower in socioeconomic status), but it is still statistically significant in the UK even if one considers only those with home access.

However, in several other European countries, the evidence points in the opposite direction, with lower class children being more exposed to online risk. It seems that further research is needed to determine whether online risks compound other forms of socioeconomic disadvantage or, as seems the case in the UK, are instead associated with relative privilege. As regards the UK Children Go Online findings, it should be stressed that these findings need not imply that middle-class children deliberately seek out more risks online; rather, that their better access and experience (more years online, more locations for internet use) means that they use the internet more, gain more skills online, take up more online opportunities and so encounter more online risks. After all, learning to read, or to make friends, or to ride a bicycle may result in a variety of activities – some of them approved of by parents, others not; the same is surely true of learning to use the internet.

Disadvantage may also matter when we ask what resources teenagers can call upon to cope with online risks. Equally little research exists here (Staksrud and Livingstone, in press). However, a multiple regression analysis of the survey points to the importance of socio-psychological factors as much or more than demographic ones. It found that going to an offline meeting with a contact made online is more typical of older teens, both boys and girls, especially those who have not been using the internet for very long, those who are less shy offline (compared with those who have not attended a meeting), more likely to be sensation-seekers and more likely to be dissatisfied with their lives (Livingstone and Helsper, 2007b). It also seems that those who meet online contacts offline are those who feel more confident communicating online than offline and who value the anonymity afforded by the internet. Last, these teenagers seem to have relatively greater difficulty discussing personal issues with their parents or feel their parents to be more conformity-oriented rather than conversation-oriented (see also Cottrell, Branstetter, Cottrell, Rishel and Stanton, 2007).

In the American Youth Internet Safety Survey, those who encountered online risks (e.g. embarrassing others, meeting new people, and talking about sex online with strangers) were more likely to be depressed and, possibly in consequence, to cope less well with risky encounters. Specifically, among a national survey of 10–17-year-old internet users, those who reported major depressive-like symptoms were 3.5 times more likely to also report an unwanted sexual solicitation online compared to youths with mild/no symptoms. Among youths reporting an internet solicitation, those with major depressive-like symptoms were twice as likely to report feeling emotionally distressed by the incident compared to youths with mild/no symptoms. Thus it seems that depression both predicts unwanted sexual contact and also exacerbates the distress experienced as a result of such contact (Wolak, Mitchell and Finkelhor, 2007; Ybarra and Mitchell, 2004a; 2004b; Ybarra, Mitchell, Finkelhor and Wolak, 2007).[14]

In most of the foregoing discussion, I have treated findings regarding online risk as more or less constant across countries. Yet the range of variation in incidence observed for specific risks above includes considerable cross-national differences. The EU Kids Online network therefore examined whether or not systematic patterns could be identified, following this with an examination of possible explanations for observed patterns (Hasebrink, Livingstone and Haddon, 2009). Based on pan-European data on children's internet use, plus the review of national studies regarding the incidence of online risk experienced by children in each country, the following classification was tentatively put forward.

Online risk	Children's internet use		
	Below EU average (<65%)	**Average (65%–85%)**	**Above EU average (>85%)**
Low	Cyprus Italy	France Germany	
Medium	Greece	Austria Belgium Ireland Portugal Spain	Denmark Sweden
High		Bulgaria Czech Republic	Estonia Netherlands Norway Poland Slovenia UK

(Source: EU Kids Online; Hasebrink, Livingstone and Haddon, 2009)

On this basis, it appears that high use of the internet is rarely if ever associated with low risk. Clearly, high-use, high-risk countries are, for the most part, wealthy Northern European countries though high risk has also became evident in new entrants to the European Union.

Even medium use may, it seems, be associated with high risk, suggesting particular problem in Eastern European countries when regulatory infrastructure and safety awareness is underdeveloped. Last, Southern European countries tend to be lower in risk, though there are differences among them. Putting this another way around, Hasebrink *et al.* concluded that,

> As a broad generality, (i) Northern European countries tend to be 'high use, high risk'; (ii) Southern European countries tend to be 'low use, variable risk', and (iii) Eastern European countries can be characterized as 'new use, new risk'.

Why this should be the case is far from straightforward, as there are multiple competing explanations to take into account. After reviewing a considerable body of cross-national contextual information, the EU Kids Online network concluded that, over and above the importance of the trajectory of internet diffusion across countries, national internet regulation appears lower (or less interventionist) in countries where internet use is lower (or more recently introduced to a mass market), resulting in turn in greater risk to children in these countries. It also observed that higher-use countries had higher levels of general education, while higher-risk countries often had low engagement from child welfare/NGOs in awareness-raising and fewer sources of positive online content for children. The array of factors that may play a role in accounting for online risk, it seems, grows as we adopt a wider comparative lens.

Linking risks and opportunities

The internet promises such wonderful opportunities for education, communication, participation and creativity. Yet the very same medium represents, it seems, the means of bringing into the privacy of the home the very worst of society. This struggle is itself exacerbated by the use of rhetoric that polarizes discussion of opportunities and risks – as in the start of this paragraph. Beck and others stress that, in reflexive modernity we must be aware that risks and opportunities go hand in hand. Pleading ignorance regarding the potential risks associated with newly developed online opportunities is no longer plausible.

The inextricable linking of opportunities and risks also characterizes the everyday experiences of individuals, for risks emerge from everyday social relations and processes of our (society's) own making. Not only do young people engage in some activities of which society approves and others of which society disapproves, but often these are the same activities – to take up an opportunity one may have to take a risk. To make a new friend online, one risks meeting someone ill-intentioned. To engage even with the children's BBC website, one must provide personal information online. To search for advice about sexuality, one will encounter pornographic content also, since there is no consensual line between them. These interconnections are not 'natural' to the internet but rather inhere in the ways that websites and services have been designed, socially shaped by producers, content providers and users based on assumptions and interests that could have been otherwise. The internet thus does not create risk for children so much as it mediates the balance between societal risks and opportunities.

This is not mere semantics, but rather an insistence that the internet has been socially shaped to mediate social relations in particular ways and not others. The advantage of such recognition is that the internet, and the processes that shape it, become amenable to risk management (as discussed in chapter 8). Further, the importance of the social shaping argument is that it complements our attention to risk-taking activities of teenagers with a recognition of the potentially dangerous contexts within which they engage in these activities. Teenagers may search for 'sex', but it is not they who put pornography high in the top ten sites listed instead of advice on sexual relationships or health. Since www.martinlutherking.org is a white supremacist site and www. whitehouse.com is a pornography site, an explanation for online risk lies not simply with youthful behaviour but with the infrastructure of domain names, search engines and browsers. The economics and the cultural politics of online content is only just beginning to be mapped (see, for example, Machill, Neuberger and Schindler, 2003).

With this in mind, we may better understand one surprising finding from the UK Children Go Online project. When I began the research, I had perhaps naively imagined that some would enjoy the opportunities of going online (educational, entertaining, civic, participation) while others, possibly those 'at risk' in their personal circumstances, or those inexperienced in using the internet, would encounter the risks of going online (happening upon pornography, meeting online friends offline, giving out personal information online). On the contrary, analysis of the survey findings showed that the range of opportunities and risks children experienced (as set out in chapter 1) were positively correlated. In other words, the more opportunities they take up, the more risks they encounter, and vice versa (Livingstone and Helsper, in press).[15]

Also unexpectedly, those who were more experienced or skilled in using the internet had more experience of both the opportunities and risks compared with novice users. Being more skilled does not, it seems, provide a means to avoid the risks (and though it may enable youth to cope with what they find, this question has been little investigated). These findings suggest that policy interventions designed to increase young people's internet literacy, and their take up of online opportunities, will have the unintended consequence of increasing their online risk of harm. Conversely, seeking to reduce the risks tends also to reduce their online opportunities, either by generally limiting internet use or by specifically restricting interactive or peer-to-peer activities online. Overall, four groups of teenage internet users were identified:

- The 'low-risk novices' tended to be younger, more likely to be working-class children, especially girls, with parents who lack confidence in using the internet but who monitor their children closely; these children encounter few online risks, but their take up of online opportunities is also very limited, and they develop few online skills in consequence.
- The 'inexperienced risk takers' were a little older, more likely to be working-class boys, also with parents low in internet literacy; these teenagers are also low in online skills, they concentrate on peer-to-peer opportunities, and they encounter a relatively high degree of risks, both accidental and deliberate.
- 'Skilled risk takers', by contrast, tended to be middle-class boys who are highly skilled online, and who both take up a fair number of opportunities and encounter a range of online risks.
- Last, the 'all-round experts', often slightly older middle-class boys, have the greatest online expertise, take up far more opportunities than the other groups and also encounter a high degree of risks.

What is noticeable is that none of these groupings contain those high in opportunities and low in risks, or vice versa. One reason for this is that the very activities that adults perceive to be risky on the internet – social networking, disclosing personal information, downloading music, visiting chat rooms, playing first person shooter or hack and slash games – are valued as new opportunities by children. Some of these activities contravene adult norms of taste or morality, and some undermine guidelines designed to ensure online safety. Examples include posting pictures that reveal identity/location (sports team, school, and so forth) or sexually provocative/indecent images (via mobile or webcam), circulating messages to 'friends of friends' whose identity is unclear, expressing insecurities and fantasies in blogs, circulating hostile or bullying content about peers, tricking others into embarrassing or indecent acts on webcam, choosing sexual nicknames (e.g. Lolita, sxcbabe), and encouraging peers to visit sites that promote suicide, anorexia, drug-taking or self-harm.

This risk-taking is not purely a matter of sensation seeking. Consider another area of youth socialization that generations of adults have failed to address sensitively or well – that of sexuality. Having listened to teenagers discussing how they did, and would like, to learn about sexuality, a process in which parents and teachers play at best a partial and flawed role, Buckingham and Bragg conclude,

> Learning about sex and relationships thus appeared to be seen as a form of *bricolage*, a matter of 'piecing it together' from a range of potential sources. It was also often a collective process, conducted among the peer group. (2004: 61)

Teenagers need, and will actively seek out, opportunities to discuss sexuality among their peers, and here the internet offers a valued opportunity. As Stern (2002) shows, teenage girls use the internet not only to express their identity but also to explore, often in a private, intimate, sometimes anonymous, sometimes confessional manner, their confusions, vulnerabilities, uncertainties and ignorance regarding sexuality, including sexual norms, emotions and health (see also Leung, 2007; Ito *et al.*, 2008):[16]

> Communicating in their own words helps girls develop not only their sense of self and identity but also allows them to construct their own social reality as members of peer groups ... girls will be most free to explore and construct their identities and express feelings about the issues of greatest importance to them when they are in a space they consider safe – that is, free from the potentially judgemental or inhibiting influence of adults or male peers. (Grisso and Weiss, 2005: 31–2)

Online, perhaps more than offline, the opportunities for information, advice and intimacy are clearly and closely linked to the risks of misinformation, inappropriate influence and exploitation. Research suggests that those particularly in need of sexual information (e.g. early maturing girls or those without offline forms of social support) are more likely to turn to teen media, including the internet, precisely because their immediate peers (or parents) are not yet ready to engage with such issues (Brown, Halpern and L'Engle, 2005; Suzuki and Calzo, 2004). Yet what they find may be negative or oppressive rather than positive and empowering (Buckingham and Bragg, 2004).[17] In short, to judge the balance of opportunities and risks experienced by children online, one must recognize that these are linked – in both the shaping of the online environment and children's own practices of use, including exploratory and risk-taking activities; additionally, one must recognize that there are some genuine uncertainties over what benefits or harms children, including the likelihood that what benefits some may harm others. So, while this chapter has examined online risks, it should be read in relation to the preceding chapters on opportunities.

The identification of risk in the risk society

No one expects a zero-risk childhood, yet society seems loath to specify a level of acceptable risk when it comes to children. One result is that media panics effectively construe all risk as unacceptable. In reaction, critics counter by pointing to children's resilience to harm, their sophistication in using the internet, and the historical fact that risk has always been part of childhood. The challenge is to move beyond these polarized positions, for we can neither conclude that the internet is too risky to allow children access nor that it has made no difference whatsoever. The theory of the risk society offers three useful directions for thinking about how risk is being reconfigured for (and by) today's children and young people – the identification of risk, the intensification of risk and the individualization of risk.

The theory of the risk society problematizes the *identification of risk*, rejecting the notion of risk as a natural hazard 'out there' and seeking to understand how it is precisely a consequence of the institutions, innovations and practices of modernity. These institutions, innovations and practices include not only the internet (and its infrastructure, content provision and regulation), and not only the science of risk assessment by which we come to know of internet-related risks (mainly, the uneven body of survey evidence reviewed above) but also, most importantly, society's reshaping of the ubiquitous networks in which we all, including children, are now willingly embedded. Following Beck, Klink and Renn (2001) stress that risk concerns the way in which people's actions adversely (and often inadvertently) affect precisely what people value. Online risk, as we have seen, is generally held primarily to pose sexual or violent threats to and from children; these, it seems, threaten what society values about childhood both in the present and for the future.

For example, as noted in chapter 1, the social practice of young children walking to school on their own almost disappeared in the UK over the two decades to 1990, a change attributable to the mix of increased car ownership, worry about traffic risks, and a growing fear of child abduction. Leaving aside the irony that traffic has consequently worsened, it is noteworthy that this trend is culturally specific: in 1990, Hillman *et al.* (1990) found that three quarters of German primary school children came home from school on their own, compared with only a third of English children, the latter also being more restricted as regards permission to cross roads, visit other places, use buses after dark or cycle on the roads. During those same decades, screen-entertainment media were adopted by many homes, and more in the UK than in Germany. For example, by the late 1990s, 2 in 3 British but only 4 in 10 German children aged 6–17 had a television in their bedroom (Bovill, 2001). Risks faced by children, both in the popular imagination and in reality, were thereby reconfigured.

Just a few years later, online chat rooms appeared to be the new and exciting opportunity for children. Millions rapidly became regular users but, following some highly publicized cases of stranger grooming for sexual abuse, chat rooms were instead regarded as risky, children were warned away (Internet Crime Forum, 2000), and in 2003 Microsoft closed its chat rooms to children.[18] This cleared the way for the rapid uptake instead of instant messenger services, seen still by young people as a great opportunity and, by their parents, as a new source of risk. While chat rooms were acknowledged to contain 'strangers', instant messaging is conducted among 'friends', raising new issues regarding intimacy and privacy in social relations. As we saw in chapter 4, social networking sites came next, with each step on this path reconfiguring just who children could and did talk to online, what others knew about them, and what kinds of risk they encountered. Lash and Wynne note that in the risk society:

> Risks are always created and effected in social systems, for example by organizations and institutions which are supposed to manage and control the risky activity [with the magnitude of the risk being] a direct function of the quality of social relations and processes ... [Consequently] the primary risk, even for the most technically intensive activities (indeed perhaps most especially for them), is therefore that of social dependency upon institutions and actors who may well be – and arguably are increasingly – alien, obscure and inaccessible to most people affected by the risks in question. (1992: 4)

Use of the internet, we may conclude, exacerbates the risks in children's lives to the extent that a generation comes to rely upon it for their social lives.

In identifying the risks associated with internet use, we should also observe that the media panic agenda not only draws attention to certain risks but also distracts from others. Worries about paedophiles, notably, mask the threat to children from known rather than unknown adults. Yet offline and, arguably, online also, most physical and sexual risk to children derives less from 'stranger danger' than from parents and other relatives, at least until the age of fifteen or sixteen (Jackson and Scott, 1999; Munro, 2008). The policy difficulty is evident – if parents are to be positioned as part of the regulatory solution, they can hardly be acknowledged as the potential villains. Yet policy must, surely, begin with an accurate assessment of threats to children online – primarily adults known to them, older teenagers in their social circle and 'friends of friends'.

Equally, public discourses centred on content and contact risks distract attention from the overwhelmingly commercial nature of the online environment. Some have argued that commercialism too may undermine children's well-being, both because of its content (such as promoting thin girls, shopping for self-esteem or wealth as achievement) and its often covert advertising and sponsorship practices (Boone, Secci and Gallant, 2007; Fielder, Gardner, Nairn and Pitt, 2007; Kenway and Bullen, 2001; Montgomery and Pasnik, 1996). Yet this attracts less attention, with the media seemingly little concerned about the degree to which the modern child is surrounded with persuasive messages and cross-media merchandising on a historically unprecedented scale (Schor, 2004). One might continue, pointing to the relative lack of concern about, and research on, children's encounters with racist content, the commercial use (or abuse) of their personal information (although see Turow, 2000), the plethora of pro-anorexic sites online, and so forth. We worry primarily about children's sexuality, it seems, and their physical safety, and in so doing, we have discursively divided the world of 'others' into strange adults and friendly peers, irrespective of the realities of children's lives.

The intensification of risk in the risk society

Beck's critics note some ambivalence in his position regarding the real or socially constructed nature of risk (Elliott, 2002; Lupton, 1999), which raises the question of whether the rise of the discourse of risk on the public agenda means that risk itself has increased. Nonetheless, the theory of the risk society invites us to inquire into the social, political and economic as well as the technological reasons for the *intensification of risk* in late modernity. Disentangling the contributory role of the internet remains difficult, not least because there are few sound points of comparison with pre-internet times. Both parents and children said in the UK Children Go Online survey that they considered the internet more risky than any other medium.[19] But a rigorous assessment of the claims for social change requires clear answers to the question of whether the risks facing children today are fundamentally different from or, particularly, greater than those of earlier periods. We do not know whether the nature or scale of bullying or sexual harassment or self-harm has become more harmful to children now that some of these risks are mediated by the internet. This is both because rigorous statistics for previous decades are largely lacking and because there appears to be no systematic recording, as yet, of any involvement of the internet in government statistics on clinical, medical or criminal harm to children.

The review by ECPAT International for the United Nations concludes that the internet affords multiple opportunities for harm to children (Muir, 2005). For a child victim, an image of abuse may now be distributed anywhere worldwide in a matter of seconds and never eradicated (IWF, 2008). For the bullied child, a hostile site morphing their image and inviting ridicule may harm them whether or not they are aware of its existence (Nightingale, Dickenson and Griff, 2000). For a teenager in despair, a community of suicidal others, advocating the means of self-harm, may be reached at the click of a mouse with a convenience that is historically unprecedented (Alao, Soderberg, Pohl and Alao, 2006). And for the young bully, racist or abuser, the creative potential of the internet invites new opportunities to harm others, unobserved and not easily detectable, even reaching into the privacy of their victim's bedroom (Barak, 2005).

At the least, the internet has become a new locus for familiar but still significant problems – bullying, sexual harassment, hostility, and more. Some long-familiar risks are now reconfigured – more frequent for some, potentially more pernicious for others, more or less detectable or avoidable compared with their offline equivalents. Further, the evidence points to an intensification of risk to children's well-being because of their fast-changing practices of communication, disclosure and privacy. These changing practices are, in turn, shaped by the changing conditions of childhood and youth. And they are also shaped by the specific affordances of the internet: notably, convenience of access and distribution, global connectivity, speed, persistence or permanence of content, searchability, replicability and manipulability of messages and the conditions of privacy and anonymity. As I explore in chapters 4 and 7, risks are also intensified insofar as children (and parents) may not recognize the consequences of their actions online – a matter of media literacy, though the conditions of legibility (i.e. the ease by which online sites and services enable or impede such recognition) must also be noted.

For example, although many would argue that there is little new about the content of online pornography, one may surely agree with Waskul that 'what is most new about internet sex is its unprecedented access' (2004: 4). Previous formal and informal access controls for pornography, from the informal embarrassment of buying a 'top shelf' magazine to the formal age restrictions of the sex shop or the planning requirements imposed on the location of such shops (not near schools or swimming pools, for example), have all changed now that a vast range of content can be accessed at home with anonymity. Such access, many argue, alters the market, expanding the potential for niche and specialized content addressing any and all sexual tastes, linking the mild through a series of easy steps to the hardcore. Thus, 'the old and the new are reconfigured, sometimes in ways that are predictable and sometimes in ways that surprise' (p. 5).

For most children, the evidence reviewed in this chapter suggests that one should not overstate the case. Online risks do not merit a moral panic, and nor do they warrant seriously restricting children's internet use, especially as this would deny them many benefits. However, some degree of risk of harm is widespread, and it is experienced by a sizeable minority of children as worrying or problematic, thus warranting serious attention and intervention by government, educators, industry and parents.

The individualization of risk in the risk society

> Risks may be produced by social conditions, but we are expected to assess and manage them as individuals. (Jackson and Scott, 1999: 88–9)

Developing the findings regarding inequalities in the incidence and management of risk, a third dimension of the risk society thesis comes into focus, namely the *individualization of risk*. In Western capitalist societies, the discourse of risk is closely accompanied by a discourse of empowerment, carried forward from life-political movements such as feminism and, perhaps curiously, re-embedded within official establishment discourses as a means of rationalizing the increasing exposure of the individual to the consequences of their own risk-related decisions (Lunt and Livingstone, 2007). Thus official optimism regarding the individual benefits afforded by the internet goes hand in hand with a strategy to encourage individuals voluntarily to engage in self-regulation – regarding parenting responsibilities or 'positive parenting', for example (Oswell, 1999), rather than, say, enforcing regulatory compliance for child protection from firms. Since it appears the public has lost its trust in those institutions which, traditionally, were relied upon to mitigate or protect against risk, this contemporary stress on individual agency may seem pragmatic.

But looked at more critically, the rhetorical emphasis on empowerment suits the neoliberal move, driven by the pressure to liberalize (and deregulate) markets both nationally and globally, away from the hierarchical, 'command-and-control' approach of both self-regulatory bodies and government departments (Black, Lodge and Thatcher, 2005; Jessop, 2002). Thus regulatory regimes are moving towards a 'softer', more indirect approach that disperses the role of the state by establishing more accountable national and transnational regulatory bodies, by engaging civil society in processes of governance and by encouraging in the 'responsible' or 'empowered' citizen the new task of personal risk assessment – 'the need to adopt a calculative prudent personal relation to fate now conceived in terms of calculable dangers and avertable risks' (Rose, 1996: 58). But for children and parents already absorbed in the fraught emotional conflicts of negotiating boundaries of public and private, dependence and independence, tradition and change, this presents a new burden, adding official responsibilities to what were hitherto private struggles.

The public resolution to a moral panic is, in short, repackaged as the private individual's problem, and this precisely at the same time as many parents feel undermined by the considerable technological and moral complexities involved. Harden observes that, 'while anxieties about risk may be shaped by public discussion, it is as individuals that we cope with these uncertainties' (2000: 46). Moreover, this strategy of reducing the regulatory burden on industry and the state has the interesting consequence of bringing everyday public beliefs and actions into the policy process. People's perceptions and misperceptions, fears and anxieties, confusions and misunderstandings – as well as their good intentions and sound common sense – have all become central, rather than peripheral, to policies designed to ensure child protection on the internet. If parents, in the privacy of their own homes, cannot install a content filter or update their virus software, if teenagers reveal all to the world online but reveal little or nothing to their parents, if children click mistakenly on a popup and find pornography on their screen, all this becomes a new and somewhat intractable problem for public policy.

However, the individualization thesis does not treat all individuals as equivalent. On the contrary, inequalities in socioeconomic and other resources make for inequalities affecting both which individuals experience risk and how they may cope with it. In many areas of child protection, social stratification has brought the disadvantaged in particular – discursively labelled as 'vulnerable' or 'at risk' – into the purview of state welfare organizations and institutional risk management (e.g. Kelly, 2000; McWilliam, 2003; Rose, 1990). But on the internet, it is far from clear just who is at risk, making an entire generation subject to such attention. For example, since girls are particularly 'at risk' of contact with potentially abusive strangers, they have become the target of a considerable edifice of well-meaning but highly controlling advice on the micro-conduct of their daily interactions with friends, with official surveillance extending to matters hitherto regarded as both trivial and, more importantly, private.

With parents peering over children's shoulders, websites advising on what information to disclose and when, and safety initiatives providing guidelines on how to test if people are really who they say they are, there is surely little left ungoverned in young people's lives. On the other hand, Wolak *et al.* are surely right to argue that, rather than worrying about youth in general, 'particular attention should be paid to higher risk youths, including those with histories of sexual abuse, sexual orientation concerns, and patterns of off- and online risk taking' (Wolak, Finkelhor, Mitchell and Ybarra, 2008: 111; see also Finkelhor, 2008; Shim, Lee and Paul, 2007). To address the risks faced by a vulnerable minority in a proportionate manner without extending surveillance and restrictions to the occasionally naive, sometimes risk-taking majority is undoubtedly a difficult problem for public policy.

7

Media and Digital Literacies

In support of media literacy

Every dimension of social, political, economic and cultural life is, to a greater or lesser extent, mediated by the internet. Such mediation has become ubiquitous – everyone is affected by online networks and flows, even if they don't use them directly. As technologies, digital forms and spaces of mediation converge, we are witnessing the blurring of hitherto distinctive social practices of information and entertainment, work and leisure, public and private, national and global, even childhood and adulthood. Relations of production, representation and consumption are altered, and the user – whether conceived as citizen or consumer, actor or recipient – is repositioned. Individually and collectively, the public is becoming, as it must, more knowledgeable about, critical of and engaged in contemporary processes of mediation (Silverstone, 2005).

This 'public' includes children and young people, both because they are citizens with rights and responsibilities, as argued in chapter 5, and because they are avid consumers of online information and services. Yet a certain complacency has arisen regarding children in this regard, for they are widely heralded as 'the digital' or 'internet generation', supposedly natural 'experts' in using the internet and so, for once, a source of wisdom rather than innocence or ignorance. This perception is almost unprecedented in the history of childhood as children are generally held to know less than their 'elders and betters', and their 'childish' perspective on life denigrated or sidelined, for all their imaginative play is cherished. The result is a reverse generation gap much celebrated in public discourse, as we saw in chapter 2.

This celebratory discourse is on the lips of many observers, creating curious alignments among cultural studies critics, public policy-makers, industry stakeholders and children themselves. Who could demur? It is ironic, therefore, that since children are seen to use the internet so adeptly, using services unheard of by adults, fixing technical problems where parents or teachers have failed, this very expertise threatens to disempower children, for it undermines their claim on public policy resources. 'Experts' need little guidance or support and can be left to their own devices, and the more sophisticated they are, the less they need protection from online risks. Without in any way denigrating children's abilities, I suggest that so comfortable a consensus demands critical scrutiny. For 'using the internet', the foregoing chapters have argued, is no simple matter, and the expertise required can no more be straightforwardly attributed to the child conceived as media-savvy sophisticate than its absence can be deplored in the child conceived as vulnerable innocent.

This chapter begins with the observation that, over the past few years, strikingly diverse commentators have converged on the notion of literacy as a way of framing and recognizing the complexity of 'use'. Whether labelled internet literacy, cyber-literacy, digital literacy, information literacy or, rapidly becoming the all-encompassing term, media literacy, there are some crucial theoretical, empirical and political debates at stake, not to be masked by the consensus that media literacy is ever more crucial for children, parents and, indeed, the wider public. These interrelated debates are separated analytically in this chapter.

Thus I explore, first, the relation between new media literacies and the longer legacy of print; second, the nature of the different elements of media literacy and, especially, their potential to democratize knowledge and participation; third, the conception of literacy as an individual skill or a social practice; fourth, the relation between the knowledge of the user and the design of the technological interface; and, fifth, the direction that policymakers should take in promoting media literacy. My aim is to advance discussion beyond the question of simple practical skills so as to address, more fundamentally, the individual demands, the societal purposes and the implicit politics of media literacy.

But since it was only a few years ago that the very mention of 'literacy' in relation to new media and the internet caused eyebrows to be raised – surely the comparison with print is neither appropriate nor desirable, sceptics implied – I shall open and close this chapter with a discussion of definitions. These range from the tautological (internet literacy is the ability to use the internet) to the idealistic –

'literacy is shorthand for cultural ideals as eclectic as economic development, personal fulfilment, and individual moral fortitude' (Tyner, 1998: 17). To those for whom 'literacy' means 'just' reading and writing, the notion of media literacy (and related literacies) may seem puzzling. To non-native English speakers, the lack of a ready translation for 'literacy' into some languages also poses a difficulty (Livingstone, 2008a).[1] But definitions are rarely contested just to play games with words; rather, they are contested because real matters of power and resources are at stake. Hence the importance of integrating academic and public policy debates over media literacy, as I explore below.

The legacy of print literacy

The concept of media literacy, like that of literacy itself, has long been contentious (Luke, 1989). What are the literacies required for today's communication and information environment? Are they singular or multiple? Are they an extension of or a radical break from past traditions of representation and learning? More normatively, how should we conceptualize the public's relation to knowledge, participation and critique? (Hobbs, 1998, 2008; Warnick, 2002).

Williams (1983) traces the historical emergence of the English term 'literacy' not to knowing one's ABC or being able to use 'pen and paper' but to 'literature'. This term once combined an adjectival meaning – being discerning and knowledgeable according to 'standards of polite learning', with a noun – a body of writing of nationally acknowledged aesthetic merit. By the end of the nineteenth century, 'literature' (and 'literary') came to refer exclusively to the high culture canon. But, since over that century there had arisen a new category of the 'mass public' – people who could read and write but who lacked cultural capital and were not 'literary' – a new word was needed. Hence, 'literacy' (and 'literate') was 'invented to express the achievement and possession of what were increasingly seen as general and necessary skills' (p.188).

With the advent of mass education, spreading mass literacy far beyond the confines of elite society, the 'uses of literacy' (Hoggart, 1957) became increasingly subject to regulatory scrutiny and governance, occasioning a series of moral panics accompanying each new mass medium. Drotner (1992) observes that the progression of each media panic following the introduction of the latest technology involves a shift from 'pessimistic elitism', in which the establishment seeks to control, from the top down, the media enjoyed by the mass public, to 'optimistic pluralism', in which diverse media tastes are accepted within a positive affirmation in the public's good sense and legitimate variability. Tensions throughout this history centre on the political consequences of disseminating knowledge among 'the masses' who lack the critical discernment to appreciate it or use it in an 'approved' fashion and, following this, on the repositioning of established authorities and elites as alternative sources of knowledge and alternative networks of power arise. As Luke's (1989) subtly interwoven history of pedagogy and printing clearly shows, European states, both Catholic and Protestant, have always paid close attention to managing exactly which segments of society have access to what forms of knowledge.

The twentieth century saw the multiplication of textual forms, resulting in plural 'literacies' which first draw into the frame the even older legacy of oral history from anthropology and visual literacy from the humanities, and then encompass new literacies. Over time, these have included film literacy, television literacy, advertising literacy, computer literacy, games literacy and network literacy. Unsurprisingly, this multidisciplinary convergence of intellectual traditions and analysis has resulted in a multiplication of definitions (Buckingham, 2005; Christ and Potter, 1998; Livingstone, van Couvering and Thumim, 2008). Even focusing just on 'media literacy' within the social sciences, pedagogy and the humanities, Potter (2004) identified over twenty definitions. Yet commonalities can be identified. Many of these broadly concur with the clear and concise definition proposed by the National Leadership Conference on Media Literacy held in the USA in 1992 and endorsed by the National Association of Media Literacy Education, namely that media literacy is:

> the ability to access, analyze, evaluate and communicate messages in a variety of forms. (Aufderheide, 1993)

In the parallel realm of information science and computing, the recent transition in the dissemination and management of information sources, from authoritative and controlled forms (encyclopaedias, libraries, expert databases) to networked, diverse, flexibly specialized forms of representation of the information or knowledge society (for example, Wikipedia) has necessitated a rethinking of the notion of information literacy. The UNESCO-funded multinational gathering of experts organized by the US National Commission on Library and Information Science and National Forum on Information Literacy stated that information literacy encompasses:

the ability to identify, locate, evaluate, organize and effectively create, use and communicate information to address issues and problems at hand. (Information Literacy Meeting of Experts, 2003)

This evident convergence in definitions provides a useful consensus regarding the convergent literacies required for today's digital world. Within these, some distinctions can be made, depending on the specificity of the technologies and texts at issue. 'Internet literacy' may thus be distinguished from other forms of literacy to the extent that the specific skills, experiences, texts, institutions and cultural values associated with the internet differ from those associated with print, audiovisual or other forms of communication (Livingstone, 2008b).

Yet the legacy of print literacy remains strong, as evident from the persistence of the metaphor of 'reading', which extends well beyond books to encompass not only the screen (Snyder, 1998) but the whole of society – as in 'reading the world' (Freire and Macedo, 1987). At issue here is not only the ability to know and interpret the world as a given but, crucially, the critical ability to analyse and evaluate that world, to conceive how it might be otherwise. As we turn to the internet in the twenty-first century, it is notable that much online content is still written linear text and, additionally, that our metaphorical language for understanding this internet shares the print legacy – consider the language of webpages, email, files and folders and encyclopaedias. And critical literacies are even more important in multimedia online domain.

As the history of print literacy further reveals, while teaching the population to read was itself highly contentious, teaching people to write required yet a further struggle between the elitist interests of the establishment and the democratizing trends of the Enlightenment (Luke, 1989). Kress observes that 'writing has been the most valued means of communication over the last few centuries – the one that has regulated access to social power in Western societies' (1998: 55). In audiovisual media education, a parallel struggle has been apparent over whether children should be taught not only to critically interpret media texts but also to create their own (Sefton-Green, 1999). And now in relation to the internet, the ability to 'communicate' or 'create' must remain a central element of media or internet literacy for, as with previous media, it is this element that may democratize knowledge and challenge the authority of elites (Kellner, 2002).

The tendency to downplay or omit the critical and creative or participatory elements of media literacy in policy definitions marks a vital point of contestation in contemporary policy debates, as I shall argue later. But first let us consider the issues addressed by all four elements of the broad definition of media literacy in order to unpack the ways in which internet literacy both typifies and can be distinguished as a specific type of media literacy.

Access, analysis, evaluation and creation

'Using' the internet is clearly not as simple as turning on the computer and checking email or clicking on Google. Use depends on the abilities to access, analysis, evaluate and create and each of these is, further, part of a dynamic and mutually supporting process of engagement and learning. For example, analytic literacies are 'not only gained through critical analysis; they can also be developed – in some instances, more effectively and enjoyably – through the experience of media production' (Buckingham, 2007b: 49); similarly, skills in analysis and evaluation open the way for new creative uses of the internet, in turn extending access, while critical literacies are vital for creative participation:

> In the 21st century, critical media literacy is an imperative for participatory democracy because new information communication technologies and a market-based media culture have fragmented, connected, converged, diversified, homogenized, flattened, broadened, and reshaped the world. (Kellner and Share, 2007: 59)

Including access as a dimension of literacy may seem counterintuitive, for most obviously, use follows access. But, it takes economic, educational, social and cognitive resources to know which digital goods and services to acquire and update, and how to fit them meaningfully into one's life, as argued in chapter 2. And, although there are continuities with other media literacies, especially when it comes to understanding those who are excluded (or 'illiterate'), it is also evident that accessing the internet is far more demanding than turning on the television, going to the cinema or opening a book. Expanding the conception of access beyond hardware to encompass accessing information and communication further increases the literacy requirements on users, for they must navigate complex portals, databases and other information sources effectively and efficiently if they are truly to 'access the internet'. Last, the access dimension of literacy includes the skills required to avoid undesired contents, thus managing one's exposure to content and contact risks, whether through technical means or social practices.

A satisfactory engagement with media texts also demands a range of analytic competencies. Buckingham (2007b) argues that media literacy should enable users to analyse, or understand, four aspects of the internet. First, representation – as with any other medium, the internet does not simply reflect the world but it represents it in particular, selective and motivated ways, while also marginalizing other voices; here arise crucial questions of authority, authorship, ex/inclusion, reliability and bias. Second, language – the codes, conventions and genres of online communication are as crucial as for any other form of communication, and users should understand the 'grammar' and 'rhetorics' of, say, the design of websites and the significance of the links that connect them (Burbules, 1998; Torow and Tsui, 2008) or, as discussed in chapter 4, of the blogs, groups and other applications afforded by social networking sites. Third, production – the internet, like other media, mediates between social actors, and users must understand who is communicating to whom and for what purpose, particularly as distinctions among public and commercial bodies, or individuals and institutions, are often unclear online (Livingstone, 2004). Fourth, audience – here Buckingham requires the user to be reflexive, understanding their own position as a reader or user, as steered more or less firmly down a particular path, as specifically targeted or part of an unintended audience, and as visible or private, accountable or anonymous.

Critical evaluation is the third key element of internet literacy, and this too reveals both continuities and discontinuities with earlier forms of media literacy. The mass media – characterized by limited spectrum, expensive distribution channels, centralized organization and strong state regulation – maintained a strong distinction between producers and consumers. They also maintained a range of elite filters to select material to be distributed in accordance with criteria of cultural quality, editorial values, professional production conventions and, not least, political and market pressures. Consequently, audiovisual media literacy education centred on recognizing and critiquing the operation and effects of these elite filters and the organizations behind them. Although these have their online equivalents, for the mass media have substantially adjusted their operation to incorporate the internet, the internet also enables cheap, accessible, diverse and dispersed forms of knowledge distribution. Thus 'critical literacy' must be broadened to include information searching, navigation, sorting, assessing relevance, evaluating sources, judging reliability and identifying bias. All these tasks increasingly fall to the ordinary user in a fast-changing environment in which familiar markers of authority, value, trust and authenticity are lacking (Warnick, 2002). Nor are these tasks inconsequential, for they matter not only to the entertainment and hobbyist activities characteristic of engagement with traditional media, but also to the worlds of work, personal finance, civic engagement, health advice and education now accessed through online media.

Last, media literacy underpins the hopes that online opportunities enable people to be not only receivers but also producers of content. Put simply, we would not call a person who can read but not write literate, so nor should we call media literate a person who can access content online but is unable to contribute to it. More than for any previous media, the internet makes it possible for anyone with a certain level of skills and technical resources, now fairly accessible if far from universal, to create their own content, for any purpose, and make it widely available on a hitherto unprecedented, even global scale. Online, one and the same technology can be used for sending and receiving, with desktop publishing software, easy-to-use web creation software, digital cameras and webcams putting professional expertise into the hands of everyone. This eases the case for making communication tools available to the 'voiceless', thereby furthering possibilities for self-expression and cultural participation and so potentially democratizing content creation, dissemination and participation in unprecedented ways.

Are children media, or internet, literate in each of these four respects? As reviewed in the preceding chapters, a considerable body of empirical work shows that, although the vast majority of children have access to the internet in the simplest terms (i.e. there is a connected computer in their home or school), there are significant limits on the degree to which they are benefiting from online opportunities. Children and, indeed, adults, vary considerably in their resources and ability to access the range of online contents and services. Systems of selection, control and user protection are only unevenly understood or used. Many have a weak understanding of how contents are produced, disseminated, financed or regulated, undermining decisions regarding trustworthiness or authenticity. And opportunities to create and participate are taken up in part but are not always followed through except by the already dedicated. In short, there are clearly grounds to support efforts to enhance media literacy – whether via an educational curriculum directed at children, a media campaign to the general population, targeted interventions to disadvantaged or 'vulnerable' groups, or through some other means.

Many diverse initiatives are underway nationally and internationally, yet there are challenges here too. The 'knowledge gap' thesis means that initiatives directed at the population as a whole tend more effectively to reach the information rich than the information poor, so that the former sustain their relative advantage over the latter (Bonfadelli, 2002; Süss, 2001). Lower levels of media literacy are, further, associated with other forms of social exclusion and relative deprivation (Bradbrook *et al.*, 2008; Selwyn and Facer, 2007; Warschauer, 2003). Even when media literacy is increased, the persistence of a knowledge/behaviour gap (Azjen and Fishbein, 1980; Kunkel, 2001) means that critical media skills of interpretation and evaluation may not always be practised in real-life circumstances. Unfortunately, media literacy initiatives tend to be evaluated only insofar as they 'work' as resources or teaching materials, not whether they deliver outcomes that transfer to real life situations of internet use – whether enhanced participation, greater critical awareness, stronger 'cognitive defences' against harm, or richer creative depth in online activities.

Indeed, it has not been established that media literacy does work, despite the many confident claims made for it (John, 1999; Kunkel *et al.*, 2004). Assuming it will eventually be shown that media literacy initiatives have a positive effect, it may still be that, as children grow older and more media literate, they will encounter more subtle texts employing different or more complex persuasive tactics. Media literacy initiatives may even have a counter-intuitive effect – some theories of persuasion suggest that a sceptical approach results in greater not less persuasion, provided the person is motivated and interested in the message content and provided the arguments in the message are strong (Petty and Cacioppo, 1986). Livingstone and Helsper (2006) found that in the field of advertising to children, the evidence is consistent with the view that different processes of persuasion operate at different ages, precisely because literacy levels vary by age: thus children's media literacy may always be outpaced by the growing sophistication and complexity of the media with which they engage.

Thus far I have painted a glass-half-empty scenario; others might reach a more optimistic conclusion as, undoubtedly, the public is rapidly attaining new skills and enjoying new forms of expertise of which, a few years ago, they had no conception. My purpose in stressing the gap between great expectations and mundane realities is, first, to critique the hyperbole surrounding the notion of youthful expertise; second, thereby to establish the justification for expanding public efforts to enhance youthful media literacy; and, third, the main task of this chapter, to provoke a deeper analysis of the social, institutional and technological conditions that sustain or undermine media literacy.

Individual skills or social practices?

Definitions of literacy tend to frame it as an individual accomplishment. In some ways, it is – some people can or cannot read, some can or cannot find what they want online. Identifying just which competences explain variation in performance is a crucial question for educators and policymakers. In seeking to identify the individual skills that, taken together, constitute internet literacy, Hargittai (2007: 132) argues that users require knowledge of the following:

- Effective and safe ways of communicating with others
- Knowledge of how to contribute to group discussions and share content
- Knowledge about and use of tools
- Knowledge of what is available
- Ability to find content
- Efficiency in Web navigation
- Ability to assess source and message credibility
- Understanding of privacy issues
- Understanding of security issues
- Knowledge of where and how to seek assistance with questions
- Customization

Others might produce different lists, but this is a good start, encompassing access, analysis, evaluation and creative/participatory skills and thereby sketching out a feasible research and policy agenda. Empirical studies thus far, albeit mainly conducted on American university students, suggest that 'these eleven areas all pose both challenges and opportunities to users' (p.132). As we saw in earlier chapters, children and young people may be good at some and, even, better than adults on many, but one could hardly conclude that they 'know it all', leaving much for educators, industry and public policy-makers to do.

However, literacy can also be framed as a property of a society, instantiated through distinct social and cultural practices, and adding to the above psychological approach also a sociology and a politics of literacy:

> literacy is not and never has been a personal attribute or ideologically inert 'skill' simply to be 'acquired' by individual persons... It is ideologically and politically charged – it can be used as a means of social control or regulation, but also as a progressive weapon in the struggle for emancipation. (Hartley, 2002: 136)

Advocates of the social practices or 'new social literacies' approach (Snyder, 2007; Street, 1995) concede that literacy emerges as users rise to a series of everyday challenges – in the case of the internet, from the initial difficulties posed by hardware accessibility through to more complex interpretative and evaluative competences regarding the nature and value of online contents and services. But, they stress, users face these challenges not as isolated individuals but as members of a society within which the necessary financial, social and cultural resources are unequally distributed. The increasing attention is paid to the significant financial, social and cultural capital required to benefit from the internet (DiMaggio, Hargittai, Celeste and Shafer, 2004; Seiter, 2008), drawing especially on the work of Bourdieu (1984), poses a theoretical, empirical and political challenge to the individual skills model.

What the social literacies approach adds is a theoretical account of the relations between the cultural and economic capabilities of a society (Mansell, 2004) and the social contexts of technology use (Selwyn, 2004) as shaping the interpretative practices of engagement with digital texts. Taking issue with the individual stills view (as illustrated by the UK's communication regulator's claim 'media literacy is a personal attribute'; Ofcom, 2006b: 8), Buckingham asserts that,

> literacy is a phenomenon that is only realized in and through social practices of various kinds, and it therefore takes different forms in different social and cultural contexts. (2007b: 44)

For example, changes in pedagogic practice within educational institutions led to the gradual prioritization of visual over print literacy in the design of school textbooks. As Kress convincingly shows, half a century ago visual illustrations were used merely to break up lengthy sections of printed text; today the latter has been reduced to brief labels used to amplify the primary form of representation, the colourful image (whether photographs, diagrams, flow charts or other visual forms). As a result, 'the exponential expansion of the potentials of electronic technologies will entrench visual modes of communication as a rival to language in many domains of public life' (Kress, 1998: 55). Crucially, the reader's task is changed, in consequence, from reading in a linear fashion, from top to bottom and filling out the imagery for oneself, to reading nonlinearly, tracing paths from the centre to the periphery and filling out the narrative for oneself. But this is not simply a matter of individuals each learning new interpretative strategies, for a host of cultural norms, institutional processes and social expectations have accompanied this evolution in 'the textbook'. Together, these shape the discourses through which knowledge is constituted in particular times and places, in accordance with particular socio-political interests at stake.

The social literacies argument thus refocuses attention away from individual learning to encompass the institutions that establish value for particular learning outcomes. One form of institutional struggle is evident when employers deplore as 'trendy' or irrelevant the skills of contemporary school-leavers, calling instead for a return to 'traditional educational standards'. Seiter (2005) shows another form of struggle operating in a preschool setting when she reveals the micropractices by which teachers routinely construe children's knowledge of computer games as illegitimate in an educational context – for example, by disapproving of children's enthusiasm for popular media and, even, of their parents for permitting it. Thus Şnyder (2007) argues that literacy cannot be understood as 'a neutral technical skill'. Rather, it comprises a set of culturally regulated competences that specify not only what is known but also what is normatively valued, disapproved or transgressive.

From this perspective, Hargittai's list of skills above raises more questions than it answers – who is to say what is 'effective and safe', what constitutes a contribution to group discussions, or how to evaluate source and message credibility? The role of social and institutional practices in shaping the individual skills in her list, though often tacit, demands critical analysis. Yet, in support of the skills approach, I note that it is difficult to escape the language of skills: as academics, policymakers and ordinary people, we all adopt this language, routinely, in characterizing our own competence or struggle with the online environment. Further, we do generally expect an enhancement of individual skills to result from education, and many also hope that research will produce the reliable measures of skills necessary if public policy interventions designed to equalize skills can be evaluated and promoted.

Perhaps a compromise can be reached, one that draws on the social literacies approach to critique, challenge and contextualize the skills approach, while also drawing on the skills approach to measure, check and evaluate the claims of the social literacies approach. Such a convergent approach, ideally integrating media literacy and information literacy and understood at both societal and individual levels of analysis, has been adopted by UNESCO:

'Empowerment of people through information and media literacy is an important prerequisite for fostering equitable access to information and knowledge, and building inclusive knowledge societies. Information and media literacy enables people to interpret and make informed judgements as users of information and media, as well as to become skillful creators and producers of information and media messages in their own right.' (UNESCO, n.d.)

Reading the online world – a matter of design

Challenging the notion of literacy as an individual skill complicates not only the relation between individuals and the social but also the relation between the knowledge of the user and the design of the technological interface – as also illustrated by the textbook example from Kress (1998), above. Just as for print, 'readers' have been theorized not merely in terms of learning their ABC but also in terms of the complex interpretative relation between readers and texts (cf. theories of reader-response or reception aesthetics; Hohendahl, 1974; Iser, 1980; Suleiman and Crosman, 1980), so too can this be argued for 'users' of the internet.

Literacy, whatever the medium, concerns the hermeneutic dynamic at the interface of the interpreter and that which is interpreted. Put simply, literate readers require legible texts and, however skilled they may be, the more impenetrable, opaque or ill-designed the text, the more they will struggle. Central to the interpretability of texts (and I include here the notion of technology as text; Woolgar, 1996) is a host of considerations that includes institutional purposes and culture, organizational norms and structures and communicative design and intent (Yates and Orlikowski, 1992). The outcome is the discursive management of the interpreter – the 'model reader' (Eco, 1979) or 'implied reader' (Iser, 1980; extended to the implied audience in Livingstone, 1998a) that is designed into the very construction of the text or interface.

Applying insights from the text-reader metaphor to reveal the interpretative dynamics of users' engagement with the affordances of the online environment is producing a critical analysis of how, for example, websites enable, direct or impede particular interpretations by users (Burbules, 1998; Snyder, Angus and Sutherland-Smith, 2004). This in turn is opening up new questions of how people interpret, diverge from, resist, conform to or re-create meanings in the process of engaging with multiple forms of media texts and technologies (Fornäs, 2002; Jenkins, 2003; Livingstone, 2004). However, if such practices of engagement are conceived only in terms of competencies or skills as properties of the individual, then the ways in which texts themselves enable or impede creative, critical or even just usable interpretations become obscured.

To illustrate, consider the market shift from producing user-installed to plug-and-play peripherals. This transformed the task of installation from one to be managed skilfully (or not) by individual users to one to be built (fallibly or not) into the process of design and manufacture. Or, consider the distinction between information and advertising. On television, clear content demarcation as a matter of routine design has long been regulated by the state, enabling parents to teach their children 'advertising literacy' successfully; by the age of eight, children can distinguish these effectively, first by learning the conventions of design demarcation, later learning the differences in communicative intent (Kunkel *et al.*, 2004). But online, no such distinction is regulated or demarcated by familiar textual conventions; consequently, neither children nor their parents are able reliably to identify advertising or sponsorship online (Fielder, Gardner, Nairn and Pitt, 2007). Or, thirdly, consider how the symbolic cues by which people have traditionally judged credibility or trustworthiness (of a speaker, or a book) are rendered more complex or, worse, more obscure by the online interface: a blocked site that returns the same 'site not found' message as that obtained if the user mistypes the url; the 'link-popularity' metric embedded in search engines operation which teaches users that 'popularity equals credibility' (Machill, Neuberger and Schindler, 2003). As Lankes (2008: 104) observes:

> End users are becoming more responsible for making information determinations, but because they have fewer physical cues to work with, they are becoming more dependent on the information provided to them by others.

In short, critical scholars must ask not only whether people have or lack certain skills but also whether society has so constructed certain resources, or so positioned particular groups, as to facilitate, undermine or restrict the knowledge or opportunities available (see Turow and Tsui, 2008). Indeed, without a critical analysis of media institutions and of the social shaping of information texts and technologies, the force of any critique of new media uses will be turned onto the user. In other words, if uses of the internet are judged to be narrow, limited, harmful or unequal, on a skills-based view, the finger will be pointed at the user for being unskilled, incompetent, gullible or naive. On the other hand, if internet literacy includes recognition not only of the activities of the user but also the nature of the text they engage with, then the finger of blame can also be pointed at those who provide biased, incoherent, manipulative or inadequate (rather than lucid, eloquent and stimulating) texts (Livingstone, van Couvering and Thumim, 2008).

In the case of demarcating online advertising (and sponsorship, product placement and other forms of embedded marketing; Moore and Rideout, 2007), the task facing parents in teaching children advertising literacy is greater than for television. The same may be said for the task of teaching children to avoid, cope with or respond appropriately to online violent, hateful or sexual material, all of which are not only more abundant and more extreme on the internet but which are also less clearly labelled or segregated from other contents. Indeed, charging parents and teachers with the responsibility of ensuring that children are sufficiently literate to determine trustworthy or authoritative information online in a world where content providers are under no equivalent obligation to avoid misleading, exploitative or opaque strategies of content presentation and organization raises a crucial question – who, really, is responsible for limitations on children's media literacy?

The often problematic or suboptimal relation between users and design has emerged as a vital consideration over and again in the foregoing chapters, limiting children's learning online, their privacy protection and their participation in civic forums. For this reason, I have urged a hermeneutic account of the dynamic or transactional relation between what, in audiovisual and audience studies, was called 'active subjects' and 'polysemic texts' (Eco, 1979; Fiske, 1987; Hall, 1980) and what, in human-computer interaction and social shaping of technology studies, is called skilled (or unskilled) users and well-(or poorly) designed interfaces (Bijker, Hughes and Pinch, 1987; Isaacs and Walendowski, 2002).

In pointing not only to the nature of interface design but also to the practitioners, institutions and designers that produce them, it should be observed that the social practice critique of the individual skills model of media literacy has converged with the text-reader critique elaborated in this section. Let me illustrate how these matters of design shape and limit children's burgeoning media literacy by presenting two extended accounts from my observational work with children in front of the screen.

A pair of 10-year-old boys are playing a maths game on the computer in their after-school club. The task is to navigate a ship around a map of Scotland, calling at two ports on the way. This must be completed within some 90 moves, by entering the direction (in degrees) and the distance (in km) of each leg of the journey, which turns out to be hard to estimate. This particular pairing is of one very bright child, as the head teacher describes him, and one very stubborn child, as a teacher passing by confirms. This is a successful combination: with one boy's understanding and the other's determination, after nearly an hour of crashing a few times and playing around a bit and typing in rude words, they eventually succeed. They are rightly pleased with themselves, and have learned something about navigation, direction and distance. Next to them is a 10-year-old girl working on her own and far less successful. She crashes the boat several times in rapid succession and becomes frustrated. I find myself sitting down next to her and gently trying to help. I find she hasn't read the instructions and so has missed the point about the compass. Even when I point out the importance of this, she cannot manage this game, continuing to crash and, receiving no feedback either from the game itself or from her teacher, she gives up and plays a simpler game – a drawing programme – with which she slowly but happily makes a coloured rainbow. The teacher, understandably, was busy with a large class and had little time to help. But could the game itself have been better designed? This maths game represented an intolerant piece of software – one small mistake and the whole game is lost, no matter how near one is to succeeding and how much effort has been put in. And the error message when you crash the boat is always the same, whether this occurs after five minutes through a serious mistake or, frustratingly, after 30 minutes and a very minor mistake. Learning from one's mistakes seems positively impeded rather than enabled by such an 'educational' game and an entirely unnecessary tension was created by knowing that, even if the maths had been understood, a simple mistake made late on would crash the game entirely.

As a second example, recall Megan who, when aged eight, I observed diligently and accurately typing complex and personalized questions into Ask Jeeves, a search engine that could only respond to simple, standardized questions. Wanting to research the purchase of a hamster for her friend, Megan asks Jeeves, 'what breed of hamster is friendlier than russian hamsters?' Jeeves answers, 'how do I say a word in Russian?' and 'what is the alphabet in Russian?' Observing this frustrating encounter, shall the observer conclude that Megan lacks search skills, and should be better taught? Or should criticism focus on Jeeves instead? Megan asked an intelligent question of what she thought to be an intelligent interlocuter. But Jeeves is programmed to respond to key words, and he lamentably underestimates the intelligence of his young user. Perhaps eventually Jeeves will be better designed. But for the present, it is Megan who has to adjust. And being bright – witness her correct spelling of 'friendlier', Megan learns. I watch her give up on her complex questioning of Jeeves and reframe her questions in terms of everyday key words and 'tell me more about . . .' follow up questions. From a critical pedagogy point of view, Megan has accommodated to the system before her by intelligently learning to be less intelligent. More generally, I suggest that to the extent that online knowledge resources encourage 'right answer' learning, they support a model of learning that promotes answering questions rather than questioning answers (Quinn, 1997).

In conclusion, it seems that only rarely does the internet invite children to judge for themselves the truth or value of the information it offers them, nor do websites advise on the criteria by which such an evaluation might be reached. Rather, the design even of educational and participatory public sector sites encodes what Hall (1980) called the preferred reading – formats such as frequently asked questions, recently asked questions, top ten lists, fact of the week, our favourites – all asserting knowledge as factual and incontestable, all therefore discouraging critical literacy on the part of the user. For Joyce (1998: 167), this reproduces (rather than challenges) the linear hierarchies familiar from the era of print. The effect is to undermine the creative and participatory potential of the internet by imposing behind the scenes, often commercially led editorial decisions that collate, filter, prioritize and re-present the potential of the internet in terms of a series of pre-given menus, buttons, lists, hotspots and preferences (as in, 'other people bought this . . .', 'you went here before . . .', 'music of the day'). As a result, he suggests (with more than a nod to Adorno and Horkheimer, 1977), users experience:

> a constant hunger for newness without a taste for detail. The eye gets tired of watching passing patters and we settle into a commercial glaze. We are so used to thinking something new will come, and so tired of seeing only patterns, that we never really see or settle into the particularity of where we are. (Joyce, 1998: 167)

To the extent that lucidity and transparency is not built into the design of online content and services, the demands on parents and teachers to support children and young people's critical literacy are increased commensurately. Lankes suggests that,

> If society wants youth to be truly able to make credibility decisions in digital networks, then youth must understand the technical nature of the network itself – from the use of tools to the creation of tools. Simple use skills, such as browsing the Web, are insufficient to truly understand the role that tools play in the credibility of Internet-based information. (2008: 111)

But since, as we saw in chapter 3, only a minority of pupils are guided even minimally in effective web-searching skills, this is a demanding ambition. We should not confuse the ordinary competences of most children with the impressive but rare skills of the 'digirati' who have the resources to sustain, as Burbules (2006) advocates, a 'self-educating community' based on collaborative peer learning. For the former, rather than meet Lankes' high demands, most children (and adults) will simply turn to the trusted global brand that shows up in the top ten hits on a search, and ask few further, searching questions of their own.

Media literacy – a concept whose time has come

Though debates over media literacy are far from new, media literacy is increasingly occupying a prominent place on the policy agenda. Once a rather specialist issue for media practitioners and educators, though drawing on a longer, contested history of print literacy, media literacy is now a central issue for everyone concerned with people's – especially but not only children's – critical, participatory and creative engagement with all forms of media and communications. Particularly welcome and much needed is the importance accorded to 'new media literacies,' recognized well beyond the domains of entertainment and personal expression to encompass also educational outcomes, labour market competences and civic participation.

Ofcom, the UK's media and communications regulator, broke new ground when it gained, somewhat unwillingly, the legal duty to promote media literacy in the Communications Act 2003 – this in advance of any clear and consensual definition of media literacy. Mirroring the academic definitions noted earlier (especially that of Aufderheide, 1993), Ofcom now defines media literacy as 'the ability to access, understand and create messages in a variety of forms'. In practice, Ofcom tends to emphasize access and choice over creation, participation and critical evaluation, as might be expected from an economic regulator, and it tends to emphasize easily quantifiable measures of media literacy over the more ambitious benefits held out for it, as might be expected of a body that contracts out its research to market research organizations. Nonetheless, its strategy is proving fairly effective in mobilizing new levels of attention and resources in the UK.

Media literacy is also prominent on the European policy agenda, reflecting a widespread sense that today's technologically convergent, globalized market is increasingly difficult, perhaps impossible to regulate by individual states. As the European Commission's Information Society and Media Commissioner, Viviane Reding, said in December 2007:

> In a digital era, media literacy is crucial for achieving full and active citizenship . . . The ability to read and write – or traditional literacy – is

no longer sufficient in this day and age... Everyone (old and young) needs to get to grips with the new digital world in which we live. For this, continuous information and education is more important than regulation. (Europa, 2007)

As a result, diverse government, industry and civil society initiatives are working to advance these objectives across Europe. The European Commission (EC) has mapped trends and approaches to media literacy in Europe, observing that although 'still in the early stages ... Media literacy in Europe has become very dynamic' (The European Commission, 2007d). The Council of Europe, which represents many more European countries than those formally included in the European Union, published an 'Internet Literacy Handbook'.[2] UNESCO has published a Media Education Kit (January 2007) and is developing information literacy indicators for cross-national evaluations (UNESCO, n.d.). What is being promoted here? The European Commission defines media literacy as:

> the ability to access, analyse and evaluate the power of images, sounds and messages which we are now being confronted with on a daily basis and are an important part of our contemporary culture, as well as to communicate competently in media available on a personal basis. Media literacy relates to all media, including television and film, radio and recorded music, print media, the Internet and other new digital communication technologies.[3]

While seemingly comprehensive, it is noteworthy that this definition omits the crucial element of 'creating' messages, downplaying communication to a personal rather than, say, a civic matter. Yet content creation is not an optional extra: Article 13 of The UN Convention on the Rights of the Child states that 'The child shall have the right to freedom of expression; this right shall include freedom to seek, receive and impart information and ideas of all kinds, regardless of frontiers, either orally, in writing or in print, in the form of art, or through any other media of the child's choice.'[4]

Concerns with protection come to the fore in the definition set out by the key legal framework in this sector, the Audiovisual Media Services Directive (AVMS), approved by the European Commission in November 2007 as a revision of the Television Without Frontiers Directive:[5]

> Media literacy refers to skills, knowledge and understanding that allow consumers to use media effectively and safely. Media-literate people will be able to exercise informed choices, understand the nature of

content and services and take advantage of the full range of opportunities offered by new communications technologies. They will be better able to protect themselves and their families from harmful or offensive material.

In this definition, media literacy is wholly individualized. It prioritizes consumers and consumer choice over citizens and citizens' rights, and it prioritizes protection over empowerment and participation (see Livingstone and Lunt, 2007, for a wider analysis of these regulatory regime changes). Consider, by contrast, the broad definition offered by the European Charter for Media Literacy,[6] which identifies seven competences for media literate people, stating that they should be able to:

–   Use media technologies effectively to access, store, retrieve and share content to meet their individual and community needs and interests;
–   Gain access to, and make informed choices about, a wide range of media forms and content from different cultural and institutional sources;
–   Understand how and why media content is produced;
–   Analyse critically the techniques, languages and conventions used by the media, and the messages they convey;
–   Use media creatively to express and communicate ideas, information and opinions;
–   Identify, and avoid or challenge, media content and services that may be unsolicited, offensive or harmful;
–   Make effective use of media in the exercise of their democratic rights and civic responsibilities.[7]

This definition includes all four elements of access, analyse, evaluate and create, it emphasizes the social as well as the individual benefits, and the civic as well as the expressive dimension of 'create'; it also adds two further elements: exercising informed cultural choice and avoiding harm. This ambitious attempt to balance empowerment and protection is also evident in the Council of Europe's aim to:

give special encouragement to training for children in media literacy, enabling them to benefit from the positive aspects of the new communication services and avoid exposure to harmful content [and] support steps to promote, at all stages of education and as part of ongoing learning, media literacy which involves active and critical use of all the media, including electronic media.[8]

Paying attention to definitions matters especially because definitions are still in flux. Once a consensus is reached, the policy window will surely close and attention will move on to the challenges of implementation. Yet these policy deliberations tend to proceed with little explicit attention paid to the crucial question: what is media literacy for? Once the lists of skills can be checked off, for the majority of the population, what will have been gained? After all, being able to use the internet is of little value in and of itself; rather, its value lies in the opportunities that it opens up.

These have been more clearly articulated within public policy in relation to information than media literacy. As we saw in chapter 3, information and communication technology skills are now recognized 'as a third skill for life alongside literacy and numeracy.' Similarly, information literacy is considered 'a prerequisite for participating effectively in the Information Society', 'part of the basic human right of life long learning' (Information Literacy Meeting of Experts, 2003). And they are vital for social inclusion: as Warschauer puts it:

> the ability to access, adapt, and create new knowledge using new information and communication technology is critical to social inclusion in today's era. (2003: 9)

The public policy importance of media literacy has not been so wholeheartedly recognized. Buckingham (1998) argues that media education has never resolved the tension between a positive approach to education-as-democratization and a paternalist approach to education-as-discrimination (or cultural demarcation). Just this tension continues to shape contemporary discussions of new media literacies, with the vague term, 'empowerment', ambiguously open to both democratic and defensive or protectionist constructions. In short, while questions of access, analysis and creating content can be straightforwardly understood, the place of critique in media literacy is particularly contested.

Kellner and Share identify four distinct notions of critique in media literacy policies and programmes: first, the protectionist approach, with media literacy required to defend against harmful media contents; second, the approach of media arts educators, for whom social critique results from encouraging new spaces for self-expression from those whose voices are marginalised by society; third, the media literacy movement, which downplays ideological critique in order to persuade mainstream educators to include media literacy alongside print literacy in the curriculum; and fourth, the critical media literacy approach which emphasizes ideology critique and the politics of representation as part of 'a political project for democratic social change' (2007: 62). Arguably, all are needed by children and young people today. However, as with print literacy, public policy imperatives are often more directed towards developing a skilled work force to advance economic competitiveness than towards encouraging a critically engaged citizenry. Given some tension between these two goals, I advocate an ambitious definition of and agenda for media literacy so as to preclude the imperatives of the former imperilling the success of the latter.

Thus media literacy should address three central purposes. First, equality of opportunity in the knowledge economy: in a market economy increasingly based on information and communication networks, media and information-literate individuals contribute to a skilled, innovative and competitive work force, making equality of opportunity and an end to the digital divide a priority. Second, active participation in a democracy: in a democratic society, media and information-literate citizens gain informed opinions on matters of the day and are equipped to express their opinions individually and collectively in public, civic and political domains, thereby supporting a critical and inclusive public sphere. Third, the agenda of human rights and self-actualization: since a highly reflexive, heavily mediated symbolic environment informs and frames the choices, values and knowledge that give meaning to everyday life, media and information literacy contributes to the lifelong learning, cultural expression and personal fulfilment that is the right of every individual in a civilised society. In short, just as debates over print literacy have been, at heart, debates over the manner, inclusiveness and purposes of public participation in society, this is equally important for media and information literacies today.

Media literacy and media regulation

In addition to debates over the definition and implementation of media literacy, media literacy is increasingly positioned as part of a dual strategy of citizen (or consumer) empowerment and private sector liberalization and deregulation. In other words, in policy terms, not only does the promotion of media literacy support economic competitiveness by increasing consumer knowledge and awareness but in a convergent media market characterized by strong pressures towards market liberalization and industry de-regulation (or, at least, self-regulation), it also legitimates the reduction of top-down regulation of firms (Livingstone, Lunt and Miller, 2007). Put simply, if children can discern good content from bad, use media to express themselves, and protect themselves from mediated harm, then the burden of regulation on the industry and government can be lifted.

Given the difficulties of regulating the internet nationally and internationally, calls to the individual to 'take responsibility' for their activities online can be heard on all sides, notwithstanding that this is to expect individuals to manage a medium which tends to escape the powers of government. Indeed, unsurprisingly, the promotion of media literacy is rising up the agenda of regulators and policymakers: the hope is that media literacy can deliver individual protection against potential media harm in a manner that legitimates transferring the burden of responsibility from the industry or state to the individual. As Tessa Jowell said tellingly when Secretary of State for Culture, Media and Sport, 'if people can take greater personal responsibility for what they watch and listen to, that will in itself lessen the need for regulatory intervention' (*Daily Mail*, 21/1/04: 23). The UK's communication regulator, Ofcom, followed suit:

> Media literacy is increasingly becoming a fundamental component of European and national regulatory policy agendas in the communications sector, especially as developments in the creation and distribution of content challenge current approaches to regulation in this area. (2006b: 1)

When twenty-first-century European policy advocates a shift from state to industry self-regulation, encompassing codes of conduct, content management systems (rating, filtering and access controls), what is less clearly stated is the position being allocated to the individual in this emerging regulatory regime. They too, it seems, must be self-regulating. As Ofcom (2006b: 4) acknowledges, 'these schemes rely for their effectiveness on consumers actively taking measures to protect themselves and their families.' Or as The UK's Department for Culture, Media and Sport puts it in its 'media literacy statement' (DCMS, 2001):

> A future system of regulation ... will involve a greater degree of self regulation on the part of viewers and parents ... there will be an expectation that people will themselves take greater responsibility for their use of these media. That expectation will be a fair one only if people have the tools (both material and intellectual) with which to make those informed choices. That demands a greater degree of media literacy and critical viewing skills than is apparent at present.

Implicit in these statements is the possibility that individuals will not so self-regulate, failing in their duty as good consumers. Hence the tacit threat in the above statement – provided the government (or industry) have supplied the tools to support media literacy, if people fail to use them, the costs too must be borne by them. Although what these costs might be, and whether it is fair that individuals should bear them, remain unclear, it does seem that familiar limitations on the public's media literacy, especially that of parents and children, gain a new significance. These now represent not only a limit on what people can do online and on the likely competitiveness of a national work force but they also place a brake on the deregulation of the media and communication industries. As research shows, media literacy, like any other form of knowledge, is uneven in its implementation, unequal in its adoption by those of differential social status, inconsistently translated into everyday practices, under-resourced in its delivery and, in any case, unproven as a strategy for protection.

Lest observers of contemporary policymaker's interest in media literacy doubt the above analysis, I would point to the recent prominence of all forms of literacy, not just media literacy, on the policy agenda: a search of the UK press for the first two months of 2007 revealed references to print literacy, financial literacy, scientific literacy, ICT/computer literacy, emotional literacy, spatial literacy, Gaelic literacy, political literacy, technical literacy, film literacy, media literacy, Catalan literacy and theological literacy; a little further searching added ethical literacy, environmental literacy, information literacy, health literacy and critical literacy (Livingstone, 2008a). In several of these instances, a parallel analysis linking individual responsibility with market liberalization is evident. For example, the first mention of health literacy in the UK was in 1994, when the Conservative Secretary of State for Health 'emphasized the importance of encouraging greater health literacy in the population' when reviewing to ration health care in the face of rapidly rising costs (*Guardian* 9/11/04, Society Section, p. 7). Two contrasting reports illustrate what's at stake. One report, in the (Conservative) *Financial Times,* illustrated how the notion of health literacy was mobilized to reduce business costs by promoting 'empowerment' among consumers.[9] Taking a very different approach, a report in the Communist Party's *The Morning Star,* used the same term to point out how inequalities in knowledge resources compound existing inequalities in financial resources.[10]

The critical observer is posed with something of a dilemma. One would surely wish to support the individual empowerment and investment in education and awareness that the promotion of media literacy promises. Yet at the same time, these moves must be recognized as part of a broader shift from direct control by government to governance through 'action at a distance' – regulating parents, for example, through discursively established norms of 'good parenting' and 'appropriate children's conduct' (Oswell, 1999: 52; see also Rose, 1990). One consequence is that this creates a skills burden which parents and children neither can nor should bear alone, and this burden falls unequally, as we have seen in previous chapters and as theorized by Beck (1986/2005) in his thesis of the individualization of risk.

Arguably, the way forward is, first, to resist minimal definitions of media literacy, as the more readily the demands on media literacy are met, the more readily is a neo-liberal deregulatory policy for the media and communication sector legitimated. Second, I would argue for an ambitious definition of media literacy in the service of an empowered public (i.e. not just for 'consumers'), for only then can the social, economic, cultural and political ambitions held out for the so-called 'internet generation' be met. And third, since children and young people will, inevitably, fail to match up to an ambitious specification for media literacy (while they will more easily 'pass' a minimal threshold), one must call for the equitable provision of resources to ensure the social, institutional and technological conditions required to sustain a media literate population.[11]

Conclusions

This chapter has sought to place a structured framework around the emerging evidence for children and young people's strengths and weaknesses in relation to four key dimensions of media literacy – access, analysis, evaluation and creation. This has produced a balanced picture neither of cyber-experts nor of cyber-idiots which, in turn, bodes well for further initiatives to encourage, celebrate and support children's effective use of the internet while not legitimating any withdrawal of the public resources that such initiatives will require. However, conceptually, the limitations of this largely individualistic, skill-based model have become apparent: it can offer little explanation for the specific pattern of strengths and weaknesses observed; it cannot explain why media literacy is on the agenda now; and it cannot encompass the relations between individual competence, societal capability and interface design.

To be sure, new media literacies can be conceptualized at several levels, from the basic (using the pen, the remote control, the mouse) through to intermediate skills (finding a book in the library, identifying a reliable webpage, contributing to a forum) and then to advanced competences (creativity, specialized learning, participation and critique). But so too, I have argued, can the social structures that underpin these competences. Thus at the micro level, new media literacies are enabled by and dependent on the design of interfaces, software, technical provision. At a more macro level, literacy requires institutional supports (education and other learning environments, accountable gate-keeping practices, well-resourced curricula and information resources). Most ambitiously, literacy requires societal encouragement for online and offline democratic engagement, open and responsive civic organizations, an innovative and flexible economy, and a rich and diverse culture.

In short, media literacy does not simply concern the ability to use the electronic programme guide for digital television or to complete one's income tax return online. Nor are its benefits restricted to becoming an informed consumer or getting a better paid job. Crucially, once a more ambitious definition of media literacy is endorsed, the limits on its achievement become apparent. I have argued that pointing the finger of blame at the individual's failure of intelligence, motivation or effort is unhelpful in practical terms and dubious in political terms, for this is to neglect the degree to which interfaces are poorly designed or necessary resources and contexts for action are lacking. Nor is it evident that internet literacy can be promoted by simply training individuals in a specific skill set, especially in a fast-developing and sophisticated media and information environment, where emergent cultural forms are unfamiliar, knowledge representations are not yet conventionalized, textual cues to interpretation are inconsistent or confusing, and a popular critique of the online offer is undeveloped. Thus we must accommodate an analysis of the institutions and businesses that design, disseminate and interface with users and the variable socioeconomic circumstances that shape the conditions by which users come to learn about or gain access to or support in using digital technologies.

In future research and policy, a satisfactory analysis of media or internet literacy will require – similar to that long been argued for theories of print literacy – recognition of the historically and culturally conditioned relationship among three processes, no one of which is sufficient alone: (i) the symbolic and material (textual, technological) representation of knowledge, culture and values – especially as these are now being rewritten for a convergent, multimodal, globalizing digital age; (ii) the distribution of socially situated practices across a (stratified) population – in which socio-economic processes that actively sustain symbolic distinctions and privilege in everyday contexts are thoroughly integrated into an account of online literacy skills and practices; and (iii) the institutional (state, regulatory, educational) management of the power that skilled access to knowledge brings to the 'literate' – including a critical analysis of the public and private sector interests at stake in promoting or undermining mass media literacy.

In conclusion, young people's internet literacy does not yet match the headline image of the intrepid pioneer. This is not because young people lack imagination or initiative but because the institutions that manage their internet access and use are constraining or unsupportive – anxious parents, uncertain teachers, busy politicians, profit-oriented content providers. In recent years, popular online activities have one by one become fraught with difficulties for young people – chat rooms and social networking sites are closed down because of the risk of paedophiles, music downloading has resulted in legal actions for copyright infringement, educational institutions are increasingly instituting plagiarism procedures, and so forth. Thus in practice, the internet is not quite as welcoming a place for young people as popular rhetoric would have one believe and in this respect, of course, it is not so different from offline social institutions concerned with young people (Qvortrup, 1995). Yet the promise of media literacy remains. For, insofar as the internet mediates and reconfigures pathways to learning, communicating and participating in society, media literacy must be central to any strategy to reposition the media user – from passive to active, from recipient to participant, from consumer to citizen.

8

Balancing Online Opportunities and Risks

Online opportunities and risks – a balancing act

> Self-actualization is understood in terms of a balance between opportunity and risk. (Giddens, 1991: 78)

Governments in many countries around the world are actively promoting internet infrastructure, diffusion and use in the workplace, schools, communities and households. In Europe, this is specified in the eEurope 2005 Action Plan, designed to facilitate Europe's Information Society through a series of targets and milestones through to 2010 to maximize opportunities for European business, public sector and citizens, including initiatives for e-learning, e-inclusion and media and information literacies (The European Commission, 2007b).[1] Within this framework, policymakers are deliberating on how best to facilitate the opportunities for children and young people online (i.e. positive regulation) while also reducing or managing the associated risks (i.e. negative regulation). The growing consensus is that this is a task for multiple stakeholders, requiring not only financial investment but also adaptation to rapid change, apportioning responsibility flexibly among relevant parties, applying local or national experience to confront a global phenomenon, learning new forms of expertise and, last, acknowledging some limits to regulatory power.

Some tension exists between these positive and negative goals, evident in phrases such as 'a secure information society' or a 'safer' (but not 'safe') internet, as well as in the competing objectives of the European Commission's Audiovisual Media Services Directive (2007a), designed to further liberalize markets, and its

Recommendation on the Protection of Minors and Human Dignity.[2] It seems that policy is particularly contested when children's safety is framed as a brake on commercial freedoms or when the enforced regulation of firms can be rolled back only by increasing expectations for the public's (especially parents' and children's) media literacy. Yet although 'children' often figure in policy discourses as an impediment to market developments, their activities also drive the market – witness their eager adoption of mobile and social networking services, their music consumption, the fast-growing e-learning sector, and so forth. Indeed, insofar as young people do the unexpected in initiating new trends, which are subsequently capitalized upon by the corporate sector – examples include 'grunge' fashion, rap music, text messaging – their creativity is significant in influencing both youth culture (within the 'lifeworld', in Habermas' terms)[3] and the economy (part of the 'system world'; Habermas, 1981/7).

In many ways children and young people are motivated and knowledgeable regarding the internet, more so than many adults. However, my focus in this last chapter concerns adult responsibilities, institutional and individual, for children and the internet. To be sure, children relish the peer-to-peer opportunities the internet affords, and once they have gained access, they can provide for themselves and each other the responsiveness, criticism, humour, feedback, openness and networking that so often eludes content designed for children by adults. Yet since it is society's ambition to use the internet to open up new routes to informal and formal education, employment skills, health and therapeutic advice, civic participation and much more, we must go beyond children's self-generated enthusiasms, also ensuring fairness of opportunity, ambitious expectations for participation and literacies and reasonable expectations of safety. Simply celebrating young people's enterprise and enthusiasm while failing to support, respond to or engage with the range and potential of their online activities risks will, in turn, fail to bring to fruition the great expectations society holds not only for the internet but, more significantly, for children and young people.

Maximizing opportunities – a matter of children's rights

The child/media relationship is an entry point into the wide and multifaceted world of children and their rights – to education, freedom of expression, play, identity, health, dignity and self-respect, protection ... in every aspect of child rights, in every element of the life of a child, the relationship between children and the media plays a role. (The Oslo Challenge, UNICEF, 1999)

Issued on the tenth anniversary of the UN Convention on the Rights of the Child (United Nations, 1989), this statement challenged nations to take forward the media and communication element of the convention, now ratified by nearly all countries, though not the USA. These elements include children's rights to express their views freely in all matters affecting them (Art. 12), freedom of expression (i.e. to seek, receive and impart information of all kinds) through any medium of the child's choice (Art. 13), freedom of association and peaceful assembly (Art. 15), protection of privacy (Art. 16) and to mass media that disseminate information and material of social and cultural benefit to the child, with particular regard to the linguistic needs of minority/indigenous groups and to protection from material injurious to the child's well-being (Art. 17).

Within the broader framework of the UN's Universal Declaration of Human Rights, Hamelink collects under the heading of 'communication rights' all those rights that relate to information and communication, arguing that:

> Communication is a fundamental social process and the foundation of all social organization ... Communication rights are based on a vision of the free flow of information and ideas which is interactive, egalitarian and non-discriminatory and driven by human needs, rather than commercial or political interests. These rights represent people's claim to freedom, inclusiveness, diversity and participation in the communication process. (2003: 1)[4]

A communication rights framework deliberately counters the assumption that media and communications remain somehow incidental, rather than increasingly central to the infrastructure of a networked, global information society. Even if the mass media were, historically, just an optional part of the leisure sphere, this could not be argued of today's mediated communication, for without this, many forms of political, social, cultural and educational participation are now all but impossible. For children, as for adults, a rights framework can point the way ahead without pitting adult (or commercial) freedoms against child protection. Instead, it is more productive to balance children's freedoms against children's protection, for both are encompassed by a children's rights framework. Moreover, freedoms should be understood positively as well as negatively (Berlin, 1958), for 'empowerment' is not just free access to any information, but rather means enabling children to do what they can do best (Quinn, 1997) – a matter of positive regulation as well as limiting restrictions. In this chapter, I examine the emerging balance between children's online opportunities and risks, in order to critically evaluate present initiatives and identify prospects for future ones.

The internationally endorsed though rarely enacted Children's Television Charter, formulated in 1995 (Livingstone, 2007b: 164), proposes a series of principles for television that can, by substitution of terms, be readily extended to the internet, indeed to media generally. Rephrasing these principles instead as a Children's Internet Charter reads as follows:

(1)   Children should have online contents and services of high quality which are made specifically for them, and which do not exploit them. In addition to entertaining, these should allow children to develop physically, mentally and socially to their fullest potential;

(2)   Children should hear, see and express themselves, their culture, their languages and their life experiences, through online contents and services which affirm their sense of self, community and place;

(3)   Children's online contents and services should promote an awareness and appreciation of other cultures in parallel with the child's own cultural background;

(4)   Children's online contents and services should be wide-ranging in genre and content, but should not include gratuitous scenes of violence and sex;

(5)   Children's online contents and services should be accessible when and where children are available to engage, and/or distributed via other widely accessible media or technologies;

(6)   Sufficient funds must be made available to make these online contents and services to the highest possible standards;

(7)   Governments, production, distribution and funding organizations should recognize both the importance and vulnerability of indigenous online contents and services, and take steps to support and protect it.

In short, a Children's Internet Charter would assert, in advancement of children's communication rights, as part of their human rights, the seven principles of quality, affirmation, diversity, protection, inclusion, support and cultural heritage. Addressing the whole population, not just children, the Council of Europe made just such a call in November 2007:

> The Council of Europe advances the concept of public service value of the Internet, understood as people's significant reliance on the Internet as an essential tool for their everyday activities (communication,

information, knowledge, commercial transactions) and the resulting legitimate expectation that Internet services are accessible and affordable, secure, reliable and ongoing.'[5]

What could this mean in practice for the positive provision of online opportunities for children?

Improving provision – some practical challenges

In chapter 6, I presented a classification of online risks from the EU Kids Online network. The network also proposed an equivalent classification of online opportunities (Hasebrink, Livingstone and Haddon, 2009). The assumption is that a good way to avoid the negative dimensions of internet use is to direct children towards the positive, thereby avoiding harm and empowering children in terms of learning, participation, creativity and identity. Thus a strategy for risk reduction can be combined with the advancement of children's communication rights.

Again, by distinguishing among content opportunities which position the child as recipient, contact opportunities which position the child as participant, and conduct opportunities which position the child as actor, and crossing this with the values or motivations from online providers, twelve cells result (see table below). These scope the array of online opportunities for children, with examples of provision in each cell.

	Learning	**Participation**	**Creativity**	**Identity**
Content – *child as recipient*	In/formal e-learning resources	Civic global or local resources	Diverse arts/ leisure resources	Lifestyle resources, health advice
Contact – *child as participant*	Online tutoring, educational games/tests	Invited interaction with civic sites	Multiplayer games, creative production	Social networking, personal advice
Conduct – *child as actor*	Self-initiated/ collaborative Learning	Concrete forms of civic engagement	User-generated content creation	Peer forums for expression of identity

With this as a tool, it becomes possible to audit current provision to determine the extent to which it meets children's needs, interests and desires. Such an audit poses no easy task, however. Many different contents and services online, whether or not designed specifically for children, may meet these expectations. Children, like adults, are difficult to predict in what may benefit them, for much depends on the interpretative contexts of use, and these are as heterogeneous for children as for any other population. Thus we may place few *a priori* limits on just what online contents present opportunities for young people. At the same time, much online content is, one can easily recognize, uninspiring, banal, superficial or worse – misleading, hostile or exploitative. So, what kinds of content are genuinely in children's interests? When we – parents, educators – look over children's shoulders, what do we hope to see on the screen? What do children themselves hope to find and want there to be more of? And of this, what should be provided by the public sector or encouraged in the private sector?

Notwithstanding the clamour of hyperbolic claims from content providers, both public and private, the answers are not obvious. It is too often taken for granted that 'the internet' is a good thing, with little more said about what, why or for whom. To be sure, we might agree in highly abstract terms: the internet can be used to facilitate children's education, participation, communication and expression. We might also agree on 'good' sites – Children's BBC Online is a fantastic resource[6], Google Earth has excited adults and children alike with its accessible vision of everywhere and anywhere, YouTube has enabled amateur youthful creativity like nothing we've seen before. But between the abstractions and the examples, everything remains contested.

Having asked many people – experts, policymakers and parents – to identify some great online resources for children, I was surprised to find them scratch their heads in puzzlement. One problem is that much depends on the child – children can and often do make much of apparently uninspiring content, just as they can fail to get any benefit from great content. Another problem is that much of what children enjoy occasions a certain degree of adult ambivalence or even disapproval. This includes such sites as Neopets, Habbo Hotel, Club Penguin, YouTube, MySpace, LiveJournal, Limewire, Wikipedia, multiplayer games (e.g. Simtropolis, World of Warcraft), sports-related sites, television/film-related sites[7] and so forth, all of which may or may not offer genuine benefit.

Of course, my colleagues did have some excellent suggestions, although not everyone will agree on 'good' (or 'bad') examples.[8] These include, somewhat *ad hoc*, a French children's search engine, *Takatrouver*, designed for 7–12 year olds with pre-moderated content,[9] a Greek portal for children by the Hellenic World Foundation, which provides virtual reality projects (e.g. the life and history of the olive tree, the chronicle of an excavation, the ancient Agora),[10] a Slovenian storytelling site for young children that mixes educational content with games and entertaining activities, including a publicly funded children's portal,[11] an Australian resource for indigenous populations, *Digital Songlines*, to support 'the collection, education and sharing of Indigenous cultural heritage knowledge' in forms accessible to children and others,[12] and a Californian project, *Digital Underground Storytelling for Youth*, which supports local communities and educators in children's creation of digital stories to express and explore their identities using multimedia tools.[13] One might also point to the often substantial sites produced by European public service broadcasters[14] or other public bodies (e.g. NASA), to civic sites for youth participation,[15] to children's helplines and advice services,[16] and to online fanzines.[17]

These resources vary considerably in scale and scope, and they are far more plentiful in some countries (or languages) than others. Small-scale projects are often dependent on one or a handful of enthusiastic individuals, reliant on temporary project funding and so difficult to sustain and update. They often struggle to reach a wide audience, for both promotion and navigation are difficult to achieve in an age of information abundance. Those sites adequately resourced by government organizations must meet official objectives and so may be seen by children as irrelevant and dull, as we saw in chapter 5. The best resourced are the commercial sites, able to employ high production values, sophisticated games, updated content, desirable freebies and expensive downloads. Yet even these must decide between targeting a general population (e.g. Google Images, Wikipedia) or, if specifically dedicated to (and safe for) children, they must employ a commercial strategy equally specifically directed towards children, with advertising/ sponsorship prominent in the online offer and with little reason to reach out to the digitally or socially disadvantaged. As safety considerations make interactivity particularly expensive (e.g. requiring pre-moderated content and age-tailored interactive services), sites for younger children especially are often non-interactive (Kenix, 2007) or, to pay their way, highly commercialized (Grimes and Shade, 2005).

There are few publicly reported evaluations of even public sector sites and resources,[18] so we know little about whether, why and which children use them, or whether they prefer them to other online or, indeed, offline resources. Wartella and Jennings (2000: 40, Box 1) propose a set of evaluation criteria which usefully echo several of the seven principles of children's communication rights noted earlier. They frame these in terms of questions 'to consider when creating new media content for children', as I paraphrase below:

- Diversity (and affirmation) – is the content relevant to diverse social groups, by ethnicity, gender or class, and does it either reinforce stereotypes or provide positive role models of marginalized groups?

- Accessibility (or inclusion and support) – is the technology and content accessible to children with different resources and needs, so as to be universally available?
- Interactivity – does the content use the interactive potential of the medium to best effect, enabling children to be creative, including creating a community of young people, and providing real choices with real consequences?
- Education – does the content offer age-appropriate, context-appropriate educational, informational or cultural opportunities? (cf. cultural heritage also)
- Value (or quality) – is it fun, engaging to children, so they will want to explore further? 'Does the content have something to tell, instead of just something to sell?'
- Artistry – is the content of high quality, with excellence in design elements, and an understandable, easily navigable interface?
- Safety (or protection) – are the links carefully chosen, the requirements for disclosing personal information appropriately managed, and does the content include inappropriate violent or sexual content?

An audit of online opportunities for children and young people would surely be timely, evaluating them using criteria such as these in order systematically to map current provision and, taking into account the needs of children by country, gender, age and so forth, to identify key gaps and prioritize the development of future online resources. As the principles of inclusion and support require, such an audit should include a determination of which bodies are, and should be, tasked with the responsibility for providing and funding children's online resources, a promotional strategy for ensuring that children, parents and teachers become aware of positive provision for children online, both current and future, and a network of providers, with a forum in which to meet/communicate, to ensure that experiences are shared, lessons learned and best practice disseminated.

No doubt much of this could and will be provided by the private sector. But the Council of Europe's call for public provision is significant, particularly since of all the various social influences on children (notably, family, school and community), media and communications provision stands out as being left largely to the private sector. To be sure, there are many ways, often genuinely motivated by children's welfare, in which state, third sector and commercial providers are creating stimulating online resources for children. There are also valiant efforts by those in corporate social responsibility to take on 'public' concerns, especially regarding children's safety and privacy online.

Nonetheless, there are two problems with such a strategy. First, insofar as the interests and anxieties of young people all become grist to the mill of mass consumerism, what results is both the further commercialization of childhood and the further individualization of society – promoted by sophisticated marketing that simultaneously addresses ever more diverse taste categories or esoteric niche audiences while being ever more global in its reach (Bauman, 2001). Peer culture, and youth culture, become indistinguishable from consumer culture, transacted and disseminated on a global stage; and few find it possible or desirable to stand outside (France, 2007). Second, following Habermas' (1981/7) critique of the inter-penetration of the lifeworld by the system world, we can see that even public sector provision is becoming increasingly dominated by administrative and market logics (Clarke, Newman and Smith, 2007). Recall the difficulties faced by civic website producers (discussed in chapter 5) in encouraging youthful participation when they are evaluated in terms of reaching promoting brands, target audiences, maximizing take-up, achieving stakeholder 'ownership' and so forth rather than, or as well as, in terms of changes in policy or practice resulting from young people's agency.

Neither commercial nor public provision framed within a commercialized environment necessarily serves the best interests of children, not least because ultimately, neither is evaluated primarily in those terms. The concept of the 'sticky' site, popular among both commercial and many public websites, is symptomatic. Such sites are designed to contain the user, to keep them on the site, enticing them with commercially themed contents, working rhetorically to make it unattractive or difficult to leave. Each site offers a 'whole community', 'all' one could ever want to know, all the services one might want 'in one place'. Such content design implicitly but firmly undermines the optimistic rhetoric of the internet as a democratic and open space of links and connections, freedom and choice.

If this optimism is to move significantly beyond the rhetorical, a rather different public strategy is required, one that not only complements private with publicly provided opportunities, but one that balances opportunities and risks. If children and young people are to engage freely and creatively with the online environment, issues of trust, legibility, safety and accountability must also be addressed. These are, I have argued, partly a matter of internet literacy (searching, navigation, evaluation) and partly a matter of design (ensuring that indicators of reliability and quality are clearly marked). Also crucial are answers to such questions as, if youth has its say online, who will reply, who will take action, and will youth be informed of the consequences?

Only if the internet appears a trustworthy and accountable route to participation, embodying principles of respect and connecting structures of decisionmaking – for which the internet could be admirably suited if only it was so used – might it contribute to the great expectations held out for children. Trust and accountability also depend on effectively balancing opportunities and risks. To give a simple but telling example, in the UK Children Go Online civic participation interviews, I watched two teenage girls respond to the invitation of Mykindaplace[19] which announced, 'we want your real life stories' (Livingstone, 2007a). Mia noted, 'you can send a photo as well', but Natasha's rejection of this opportunity was immediate – 'why would you send in a photo, that's just stupid. . . . I'd give out my name, I wouldn't give out my phone number or my address or anything like that.' In short, if it isn't reasonably safe, it isn't trustworthy, and children will not participate.

Minimizing risks through top-down approaches

In 2007, the European Commission (2007c) held a public consultation on 'Safer Internet and Online Technologies for Children', with another on mobile communication in 2008. In the UK, the Prime Minister Gordon Brown set up 'The Byron Review on Children and New Technology' to examine the risks to children's safety and well-being from exposure to potentially harmful or inappropriate material on the internet and in video games, closely followed by a similar review by the House of Commons' Culture, Media and Sport Committee (2008). With the Byron Review's (2008) recommendation to establish a UK Council for Child Internet Safety, it appears that the notion that Britain 'won't regulate the internet' – stated confidently by the government (along with others) until recently – is fast fading. With a parallel call to the Obama administration for a United States Council of Internet Safety,[20] it seems that the struggle is on between advocates of state regulation versus self-regulation. Everyone's favourite solution – media literacy – is suddenly a phrase on many lips, raising the question of whether society can enable media-savvy kids to cope with online pornography, grooming and race hate when they encounter it or whether it should restrict their online opportunities in order to spare them the risks.

Risk reduction strategies fall into several categories, some of which are primarily top-down in orientation. The first and most obvious is legislation – requiring technology and content providers to alter the conditions that give rise to risk, and empowering law enforcement agencies to act against those who pose a risk of harm to children online. In most if not all countries, the emphasis has been on applying or extending existing legislative frameworks to online contents, services and activities. As understanding has grown of specific risks associated with the internet, some new laws have resulted (e.g. laws on online grooming), some new organizational structures have been established (e.g. linking law enforcement, technological expertise and public engagement), and various forms of legal guidance and case law have been developed to interpret existing regulation in relation to new circumstances (essentially, applying 'offline' law to the online domain). This approach is, in many respects, effective (for critical discussion, see Akdeniz, 2001; Finkelhor, 2008; Flint, 2000; Heins, 2001; Oswell, 1999).

There are three difficulties that give rise to concern, however. One is that laws take a long time to be introduced or changed (and hasty laws are often repented). Another is that, for the most part, laws are established and enforced nationally, creating challenges in regulating an international phenomenon such as the internet. The last is that legislative solutions are generally sought only for high-risk circumstances, for necessarily their effect is to constrain freedoms by making certain actions illegal.[21] Distributing photographs of child abuse is internationally recognized as illegal. That grooming a child online in order to abuse them sexually is unacceptable is also uncontroversial, though fewer countries have made this illegal. But many other activities accepted as likely to be harmful to children are not illegal and are unlikely to be made so. Examples include peer-to-peer bullying, websites promoting anorexia or self-harm, making adult, even extreme or violent, pornography accessible to children, games based on racial hatred, and peer-to-peer or user-generated content. For the diversity of risks that are potentially harmful but not illegal, alternative risk reduction strategies are required.

A second strategy is not to seek to alter the online offer but rather to alter people's approach to it. In the short term, this strategy encompasses a range of awareness raising activities, variously undertaken by the industry, governments, educators and NGOs.[22] Typically following the model of public health or similar campaigns (road safety, for example; see Criddle, 2006, for the extension of this analogy to the 'information superhighway'), awareness raising activities include the production of safety guidance materials, delivered via schools, the mass media or other means so as to reach as wide or as targeted a population as required. While many young people are reasonably responsive to safety guidance, considerable efforts are still required here. The cross-national Mediappro project concluded:

> In France, the young people were aware of a wide range of risks, and expressed sensible, cautious attitudes, which the French study attributed to extensive and successful public information campaigns and

teacher training. Similarly, in Estonia, respondents were well aware of a wide variety of risks, from communicating with strangers to the dangers of Internet shopping. By contrast, the Polish study found evidence that young people were sometimes too trusting of websites and in need of education to evaluate risk; while the Greek study found generally low awareness of risk. (2006: 14)

Other research supports this variable picture.[23] Specifically targeting vulnerable or at-risk groups is especially difficult because interventions or campaigns designed for the general public are least likely to reach them, thus failing the very groups – the so-called 'hard to reach' – that may need them the most. Also demanding is the considerable expense involved in sustaining campaigns to update public awareness as risks evolve. The 'free' route to raising awareness is by gaining media attention to messages of high risk (such as, 'Do you know who your child is talking to online?'), but this tends to amplify media panics and raise parental anxieties.[24] More important perhaps is the question of the limits of awareness-raising initiatives – what happens to those not reached by the safety messages, or those who forget them when they are needed, or even those who wilfully ignore 'good' advice? Dovetailing multiple strategies so that one steps in where another leaves off requires more coordination among stakeholders than exists at present.

If extended over the longer term, awareness raising falls under the heading of media literacy, discussed in chapter 7, for a more skilled and aware population will surely engage with the internet more wisely and carefully, knowing both how to avoid or manage the risks and how to cope with them if encountered. For educators and critical scholars, safety awareness is usually accepted as one small part of media literacy, the broader focus remaining on positive empowerment, freedom of expression and critical engagement. However, for regulators and governments, safety awareness often figures more prominently in programmatic statements regarding media literacy, seemingly downplaying the value of more ambitious specifications. The result, too often, is the undue narrowing of the concept of media literacy, conceived negatively as a means of self-protection from harmful aspects of the new media and information environment, this tending to displace its importance for empowering users. Whether understood positively or negatively, the advantages of media literacy – to enable people's skills, choice and independence are considerable. But so too are the disadvantages. As argued in chapter 7, and as for many other forms of public knowledge, media literacy is uneven in its implementation, unequal in its adoption by those of differential social status, inconsistently translated into everyday practices, under-resourced in its delivery and, in any case, largely unproven as a strategy for protection.

Minimizing risks – a matter of parental mediation

A third strategy, involving more collaboration among individuals, industry and the state, positions parents as the key means of protecting (and empowering) children online. The role of industry here lies mainly in the provision of 'parental control' tools, usually filtering and monitoring software, while the role of the state lies in encouraging both industry and parents to play their part. This strategy is, for legal and moral reasons, often the first to be called upon; it is uncontentious that parents are responsible for their children. It is also, for rhetorical and pragmatic reasons, often the last to be called upon; if and when all else fails, one can surely expect parents to provide the backstop or final safety net for children.

Perhaps tellingly, although there is rather little research on how parents help their children towards online opportunities, there is a fair amount on whether and how they help their children avoid or manage online risks. The task before them has been scoped in chapter 6 – in brief, and notwithstanding the many difficulties of measurement, research suggests that the majority of young internet users encounter risks online one way or another, that half have encountered some form of problematic content or contact, and that for a fifth, this has been experienced as upsetting or disturbing. For most parents, the starting point is their familiar role in mediating or regulating children's use of media, especially television (Nathanson and Yang, 2003; Valkenburg, Krcmar, Peeters and Marseille, 1999), though also video games (Nikken and Jansz, 2007). Generally, several strategies are employed, including active mediation (talking about the media content), restrictive mediation (setting rules and restrictions) and co-use (sharing the experience).

For the internet, an altered set of strategies are used, partly because technical forms of mediation (filtering and monitoring) are available for the internet especially (Livingstone and Helsper, 2008). More importantly, for the internet it appears that the strategies of talking about content and sharing the experience of use are indistinguishable (i.e. they are coterminous), resulting in what we called 'active co-use' – parents and children go online together and talk about the experience as they do so. Further, possibly because of parental concerns regarding risk, it seems that the internet occasions a specific set of parental restrictions concerning interactivity – parents may ban their child's use of chat, instant messaging, games or downloading (these being, of course, precisely the activities that children enjoy most).[25]

Overall, despite the array of parental control tools available, it appears that parents prefer social practices such as active co-use over technical restrictions and monitoring practices. One reason concerns parental expertise – the UK Children Go Online survey found only 15 per cent of parents said they were good at installing a filter, and 23 per cent were unsure if one was installed on their child's computer or not (Livingstone and Bober, 2006). This may explain why the Eurobarometer survey (2006) found that, especially in countries new to the internet, there is what we might term a 'regulation gap', with more parental rules for television than for the internet. Since parents do not consider television more risky than the internet, their greater mediation of television may be taken to reveal their willingness to mediate in general, while their lower mediation of the internet may be taken to reveal their insufficient competence (or confidence) in managing their children's activities online (Hasebrink, Livingstone, and Haddon, 2009). This is confirmed by the 2008 survey, showing that parents who do not themselves use the internet are more worried about risks to their children online and they also do less to mediate their children's internet use (Eurobarometer, 2008).

Also problematic for efforts to encourage parental mediation is that parents prefer to trust their children than to check up on them – as Ofcom (2008a: 43) observes when noting the use of parent control tools in the UK has declined, rather than increased, in recent years,[26] though they use them more than most other parents in Europe (Eurobarometer, 2008). Thus filtering software may appear authoritarian, while the secrecy associated with monitoring software offends against the principles of the democratic family. Consider the naming of *Cybersnoop*, for example, or *Cybersitter*, which 'works by secretly monitoring all computer activity' so as to close the door on 'unrestricted cybersmut' (including that stored in parents' files). Similarly, *Childsafe* allows parents to 'see exactly what your children have been viewing online . . . [and to] monitor chat room sessions, instant messaging, email.'[27] In focus groups, young people reacted strongly against such practices.

> My parents don't ask me 'ooh, what did you go on?' because I wouldn't like it if I came from school, came home, and they search my pockets. I'd say 'what are you doing – that's personal.' What if I had something I didn't want them to see? Just like I wouldn't search my mum's bedroom. (Amir, aged 15)

> You just like don't want your mum spying on you and knowing everything about you. (Nina, aged 17)

> Because you want your independence, really, you don't want your mum looking over your shoulder checking what you're doing all the time. (Steve, aged 17)

To maintain their privacy, young people engage in a variety of tactics for evading parental or school monitoring and controls – hiding folders, minimizing windows when parents are looking over their shoulder, and so on (Livingstone, 2006).[28] The UK Children Go Online survey found that two thirds (63%) of 12–19-year-old home users have taken some action to hide their online activities from their parents, and 69 per cent of 9–17-year-old daily and weekly users say they mind their parents restricting or monitoring their internet use. Such activities clearly threaten to undermine parental control, albeit for understandable reasons. Thus although many parents practise one or more mediating strategies, it is less clear that these are effective.

Crucially, the project found that the expectation that increasing mediation would reduce risks was not generally supported, except insofar as parental restriction of online communication was associated with a significant reduction in the range of online risks encountered by 12–17 year olds (Livingstone and Helsper, 2008). The preferred strategy of active co-use, in short, is not (yet) evidently associated with reduced experience of online risk, and though 'old-fashioned' restrictions seem to work better, this is only by reducing children's online freedoms.[29] The challenge of identifying effective and constructive strategies of parental mediation remains. For without these, children will be reluctant to share their experiences with parents for fear of losing freedoms. Hazel (aged 17) is very aware of the costs of letting parents know what children are up to:

> my dad ... doesn't let me go on the internet very often because we had an incident one day where my sister ... she was on MSN, and someone sent her something through. And it was actually like – it was like porn. So my dad saw it, and he was like very angry, so he doesn't let us use MSN now.

Reassuringly, however, 61 per cent of children say they would tell their parent(s) if something on the internet made them uncomfortable, this including 71 per cent of 9–11 year olds (– by implication, a fair minority would not). In practice, though, of those who had received pornographic junk mail, however, only 8 per cent told either a parent or a teacher. Yet some degree of mutual understanding between parents and children is important. Research consistently shows that parents and children give different accounts of domestic rules and practices regarding the internet.

The UK Children Go Online survey found that 81 per cent of parents claim to show an interest in what their child does online, 63 per cent keeping an eye on the screen, 57 per cent offering some help, 50 per cent staying in the same room, 41 per cent checking the computer later, 32 per cent sitting with the child, and 25 per cent checking their email. But the equivalent reports from children are much lower – only 25 per cent say their parents ask what they are doing online, only 17 per cent keep an eye on the screen, 32 per cent offer help, 22 per cent stay in the same room, 9 per cent check the computer later and so on (Livingstone and Bober, 2006). Since 31 per cent agree that a parent sits with them when they go online, these discrepancies need not reveal that either side is not telling the truth; rather that – as with the discrepancy in reporting the incidence of risks (reported in chapter 6) – parents and children may not recognize what the other does. It is noteworthy that, in our further analysis, it seemed that only when children recognized a parental rule was it associated with reduced risk behaviour (Livingstone and Helsper, 2008), a finding confirmed by others (Cottrell, Branstetter, Cottrell, Rishel and Stanton, 2007; Fleming, Greentree, Cocotti-Muller, Elias and Morrison, 2006).

While parents and children continue to develop their expertise online as well as their negotiation practices at home, possibly catching up with – but perhaps always lagging behind – developments in online risk, it is noteworthy that these activities are no longer merely a private matter. They now have public policy implications. Put simply, the more effectively parents keep their children safe online, the less emphasis need be placed on regulating (or self-regulating) the activities of the industry and other institutions (e.g. schools).[30] Conversely, the more parents struggle – in terms of time, effort, cost, technical competence and parenting skills – the more reliance society must place on the efforts of other stakeholders. As Oswell (1998) observes, in considering the division of responsibilities among government, industry and parents, it is important to think carefully about the nature of the task and the consistency and effectiveness of approach being expected of parents when striking this difficult balance.

Minimizing risks through safety by design

A fourth and final strategy is that of safety by design. This concept is well established in the domains of traffic/transport safety, health and safety regulations and planning for built environments. This strategy incorporates risk and safety considerations into the design stage of innovation and manufacture, seeking to anticipate the risks likely to be encountered by users. It recognizes that parents, children and, indeed, those whose activities might harm children, intentionally or otherwise, all operate within an environment that has been substantially planned for, paid for, designed and institutionally supported in particular ways, according to particular understandings of anticipated use and in order to further certain interests. In short, this environment could be arranged otherwise, and if the alternatives would reduce risk in a proportionate manner – in other words, without inappropriate cost to the freedoms or opportunities of children or adults – this could and should be implemented.

Countering the assumption that technology itself determines the nature of any artefact, Mansell and Silverstone argue for a recognition and critical analysis of the degrees of freedom available to both technology producers and users in selecting one design over another. As they note, there is

> a politics deeply embedded not just within the institutions that design and distribute technologies and services, but within the technology itself, as software products and information networks both prescribe and proscribe, configuring suppliers and users, containing and constraining behaviour, and embodying in their algorithms and their gateways both the normative and the seductive (1996: 213)

Theoretically, these degrees of freedom exist at the level of institutions, innovation practices, funding decisions, promotional strategies and, in the design of the technologies themselves. Thus one must consider not only the technological artefact but also everything that surrounds it, including marketing, policies and social expectations. Together, these have the effect of prioritizing or favouring some activities on the part of users and impeding or even precluding others.

A useful analogy here is that of road safety (Criddle, 2006), evident for example in notions such as the European Computer Driving Licence[31] or surfing proficiency test (Livingstone, 2001). This points not only to the importance of learning to navigate 'cyberspace' as safely as the offline environment but also to the importance of the design and planning of that space. In short, we teach children to cross roads safely (and adults to drive safely) only in an environment in which roads have been designed with safety in mind – they have traffic lights, width restrictions, road bumps, marked crossing points, and so forth.

This design is both physical and social – the many rules of the road are known, accepted and enforced. It is taken for granted, especially in the minds of parents or schools who teach safety to young children, that children should be taught both how to take care of themselves and about the social rules by which they may expect others to act; they are also taught what to do, how to complain, report or get help if something goes wrong. As I argued in relation to media or internet literacy, safety depends on both the user and their environment. To be sure, every child should be taught how to cross the road, but we do this in a managed environment, even placing 'lollipop ladies' (or 'crossing guards') outside schools; we don't teach them to cross a four-lane highway or an unlit road at night or a road on which the cars have no vehicle testing, insurance or drink/drive laws. Further, if the roads are unregulated and badly designed, or if drivers drive badly, it is hardly a simple failing or lack of skill of the individual child if they are knocked down.

To extend the road safety analogy, think of the wider context of town planning. Town planners ensure that children's playgrounds do not open onto major roads, that sex shops are not sited next to schools, that commercial areas are treated differently from residential ones. It is within this wider context that we teach children when to be wary of strangers or to deal with traffic and when they can play freely. Only thus can the safety awareness task be rendered feasible. Note, however, that achieving such a balance between regulation and education in relation to the physical environment is not widely regarded as restricting adult freedoms or as trading the free market against child protection – largely, perhaps, because the planning system offline has evolved over generations and so its principles and practices are accepted, embedded in everyday 'common sense'. Online, this is being attempted in a matter of a decade or two and, it seems, the charge of censorship is ever-present.

But introducing planning into an environment is not simply a matter of banning this or that but rather one of managing the conditions of accessibility. A common criticism of such efforts online is that, for example, many boys and some girls always had soft-core pornography under their beds, and that since such 'risks' have always existed, this provides no justification for online restrictions. But online, the top shelf material is a click or two from the next step – extreme material that was really hard to find thirty years ago and that many children didn't know existed. Similarly, thirty years ago an anorexic teenager was doubtless as unhappy as today, but a supportive network of other anorexics swapping tips on how to hide dieting and vomiting from parents was much harder to come by. For legal material, setting aside the questionable legality of permitting adult content to be accessible to children, at issue is not the wholesale elimination of such material but rather that of setting conditions by which one is unlikely to find it accidentally, and making it hard to find even if a child seeks it out deliberately.

Over the past decade or so, the management of these conditions of accessibility – 'rules of the road' or 'planning' regulations – is unfolding online, complementing the efforts of awareness raising and media educators to teach children to navigate the internet safely and effectively. Examples of online 'traffic safety' include provision of filtering preferences, specification of child-friendly default settings, age verification systems, content rating and labelling, design standards (e.g. for filtering software), opt-in/opt-out points (e.g. for 'adult' content), and so on. As each policy is developed, so too it must be researched to ensure the match with anticipated user behaviour. It must also be evaluated for its effectiveness – not only in usability but also in risk reduction outcomes and, equally important, in terms of any trade-off in restricting freedoms. Then it must be translated into guidance for users, both institutional and individual, for internet literacy depends on a 'legible' environment, with rules and conventions understood by the users.

Practically speaking, then, safety by design encompasses a range of initiatives, often self-regulatory and industry led, or resulting from cooperation among multiple stakeholders. In the UK, the Home Secretary's Task Force for Child Protection on the Internet, now transmuted into the UK Council for Child Internet Safety and, recently, called for from the Obama government also in the USA by the Family Online Safety Institute[32], is a good example (Home Office Police, n.d.). Set up in March 2001 following a report by the Internet Crime Forum (2000), this has produced widely implemented guidance – both in the UK and emulated elsewhere – regarding safety messages, searching, moderation of chat rooms and instant messaging, reporting of abuse, and social networking services, much of it later implemented also on a European and international level (e.g. see Safer Social Networking Principles for the EU, 2009). The UK's Child Exploitation and Online Protection Centre explicitly champions a policy of encouraging safety by design, as part of its broader remit to protect potential and actual child victims of online abuse (CEOP, 2008). Further instances could be cited, including regulations concerning the collection of personal data from children, care regarding defaults on privacy settings, provision of moderation services, warning pages before pay-for pornography, child-friendly advice on sites where this may be needed, report abuse buttons in chat rooms, and so forth.

In practical terms, the pace of change sets tough demands. As Balkam (2008: 4) observes, 'as we catch up with and provide solutions to technologies and content that could prove harmful to kids, new devices, new strange meeting places spring up and thwart our earlier efforts'. There are political dangers here also. Esler (2005) stresses the dangers of embedding social choices (and prejudices) into filtering technology, arguing that restricting children's access to the range of information online will result in a narrowing of their world, centring it on normative values and commercial culture. Many bodies, rightly, fight the cause of keeping the internet free of regulatory interference for reasons of political freedom, of whom McChesney (2000) and Lessig (1999) are among the best known advocates. Yet in claiming that in these debates 'the idea of 'freedom' presides as a stirring but deeply deceptive first principle', Corner argues that:

The deceptiveness follows largely from the way in which 'media freedom' is routinely invoked to indicate a desirable absence of constraint on the media industries themselves rather than to indicate the desirable conditions for members of a democratic public to access a range of information and to encounter and express a range of opinions. (2004: 893)

I reference this discussion not under the earlier heading of legislative solutions but rather under that of safety by design, in order deliberately to sidestep the debate over freedom of expression or censorship and instead to focus on the access conditions by which children may encounter (or themselves produce) potentially harmful material (Millwood Hargrave and Livingstone, 2009).

Two final points are worth noting. First, the internet marks a significant difference from the world of print, in which content regulations have been both attacked and defended for centuries (Winston, 1996), and from which many of our expectations regarding freedom of expression derive – television, after all, has always been both regulated and restricted. Yet not only has print also been subject to some degree of national regulation through the law, something difficult to apply to so international a medium as the internet content, but its principles of distribution and access are very different. The internet, unlike the print market, is not organized into mainstream and specialist outlets – a simple online search may bring 'specialist' content to anyone, intentionally or otherwise. Further, institutional practices have long managed the conditions of access even within the law. Libraries do not generally subscribe to pornographic magazines or neo-Nazi information or pro-anorexia content, and nor is there a call for them to do so on the grounds of free speech (Banks, 2003). Introducing the internet into a library, school or home demands decisions not about what to include – as for books or television – but rather, decisions about what to exclude: this too comes with increased choice. As Rose notes, these are the consequences of a societal shift in which the state,

does not seek to govern through 'society', but through the regulated choices of individual citizens, now construed as subjects of choices and aspirations to self-actualization and self-fulfilment (1996: 41)

Second, there is something else to be learned from the planning analogy. Offline, to the extent that planning regulations are contested, which of course they are, there is recourse to an independent, transparent and public process of management and arbitration, including published codes of practice and a clear appeals process, whereby competing interests are fought out. Online, many initiatives – other than legislative approaches that demarcate the legal from the illegal – are self-regulatory. This may work well and be widely accepted, but it may not. It must be a concern that hitherto these self-regulatory initiatives have been largely unaccountable, with few if any public evaluations or independent reports on rates of compliance. Even though large companies invest in 'customer care' procedures, it remains the case that public information regarding their complaint handling, filtering decisions or moderation processes, for instance, is rarely available. In the UK, the Byron Review (2008) points the way beyond road safety towards town planning by establishing a UK Council for Child Internet Safety. Thus a degree of independent evaluation, transparency of process, and right of appeal should now be incorporated into risk reduction strategies. Possibly, as a government-run body to oversee the self-regulatory activities of the private sector, the Council will be as unpopular as planning departments, but equally, for those who live everyday in the environment that results, it may soon become a familiar and valued part of the regulatory regime.

Looking ahead

What is a good or proper childhood? (James and James, 2008: 3)

Children are growing up in an immersive media culture that has become a constant and pervasive presence in their lives (Montgomery, 2007: 212).

In characterizing 'European childhoods', James and James observe that the question of a 'good childhood' is being discussed widely among governments, policymakers, academics and the public (e.g. The Children's Society, 2006; UNICEF, 2007). The importance of the internet to those same childhoods must be clearly recognized, as Montgomery (speaking for the USA and elsewhere) suggests when she characterizes them as 'Generation Digital'. Compared with previous media, the internet both extends and intensifies the media experience, bringing the very best and very worst of society to children while simultaneously disintermediating parents. Not only are children often significantly more expert online than their parents, but the internet also offers children more subject positions, not just recipient of mass-produced content but also player, searcher, communicator, content creator, victim and, on occasion, perpetrator. However, contrary to media hype, the pace of technological change is far from straightforward and it interacts in complex ways with social practices, both institutional and individual. To be sure, some aspects of the media and communication environment change very fast – such as the rise of texting or social networking as new forms of communication. Others change more slowly than expected – the fragmentation of the mass audience, the shift from broadcasting to the internet, the move from desktop to mobile internet.

In this book, my starting point was that the very multiplicity of contextualizing processes undermines the popular account of the impact of technology on society, including on childhood. In relation to each of learning, communication, identity, participation and risk, it has been vital to ground an account of internet use in the historical, cultural, economic and political contexts of children's lives. And these contexts, in turn, are shaped by societal structures of family, education, commerce, state. But I have also sought not to position the internet as a neutral medium – for it enters into these relations of action and structure in particular ways, with particular effects, this mainly because we have designed it that way. Perhaps most crucial, I have sought not to position children as the passive recipients of these many and multilayered influences, for they are agents – though not the sole agents, nor necessarily the most powerful or expert – in the production and reproduction of the opportunities and risks that surround them. In writing this book, I found the figure below helpful (Livingstone, 2005c), and so I reproduce it here to illustrate this position.

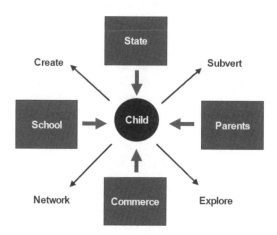

Source: Livingstone, S. (2005c). Opportunities and constraints framing children and young people's internet use. In M. Consalvo and C. Haythornthwaite (eds), *Internet Research Annual* (Vol. 4, pp. 59–75). Oxford: Peter Lang. Reproduced with permission.

In order to understand these shifting relations of structure and agency (Giddens, 1984) and thereby to inform unfolding policy deliberations as society seeks ways to balance online opportunities and risks for children and young people, social scientists are conducting new research, critically reviewing the evidence base, advising inquiries, responding to consultations and debating with each other. In so doing, they face some methodological challenges – clearly it is unethical to test the consequences of exposing children to harmful contents and, perhaps, even to track the activities of children online, and it is expensive to examine or measure the effects of exposure or online activities longitudinally; the result is some significant gaps in the evidence base. They also face some political challenges. Traditionally advocates of freedom of expression rather than in favour of content regulation, even the most libertarian researcher confesses to private concerns faced with some of the truly grim content to be found online – from beheadings and rape to pro-suicide sites and child-abuse networks. Also, while often inclined to argue for the media-savvy child, the alignment this occasions with the neo-liberal media industry, and the consequent undermining of public policy investment, also poses some dilemmas. In terms of policy effectiveness, the scholar's careful conclusions – 'it depends on the context', 'different children react in different ways', 'the findings are indicative but not conclusive' – play out poorly in a fast-paced and hotly contested policy process.

Eschewing the moral panics and problem-oriented approaches that have characterized youth studies, France (2007: 164) calls for a 'new' public social science, with 'a critical role to play' in shaping public debates. Somewhat in parallel, Wellman (2004: 124) welcomes the end of the first 'age of internet studies' which he labels as 'punditry rides rampant', an optimistic celebration of the transformative potential of the internet during the mid 1990s, peppered with dystopian prognostications from the sceptics. Wellman argues that we are now also moving beyond the second age, which had turned to a more serious engagement with evidence in seeking to document users and uses of the internet. As Wellman and Haythornthwaite put it, this was to study the internet 'as it descends from the firmament and becomes embedded in everyday life' (2002: 4). The hope is that the third age – the present – will make the move 'from documentation to analysis' (Wellman, 2004: 27), a move that must – notwithstanding the preferences of policymakers – necessarily prioritize provisional and contingent claims in 'work which seeks to analyse 'newness' through comparison between the old and the new, in their social and cultural contexts' (Jankowski, Jones, Samarajiva and Silverstone, 1999: 6).

The gist of my present analysis is that, for most children and young people, the internet is not yet used to its full potential. As an information medium, the internet has rapidly become central in children's lives, and as a communication medium, it represents a significant addition to the existing means of communication available to them. In a plethora of ways, children and young people are taking steps towards deepening and diversifying their internet use, many of them gaining in sophistication, motivation and skills as they do so. But many are not yet taking up the potential of the internet: children and young people lack some key skills, they also worry about the risks, and many of them visit only a few sites or fail to upload and maintain personal websites, in effect treating the internet more as a ready-made source of entertainment or information than as an opportunity for critical engagement, creative content production or active participation.

Too often, it seems that societal decisions downplay children's rights to participate fully in their communities. As societies, we invest in roads and cars rather than cycle paths. We are building multiplex cinemas on what were once children's playing fields. Such decisions affect their offline opportunities, but how will we invest in their online opportunities? Commercially, the investment is considerable. The lively and creative interests of children and young people are increasingly the target of a vast, commercial leisure industry devoted to the sophisticated targeting of youth. This is resourceful in the cross-promotion of media and consumer goods on and offline and it is alert to the possible exploitation of counter-normative tastes or interests as these evolve among youth; it also reflexively capitalizes on the same child-centred discourses of children's rights, empowerment and identity that cultural critics use to oppose the commodification of childhood and youth. Thus the market benefits considerably from teenagers' desire to have the latest product, to try the newest service, to seek out the niche media that make them both 'individual' and 'cool' (Kenway and Bullen, 2008; Wasko, 2008). Children are not only bombarded with advertising and marketing for the latest commodity but, arguably, as a new and profitable market, they have been themselves commodified, sold to marketers and advertisers as 'tweenies', 'kids' and 'teens' (Seiter, 1993; Smythe, 1981). To be sure they creatively appropriate the commercial offer but, in turn, the market watches closely and learns, reappropriating peer practices and preferences to further perfect its approach to children and young people (Ito, 2008; Jenkins, 2003). The public sector appears both reluctant to counter what has been called 'the commercialization of childhood', especially online, and to plan for positive alternatives.[33]

But now that we live in a ubiquitous and complex media and communication environment, it is timely to recognize that this environment contributes significantly to shaping our identities, our culture and learning, our opportunities in relation to others and thus the conditions for participation in society. No one can live outside it, no child wants to. In this book I have not argued that children should spend more or less time with the internet. Rather, I have argued that, looked at from a range of perspectives, when they do go online, it should be – however defined – to their benefit. Children always have been, and always will be, motivated to play, learn, explore, create, share, subvert and take risks. However, the environment in which they do so, online as offline is, in many ways, beyond their control. And thus the responsibility for shaping children's opportunity structures, and the risks they encounter, remains with the society they live in.

Appendix

The empirical material discussed in this book draws on a series of original research projects conducted between 1995 and 2007. I summarize below these projects' main methods and research samples. Complementing this work with individual children and parents, these projects also included interviews with teachers and information technology coordinators, and observations of children in computer classes, after-school clubs and cybercafés, as noted below.

Research ethics

Throughout this book, all children's names have been changed to pseudonyms to preserve their anonymity. Household socioeconomic status (SES) is categorized according to standard UK market research categories – AB (professional middle class), C1 (lower middle class), C2 (skilled working class) and DE (semi/unskilled working class).

All interviews were recorded and transcribed before coding. Each project was conducted according to clear guidelines regarding research ethics in order to protect the interests and identities of the children with whom we worked. Children were all asked for their written consent to participate in the research, and for children under the age of 16 years old (or, for some projects, under 18 years old), written parental consent was sought in addition. Further details of any research methods, sample details or ethical procedures can be provided by the author upon request.

UK Children Go Online

As director of the ESRC-funded research project 'UK Children Go Online' (UKCGO), I conducted a thorough investigation, integrating qualitative and quantitative methods, of 9–19 year olds' use of the internet between 2003 and 2005 (see http://www.lse. ac.uk/collections/children-go-online/ for project details, interview schedules, the survey questionnaire, and a statement on research ethics). This project provides much of the empirical material on which I draw throughout this book. In all phases of the research I and my colleagues, first Magdalena Bober and then Ellen Helsper, worked with children from diverse backgrounds in terms of socio-economic status, ethnicity, family status and geographic region. It addressed four aims: (i) access, inequalities and the digital divide, (ii) undesirable forms of content and contact, (iii) education, informal learning and literacy, and (iv) communication, identity and participation.

The project included paired interviews with parents and children (conducted separately), in-home observations of children in front of the computer screen, focus group discussions and paired interviews in schools, a week-long discussion on a password-protected message board hosted by the project (convened twice), and a major national in-home face-to-face survey in spring 2004 of 1,511 children and young people aged 9–19 years old, with self-completion question-naires from 906 of their parents. In design and execution, the project followed a child-centred approach, regarding children as active, moti-vated and imaginative, though not necessarily always knowledgeable or sophisticated agents, who contribute to shaping the meanings and consequences of the 'new' through the lens of their established social practices (Corsaro, 1997; Graue and Walsh, 1998; Livingstone, and Lemish, 2001; Lobe, Livingstone and Haddon, 2007; Mahon, Glendinning, Clarke and Craig, 1996).

Focus group interviews
Fourteen group interviews of around one hour were held with mostly same-sex groups of approximately four children each (a total of 55 children) in 2003. For the most part, each school provided a group of girls and a group of boys from the same class, apart from school D which provided two groups of boys and two groups of girls. The teachers were asked to select the children at random (every fourth or fifth girl or boy from the register). Main findings are reported in Livingstone and Bober (2003).

School type	Size	Location	Social grade	Achievement	Age	Number interviewed
Primary	97	Hertfordshire (rural)	Mixed	Above average	10–11	8
Secondary	369	Derbyshire (town/rural)	Middle class	Above average	12–13	8
Secondary	928	London (city)	Working class	Above average	14–16	8
Secondary	1,148	Essex (town)	Mixed	Above average	13 14–15	14
Post-16	2,010	Essex (town)	Middle class	Slightly above average	16–17	10
Post-16	2,911	Greater Manchester (city)	Working class	Below average	17–19	7

Note: Information about schools was taken from the most recent OfSTED (Office of Education) inspection report and the school website. Ability levels were determined according to how the school had performed in relation to National Average Performance levels cited in the 2002 school league tables.

Paired interviews focused on civic participation

In 2004, the project specifically focused on civic participation, conducting five in-depth semi-structured interviews (one to two hours each) with those responsible for youth websites, conducted at the respondent's place of work. Those interviewed represented the following organizations (and websites): Department for Education and Skills (www.need2know.co.uk), Epal – Greater Manchester Connexions (two producers interviewed together; www.epal.tv), Childnet Academy (www.childnetacademy.org), BBC Children's Online (www.bbc.co.uk/cbbc and /cbeebies) and BBC Teens (www.bbc.co.uk/teens).

Second, nine paired depth interviews were conducted in secondary schools with twelve girls and five boys aged 14–15 years old. These lasted approximately one hour and took place in front of a computer connected to the internet. Using a detailed open-ended interview schedule, the teens were shown several youth-oriented public sector websites selected from a varied list (including Connexions' Epal, BBC Teens, Need2know, Young.gov, Dubit, UK Youth Parliament, Talk to Frank, Mykindaplace, TheSite.org, Children's Express, and Rock the Vote), and asked to navigate, select and discuss the content together, with prompting where needed from the interviewer. The main findings – discussed in chapter 5 – are reported in Livingstone (2007a).

Schools	Participant pairs interviewed	
Oxfordshire (children from mixed backgrounds, achieving results above national average)	Natasha, 15 (f)	Mia, 14 (f)
	Chloe, 15 (f)	Georgia, 14 (f)
	Samantha, 15 (f)	Zhen Juan, 14 (f)
London (mainly working class children, achieving results above national average)	Tabia, 15 (f)	Faseeha, 15 (f)
	Sally, 14 (f)	Zara, 14 (f)
	Luke, 15 (m)	Mumtaz, 15 (m)
Yorkshire (mainly working class children, achieving results below national average)	Ethan, 14 (m)	Kanita, 15 (f)
	Molly, 14 (f)	(No show)
	Joe, 14 (m)	Bailey, 14 (m)

The UK Children Go Online survey
This national survey was conducted through an in-home, 40 minute, face-to-face, computer-assisted interview with children and young people aged 9–19, using random location sampling across the UK. In random location sampling, interviewers are given little choice in the selection of respondents, and respondents are drawn from a small set of homogenous streets selected with probability proportional to the population after stratification by their postcode characteristics and region. Quotas are set in terms of characteristics known to have a bearing on individuals' probabilities of being at home and so available for interview, and strict rules are given which govern the distribution, spacing and timing of interviews.

Following the design and piloting of the survey questionnaire by the research team, the fieldwork was carried out by a reputable market research company (BMRB International). This was conducted via multimedia computer-assisted personal interviewing with children, together with a paper questionnaire completed by one parent of each of the 9–17 year olds, in spring 2004. In total, 1,511 interviews with 9–19 year olds were completed. Further, 1,077 parents of those aged 9–17 agreed to complete a questionnaire of which 920 paper questionnaires were received and 906 were usable. Percentages have been weighted to data from BMRB's Target Group Index and Youth surveys. The weighting efficiency was 91 per cent and the effective sample size was 1,375. The children's and parents' surveys are available at www.eprints.lse.ac.uk. Main findings are reported in Livingstone and Bober (2004b; 2005).

Demographics	Subgroup sample sizes			
Age	9–11 years (N = 380)	12–15 years (N = 605)	16–17 years (N = 274)	18–19 years (N = 251)
Gender	Boys (N = 669)	Girls (N = 842)		
Socioeconomic Status (SES)	AB (N = 264)	C1 (N = 418)	C2 (N = 407)	DE (N = 422)
Region	England (N = 1,228)	Wales (N = 69)	Scotland (N = 166)	Northern Ireland (N = 48)
Ethnicity	White (N = 1,336)	Non-white (N = 171)		

Note: The frequencies in this table are based on unweighted data.

Young People, New Media

The UK Children Go Online project built on two earlier projects, conducted with Moira Bovill. The first, 'Young People, New Media' (1995–1999), resulted in a book that critically examined the implications of the changing array of new and old media in children and young people's lives by combining a national survey with qualitative interviews and observations in homes and schools (Livingstone, 2002).

This was also part of a pan-European project that compared children's uses of media in twelve countries, entitled 'Children and Their Changing Media Environment' (Livingstone and Bovill, 2001b). Although this study was conducted when the internet was only just on the horizon for most children, a comparison across projects reveals both continuities as well as changes in children's media environments in the past decade.

Families and the Internet

The next project, 'Families and the Internet' (1999–2001), involved an in-depth study of thirty families as they went online at the turn of the century, marking their struggles and pleasures as they appropriated the internet into their homes and daily lives. I especially draw on this material in the discussion in chapter 2 of families going online (the three cases – Megan, Anisah and Ted), and when considering dilemmas of privacy in chapter 4 (Livingstone, 2006; Livingstone and Bovill, 2001a).

Between 1999 and 2001, 30 families were recruited, each with a child between 8 to 16 who uses the internet at home at least once a fortnight. The families were selected to represent a spread of social grades

(11 AB, 11 C1, 8 C2DE), ethnic origin, family type (nuclear, single parent) and geographic location (urban, suburban, rural) across the South East of England. The sample contained 16 boys and 14 girls, of whom 11 were of primary school age and 19 of secondary school age. A reputable market research company conducted the recruitment. The author and members of the research team conducted four visits of around two hours, over a period of several months, resulting in 114 interviews with the child and at least one parent together with a series of periods of structured and unstructured observation of the child's internet use. Through these visits, time was spent informally sitting with children while they went online, observing their decisions about what to do and how it turned out, as well as the nature of the domestic context. Each family received £90 as a recruitment incentive and contribution to phone costs. Findings are reported in Livingstone and Bovill (2001a).

As part of the UK Children Go Online project, nine of these families were revisited in summer 2003 or 2004. Again, the research team conducted separate interviews with one parent and the child before

Family	Age	Gender	Area	Location	Social grade	Family type
Ted	18	Male	Town	Surrey	B – Middle class	Couple, single child
Anisah	15	Female	City	London	C2 – Skilled working class	Couple, one older brother and sister
Megan	12	Female	Suburb	Essex	C1 – Lower middle class	Couple, one older brother
Jane	18	Female	Rural	Surrey	C1 – Lower middle class	Couple, one older brother
Poppy	16	Female	City	London	B – Middle class	Couple, one older brother
Eve	13	Female	Town	Surrey	C1 – Lower middle class	Couple, one younger sister
Simon	13	Male	Town	Surrey	C1 – Lower middle class	Couple, one older, two younger sisters
Wilf	13	Male	Rural	Hertfordshire	C1 – Lower middle class	Couple, one younger brother
Daniel	20	Male	City	London	B – Middle class	Couple, single child

observing the child using the internet in an informal and unstructured manner for up to two hours. The age of the child given below is that recorded at the time of the return visit.

EU Kids Online

Coming back to the present, this book draws on two further projects, one complete and one ongoing. First, the 'EU Kids Online' network includes research teams in 21 European countries (see www. eukidsonline.net). Together with Leslie Haddon and Panayiota Tsatsou at LSE, and some 60 colleagues across Europe, this network is examining children and young people's online opportunities and risks in cross-national perspective, and is funded by the European Commission's Safer Internet plus programme from 2006–9 (as part of the DG for Information Society and Media).

Social Networking Study

Second, the 'Social Networking Study', conducted as part of the 'Mediatized Stories' project (Lundby, 2008), involved sixteen in-depth

Gender	
Girls	**Boys**
Danielle, 13, C1, Piczo	Paul, 13, C2, Bebo, ex-MySpace
Nicki, 14, AB, MySpace	Joshua, 14, AB, Facebook
Daphne, 14, C2, MySpace, Bebo, ex-Piczo	Billy, 14, C2, MySpace
Jenny, 14, DE, MySpace, Bebo	
Elena, 14, DE, MySpace, Facebook, Bebo	
Ellie, 15, AB, Facebook, ex-MySpace	Ryan, 15, C1, Bebo, MySpace, ex-Piczo
Nina, 15, C1, Facebook, ex-MySpace	Leo, 16, AB, MySpace
Sophie, 16, C2, MySpace	Danny, 16, C1, MySpace, Facebook
	Simon, 16, DE, MySpace
	Jason, 16, DE, MySpace

Note: Each interviewee's pseudonym is followed by their age, socioeconomic status (SES), and the social networking site they use/used.

interviews and observations at home with teenagers regarding their use of social networking sites during summer 2007 (reported in Livingstone, 2008c); these are mainly discussed in chapter 4 of this book.

A series of open-ended individual interviews were conducted with sixteen teenagers in their homes in summer 2007. All had home access to the internet and their own personal profile on MySpace, Facebook, Bebo, Piczo or similar such sites, which they had visited at least once per week in recent months. They were recruited by a market research agency in July 2007 and interviewed by the author. Teenagers and their parents received a written explanation of the research aims, methods and ethics (addressing the answering of sensitive questions, respondent anonymity and confidentiality, data storage and publication of findings) before signing a consent form. Each received a modest honorarium. Interviews lasted around one hour, and comprised a free-flowing, open-ended discussion in front of the computer, while simultaneously going online to visit the interviewee's personal profile and those of others. Full findings are reported in Livingstone (2008c).

Notes

Preface

1   This was funded by the Economic and Social Research Council (RES-335-25-0008), with additional funding from AOL, BSC, ITC, Citizens Online and Ofcom. See Appendix.
2   This project networks research teams in 21 European countries – see www.eukidsonline.net, accessed 15/9/08, and Appendix.
3   These are referenced in the book as appropriate, including Livingstone (2005a, 2006, 2007a, 2007c, 2008a, 2008b, 2008c, 2008d), Livingstone and Bober (2003, 2004b, 2005) and Livingstone and Helsper (2007).

Changing Childhood, Changing Media

1   It should be noted that to start with children rather than the internet brings its own problems – much work on children is marked by a surprising lack of attention to the importance of media, including the internet, in their lives (Livingstone, 1998b). This problem too I shall hope to rectify in the chapters that follow.
2   For example, Coleman and Hendry (1999) argue that sexual experimentation among adolescents represents a growing historical trend (as measured, for example, by age of first intercourse), partly because society has become increasingly open in its representation of sex, including through the media.
3   See http://www.ed.gov/policy/elsec/leg/esea02/index.html, accessed 15/9/08
4   For example, Dollman, Norton and Norton (2005: 892) review evidence that 'physical activity in clearly defined contexts such as active transport, school physical education, and organized sports is declining in many

countries; young people would like to be active but are often constrained by external factors such as school policy or curricula, parental rules in relation to safety and convenience, and physical environmental factors.'

5 Ofcom's figures from October 2007 show that 80% of parents of a child aged 5–17, but only 57% of non-parents, say they have internet access at home.

6 There has been a recent explosion of books and articles using or critiquing versions of the concept of 'digital native' – for example, see Buckingham (2006) Facer and Furlong (2001), McKay, Thurlow and Toomey-Zimmerman (2005), Montgomery (2008), Palfrey and Gasser (2008) and Tapscott (1997, 2008).

7 Crucially, affordances are not independent features of a technology or organism but are defined in relation to the user. Jones (2003) gives the example of a staircase: if the steps are less than 88% of a person's leg length, they can climb the stairs. The stairs are climbable, therefore, depending on the relationship between the stair and the person climbing them; it is neither a feature of the staircase nor a skill possessed by the individual. Similarly, a certain smell will communicate 'edible' to one animal and poisonous to another. But being climbable or edible are not features of stairs or food, only of their relationship with particular categories of user. Now consider what makes a website 'interesting' or 'legible' or 'dangerous' (or a user 'skilled' or 'literate', 'motivated' or 'risk-taking') – only by understanding the relation between the design of the artefact and the interpretative capacities of the user can we grasp the opportunities and the risks afforded by the internet to children.

Youthful Experts

1 Quotations from children and parents are drawn from the 'UK Children Go Online' project (Livingstone and Bober, 2003).

2 I could instead have dwelt on Wilf, a farmer's son aged 10 years old, for whom the internet offers an 'approved' opportunity to play games based on his favourite cartoons, plus a quick way of finding information for school when needed, via AskJeeves. But it is of far less importance in his life than going fishing or meeting friends outside. Wilf, however, is notably more competent than Charlie (also 10 years old), whose mother manages his internet use for him; he has not yet figured out how to go beyond the AOL home page and so finds the internet boring. Middle-class Kate (aged 15) sees the internet primarily as a communication device, chatting with school friends while simultaneously phoning or texting them, meeting new people (friends of friends, often), networking enthusiastically, multitasking all this with homework tasks when required. Sally, a lively 15 year old, takes a similar approach, whisking between multiple chat and multiple email identities to sustain a complex

matrix of social contacts. Manu (aged 14), son of parents from India, visits Indian chat rooms, but then pretends he's an aggressive adult to get everyone to leave the chat room. Jim (aged 16), who uses the internet mainly to find material which his teachers can't trace, which he alters minimally and passes off as his own homework.

3 In this regard, they appear more active than general (adult) users, where research suggests that only a fraction of internet users actually participate in online interactions. For example, less than two in 1,000 visitors to YouTube upload videos; most just view content uploaded by others (Auchard, 2007).

4 Note that it is particularly difficult to locate reliable information on children and young people's internet use, since most commercial services track website use either generally or for adults only (such as Google, Alexa, Nielsen NetRatings, ComScore).

5 Of the 20, eight are primarily for game-playing, seven are related to television channels, three are for social networking, and two are mainly advertising (or advergames; Grimes and Shade, 2005). All but the BBC sites are, also, walled gardens; their aim is to be 'sticky', to keep children on the site and precisely not to lead them to explore further, closing off rather than affording connections to the diversity and range of online opportunities.

6 The divide between adult 'haves' and 'have nots' is, in reality, far from simple also, but the point here is that one can, still, compare those with and without access among the adult, but no longer the child, population.

7 See http://www.dprophet.com, accessed 15/9/08. For Harry Potter fan fiction, see www.fictionalley.org, accessed 15/9/08.

8 See youtube.com/fred. According to the blogosphere, he has over 100,000 subscribers and reaches several million people per episode (3 to 4 million hits for each video posted on YouTube, according to David Sarno, LA Times Internet culture and online entertainment writer. http://latimesblogs.latimes.com/webscout/2008/06/fred-the-puzzle.html).

Learning and Education

1 See http://www.teachernet.gov.uk/wholeschool/ictis/, accessed 15/9/08. Note: DCSF is the UK Government Department for Children, Schools and Families.

2 See http://about.becta.org.uk/, accessed 15/9/08.

3 There are, of course, many problems with formal learning, including the cultural gap – larger for working-class than middle-class children – in which 'the problems and techniques of the school are not the problems and techniques of practical life or the traditional home' (Scribner and Cole, 1973: 558).

4 Schools Minister Jim Knight, announcing the Home Access initiative at BETT, 2008.

5 Chris Price, Director, Digital Development and Communities, Digital Birmingham, speech presented to 'UK Kids Online', a Westminster eForum Keynote Seminar, 24 April 2007.

6 These include, notably, the anti-technology stance of the Alliance for Childhood (2004), though see also Attewell *et al.* (2001; 2003), Seiter (2008) and, for a review, Buckingham (2007a).

7 Note that children were asked to choose the single most helpful tool, whereas parents were asked to choose all in the list that help their child.

8 The UK Children Go Online findings that follow were originally reported in Livingstone and Bober (2004a).

9 Only 19% of 9–11 year olds say they have had no lessons in how to use the internet, compared with 26% of 12–15 year olds, 45% of 16–17 year olds and 51% of 18–19 year olds in full-time education (Livingstone and Bober, 2004b).

10 Frustratingly, the research basis behind product development and testing is generally proprietary and rarely made available to public scrutiny (Buckingham, Scanlon and Sefton-Green, 2001). Can we learn from earlier efforts in relation to television to establish the uncertain boundaries between 'pure' entertainment, 'instructional' or curriculum-oriented content, and more informal educational content? Calvert (1999: 185; see Lemish, 2007, for an overview) lists eleven features of educational television which might apply to the internet; yet on close examination, these concern the avoidance of impediments to learning (e.g. uses comprehensible language, age-appropriate content, and so forth) or require the inclusion of features which are, really, important for all effective programmes for children, educational or not (e.g. includes familiar settings, fun, interactive, special effects). The only criterion which was specifically educational – namely that 'each show should emphasize a specific lesson' – is more tautological than enlightening, tying 'educational' content narrowly to the acquisition of approved (though not necessarily curricular) knowledge.

Communication and Identity

1 Quoted from *The Sunday Times*, 25/2/07.

2 Tony Elison, senior vice president at Viacom International Japan, which produces the Japanese social networking site, Mixi, says: 'In Mixi, it's not all about me. It's all about us.' *Technology Review*, 16 February 2007, www.technologyreview.com.

3 I do not here attend to those who do not communicate online, those who may be 'disenfranchised', as boyd (2008) puts it, because they lack access or are restricted by parents, or because they are what boyd calls

'conscientious objectors' (considering social networking, for example, as objectionable, stupid or, say some, too cool for them).

4   Specifically, those in year 11 (aged 15–16) were a little *more* likely than those in year 9 (aged 13–14) to say that talking online 'is less satisfying than in real life' (51% vs. 45%) and more likely to say they have never pretended about themselves online (50% vs. 43%). On the other hand, they were *less* likely to say 'I feel more confident [online] than I do in real life' (28% vs. 33%), less likely to find it 'easier to keep things secret' online (25% vs. 34%) and less likely never to have given out personal information online (38% vs. 53%). Source: UK Children Go Online survey of 9–19 year olds, 2004 (N = 1,511). Percentages are weighted, and apply only to those who use the internet at least once a week.

5   Note that, generally, teenagers are acutely aware of the subtle differences between those a school year younger or older, these indicating perceived differences in identity, social position or maturity. Media choices are often used as markers of relative maturity (have you got your own television set yet? Or seen a film classified for those older than you? Livingstone, 2002).

6   See   http://www.law.cornell.edu/uscode/15/usc_sup_01_15_10_91.html, accessed 17/12/08.

7   These difficulties in managing privacy via privacy settings reflect broader internet literacy issues (see chapter 7). For example, the top bar of a MySpace profile lists 'blog', 'groups', 'forum', 'events', 'music', 'film' and more. While I observed most of the teenagers to include music on their profile, when I asked about blogs, groups or forums, I was often met with blank looks. Even 16-year-old Danny, whose father works in computers and who says confidently, 'I know a lot about computers', was confused when asked about the group facility, saying 'I don't know if I've got a group ... I didn't even know there was groups.' Ellie, on the other hand, has joined 163 groups, including the appreciation society for her local bus, one for a favourite programme, another for a charity she supports, etc. But she had hardly noticed and certainly does not use the blog, noting that 'I don't think any of my friends have either.' The limits of teenagers' supposedly exploratory and creative approach to social networking are, it seems, easily reached.

Participation and Civic Engagement

1   See also the Civic Web project at http://www.civicweb.eu/, accessed 11/9/08.

2   These quotations are reported in Livingstone (2007a).

3   In the UK in 2003/4, prominent public protests were organized against the invasion of Iraq, both for and against fox-hunting, and by the divorced fathers' lobby group, *Fathers for Justice*.

4 This site is no longer active, perhaps reflecting its ineffectiveness.

5 Later, when I tried by using the 'search this site' facility, I received an unhelpful but not atypical message: 'You can't access this page because either your session has expired or you don't have a high enough user status to access this page.'

6 For example, Joe, being interested in golf, read Epal's career advice about professional golfing but was unimpressed. Kanita, finding little about China on the site, visited a Chinese site instead. Mia was easily sidetracked by reading personal stories and didn't read the information that accompanied it.

7 Examples of such organizations in the UK include the British Youth Council, Children's Express, Children's Rights Alliance for England, and the United Kingdom Youth Parliament. See Montgomery (2008) for a recent survey of American organizations contributing to the 'youth civic web', and Civic Web at http://www.civicweb.eu/, accessed 11/9/08 for such sites in Europe.

8 See http://www.youthforum.org/, accessed 15/7/08.

9 Cynically reinforcing children's perception that they are not listened to, this protest was widely reported in the press as 'skiving' (i.e. cheating to get a day off school).

Risk and Harm

1 For example, a headline in the *Sunday Mirror* (27/8/06) read, 'Internet sex beast controlled his victims with their own computers. Exclusive story that will put fear in every parent.'

2 To be sure, bullying remains more widespread offline (Lenhart, 2007). A 2006 survey of 4,772 school pupils reported that 69% pupils were bullied in the past year and that half of those were physically hurt; overall, only 7% said they had received unpleasant or bullying emails/IM/text messages (Bullying UK, 2006: 3). However, a smaller survey (N = 770) of 11–19 year olds found that 20% had been bullied/via text/internet/email and that 73% knew the person, though for 26% this was by a stranger. Further, 10% had a photo taken of them that made them feel uncomfortable, embarrassed or threatened, and 17% said it was sent to others. Last, 11% said they'd sent a bullying or threatening message to someone. This problem, like other online risks, is made worse insofar as children often tell no one of these experiences (NCH/Tesco Mobile, 2005).

3 The authors detail typical practices depicted in X-rated videos, including anal intercourse, men ejaculating onto women's faces, fisting and intercourse with multiple partners. Other researchers note the prevalence of extreme or violent pornography, including debasing, brutal and humiliating scenes of rape and aggression against women (Dahlquist and Vigilant, 2004).

4 Their example comes from a message board visited by teenage girls (and, as we also learned in chapter 4, these and other examples raise difficulties in distinguishing serious from playful interactions):

> Poster 1: Does anyone know how to cut deep without having it sting and bleed too much?

> Poster 2: I use box cutter blades. You have to pull the skin really tight and press the blade down really hard. You can also use a tourniquet to make it bleed more.

> Poster 3: I've found that if you press your blade against the skin at the depth you want the cut to be and draw the blade really fast it doesn't hurt and there is blood galore. Be careful, though, 'cause you can go very deep without meaning to.

> 'Poster 1: Okay, I'll get a Stanley blade 'cause I hear that it will cut right to the bone with no hassle. But I'll be careful if I do use a tourniquet and I won't cut that deep.

In a related domain, that of video games, Gee (2003) discusses post September 11th 2001 games featuring US soldiers killing Arabs and Muslims or Palestinians expelling Israeli soldiers. Though he offers the possible defence that these games allow one to experience 'the other' from the inside, and encourage the player to reflect on political conflict in an interesting fashion, he seems less tolerant of *Ethnic Cleansing*, one of several games produced by the American white supremacist hate group, the National Alliance.

5 Some seek alternative methods. For instance, Cragg (2000) interviewed experts (clinicians and therapists) about the likely effects of pornography on children, including reflections on trends in the cases they see in their clinics – and found evidence of immediate shock and trauma, sexualization and possible re-enactment, as well as broader effects on perceptions of sexuality and relationships especially if abusive or degrading in nature (see also Thornburgh and Lin, 2002). Most researchers, however, rely on children's self-report, whether by qualitative or quantitative methods. While this has generated much valuable information, it must nonetheless be regarded with caution for children are subject to social desirability and other pressures as are adult interviewees.

6 Reflecting on the evidence for effects of violent mass media, Browne and Hamilton-Giachritsis conclude that: 'There is consistent evidence that violent imagery in television, film and video, and computer games has substantial short-term effects on arousal, thoughts, and emotions, increasing the likelihood of aggressive or fearful behaviour in younger children, especially in boys. The evidence becomes inconsistent when considering older children and teenagers, and long-term outcomes for all ages' (2005: 702).

7 It is not, however, particularly surprising. Research on other aspects of youthful risk – for example, the age of first sexual activity or drug-taking

or smoking – reveal similar gaps in parental and child accounts (*Guardian*, 2007).

8 This suggests no improvement since 2003, when a survey of 8,991 internet users aged 12–17 found 1 in 4 met someone they first encountered online. Many had given out personal information online, and 56% had been drawn into an unwanted sexual conversation, making 30% of the children frightened (Wojtasik, 2003).

9 See http://ec.europa.eu/information_society/doc/factsheets/018-saferinternetplus.pdf

10 See https://wcd.coe.int/ViewDoc.jsp?Ref=Rec(2006)12&Sector=secCM &Language=lanEnglish.

11 Since respondents were permitted multiple responses to this question, these percentages do not add up to 100%.

12 He provides little guidance on how such a mapping might be conducted, however, partly because much of his argumentation centres on the historical trend towards the individualization of life chances, this precisely undercutting traditional class determination – a point on which he has been widely challenged by those pointing to the evident persistence of social divisions and inequalities (Elliott, 2002; Green, Mitchell and Bunton, 2000).

13 Although in the USA, Lenhart (2007) finds girls more the target than boys.

14 Overall, among 10–17-year-old internet users, 19% were involved in online aggression, most (12% of all users) as aggressors, 4% as targets and 3% as both. These last resembled those who, offline, are both bullies and victims, characterized by significant psychosocial difficulties (such as depressive symptoms, problem behaviour, and traditional bullying), but they are also intensive and competent internet users. Additionally, aggressors faced such psychosocial difficulties as poor relationships with their parents, substance use and delinquency (see also Beebe, Asche, Harrison and Quinlan, 2004).

15 For the sample of 789 UK 12–17 year olds who use the internet at least once a week, the Pearson product-moment correlation coefficient between opportunities (30 item scale) and risks (15 item scale) was 0.51.

16 Online anonymity may be beneficial or otherwise. One American study found that teenagers advise each other on the pleasures and risks of alcohol and drug-taking in chat rooms, on message boards and in the public areas of social networking sites (Nielsen BuzzMetrics, 2007).

17 What is meant by negative depictions? Arguably, depictions of sexuality that are 'out of context', that emphasize a narrow and restrictive conception of (usually female) attractiveness, that are associated with hostility or violence.

18 See http://www.timesonline.co.uk/tol/news/world/article1162487.ece, accessed 1/9/08.

19 A recent survey of American parents reported that 31% consider electronic media a positive influence, 23% think them a negative influence

and the remainder see media as having little influence (Rideout, 2007). But when asked about the internet specifically, 59% of parents of 9–17 year olds who use the internet at home considered this a positive influence and only 7% saw it negatively. Age matters: among parents of 2–6 year olds, the media generally are seen far more positively than among parents of 9–13 year olds and, especially, parents of 14–17 year olds. Parents initially welcome digital media into the home because of the promised social, emotional, linguistic and cognitive benefits (Marsh *et al.*, 2005). But as children become teenagers, parents find themselves struggling to retain control of the agenda, especially regarding values rather than those they perceive to be predominant in the media (commercialism, gender stereotypes or violence; Hoover, Clark and Alters, 2004).

Media and Digital Literacies

1 For example, in German, 'Alphabetisierung' means being able to read and write while 'Bildung' means culture/education, reflecting the separation of basic literacy from being educated or cultured; more recently, the terms 'Medienkompetenz' and 'Internetkompetenz' are spreading. The lack of an equivalent distinction between simple and advanced literacies in English is problematic – policymakers may call for the latter but often only the former is delivered.

2 See http://www.coe.int/t/e/integrated_projects/democracy/02_Activities/ 03_Internet_literacy/Internet_Literacy_Handbook/, accessed 30/8/08.

3 See http://ec.europa.eu/comm/avpolicy/media_literacy/index_en.htm, accessed 15/9/08. For the EC's high level expert group on media literacy; see http://ec.europa.eu/comm/avpolicy/media_literacy/expert_group/ index_en.htm, accessed 15/9/08. In North America, media literacy is promoted by the Center for Media Literacy (http://www.medialit.org/), the Media Literacy Clearinghouse (http://medialit.med.sc.edu/), Citizens for Media Literacy (http://www.main.nc.us/cml/), the National Association for Media Literacy Education (http://www.amlainfo.org), and the Association for Media Literacy in Canada (http://www.aml.ca/ home/).

4 See http://www.unhchr.ch/html/menu3/b/k2crc.htm, accessed 12/1/07. For adults, the imperative to enhance local and national participation in political and civic affairs also means that user-generated as well as simply receptive capacities are vital in today's information society.

5 Formally adopted by the EC on 29/11/07, the Audiovisual Media Services Directive gives Member States two years to implement its requirements stressing 'that regulatory policy in the sector has to safeguard certain public interests, such as cultural diversity, the right to information, the importance of media pluralism, the protection of minors and consumer protection and action to enhance public awareness and media

literacy, now and in the future.'. See http://ec.europa.eu/avpolicy/docs/ reg/modernisation/proposal_2005/avmsd_cons_may07_en.pdf, accessed 15/9/08.

6　Initiated to draw diverse institutional players from educators and scholars to producers and practitioners into a shared discourse on the meaning and potential of media literacy for European children and young people, The Charter's underlying aim is to inform the EC's MEDIA programme, jointly run by the Information Society and Media Directorate General and the Education, Audiovisual and Culture Executive Agency which together, as from 2007, are to advance the EU's media literacy responsibilities (Bachmair and Bazalgette, 2007).

7　See http://www.euromedialiteracy.eu/index.php?Pg=charter, accessed 15/9/08.

8　Council of Europe. (2005, 10–11 March). Integration and diversity: The new frontiers of European media and communications policy: Draft action plan and draft resolution no. 2. Retrieved 25/4/05, from http:// www.coe.int/T/E/Com/Files/Ministerial-Conferences/2005-kiev/texte_ adopte.asp.

9　This story revealed that the American drug company, Pfizer, 'is in talks with the state of Texas about a controversial scheme to fund patient education in return for fewer price controls on its drugs', building on its successful negotiation with Jeb Bush, state governor of Florida, to finance health literacy and save millions of dollars from mandatory price rebates (*Financial Times*, 18 February 2003, p. 1).

10　This story reported union activists' concern, backed by the National Consumer Council, that the (Labour) Government's proposal to allow 'patient choice' regarding hospitals would increase 'the gulf in "health literacy" between higher and lower social groups' (*Morning Star*, 4 August 2004, p. 4).

11　Ironically, therefore, the scholar concerned to support positive public policies, institutions and values, including those to empower children and young people as active citizens, finds him or herself stressing the failure to meet ambitious expectations regarding public levels of media literacy rather than, as has long been the critical tradition in media studies, celebrating the active media-savvy audience in the face of dominant media institutions.

Balncing Online Opportunities and Risk

1　See http://ec.europa.eu/information_society/eeurope/2002/news_library /documents/eeurope2005/eeurope2005_en.pdf, accessed 17/12/08.

2　Adopted by the European Parliament and Council in December 2006, this guides national legislation for combating illegal and harmful content transmitted over electronic media, and includes a call for the promotion of children's media literacy (The European Commission, n.d.).

3   By this he refers to informal ways of life, whether in the public sphere or the intimate realm of the family (Outhwaite, 1996).

4   He certainly includes children in this communication rights framework (see Hamelink, 2008).

5   *Building a free and safe internet.* Council of Europe Submission to the Internet Governance Forum, Rio de Janeiro, Brazil, 12 to 15 November 2007   (http://www.coe.int/t/dc/press/source/CoE%20submission%20 to%20IGF_100807FINAL.doc).

6   In the UK, BBC Children's Interactive and On-demand provision is developing 'a dynamic virtual hub' for those under 12 years old (CBBC for 7–11 and CBeebies for younger children). Cross-platform content links television, radio and internet through a consistent 'look and feel', including on-demand viewing, behind-the-scenes footage, extra content and interactive services (creative, gaming, community, learning, etc.), along with a pre-moderated search tool (not a search engine, but a pre-moderated resource linking to external websites that meet clear guidelines regarding content, advertising, messaging, use of personal data and suitability for 7–11 year olds). See www.bbc.co.uk/cbbc.

7   For example, the Disney High School Musical site has some innovative tools   to   remix   content: http://psc.disney.go.com/disneychannel/ originalmovies/highschoolmusical/. See also www.TheSimpsons.com and, in Norway, www.donald.no, a commercial website branded with Donald Duck, providing diverse forms of entertainment for children, including pre-moderated user-generated content and a partially post-moderated community forum. It also provides 'news for youngsters' (cultural news). This site may soon be launched in other European countries.

8   I thank my colleagues in the EU Kids Online network (see www. eukidsonline.net) for these and other suggestions, and also Alain Bossard (Takatrouver), Jo Bryce (UCLAN), Andrew Burn (Institute of Education, London), Stephen Carrick-Davies (Childnet International), Joshua Fincher, Lelia Green (Edith Cowan University), Karl Hopwood (Semley Primary School), Mimi Ito (USC), Dale Kunkel (U Arizona), Ben Livingstone, Rodney Livingstone, Rachel Lunt, and Rebecca Shallcross (CBBC).

9   See www.takatrouver.net. See also German and Dutch children's search engines at www.blinde-kuh.de and www.davindi.nl.

10   See www.fhw.gr/imeakia. The Hellenic World Foundation is a privately funded, not for profit foundation founded in 1993 by an act of Parliament.

11   See www.prazniki.net/default.aspx. Also, www.otroci.org/ and the children's portal, www.zupca.net/. The main responsibility for online content for children lies with the Ministry of Education, though the Ministry of Culture also funds some projects, especially those supporting the Slovenian language. There is little available for Slovenian teenagers, however, apart from social networking sites.

12   See Digital Songlines at http://songlines.interactiondesign.com.au/; see also the Australian Government's Indigenous Portal at http://www. indigenous.gov.au/

13 See http://gse.berkeley.edu/research/dusty.html

14 For example, VRT in Belgium, ZDF in Germany, NRK in Norway, RTE in Ireland, & CBBC/BBC Education in UK, www.hetklokhuis.nl/ sketchstudio in The Netherlands, sesameworkshop.org and pbskids.org in the USA and National Danish Television (www.dr.dk/boern/?oversigt).

15 In the USA – www.rockthevote.com, www.kidsvotingusa.org and www. vote-smart.org; in the UK – www.ukyouthparliament.org.uk.

16 e.g. in Spain, www.portaldelmenor.es (bullying, other problems); e.g. in UK, www.talktofrank.com (drugs) and www.childline.org.uk (child abuse).

17 e.g. Mugglenet.com (unofficial site for Harry Potter fans); insanebuffyfans.com (Buffy the Vampire Slayer fan site); http://www. flatoutblind.org/bb/ (for Beavis and Butthead fans).

18 Moreover, many initiatives fail. One such was the attempt to establish a Dot Kids domain (under the US domain – i.e. .kids.us). In 2002, this children's 'walled garden' appeared successful, when President Bush, signed the Dot-Kids Implementation and Efficiency Act in the USA, saying 'This bill is a wise and necessary step to safeguard our children while they use computers and discover the great possibilities of the Internet. Every site designated .kids will be a safe zone for children' (The White House Office of the Press Secretary, 2002). However, since dot.kids sites could not connect to any sites outside the domain (NeuStar Inc., 2003), this was so restrictive that few organizations invested in populating the domain and the initiative is effectively inactive.

19 A site for teenage girls, containing celebrity, music, fashion and entertainment news and chat. See http://www.mykindaplace.com/hi. aspx.

20 See http://www.fosi.org/cms/index.php/pr2008/14-pressreleases/321-fosi-conference-press-release.html, accessed 17/12/08.

21 One challenging consequence of widespread internet use is the extent to which youthful activities may be newly rendered illegal – from downloading music from p2p networks to circulating hate messages or producing indecent images of one's boy/girlfriend on a mobile phone.

22 In the EC, awareness-raising is undertaken by national nodes of the Insafe network, funded by the EC's Safer Internet Plus Program. On a national basis, awareness-raising is also undertaken by education ministries, child protection charities and the industry (internet service providers, content providers for children, mobile providers, etc.). Sites providing high-quality safety guidance for children, parents and teachers are multiplying. Good examples include, from America, http://www. fosi.org/; from New Zealand, www.netsmartz.org; from the UK, www. childnet-int.org, www.becta.org.uk, www.internetsafetyzone.com; and www.thinkuknow.com; from Spain, www.menorenlared.es; from The Netherlands, the safety training site, www.iksurfveilig.nl/; from Austria, http://www.saferinternet.at/ and http://www.stopline.at; from Denmark, http://portal.medieraadet.dk/ and http://www.dream.dk/index. php?lang=Engelsk; from Germany, http://www.klicksafe.de/, http://www.

jugendschutz.net/ and http://www.erfurter-netcode.de/; from Norway, http://www.saftonline.no/ and http://www.medietilsynet.no/; from Portugal, http://moodle.crie.min-edu.pt/ and http://www.educom.pt/; and from Slovenia, http://english.safe.si/ and http://stopline.si.

23 For example, in Bulgaria, a survey of 21 secondary schools in 2003 identified a very low level of parental awareness regarding children's online risks: only 5% of parents thought the internet could be harmful for their children, and 1 in 4 claimed not to know what their child does online. Similarly 3 in 4 pupils were unaware of online risks (though nearly half had experienced online pornography, violence, contact with strangers and even offers of virtual sex (State Agency for Child Protection, 2003). However, in Slovenia, where 77% of 12–19 year olds use the internet, teenagers are more worried by spam, viruses and advertisements than they are by other harms; nonetheless, 1 in 3 teenagers worry about the safety of online information (RIS, 2006).

24 It also tends to oversimplify or misrepresent findings from research (Ybarra, Mitchell, Finkelhor and Wolak, 2007).

25 Not all parents attempt such mediation. Vandewater, Park, Huang and Wartella (2005), as other previous researchers, report a strong association between parental mediation and parental education. Even for television, Jordan, Hersey, McDivitt and Heitzler (2006) identify a series of practical reasons that impede parents' ability to reduce their child's exposure to television (and, by implication, other media), including 'parents' need to use television as a safe and affordable distraction, parents' own heavy television viewing patterns, the role that television plays in the family's day-to-day routine, and a belief that children should spend their weekend leisure time as they wish' (p.e1303).

26 Thus in the UK, Ofcom finds that 51% of the parents of 8–11 year olds and 43% of parents of 12–15 year olds have installed parental controls. Similarly in the USA, Pew found that more than half (54%) of American families with teenagers use filters to limit access to potentially harmful online content, especially parents who themselves are frequent users of the internet and who have middle-school-age children (Lenhart, 2005).

27 Indeed, few filtering programs flag up the value of discussing such monitoring with children (*Childsafe* being one exception that displays an optimal 'Acceptable Use' policy to communicate parental rules to the child), leaving one to presume that unobtrusive monitoring, conveying little trust in the child, is generally deemed crucial. See http://www.pearlsw.com/home/index.com (for *Cybersnoop*) and http://www.webroot.com/wb/products/childsafe/index.php (for *Childsafe*), retrieved 29/5/03.

28 In a small but significant proportion of families, children need privacy from their parents precisely because their parents pose the threat through their physically or sexually abusive behavior (Russell, 1980). For these children, it is crucial that they have private channels for communication to ask for help and advice.

29 Similar doubts regarding the effectiveness of parental mediation exist
for other media. While Buijzen, van der Molen and Sondij (2007) found,
for a sample of 451 Dutch 8–12 year olds, that active parental mediation
(discussing the news with their child) did reduce children's fear, worry
and anger, though only among the younger children, Nikken and Jansz's
(2007) survey of 1,115 Dutch parents found that restrictive mediation
had no or even the opposite effect in reducing children's playing of
restricted electronic games (leading the researchers to conclude in
favour of the forbidden fruit argument, as theorized by the notion of
psychological reactance). It may also be that children who already play
more provoke their parents to criticize or restrict their play, as this too
would result in a positive correlation between restrictions and banned
behaviour.

30 Some aspects of this policy are somewhat curious – although governments have not previously advised parents to listen in on their children's
phone calls or read their diary or letters, parents are now encouraged
to look over their children's shoulders as they go online and to
install software to check on sites visited, e-mails sent, or chat rooms
visited.

31 See www.ecdl.co.uk, accessed 13/9/08.

32 See http://www.washingtonpost.com/wp-dyn/content/article/2008/12/10/
AR2008121001860.html, accessed 24/2/09.

33 Although see the UK's recent consultation on 'Assessing the Impact of
the Commercial World on Children's Wellbeing'; http://www.dcsf.gov.
uk/consultations/conResults.cfm?consultationId=1547, accessed 17/8/08.

References

Abrams, M. (1959). The teenage consumer. In *LPE (London Express Exchange) Papers* (vol. 5). London: The London Press Exchange Ltd.

Adoni, H. and Nossek, H. (2001). The new media consumers: Media convergence and the displacement effect. *Communications, 26*(1), 59–83.

Adorno, T. and Horkheimer, M. (1977). The culture industry: Enlightenment as mass deception. In J. Curran, M. Gurevitch and J. Woollacott (eds), *Mass Communication and Society*. London: Edward Arnold.

Akdeniz, Y. (2001). Internet content regulation: UK government and the control of Internet content. *Computer Law and Security Report, 17*(5), 303.

Alao, A. O., Soderberg, M., Pohl, E. L. and Alao, A. L. (2006). Cybersuicide: Review of the role of the Internet on suicide. *Cyberpsychology and Behavior, 9*(4), 489–493.

Alliance for Childhood. (2004). *Tech Tonic: Towards a New Literacy of Technology*: Alliance for Childhood.

Arnaldo, C. A. (2001). *Child Abuse on the Internet: Ending the Silence*. Paris: Berghahn Books and UNESCO Publishing.

Attewell, P. (2001). Comment: The first and second digital divides. *Sociology of Education, 74*(3), 252–9.

Attewell, P., Suazo-Garcia, B. and Battle, J. (2003). Computers and young children: Social benefit or social problem. *Social Forces, 82*(1), 277–96.

Aufderheide, P. (1993). *Media Literacy: A Report of the National Leadership Conference on Media Literacy*. Aspen, CO.: Aspen institute.

Auchard, E. (2007). Participation on Web 2.0 sites remains weak. Retrieved from http://www.reuters.com/article/internetNews/idUSN174363 8820070418

Azjen, I. and Fishbein, M. (1980). *Understanding Attitudes and Predicting Social Behaviour*. Englewood Cliffs, NJ: Prentice-Hall.

Bachmair, B. and Bazalgette, C. (2007). The European Charter for Media Literacy: Meaning and potential. *Research in Comparative and International Education, 2*(1), 80–87.

256 References

Bakardjieva, M. (2005). *Internet Society: The Internet in Everyday Life.* London: Sage.

Balkam, S. (2008). *State of Online Safety Report.* Washington, DC: Family Online Safety Institute.

Banks, M. A. (2003). Should internet access be regulated? Yes. In A. Alexander and J. Hanson (eds), *Taking Sides: Clashing Views on Controversial Issues in Mass Media and Society* (pp. 234–9). Guilford, Conn.: McGraw-Hill/Dushkin.

Barak, A. (2005). Sexual harassment on the Internet. *Social Science Computer Review, 23*(1), 77–92.

Bardone-Cone, A. M. and Cass, K. M. (2007). What does viewing a pro-anorexia website do? An experimental examination of website exposure and moderating effects. *International Journal of Eating Disorders, 40*(6), 537–48.

Barker, M. and Petley, J. (2001). *Ill Effects: The Media/Violence Debate* (2nd edn). New York City, New York: Routledge.

Barnes, S. B. (2006). A privacy paradox: Social networking in the United States. *First Monday, 11*(9).

Barnhurst, K. G. (1998). Politics in the fine meshes: Young citizens, power and media. *Media, Culture and Society, 20*(3), 201–18.

Bauman, Z. (2001). *The Individualized Society.* Cambridge: Polity.

BBC (2002). *Beyond the Soundbite: BBC Research into Public Disillusion with Politics.* London: http://www.trbi.co.uk/trbipolitics.pdf.

BBC News Online. (2007, 10 January). Pupils get home internet access. Retrieved from http://news.bbc.co.uk/1/hi/education/6245899.stm

Beck, U. (1986/2005). *Risk Society: Towards a New Modernity.* London: Sage.

Beck, U. and Beck-Gernsheim, E. (2002). *Individualization.* London: Sage.

Beebe, T. J., Asche, S. E., Harrison, P. A. and Quinlan, K. B. (2004). Heightened vulnerability and increased risk-taking among adolescent chat room users: Results from a statewide school survey. *Journal of Adolescent Health, 35*(2), 116–23.

Bennett, W. L. (1998). 1998 Ithiel De Sola Pool lecture: The uncivic culture: Communication, identity, and the rise of lifestyle politics. *Political Science and Politics, 31*(4), 740–61.

—— (2008). Changing citizenship in the digital age. In W. L. Bennett (ed.), *Civic Life Online: Learning How Digital Media Can Engage Youth* (vol. 1, pp. 1–24). Cambridge: MIT Press.

Bentivegna, S. (2002). Politics and new media. In L. Lievrouw and S. Livingstone (eds), *The Handbook of New Media* (pp. 50–61). London: Sage.

Berker, T., Hartmann, M., Punie, Y. and Ward, K. J. (eds). (2006). *The Domestication of Media and Technology.* Maidenhead: Open University Press.

Berlin, I. (1958). *Two Concepts of Liberty: An Inaugural Lecture Delivered before the University of Oxford on 31 October 1958.* Oxford: Clarendon Press.

BESA (2006). *Information and Communication Technology in UK State Schools.* London: British Educational Suppliers Association.

—— (2008). *BESA report: ICT in UK State Schools 2008 Vol 1*. London: British Educational Suppliers Association.

Bessant, J. (2004). Mixed messages: Youth participation and democratic practice. *Australian Journal of Political Science, 39*(2), 387–404.

Bettelheim, B. (1999). Do children need television? In P. Lohr and M. Meyer (eds), *Children, Television and the New Media* (pp. 3–7). Luton: University of Luton Press.

Biddle, L., Donovan, J., Hawton, K., Kapur, N. and Gunnell, D. (2008). Suicide and the internet. *British Medical Journal, 336*(7648), 800–2.

Bijker, W. E., Hughes, T. P. and Pinch, T. (eds). (1987). *The Social Construction of Technological Systems*. Cambridge, MA: MIT Press.

Black, J., Lodge, M. and Thatcher, M. (2005). *Regulatory Innovation: A comparative analysis*. Cheltenham: Edward Elgar.

Bolter, J. D. and Grusin, R. (1999). *Remediation: Understanding New Media*. Cambridge, MA: MIT Press.

Boneva, B., Quinn, A., Kraut, R., Kiesler, S. and Shklovski, I. (2006). Teenage communication in the instant messaging era. In R. Kraut, M. Brynin and S. Kiesler (eds), *Computers, Phones, and the Internet: Domesticating Information Technology*. (pp. 201–18) Oxford, New York: Oxford University Press.

Bonfadelli, H. (2002). The Internet and knowledge gaps: A theoretical and empirical investigation. *European Journal of Communication, 17*(1), 65–84.

Boone, G., Secci, J. and Gallant, L. (2007). Emerging trends in online advertising. *Doxa Communication, 5*, 241–53.

Bourdieu, P. (1984). *Distinction: A Social Critique of the Judgement of Taste*. London: Routledge and Kegan Paul.

Bovill, M. and Livingstone, S. (2001). Bedroom culture and the privatization of media use. In S. Livingstone and M. Bovill (eds), *Children and Their Changing Media Environment: A European Comparative Study* (pp. 179–200). Mahwah NJ: Lawrence Erlbaum Associates.

boyd, d. (2006). Friends, friendsters, and Top 8: Writing community into being on social network sites. *First Monday, 11*(12).

—— (2008). Why youth ♥ Social network sites: The role of networked publics in teenage social life. In D. Buckingham (ed.), *Youth, Identity, and Digital Media* (vol. 6, pp. 119–42). Cambridge: MIT Press.

boyd, d. and Ellison, N. (2007). Social network sites: Definition, history, and scholarship. *Journal of Computer-Mediated Communication, 13*(1).

boyd, d. and Heer, J. (2006, January 4–7, 2006). *Profiles as Conversation: Networked Identity and Performance on Friendster*. Paper presented at the International Conference on System Sciences, Kauai, Hawaii.

Bradbrook, G., Alvi, I., Fisher, J., Lloyd, H., Moore, R., Thompson, V., *et al.* (2008). *Meeting Their Potential: The Role of Education and Technology in Overcoming Disadvantage and Disaffection in Young People*. Coventry: Becta.

Bromley, C., Curtice, J. and Seyd, P. (2004). *Is Britain Facing a Crisis of Democracy?* London: UCL Constitution Unit.

Brown, J. D., Halpern, C. T. and L'Engle, K. L. (2005). Mass media as a sexual super peer for early maturing girls. *Journal of Adolescent Health*, *36*(5), 420–7.

Browne, K. D. and Hamilton-Giachritsis, C. (2005). The influence of violent media on children and adolescents: A public-health approach. *The Lancet*, *365*(9460), 702–10.

Bruner, J. (1996). *The Culture of Education*. Cambridge, MA: Harvard University Press.

Bruns, A. (2008). *Blogs, Wikipedia, Second Life, and Beyond: From Production to Produsage*. New York: Peter Lang.

Bryce, J., W. (1987). Family time and television use. In T. R. Lindlof (ed.), *Natural Audiences: Qualitative Research on Media Uses and Effects* (pp. 121–38). Norwood, NJ: Ablex.

Buchner, P., Bois-Reymond, M. d. and Kruger, H.-H. (1995). Growing up in three European regions. In L. Chisholm (ed.), *Growing Up in Europe: Contemporary Horizons in Childhood and Youth Studies* (pp. 43–59). Berlin: de Gruyter.

Buckingham, D. (1998). Media education in the UK: Moving beyond protectionism. *Journal of Communication*, *48*(1), 33–42.

—— (2000). *Making Citizens*. London: Routledge.

—— (2005). *The Media Literacy of Children and Young People*. London: Office of Communications.

—— (2006). Is there a digital generation? In D. Buckingham and R. Willett (eds), *Digital Generations* (pp. 1–13). Mahwah, New Jersey: Lawrence Erlbaum Associates.

—— (2007a). *Beyond Technology: Children's Learning in the Age of Digital Culture*. Cambridge: Polity.

—— (2007b). Digital media literacies: Rethinking media education in the age of the internet. *Research in Comparative and International Education*, *2*(1), 43–55.

—— (2008). Introducing identity. In D. Buckingham (ed.), *Youth, Identity, and Digital Media* (vol. 6, pp. 1–22). Cambridge: MIT Press.

Buckingham, D. and Bragg, S. (2004). *Young People, Sex and the Media: The facts of life?* Basingstoke: Palgrave Macmillan.

Buckingham, D., Scanlon, M. and Sefton-Green, J. (2001). Selling the digital dream: Marketing educational technology to teachers and parents. In A. Loveless and V. Ellis (eds), *Subject to Change: Literacy and Digital Technology* (pp. 20–40). London: Routledge.

Buckingham, D. and Sefton-Green, J. (2003). Gotta catch 'em all: Structure, agency and pedagogy in children's media culture. *Media, Culture and Society*, *25*(5), 379–399.

Buijzen, M., van der Molen, J. W. and Sondij, P. (2007). Parental mediation of children's emotional responses to a violent news event. *Communication Research*, *34*(2), 212–30.

Bullying UK. (2006). *The National Bullying Survey 2006*. North Yorkshire: Bullying UK.

Burbules, N. C. (1998). Rhetorics on the web: Hyperreading and critical literacy. In I. Snyder (ed.), *Page to Screen: Taking Literacy Into the Electronic Era* (pp. 102–22). New York: Routledge.

—— (2006). Self-educating communities: Collaboration and learning through the Internet. In Z. Bekerman, N. C. Burbules and D. Silberman-Keller (eds), *Learning in Places: The Informal Education Reader* (pp. 273–84). New York: Peter Lang.

Burdette, H. L. and Whitaker, R. C. (2005). A national study of neighborhood safety, outdoor play, television viewing, and obesity in preschool children. *Pediatrics*, *116*(3), 657–662.

Byron, T. (2008). *Safer Children in a Digital World: The Report of the Byron Review*. London: Department for Children, Schools and Families, and the Department for Culture, Media and Sport. Retrieved from http://www.dcsf.gov.uk/byronreview/

Calvert, S. (1999). *Children's Journeys Through the Information Age*. Boston: McGraw-Hill College.

Cammaerts, B. and Van Audenhove, L. (2005). Online political debate, unbounded citizenship, and the problematic nature of a transnational public sphere. *Political Communication*, *22*(2), 179–96.

CANEE (2006). *Research on Risky Behaviours of Polish Children on the Internet*. Child Abuse and Neglect in Eastern Europe. Retrieved from http://www.canee.net/

Carey, J. W. (1992). *Communication as Culture: Essays on Media and Society*. New York: Routledge.

Caron, A. H. and Caronia, L. (2001). Active users and active objects: The mutual construction of families and communication technologies. *Convergence, The Journal Of Research Into New Media Technologies*, 7(3), 38–67.

Cassell, J. (2004). Towards a model of technology and literacy development: Story listening Systems. *Journal of Applied Developmental Psychology*, *25*(1), 75–105.

Castells, M. (2001). *The Internet Galaxy*. Oxford: Oxford University Press.

CEOP (2008). *CEOP Annual Review 2007–8*. London: Child Exploitation and Online Protection Centre.

Children's Society, The (2006). *The Good Childhood Enquiry*. London: The Children's Society.

—— (2007). Childhood friendships at risk reveals new survey [Electronic Version]. Retrieved 04 September, 2008 from http://www.childrenssociety.org.uk/whats_happening/media_office/latest_news/Childhood_Friendships_At_Risk_Reveals_New_Survey_3623_pr.html.

ChildWise (2009). *The Monitor Report 2008–9: Children's Media Use and Purchasing*. Norwich: ChildWise.

Christ, W. G. and Potter, W. J. (1998). Media literacy, media education, and the academy. *Journal of Communication*, *48*(1), 5–15.

CIRCLE (2008). *Young Voters in the 2008 Presidential Election*. Medford, MA: The Center for Information and Research on Civic Learning and Engagement. Retrieved from http://www.civicyouth.org/

CivicWeb (2008). The production of civic websites for young people. Retrieved from http://www.civicweb.eu/images/stories/reports/ civicwebwp74thnovemberproducerreportfinal.pdf

Clark, L. S. (2002). U.S. adolescent religious identity, the media, and the 'funky' side of religion. *Journal of Communication*, 52(4), 794–811.

—— (2003). Challenges of social good in the world of 'grand theft auto' and 'Barbie': A case study of a community computer center for youth. *New Media and Society*, 5(1), 95–116.

—— (2005). The constant contact generation: exploring teen friendship networks online. In S. Mazzarella (ed.), *Girl Wide Web* (pp. 203–22). New York: Peter Lang.

Clarke, J., Newman, J. and Smith, N. (2007). *Creating Citizen-Consumers: Changing Publics and Changing Public Services*. London: Sage.

Cohen, S. (1972). *Folk Devils and Moral Panics: The Creation of Mods and Rockers*. London: MacGibbon and Kee.

Cole, J. (2007). *The 2007 Digital Future Report*. Los Angeles: USC Annenberg School for Communication, Center for the Digital Future.

Coleman, J. and Hagell, A. (eds). (2007). *Adolescence, Risk and Resilience: Against the Odds*. Chichester: Wiley.

Coleman, J. and Hendry, L. (1999). *The Nature of Adolescence* (3rd edn). London: Routledge.

Coleman, S. (1999). The new media and democratic politics. *New Media and Society*, 1(1), 67–73.

—— (2003). A tale of two houses: The House of Commons, the Big Brother house and the people at home. *Parliamentary Affairs*, 56(4), 733–758.

—— (2007). E-democracy: The history and future of an idea. In D. Quah, R. Silverstone, R. Mansell and C. Avgerou (eds), *The Oxford Handbook of Information and Communication Technologies* (pp. 362–82). Oxford: Oxford University Press.

Collishaw, S., Maughan, B., Goodman, R. and Pickles, A. (2004). Time trends in adolescent mental health. *Journal of Child Psychology and Psychiatry*, 45(8), 1350–62.

Compaine, B. M. (ed.). (2001). *The Digital Divide: Facing a Crisis or Creating a Myth?* Cambridge MA: MIT Press.

comScore. (2008). Social networking explodes worldwide as sites increase their focus on cultural relevance. Retrieved 15/09/08, from http://www. comscore.com/press/release.asp?press=2396

Condie, R. and Munro, B. (2007). *The Impact of ICT in Schools – A Landscape Review*. Coventry: Becta.

Cook, L. (2005). School without walls: Reconnecting the disconnected at 14 +. *Support for Learning*, 20, 90–5.

Coontz, S. (1997). *The Way We Really Are: Coming to Terms with America's Changing Families*. New York: Basic Books.

Corner, J. (2004). Freedom, rights and regulations. *Media, Culture and Society*, 26(6), 893–899.

Corsaro, W. A. (1997). *The Sociology of Childhood*. Thousand Oaks, California: Pine Forge Press.

Cottrell, L., Branstetter, S., Cottrell, S., Rishel, C. and Stanton, B. F. (2007). Comparing adolescent and parent perceptions of current and future disapproved Internet use. *Journal of Children and Media, 1*(3), 210–26.

Couldry, N., Livingstone, S. and Markham, T. (2007). Connection or disconnection? Tracking the mediated public sphere in everyday life. In R. Butsch (ed.), *Media and Public Spheres* (pp. 28–42): Palgrave-Mcmillan.

—— (2007). *Media Consumption and Public Engagement: Beyond the Presumption of Attention*. Basingstoke: Palgrave Macmillan.

Cragg, A. (2000). *R18 Pornography. Are 'Experts' in a Position to Say that Children are Harmed if they View R18 Videos?* London: BBFC/Cragg Ross Dawson.

Criddle, L. (2006). *Look Both Ways: Help Protect Your Family on the Internet*. Redmond, Washington: Microsoft Press.

Critcher, C. (2008). Making waves: Historic aspects of public debates about children and mass media. In K. Drotner and S. Livingstone (eds), *International Handbook of Children, Media and Culture* (pp. 91–104). London: Sage.

Crook, C. (2008). *Theories of Formal and Informal Learning in the World of Web 2.0*. Paper presented at the ESRC Seminar Series: The educational and social impact of new technologies on young people in Britain, Oxford. Retrieved from http://www.education.ox.ac.uk/esrcseries/uploaded/08_03 14%20ESRC%20report_web.pdf

Cunningham, H. (1995). *Children and Childhood in Western Society Since 1500*. London: Longman.

—— (2006). *The Invention of Childhood*. London: BBC Books.

Cutler, D. and Taylor, A. (2003). *Expanding and Sustaining Involvement: A Snapshot of Participation Infrastructure for Young People living in England*. Dunfermline, Fife: Carnegie Young People Initiative.

Dahlgren, P. (2003). Reconfiguring civic culture in the new media milieu. In J. Corner and D. Pels (eds), *Media and the Restyling of Politics* (pp. 151–70). London: Sage.

—— (2005). The Internet, public spheres, and political communication: Dispersion and deliberation. *Political Communication, 22*(2), 147–62.

Dahlgren, P. and Olsson, T. (2007). From public sphere to civic culture: Young citizens' internet use. In R. Butsch (ed.), *Media and Public Spheres* (pp. 198–209). New York: Pallgrave Macmillan.

—— (2008). Facilitating political participation: Young citizens, Internet and civic cultures In K. Drotner and S. Livingstone (eds), *International Handbook of Children, Media and Culture* (pp. 493–507). London: Sage.

Dahlquist, J. P. and Vigilant, L. G. (2004). Way better than real: Manga sex to tentacle Hentai. In D. D. Waskul (ed.), *Net.seXXX: Readings on Sex, Pornography, and the Internet* (pp. 90–103). New York: P. Lang.

Darton, K. (2005). *Children and Young People and Mental Health. Mind factsheets.* London: Mind (National Association for Mental Health).

262 References

Dayan, D. (2001). The peculiar public of television. *Media, Culture and Society*, *23*, 751–73.

DCMS (2001). *A General Statement of Policy by the Department for Culture, Media and Sport on Media Literacy and Critical Viewing Skills*: Department for Culture, Media and Sport Broadcasting Policy Division.

DCSF (2007). *A Summary of Current Government ICT Initiatives in Schools*. London: Department for Children, Schools and Families.

de Certeau, M. (1984). *The Practices of Everyday Life*. Los Angeles: University of California Press.

De Rutgers Nisso Groep (2006). Verliefd op Internet (In love on the Web). Retrieved from http://www.rutgersnissogroep.nl.

Debord, G. (1995). *The Society of the Spectacle*. New York: Zone Books.

—— (2002). Full text of John Denham's speech [Electronic Version]. *Guardian*,. Retrieved 29/07/08 from http://www.guardian.co.uk/society/2002/nov/25/childrensservices1.

Department for Education and Skills (2006). *Learning, Teaching and Managing with ICT: Funding Guidance for Schools and Local Authorities 2006–2007*. Annesley: DfES Publications.

DfEE (2000). *Survey of Information and Communication Technologies in Schools, England*. London: The Stationery Office. Retrieved from http://www.dcsf.gov.uk/rsgateway/DB/SBU/b000197/index.shtml.

—— (2007). *Connecting the Learning Society: A National Grid for Learning. Green Paper*. London: Department for Education and Enterprise.

—— (2005). *Harnessing Technology: Transforming Learning and Children's Services*. Nottingham: Department for Education and Skills.

DiMaggio, P., Hargittai, E., Celeste, C. and Shafer, S. (2004). From unequal access to differentiated use: A literature review and agenda for research on digital inequality. In K. Neckerman (ed.), *Social Inequality* (pp. 355–400). New York: Russell Sage Foundation.

Dollman, J., Norton, K. and Norton, L. (2005). Evidence for secular trends in children's physical activity behaviour. *British Journal of Sports Medicine*, *39*, 892–7.

Dorr, A. (1986). *Television and Children: A Special Medium for a Special Audience*. Beverley Hills, CA: Sage.

Douglas, J. Y. (1998). Will the most reflexive relativist please stand up: Hypertext, argument and realism. In I. Snyder (ed.), *Page to Screen: Taking Literacy into Electronic Era* (pp. 144–62). London and New York: Routledge.

Douglas, M. (1966). *Purity and Danger: An Analysis of the Concepts of Pollution and Taboo*. London: Routledge.

Drotner, K. (1992). Modernity and media panics. In M. Skovmand and K. C. Schroeder (eds), *Media Cultures: Reappraising Transnational Media* (pp. 42–62). London: Routledge.

—— (2000). Difference and diversity: Trends in young Danes' media use. *Media, Culture and Society*, *22*(2), 149–66.

—— (2005). Media on the move: Personalised media and the transformation of publicness. In S. Livingstone (ed.), *Audiences and Publics: When*

Cultural Engagement Matters for the Public Sphere (pp. 187–212). Bristol: Intellect Press.

du Gay, P., Hall, S., Janes, L. and Mackay, H. N. (1997). *Doing Cultural Studies: The Story of the Sony Walkman.* London and Thousand Oaks, CA: Sage, in association with The Open University.

Dutton, W. H. and Helsper, E. (2007). *The Internet in Britain: 2007.* Oxford: Oxford Internet Institute, University of Oxford.

Dutton, W. H. and Shepherd, A. (2004). *Confidence and Risk on the Internet.* Oxford: Oxford Internet Institute.

Dwyer, C. (2007). *Digital Relationships in the 'MySpace' Generation: Results from a Qualitative Study.* Paper presented at the Fortieth Hawaii International Conference on System Sciences, Los Alamitos. Retrieved from doi:10.1109/HICSS.2007.176

Dynarski, M., Agodini, R., Heaviside, S., Novak, T., Carey, N., Campuzano, L., *et al.* (2007). *Effectiveness of Reading and Mathematics Software Products: Findings from the First Student Cohort.* US Department of Education: Institute of Education Sciences.

Eastin, M. S. and LaRose, R. (2000). Internet Self-Efficacy and the Psychology of the Digital Divide. *Journal of Computer-Mediated Communication,* 6(1), doi:10.1111/j.1083–6101.2000.tb00110.x.

Eastin, M. S., Yang, M.-S. and Nathanson, A. I. (2006). Children of the net: An empirical exploration into the evaluation of internet content. *Journal of Broadcasting and Electronic Media,* 50(2), 211–230.

Eco, U. (1979). Introduction: The role of the reader. In *The Role of the Reader: Explorations in the Semiotics of Texts* (pp. 3–43). Bloomington: Indiana University Press.

EIAA (2006). Social networking to drive next wave of Internet usage. Retrieved 06/07/07, from http://www.eiaa.net/news/eiaa-articles-details. asp?id=106andlang=1

Electoral Commission, The (2004). *Political Engagement Among Young People: An Update.* London: The Electoral Commission.

—— (2005). *Election 2005: Turnout. How Many, Who and Why?* London: The Electoral Commission.

—— (2007). *An Audit of Political Engagement 4.* London: The Electoral Commission.

Elliott, A. (2002). Beck's sociology of risk: A critical assessment. *Sociology,* 36(2), 293–315.

Ellis, J. (2002). *Seeing Things: Television in the Age of Uncertainty.* London: I. B.Tauris.

Erikson, E. H. (1959/80). *Identity and the Life Cycle.* New York: W. H. Norton and Co.

Erstad, O. and Wertsch, J. (2008). Tales of mediation: Narrative and digital media as cultural tools. In K. Lundby (ed.), *Digital Storytelling, Mediatized Stories: Self-Representations in New Media* (pp. 21–40). New York: Peter Lang.

264 References

Esler, B. W. (2005). Filtering, blocking and rating: Chaperones or censorship? In M. Klang and A. Murray (eds), *Human Rights in the Digital Age* (pp. 99–110). London: Glasshouse Press.

Eurobarometer (2006). *Eurobarometer 64.4 – Special No. 250: Safer Internet.* Luxembourg: European Commission: Directorate General Information Society and Media.

—— (2007). *Eurobarometer on Safer Internet for Children: Qualitative Study 2007.* Retrieved from http://ec.europa.eu/information_society/activities/ sip/eurobarometer/index_en.htm.

—— (2008) *Towards a Safer Use of the Internet for Children in the EU: A Parents' Perspective.* Luxembourg: European Commission.

Europa (2007). Media literacy: Do people really understand how to make the most of blogs, search engines or interactive TV? Retrieved 19/7/08, from http://europa.eu/rapid/pressReleasesAction.do?reference=IP/07/197 0andformat=HTMLandaged=1andlanguage=ENandguiLanguage=en

European Commission,The (2007a). AVMSD – What is it? Retrieved 11/9/08, from http://ec.europa.eu/avpolicy/reg/avms/index_en.htm

—— (2007b). Information Society Policies at a Glance. Retrieved 27/2/07, from http://ec.europa.eu/information_society/tl/policy/index_en.htm

—— (2007c). Safer Internet and Online Technologies for Children: Summary of the Results of the Online Public Consultation and 20–1 June 2007 Safer Internet Forum Report Retrieved 11/8/08, from http://ec.europa.eu/infor- mation_society/activities/sip/docs/public_consultation_prog/summary_ report.pdf

—— (2007d). Study on media literacy: Current trends and approaches to media literacy in Europe. Retrieved 15/7/08, from http://ec.europa.eu/ avpolicy/media_literacy/studies/index_en.htm

—— (n.d.). Protection of minors. Retrieved 15/9/08, from http://ec.europa. eu/avpolicy/reg/minors/index_en.htm

Eurydice (2005). *Key Data on Education in Europe.* Brussels: Eurydice. Retrieved from www.okm.gov.hu/doc/upload/200601/key_data_2005.pdf.

Facer, K. and Furlong, R. (2001). Beyond the myth of the 'cyberkid': Young people at the margins of the information revolution. *Journal of Youth Studies, 4*(4), 451–469.

Facer, K., Furlong, J., Furlong, R. and Sutherland, R. (2003). *ScreenPlay: Children and Computing in the Home.* London: RoutledgeFalmer.

Fahey, T. (1995). Privacy and the family. *Sociology, 29,* 687–703.

Ferguson, H. (1997). Protecting children in new times: Child protection and the risk society. *Child and Family Social Work, 2,* 221–34.

Fernback, J. and Papacharissi, Z. (2007). Online privacy as legal safeguard: The relationship among consumer, online portal, and privacy policies. *New Media and Society, 9*(5), 715–734.

Fielder, A., Gardner, W., Nairn, A. and Pitt, J. (2007). *Fair game? Assessing Commercial Activity on Children's Favourite Websites and Online Environ- ments.* London: National Consumer Council and Childnet International.

Finkelhor, D. (2008). *Childhood Victimization: Violence, Crime, and Abuse in the Lives of Young People.* Oxford: Oxford University Press.

Fiske, J. (1987). *Television Culture.* London: Methuen.

Fleming, M. J., Greentree, S., Cocotti-Muller, D., Elias, K. A. and Morrison, S. (2006). Safety in cyberspace – Adolescents' safety and exposure online. *Youth and Society, 38*(2), 135–154.

Flichy, P. (1995). *Dynamics of Modern Communication: The Shaping and Impact of New Communication Technologies.* London: Sage.

Flint, D. (2000). The internet and children's rights – Suffer the little children. *Computer Law and Security Report, 16*(2), 88–94.

Flood, M. and Hamilton, C. (2003). *Youth and Pornography in Australia: Evidence on the Extent of Exposure and Likely Effects.* (Discussion paper number 52): The Australia Institute. Retrieved from http://www.tai.org.au/

Fornäs, J. (2002). Passages across thresholds: Into the borderlands of mediation. *Convergence, 8*(4), 89–106.

Fornäs, J. and Bolin, G. (eds). (1995). *Youth Culture in Late Modernity.* London: Sage.

Fornäs, J., Klein, K., Ladendorf, M., Sunden, J. and Svenigsson, M. (eds). (2002). *Digital Borderlands: Cultural Studies of Identity and Interactivity on the Internet.* New York: Peter Lang.

France, A. (2007). *Understanding Youth in Late Modernity.* Maidenhead: Open University Press.

Freire, P. and Macedo, D. (1987). *Literacy: Reading the Word and the World.* South Handley, MA: Bergin and Garvey.

Frith, S. (1978). *The Sociology of Rock.* London: Constable.

Gadlin, H. (1978). Child discipline and the pursuit of self: An historical interpretation. In H. W. Reese and L. P. Lipsitt (eds), *Advances in Child Development and Behavior* (vol. 12, pp. 231–61). New York: Academic Press.

Gee, J. P. (2008). Learning theory, videogames, and popular culture. In K. Drotner and S. Livingstone (eds), *International Handbook of Children, Media and Culture* (pp. 196–212). London: Sage.

—— (2003). *What Video Games Have to Teach Us About Learning and Literacy.* New York: Palgrave Macmillan.

Gergen, K. J. (2002). The challenge of absent presence. In J. E. Katz and M. Aakhus (eds), *Perpetual Contact: Mobile Communication, Private Talk, Public Performance* (pp. 227–41). Cambridge: Cambridge University Press.

Gibson, R., Lusoli, W. and Ward, S. (2002). *UK Political Participation Online: The Public Response. A Survey of Citizens' Political Activity via the Internet.* Salford: ESRI, www.ipop.org.uk.

Giddens, A. (1984). *The Constitution of Society: Outline of the Theory of Structuration.* Cambridge: Polity.

—— (1991). *Modernity and Self-Identity: Self and Society in the Late Modern Age.* Cambridge: Polity.

—— (1993). *The Transformation of Intimacy: Sexuality, Love and Eroticism in Modern Societies.* Cambridge: Polity.

—— (1995). Living in a post-traditional society. In U. Beck, A. Giddens and S. Lash (eds), *Reflexive Modernization: Politics, Tradition and Aesthetics in the Modern Social Order* (pp. 56–109). Cambridge: Polity.

Gill, T. (2007). *No Fear: Growing Up in a Risk Averse Society*. London: Calouste Gulbenkian Foundation.

Gilligan, C. (1993). *In a Different Voice: Psychological Theory and Women's Development* (Second ed.). Cambridge, MA: Harvard University Press.

Goffman, E. (1959). *The Presentation of Self in Everyday Life*. Harmondsworth: Penguin.

Golding, P. (2000). Forthcoming features: Information and communications technologies and the sociology of the future. *Sociology*, *34*(1), 165–84.

Golding, P. and Murdock, G. (2001). Digital divides: Communications policy and its contradictions. *New Economy*, *8*(2), 110–15.

Goldman, S., Booker, A. and McDermott, M. (2008). Mixing the digital, social, and cultural: Learning, identity, and agency in youth participation. In D. Buckingham (ed.), *Youth, Identity, and Digital Media* (pp. 185–206). Cambridge, MA: MIT Press.

Goode, S. (2008). The splendor of little girls: Social constructions of paedophiles and child sexual abuse. In A. Curry (ed.), *Territories of Evil: Inter-Disciplinary Perspectives on Evil and Wickedness*. Oxford: Inter-Disciplinary Press.

Gore, A. (1991). Information superhighways: The next information revolution. *The Futurist*, *25*, 21–23.

Goswami, U. (2008). *Byron Review on the Impact of New Technologies on Children: a Research Literature Review: Child Development*. Cambridge: Cambridge University Press.

Graue, M. E. and Walsh, D. J. (1998). *Studying Children in Context: Theories, Methods and Ethics*. Thousand Oaks: Sage.

Green, B., Reid, J. and Bigum, C. (1998). Teaching the nintendo generation? Children, computer culture and popular technologies. In S. Howard (ed.), *Wired-Up: Young People and the Electronic Media* (pp. 19–41). London: UCL Press.

Green, E., Mitchell, W. and Bunton, R. (2000). Contextualizing risk and danger: An analysis of young people's perceptions of risk. *Journal of Youth Studies*, *3*(2), 109–26.

Greenfield, P. M., Gross, E. F., Subrahmanyam, K., Suzuki, L. K. and Tynes, B. (2006). Teens on the Internet: Interpersonal connection, identity, and information. In R. Kraut, M. Brynin and S. Kiesler (eds), *Computers, Phones, and the Internet: Domesticating Information Technology* (pp. 185–200). Oxford, New York: Oxford University Press.

Grimes, S. M. and Shade, L. R. (2005). Neopian economics of play: children's cyberpets and online communities as immersive advertising in NeoPets.com. *International Journal of Media and Cultural Politics*, *1*(2), 181–98.

Grisso, A. D. and Weiss, D. (2005). What are gURLS talking about? Adolescent girls' construction of sexual identity on gURL.com. In S. Mazzarella (ed.), *Girl Wide Web* (pp. 31–50). New York: Peter Lang.

Gross, E., F. (2004). Adolescent internet use: What we expect, what teens report. *Applied Developmental Psychology*, 25(6), 633–49.

Guardian (2007). Parents and teenagers' survey. London: *Guardian*. Retrieved from http://image.guardian.co.uk/sys-files/Guardian/documents/2007/02/23/kids.pdf

Guzzetti, B. J. (2006). Cybergirls: Negotiating social identities on cybersites. *E-Learning*, 3(2), 158–69.

Habermas, J. (1981/7). *The Theory of Communicative Action. Lifeworld and System: A Critique of Functionalist Reason* (T. McCarthy, trans. vol. 2). Cambridge: Polity.

—— (1962/1989). *The Structural Transformation of the Public Sphere: An Inquiry into a Category of Bourgeois Society*. Cambridge: MIT Press.

Haddon, L. (2004). *Information and Communication Technologies in Everyday Life: A Concise Introduction and Research Guide*. Oxford: Berg.

Hall, S. (1980). Encoding/Decoding. In S. Hall, D. Hobson, A. Lowe and P. Willis (eds), *Culture, Media, Language* (pp. 128–38). London: Hutchinson.

—— (1996). Introduction: Who needs identity? In S. Hall and P. du Gay (eds), *Questions of Cultural Identity* (pp. 1–17). London: Sage.

Hall, S. and Jefferson, T. (eds). (1976). *Resistance Through Rituals: Youth Subcultures in Post-War Britain*. London: Hutchinson and Co.

Hamelink, C. J. (2003). *Statement on Communication Rights*. Paper presented at the World Forum on Communication Rights. Retrieved from http://www.globalizacija.com/doc_en/e0030ict.htm.

—— (2008). Children's communication rights: Beyond intentions. In K. Drotner and S. Livingstone (eds), *International Handbook of Children, Media and Culture* (pp. 508–19). London: Sage.

Hampton, K. and Wellman, B. (2003). Neighboring in netville: How the internet supports community and social capital in a wired suburb. *City and Community*, 2(4), 277–311.

Hansard Society. (2001). *None of the Above – Non-Voters and the 2001 Election*. London: Hansard Society.

Harden, J. (2000). There's no place like home: The public/private distinction in children's theorizing of risk and safety. *Childhood*, 7(1), 43–59.

Hargittai, E. (2007). A framework for studying differences in people's digital media uses. In N. Kutscher and H.-U. Otto (eds), *Cyberworld Unlimited* (pp. 121–37): VS Verlag für Sozialwissenschaften/GWV Fachverlage GmbH.

Hargittai, E. and Shafer, S. (2006). Differences in actual and perceived online skills: The role of gender. *Social Science Quarterly*, 87(2), 432–48.

Hargittai, E. and Walejko, G. (2008). The participation divide: Content creation and sharing in the digital age. *Information, Communication and Society*, 11(2), 239–56.

Harris Interactive. (2006). Friendships in the age of social networking websites [electronic version]. *Trends and Tudes*, 5. Retrieved 5 August, 2008 from http://www.harrisinteractive.com/news/newsletters_k12.asp

Harrison, C., Comber, C., Fisher, T., Haw, K., Lewin, C., Lunzer, E., *et al.* (2003). *ImpaCT2: The Impact of Information and Communication Technologies on Pupil Learning and Attainment.* Coventry: Becta.

Hartley, J. (2002). *Communication, Cultural and Media Studies: The Key Concepts.* London: Routledge.

Hasebrink, U., Livingstone, S. and Haddon, L. (2009). *Comparing Children's Online Opportunities and Risks across Europe: Cross-National Comparisons for EU Kids Online. EU Kids Online Deliverable D3.2 for the EC Safer Internet plus Programme* (2nd edn). LSE, London: EU Kids Online.

Hawisher, G. E. and Selfe, C. L. (1998). Reflections on computers and composition studies at the century's end. In I. Snyder (ed.), *Page to Screen: Taking Literacy into the Electronic Era* (pp. 3–19). London and New York: Routledge.

Hayward, B., Alty, C., Pearson, S. and Martin, C. (2002). *Young People and ICT 2002: Findings from a Survey Conducted in Autumn 2002.* Coventry: British Educational Computing and Technology Association.

Heins, M. (2001). *Not In Front of the Children: 'Indecency,' Censorship and the Innocence of Youth.* New York: Hill and Wang.

Helsper, E. (2005). *R18 Material: Its Potential Impact on People under 18: An Overview of the Available Literature.* London: Office of Communications.

Henry, L. A. (2005). Information search strategies on the Internet: A critical component of new literacies. *Webology, 2*(1), Article 9.

Heverly, R. A. (2008). Growing up digital: Control and the pieces of a digital life. In T. McPherson (ed.), *Digital Youth, Innovations, and the Unexpected* (vol. 4, pp. 199–218). Cambridge: MIT Press.

Hill, M. and Tisdall, K. (1997). *Children and Society.* London: Longman.

Hillman, M., Adams, J. and Whitelegg, J. (1990). *One False Move . . . A Study of Children's Independent Mobility.* London: Policy Studies Institute.

Hinduja, S. and Patchin, J. (2008). Personal information of adolescents on the Internet: A quantitative content analysis of MySpace. *Journal of Adolescence, 31*(1), 125–46.

Hjarvard, S. (2008). The mediatization of religion: A theory of the media as agents of religious change. In *Northern Lights 2008. Yearbook of Film and Media Studies.* Bristol: Intellect Press.

HM Government (2004). *Every Child Matters: Change for Children.* London. Retrieved from http://www.everychildmatters.gov.uk/publications/

Hobbs, R. (1998). The seven great debates in the media literacy movement. *Journal of Communication, 48*(1), 6–32.

—— (2008). Debates and challenges facing new literacies in the 21st century. In K. Drotner and S. Livingstone (eds), *International Handbook of Children, Media and Culture* (pp. 431–47). London: Sage.

Hoggart, R. (1957). *The Uses of Literacy.* London: Chatto and Windus.

Hohendahl, P. U. (1974). Introduction to reception aesthetics. *New German Critique, 3*(Fall), 29–63.

Holloway, S. L. and Valentine, G. (2003). *Cyberkids: Children in the Information Age*. London: RoutledgeFalmer.

Home Office (n.d.). Online child protection taskforce. Retrieved 15/9/08, from http://police.homeoffice.gov.uk/operational-policing/crime-disorder/child-protection-taskforce.

Hoover, S. M., Clark, L. S. and Alters, D. F. (2004). *Media, Home, and Family*. New York: Routledge.

Hope, A. (2007). Risk taking, boundary performance and intentional school Internet 'Misuse'. *Discourse, 28*(1), 87–99.

House of Commons Culture Media and Sport Committee. (2008). Harmful content on the Internet and in video games: Tenth Report of Session 2007–08. Retrieved 11/9/08, from http://www.publications.parliament.uk/pa/cm200708/cmselect/cmcumeds/353/353.pdf

Huston, A. C. and Wright, J. C. (1998). Television and the informational and educational needs of children. *Annals of the American Academy of Political and Social Science, 557*, 9–23.

Hutchby, I. (2001). Technologies, texts and affordances. *Sociology, 35*(2), 441–56.

Information Literacy Meeting of Experts. (2003). The Prague declaration: Towards an information literate society. Retrieved from http://68.163.78.28/libinter/infolitconfandmeet/post-infolitconfandmeet/FinalReportPrague.pdf

Internet Crime Forum (2000). *Chat Wise, Street Wise: Children and Internet Chat Services*. UK: The Internet Crime Forum IRC sub-group.

Internet Safety Technical Task Force (2008). *Enhancing Child Safety and Online Technologies: Final Report of the ISTTF to the Multi-State Working Group on Social Networking of State Attorney Generals of the United States*. Cambridge, MA: Berkman Center for Internet and Society, Harvard University.

Isaacs, E. and Walendowski, A. (2002). *Designing From Both Sides of the Screen: How Designers and Engineers can Collaborate to build a Co-operative Technology*. Indianapolis: New Riders.

Iser, W. (1980). Interaction between text and reader. In S. R. Suleiman and I. Crosman (eds), *The Reader in the Text: Essays on Audience and Interpretation* (pp. 106–21). Princeton: Princeton University Press.

Ito, M. (2008). Mobilizing the imagination in everyday play: The case of Japanese media mixes. In K. Drotner and S. Livingstone (eds), *International Handbook of Children, Media and Culture* (pp. 397–412). London: Sage.

Ito, M., Horst, H. A., Bittanti, M., boyd, d., Herr-Stephenson, B., Lange, P. G., *et al*. (2008). Living and learning with new media: Summary of findings from the digital youth project: The John D. and Catherine T. MacArthur Foundation. Retrieved from http://digitalyouth.ischool.berkeley.edu/report

IWF (2008). *2007 Annual and Charity Report*. Cambridge: Internet Watch Foundation.

Jackson, L. A., von Eye, A., Biocca, F., Barbatsis, G., Zhao, Y. and Fitzgerald, H. E. (2006a). Children's home internet use: Predictors and psychological, social and academic consequences. In R. Kraut, M. Brynin and S. Kiesler (eds), *Computers, Phones, and the Internet: Domesticating Information Technology* (pp. 145–67). Oxford: Oxford University Press.

—— (2006b). Does home Internet use influence the academic performance of low-income children? *Developmental Psychology, 42*(3), 429–35.

Jackson, S. and Scott, S. (1999). Risk anxiety and the social construction of childhood. In D. Lupton (ed.), *Risk and Sociocultural Theory: New Directions and Perspectives* (pp. 86–107). Cambridge: Cambridge University Press.

James, A. and James, A. (2008). European childhoods: An overview. In A. James and A. L. James (eds), *European Childhoods: Cultures, Politics and Childhoods in Europe* (pp. 1–13). Basingstoke: Palgrave Macmillan.

James, A., Jenks, C. and Prout, A. (1998). *Theorizing Childhood*. Cambridge: Cambridge University Press.

James, C., Davis, K., Flores, A., Francies, J. M., Pettingill, L., Rundle, M., *et al.* (2008). *Young People, Ethics, and the New Digital Media: A Synthesis from the Good Play Project* (GoodWork® Project Report Series, Number 54). Cambridge: Harvard Graduate School of Education.

Jankowski, N., Jones, S., Samarajiva, R. and Silverstone, R. (1999). Editorial. *New Media and Society, 1*(1), 5–9.

Jenkins, H. (2003). *Quentin Tarantino's Star Wars?* Digital cinema, media convergence, and participatory culture. In D. Thorburn and H. Jenkins (eds), *Rethinking Media Change: The Aesthetics of Transition* (pp. 281–312). Cambridge, MA: MIT Press.

—— (2006a). *Convergence Culture: Where Old and New Media Collide.* New York: New York University Press.

—— (2006b). *An Occasional Paper on Digital Media and Learning. Confronting the Challenges of Participatory Culture: Media Education for the 21st Century.* Chicago: The John D and Catherine T Macarthur Foundation.

Jensen, K. B. and Helles, R. (2005). 'Who do you think we are?' A content analysis of websites as participatory resources for politics, business and civil society. In *Interface://Culture: The World Wide Web as Political Resources and Aesthetic Form* (pp. 93–122). Frederiksberg, Denmark: Samfundslitteratur Press/Nordicom.

Jessop, B. (2002). *The Future of the Capitalist State.* Cambridge: Polity.

John, D. R. (1999). Consumer socialization of children: A retrospective look at twenty-five years of research. *Journal of Consumer Research, 26*(3), 183–213.

Johnson-Eilola, J. (1998). Living on the surface: Learning in the age of global communication networks. In I. Snyder (ed.), *Page to Screen: Taking Literacy into the Electronic Era* (pp. 185–210). New York: Routledge.

Johnson, J. and Dyer, J. (2005). *User-Defined Content in a Constructivist Learning Environment.* Paper presented at the m-ICTE 2005.

Jones, K. S. (2003). What is an affordance? *Ecological Psychology, 15*(2), 107–14.

Jordan, A. B., Hersey, J. C., McDivitt, J. A. and Heitzler, C. D. (2006). Reducing children's television-viewing time: A qualitative study of parents and their children. *Pediatrics*, *118*(5), E1303–E1310.

Joyce, M. (1998). New stories for new readers: Contours, coherence and constructive hypertext. In I. Snyder (ed.), *Page to Screen: Taking Literacy into Electronic Era* (pp. 162–82). London: Routledge.

Kahn, R. and Kellner, D. (2004). New media and internet activism: From the 'Battle of Seattle' to blogging. *New Media and Society*, *6*(1), 87–95.

Kann, M. E., Berry, J., Gant, C. and Zager, P. (2007). The internet and youth political participation. *First Monday*, *12*(8).

Karsten, L. and van Vliet, W. (2006). Increasing children's freedom of movement: Introduction. *Children, Youth and Environments*, *16*(1), 69–74.

Katz, E. (2003). Disintermediating the parents: What else is new? In J. Turow and A. L. Kavanaugh (eds), *In The Wired Homestead: An MIT Sourcebook on the Internet and the Family* (pp. 45–52). Cambridge, MA: MIT Press.

Kayany, J. M. and Yelsme, P. (2000). Displacements effects of online media in the socio-technical contexts of households. *Journal of Broadcasting and Electronic Media*, *44*(2), 215–29.

Kearney, M. C. (2007). Productive spaces: Girls' bedrooms as sites of cultural production. *Journal of Children and Media*, *1*(2), 126–41.

Kellner, D. (2002). New media and new literacies: Reconstructing education for the new millenium. In L. Lievrouw and S. Livingstone (eds), *The Handbook of New Media* (pp. 90–104). London: Sage.

Kellner, D. and Share, J. (2007). Critical media literacy is not an option. *Learning Inquiry*, *1*(1), 59–69.

Kelly, P. (2000). The dangerousness of youth-at-risk: The possibilities of surveillance and intervention in uncertain times. *Journal of Adolescence*, *23*, 463–76.

Kenix, L. J. (2007). In search of utopia: An analysis of non-profit web pages. *Information, Communication and Society*, *10*(1), 69–94.

Kenway, J. and Bullen, E. (2001). *Consuming Children: Education-Entertainment-Advertising*. Buckingham, England: Open University Press.

—— (2008). Dividing delights: Children, adults and the search for sales. In K. Drotner and S. Livingstone (eds), *International Handbook of Children, Media and Culture* (pp. 168–82). London: Sage.

Kerawalla, L. and Crook, C. (2002). Children's computer use at home and at school: Context and continuity. *British Education Research Journal*, *22*, 751–71

Kiesler, S., Zdaniuk, B., Lundmark, V. and Kraut, R. (2000). Troubles with the Internet: The dynamics of help at home. *Human–Computer Interaction*, *15*, 323–51.

Kimberlee, R. H. (2002). Why don't British young people vote at general elections? *Journal of Youth Studies*, *5*(1), 85–98.

Kinder, M. (ed.). (1999). *Kids' Media Culture*. Durham: Duke University Press.

272 References

Kitchen, S., Finch, S. and Sinclair, R. (2007). *Harnessing Technology Schools Survey*. Coventry: Becta.

Kitzinger, J. (2004). *Framing Abuse: Media Influence and Public Understanding of Sexual Violence against Children*. London: Pluto Press.

Kline, S. (1993). *Out of the Garden: Toys and Children's Culture in the Age of TV Marketing*. London and New York: Verso.

—— (2003). Media effects: Redux or reductive? *Particip@tions, 1*(1).

Klinke, A. and Renn, O. (2001). Precautionary principle and discursive strategies: classifying and managing risks. *Journal of Risk Research, 4*(2), 159–74.

Kraut, R., Kiesler, S., Boneva, B., Cummings, J., Helgeson, V. and Crawford, A. (2002). Internet paradox revisited. *Journal of Social Issues, 58*(1), 49–74.

Kraut, R., Lundmark, V., Patterson, M., Kiesler, S., Mukopadhyay, T. and Scherlis, M. (1998). Internet paradox: A social technology that reduces social involvement and psychological well-being? *American Psychologist, 53*(9), 1017–31.

Kress, G. (1998). Visual and verbal models of representation on electronically mediated communication: The potentials of new forms of text. In I. Snyder (ed.), *Page to Screen: Taking Literacy Into Electronic Era* (pp. 53–79). London: Routledge.

—— (2003). *Literacy in the New Media Age*. London: Routledge.

Kunkel, D. (2001). Children and television advertising. In D. Singer and J. Singer (eds), *Handbook of Children and Media* (pp. 375–93). Thousand Oaks, CA: Sage.

Kunkel, D., Wilcox, B., Cantor, J., Palmer, E., Linn, S. and Dowrick, P. (2004). *Report of the APA Task Force on Advertising and Children*. Washington, DC: American Psychological Association.

Lafrance, J. P. (1996). Games and players in the electronic age: Tools for analysing the use of video games by adults and children. *Reseaux, 4*(2), 301–22.

Lankes, R. D. (2008). Trusting the internet: New approaches to credibility tools. In M. J. Metzger and A. J. Flanagin (eds), *Digital Media, Youth, and Credibility* (vol. 2, pp. 101–21). Cambridge: MIT Press.

Larsson, K. (2003). Children's on-line life – and what parents believe: A survey in five countries. In C. Von Feilitzen and U. Carlsson (eds), *Promote or Protect? Perspectives on Media Literacy and Media Regulations* (pp. 113–20). Goteborg, Sweden: Nordicom.

Lash, S. and Wynne, B. (1992). Introduction. In U. Beck (ed.), *Risk Society: Towards a New Modernity* (pp. 1–8). London: Sage Publications.

Latour, B. (1993). *We Have Never Been Modern*. London: Prentice Hall.

Layard, R., and Dunn, J. (2009). *A Good Childhood: Searching for Values in a Competitive Age*. London: Penguin.

Leander, K. and Frank, A. (2006). The aesthetic production and distribution of image/subjects among online youth. *E-Learning, 3*(2), 185–206.

Lei, J. and Zhao, Y. (2007). Technology uses and student achievement: A longitudinal study. *Computers and Education, 49*, 284–96.

Lemish, D. (2007). *Children and Television: A Global Perspective*. Oxford: Blackwell.

Lenhart, A. (2005). *Protecting Teens Online*: Pew Internet and American Life Project. Retrieved from http://www.pewinternet.org/PPF/r/152/report_display.asp

——— (2007). *Cyberbullying and Online Teens*: Pew Internet and American Life Project. Retrieved from http://www.pewinternet.org/PPF/r/216/report_display.asp

Lenhart, A. and Madden, M. (2007a). *Social Networking Websites and Teens: An Overview*: Pew Internet and American Life Project. Retrieved from http://www.pewinternet.org/PPF/r/198/report_display.asp

——— (2007b). *Teens, Privacy and Online Social Networks: How Teens Manage their Online Identities and Personal Information in the Age of MySpace*: Pew Internet and American Life Project. Retrieved from http://www.pewinternet.org/PPF/r/211/report_display.asp

——— (2007c). Teens and social media: Pew Internet and American life project. Retrieved from http://www.pewinternet.org/PPF/r/230/report_display.asp

Lenhart, A., Rainie, L. and Lewis, O. (2001). *Teenage Life Online: The Rise of the Instant-Message Generation and the Internet's Impact on Friendships and Family Relationships*. Washington, DC: Pew Internet and American Life Project. Retrieved from http://www.pewinternet.org/report_display.asp?r=36

Lessig, L. (1999). *Code, and Other Laws of Cyberspace*. New York: Basic Books.

Leung, L. (2007). Stressful life events, motives for Internet use, and social support among digital kids. *CyberPsychology and Behavior*, *10*(2), 204–14.

Levine, P. (2008). A public voice for youth: The audience problem in digital media and civic education. In W. L. Bennett (ed.), *Civic Life Online: Learning How Digital Media Can Engage Youth* (vol. 1, pp. 119–38). Cambridge: MIT Press.

Levine, P. and Lopez, M. H. (2004). *Young People and Political Campaigning on the Internet – Fact Sheet*. Medford, MA: The Center for Information and Research on Civic Learning and Engagement. Retrieved from http://www.civicyouth.org/?page_id=154

Licoppe, C. and Smoreda, Z. (2006). Rhythms and ties: Toward a pragmatics of technologically mediated sociability. In R. Kraut, M. Brynin and S. Kiesler (eds), *Computers, Phones, and the Internet: Domesticating Information Technology* (pp. 296–313). Oxford, New York: Oxford University Press.

Lievrouw, L. (2004). What's changed about new media? Introduction to the fifth anniversary issue of new media and society. *New Media and Society*, *6*(1), 9–15.

Lievrouw, L. and Livingstone, S. (2006). Introduction. In L. Lievrouw and S. Livingstone (eds), *Handbook of New Media: Social Shaping and Social Consequences* (Updated Student Edition)(pp. 1–14). London: Sage.

Lincoln, S. (2004). Teenage girls' bedroom culture: Codes versus zones. In A. Bennett and K. Harris (eds), *After Subculture: Critical Studies of Subcultural Theory* (pp. 94–106). Hampshire: Palgrave/MacMillan.

Ling, R. and Haddon, L. (2008). Children, youth and the mobile phone. In K. Drotner and S. Livingstone (eds), *International Handbook of Children, Media and Culture* (pp. 137–51). London: Sage.

Lister, R., Smith, N., Middleton, S. and Cox, L. (2003). Young people talk about citizenship: Empirical perspectives on theoretical and political debates. *Citizenship Studies, 7*(2), 235–53.

Livingstone, S. (1998a). Audience research at the crossroads: The 'implied audience' in media theory. *European Journal of Cultural Studies, 1*(2), 193–217.

—— (1998b). Mediated childhoods: A comparative approach to young people's changing media environment in Europe. *European Journal of Communication, 13*(4), 435–56.

—— (1999). New media, new audiences. *New Media and Society, 1*(1), 59–66.

Livingstone, S. (2001). *Online Freedom and Safety for Children*. London: Institute for Public Policy Research / Citizens Online. Retrieved from http://eprints.lse.ac.uk/416/

Livingstone, S. (2002). *Young People and New Media: Childhood and the Changing Media Environment*. London: Sage.

Livingstone, S. (2003) Children's use of the internet: Reflections on the emerging research agenda. *New Media and Society, 5*(2), 147–66.

—— (2004). The challenge of changing audiences: Or, what is the audience researcher to do in the internet age? *European Journal of Communication, 19*(1), 75–86.

—— (2005a). Critical debates in internet studies: Reflections on an emerging field. In J. Curran and M. Gurevitch (eds), *Mass Media and Society* (5th edn, pp. 9–28). London: Sage.

—— (2005b). On the relation between audiences and publics. In S. Livingstone (ed.), *Audiences and Publics: When Cultural Engagement Matters for the Public Sphere* (pp. 17–41). Bristol: Intellect Press.

—— (2005c). Opportunities and constraints framing children and young people's internet use. In M. Consalvo and C. Haythornthwaite (eds), *Internet Research Annual* (vol. 4, pp. 59–75). Oxford: Peter Lang.

—— (2006). Children's privacy online: Experimenting with boundaries within and beyond the family. In R. Kraut, M. Brynin and S. Kiesler (eds), *Computers, Phones, and the Internet: Domesticating Information Technology* (pp. 145–67). Oxford, New York: Oxford University Press.

—— (2007a). The challenge of engaging youth online: Contrasting producers' and teenagers' interpretations of websites. *European Journal of Communication, 22*(2), 165–84.

—— (2007b). Children's Television Charter. In J. Arnett (ed.), *Encyclopedia of Children, Adolescents, and the Media* (pp.164).Thousand Oaks, CA: Sage.

—— (2007c). From family television to bedroom culture: Young people's media at home. In E. Devereux (ed.), *Media Studies: Key Issues and Debates* (pp. 302–21). London: Sage.

—— (2007d). Interactivity and participation on the internet: A critical appraisal of the online invitation to young people. In P. Dahlgren (ed.),

Young Citizens and New Media: Strategies for Learning Democratic Engagement (pp. 103–24). London: Routledge.

—— (2008a). Engaging with media – a matter of literacy? *Communication, Culture and Critique, 1*(1), 51–62.

—— (2008b). Internet literacy: Young people's negotiation of new online opportunities. In T. McPherson (ed.), *Digital Youth, Innovation, and the Unexpected* (vol. 4, pp. 101–22). Cambridge: MIT Press.

—— (2008c). Taking risky opportunities in youthful content creation: Teenagers' use of social networking sites for intimacy, privacy and self-expression. *New Media and Society, 10*(3), 393–411.

—— (2008d) Learning the lessons of research on youth participation and the internet. Commentary on the special issue on youth/ICT. *Journal of Youth Studies, 11*(5): 561–4.

—— (2009). On the mediation of everything. ICA Presidential address. *Journal of Communication, 59*(1), 1–18.

—— (in press). Internet, children and youth. In R. Burnett, M. Consalvo and C. Ess (eds), *The Blackwell Handbook of Internet Studies.* Oxford: Blackwell.

Livingstone, S. and Lemish, D. (2001). Doing comparative research with children and young people. In S. Livingstone and M. Bovill (eds), *Children and Their Changing Media Environment: A European Comparative Study* (pp. 31–50). Mahwah, NJ: Lawrence Erlbaum Associates.

Livingstone, S. and Bober, M. (2003). *UK Children Go Online: Listening to Young People's Experiences.* London: London School of Economics and Political Science. Retrieved from http://eprints.lse.ac.uk/388/

—— (2004a). Taking up opportunities? Children's uses of the internet for education, communication and participation. *E-Learning, 1*(3), 395–419.

—— (2004b). *UK Children Go Online: Surveying the Experiences of Young People and their Parents.* London: London School of Economics and Political Science. Retrieved from http://eprints.lse.ac.uk/395/

—— (2005). *UK Children Go Online: Final Report of Key Project Findings.* London: London School of Economics and Political Science. Retrieved from http://eprints.lse.ac.uk/399/

—— (2006). Regulating the internet at home: Contrasting the perspectives of children and parents. In D. Buckingham and R. Willett (eds), *Digital Generations* (pp. 93–113). Mahwah, New Jersey: Lawrence Erlbaum Associates.

—— (2007). UK children go online: A child-centred approach to the experience of using the internet. In B. Anderson, M. Brynin, J. Gershuny and Y. Raban (eds), *Information and Communication Technologies in Society: E-Living in a Digital Europe* (pp. 104–18). London, UK: Routledge.

Livingstone, S., Bober, M. and Helsper, E. J. (2005). Active participation or just more information? Young people's take up of opportunities to act and interact on the internet. *Information, Communication and Society, 8*(3), 287–314.

276 References

——— (2005). *Internet Literacy Among Children and Young People.* London: London School of Economics and Political Science. Retrieved from http://eprints.lse.ac.uk/397/

Livingstone, S. and Bovill, M. (2001a). *Families and the Internet: An Observational Study of Children and Young People's Internet Use. Final Report to BT:* London School of Economics. Retrieved from http://eprints.lse.ac.uk/21164/

——— (eds). (2001b). *Children and their Changing Media Environment: A European Comparative Study.* Mahwah, NJ: Lawrence Erlbaum Associates.

Livingstone, S. and Haddon, L. (2008). Risky experiences for European children online: Charting research strengths and research gaps. *Children and Society, 22,* 314–23.

Livingstone, S. and Helsper, E. J. (2006). Relating advertising literacy to the effects of advertising on children. *Journal of Communication, 56,* 560–84.

——— (2007a). Gradations in digital inclusion: Children, young people and the digital divide. *New Media and Society, 9,* 671–96.

——— (2007b). Taking risks when communicating on the Internet: The role of offline social-psychological factors in young people's vulnerability to online risks. *Information, Communication and Society, 10*(5), 619–43.

——— (2008). Parental mediation of children's internet use. *Journal of Broadcasting and Electronic Media, 52*(4), 581–99.

——— (in press). Balancing opportunities and risks in teenagers' use of the internet: The role of online skills and family context. *New Media and Society.*

Livingstone, S. and Lunt, P. (2007). Representing citizens and consumers in media and communications regulation. *The Politics of Consumption / The Consumption of Politics, The Annals of the American Academy of Political and Social Science, 611,* 51–65.

Livingstone, S., Lunt, P. and Miller, L. (2007). Citizens and consumers: Discursive debates during and after the Communications Act 2003. *Media, Culture and Society, 29*(4), 613–38.

Livingstone, S. and Markham, T. (2008). Mediating public participation: On the political significance of everyday media consumption. *British Journal of Sociology, 59*(2), 351–71.

Livingstone, S., and Thumim, N. (2008) What is Fred telling us? A commentary on youtube.com/fred. *Teachers' College Record,* 8 September 2008.

Livingstone, S., van Couvering, E. J. and Thumim, N. (2008). Converging traditions of research on media and information literacies: Disciplinary and methodological issues. In D. J. Leu, J. Coiro, M. Knobel and C. Lankshear (eds), *Handbook of Research on New Literacies* (pp. 103–32). Hillsdale, NJ: Lawrence Erlbaum Associates.

Lobe, B., Livingstone, S., Haddon, L. (2007). *Researching Children's Experiences Online across Countries: Issues and Problems in Methodology:* LSE, London: EU Kids Online. Retrieved from http://eprints.lse.ac.uk/2856/

Lopez, M. H., Levine, P., Both, D., Kiesa, A., Kirby, E. and Marcelo, K. (2006). *The 2006 Civic and Political Health of the Nation: A Detailed Look at How Youth Participate in Politics and Communities.* New Brunswick, NJ: Center for Information and Research on Civic Learning and Engagement. Retrieved from http://www.civicyouth.org/research/products/youth_index.htm

Loveless, A. and Ellis, V. (eds). (2001). *ICT, Pedagogy and the Curriculum: Subject to Change.* London: Routledge.

Luke, C. (1989). *Pedagogy, Printing and Protestantism: The Discourse of Childhood.* Albany, NY: State University of New York Press.

Lundby, K. (2008). Editorial: mediatized stories: Mediation perspectives on digital storytelling. *New Media and Society, 10*(3), 363–71.

Lunt, P. and Livingstone, S. (2007). Regulating markets in the interest of consumers? On the changing regime of governance in the financial service and communications sectors. In M. Bevir and F. Trentmann (eds), *Governance, Citizens, and Consumers: Agency and Resistance in Contemporary Politics* (pp. 139–61). Basingstoke, UK: Palgrave Macmillan.

Lupton, D. (1999). *Risk.* London: Routledge.

Lusoli, W., Ward, S. and Gibson, R. (2006). (Re)connecting politics? Parliament, the public and the internet. *Parliamentary Affairs, 59*(1), 24–42.

McChesney, R. W. (2000). *Rich Media, Poor Democracy: Communication Politics in Dubious Times.* New York: The New Press.

Machill, M., Beiler, M. and Zenker, M. (2008). Search-engine research: A European–American overview and systematization of an interdisciplinary and international research field. *Media, Culture and Society, 30*(5), 591–608.

Machill, M., Neuberger, C. and Schindler, F. (2003). Transparency on the Net: Functions and deficiencies of Internet search engines. *Info – The Journal of Policy, Regulation and Strategy for Telecommunications, 5*(1), 52–74.

Mackay, H. (ed.). (1997). *Consumption and Everyday Life.* London: Sage.

McKay, S., Thurlow, C. and Toomey-Zimmerman, H. (2005). Wired whizzes or techno-slaves? Young people and their emergent communication technologies. In C. Thurlow and A. Williams (eds), *Talking Adolescence: Perspectives on Communication in the Teenage Years* (pp. 185–203). New York: Peter Lang.

MacKenzie, D. and Wajcman, J. (eds). (1999). *The Social Shaping of Technology* (2nd edn). Buckingham: Open University Press.

McLean, S. L., Schultz, D. A. and Steger, M. B. (2002). *Social Capital: Critical Perspectives on Community and 'Bowling Alone'.* New York: New York University Press.

McMillan, S. (2006). Interactivity: Users, documents, and systems. In L. Lievrouw and S. Livingstone (eds), *The Handbook of New Media* (Updated Student Edition)(pp. 164–75). London: Sage Publications.

McPake, J., Plowman, L., Stephen, S., Sime, D. and Downey, S. (2005). *Already at a Disadvantage? ICT in the Home and Children's Preparation for Primary School.* Coventry: becta.

McQuillan, H. and d'Haenens, L. (in press). Young people online: gender and age influences. In S. Livingstone and L. Haddon (eds), *Kids Online: Opportunities and Risks for Children.* London: Policy.

278 References

McRobbie, A. and Garber. (1976). Girls and subcultures. In S. Hall and P. Jefferson (eds), *Resistance Through Ritual: Youth Cultures in the Post War Britain* (pp. 209–22). Essex: Hutchinson University Library.

McWilliam, E. (2003). The vulnerable child as pedagogical subject. *Journal of Curriculum Theorizing, 19*(2), 35–44.

Madge, N. and Barker, J. (2007). *Risk and Childhood*. London: The Royal Society for the Encouragement of Arts, Manufactures and Commerce.

Mahon, A., Glendinning, C., Clarke, K. and Craig, K. (1996). Researching children: Methods and ethics. *Children and Society, 10*, 145–54.

Mancheva, G. (2006). *'Child in the Net' National Campaign*: The National Center for Studies of Public Opinion.

Mansell, R. (2004). The internet, capitalism, and policy. In M. Consalvo, N. Baym, J. Hunsinger, K. B. Jensen, J. Logie, M. Murero and L. R. Shade (eds), *Internet Research Annual* (vol. 1, pp. 175–84). New York: Peter Lang.

Mansell, R. and Silverstone, R. (eds). (1996). *Communication by Design: The Politics of Information and Communication Technologies*. New York: Oxford University Press.

Marsh, J., Brooks, G., Hughes, J., Ritchie, L., Roberts, S. and Wright, K. (2005). *Digital Beginnings: Young Children's Use of Popular Culture, Media and New Technologies*. Sheffield: Literacy Research Centre, University of Sheffield.

Marshall, T. H. (1950). *Citizenship and Social Class and Other Essays*. Cambridge: University Press.

Marwick, A. (2005, October). *'I'm a Lot More Interesting than a Friendster Profile': Identity Presentation, Authenticity and Power in Social Networking Services*. Paper presented at the Association of Internet Researchers 6, Chicago. Retrieved from http://www.tiara.org/blog/?page_id=299

Mazzarella, S. R. and Pecora, N. (2007). Revisiting girls' studies: Girls creating sites for connection and action. *Journal of Children and Media, 1*(2), 105–25.

Mead, G. H. (1934). *Mind, Self and Society: From the Standpoint of a Social Behaviourist*. Chicago: University of Chicago Press.

Mediappro. (2006). *A European Research Project: The Appropriation of Media Youth*. Brussels: Mediappro. Retrieved from http://www.mediappro.org/

Meola, M. (2004). Chucking the checklist: A contextual approach to teaching undergraduates web-site evaluation. *Portal-Libraries and the Academy, 4*(3), 331–44.

Merchant, G. (2006). Identity, social networks and online communication. *E-Learning, 3*(2), 235–44.

—— (2007). Mind the gap(s): Discourses and discontinuity in digital literacies. *E-Learning, 4*(3), 241–55

Mesch, G. (2001). Social relationships and internet use among adolescents in Israel. *Social Science Quarterly, 82*(2), 329–39.

Mesch, G. S. and Talmud, I. (2007). Similarity and the quality of online and offline social relationships among adolescents in Israel. *Journal of Research on Adolescence, 17*(2), 455–66.

Meyer, D. and Staggenborg, S. (1996). Movements, countermovements, and the structure of political opportunity. *The American Journal of Sociology*, *101*(6), 1628–60.

Meyrowitz, J. (1985). *No Sense of Place: The Impact of Electronic Media on Social Behavior.* New York: Oxford University Press.

Miller, D. and Slater, D. (2000). *The Internet: An Ethnographic Approach.* London: Berg.

Millwood Hargrave, A. and Livingstone, S. (2009). *Harm and Offence in Media Content: A Review of the Evidence* (2nd edn). Bristol: Intellect.

Montgomery, K. C. (2007). *Generation Digital: Politics, Commerce, and Childhood in the Age of the Internet.* Cambridge, MA: MIT Press.

—— (2008). Youth and digital democracy: Intersections of practice, policy, and the marketplace. In W. L. Bennett (ed.), *Civic Life Online: Learning How Digital Media Can Engage Youth* (vol. 1, pp. 25–49). Cambridge: MIT Press.

Montgomery, K. C., Gottlieb-Robles, B. and Larson, G. O. (2004). *Youth as E-Citizens: Engaging the Digital Generation.* Washington, DC: Center for Social Media, American University (http://www.centerforsocialmedia.org/ecitizens/youthreport.pdf).

Montgomery, K. C. and Pasnik, S. (1996). *Web of Deception: Threats To Children from Online Marketing.* Washington: Centre for Media Education.

Moore, E. S. and Rideout, V. J. (2007). The online marketing of food to children: Is it just fun and games? *American Marketing Association, 26*(2), 202–20.

Morgan, A. and Kennewell, S. (2005). The role of play in the pedagogy of ICT. *Education and Information Technologies, 10*(3), 177–88.

MORI (2004). *The Rules of Engagement? Participation, Involvement and Voting in Britain: Research Analysis for the Electoral Commission and the Hansard Society.* London: MORI.

Morley, D. (1986). *Family Television: Cultural Power and Domestic Leisure.* London: Comedia.

Morris, Z., John, O. and Halpern, D. (2003). Compulsory citizenship for the disenfranchised. *The Curriculum Journal, 14*(2), 1–19.

Muir, D. (2005). *Violence against Children in Cyberspace: A Contribution to the United Nations Study on Violence Against Children.* Bangkok, Thailand: ECPAT International.

Munro, E. (2008). *Effective Child Protection* (2nd edn). London: Sage.

Murdock, G. (2002). Review article: Debating digital divides. *European Journal of Communication, 17*(3), 385–90.

Nairn, A., Ormond, J. and Bottomley, P. (2007). *Watching, Wanting and Well-Being: Exploring the Links.* London: National Consumer Council.

Nathanson, A. I. and Yang, M. S. (2003). The effects of mediation content and form on children's responses to violent television. *Human Communication Research, 29*(1), 111–34.

NCH/Tesco Mobile. (2005). *Putting U in the Picture: Mobile Bullying Survey.* Retrieved from http://www.nch.org.uk/information/index.php?i=237

280 References

Neuman, S. B. (1988). The displacement effect. *Reading Research Quarterly*, 23(4), 414–40.

NeuStar Inc. (2003). *Kids.us Content Policy: Guidelines and Restrictions* Sterling, VA.: NeuStar, Inc.

Newman, J., Barnes, M., Sullivan, H. and Knops, A. (2004). Public participation and collaborative governance. *Journal of Social Policy*, 33, 203–23.

Nightingale, V., Dickenson, D. and Griff, C. (2000). *Children's Views about Media Harm*. Sydney, Australia: University of Western Sydney and Australian Broadcasting Authority.

Nikken, P. and Jansz, J. (2007). Playing restricted videogames: Relations with game ratings and parental mediation. *Journal of Children and Media*, 1(3), 227–43.

Nocon, H. and Cole, M. (2006). School's Invasion of 'After-School': Colonization, Rationalization, or Expansion of Access? In Z. Bekerman, N. C. Burbules and D. Silberman-Keller (eds), *Learning in Places: The Informal Education Reader* (pp. 99–122). New York: Peter Lang.

Norris, P. (1996). Does television erode social capital? A reply to Putnam. *Political Science and Politics*, 29, 474–80.

—— (2000). *A Virtuous Circle*. Cambridge: Cambridge University Press.

—— (2001). *Digital Divide: Civic Engagement, Information Poverty, and the Internet Worldwide*. Cambridge: Cambridge University Press.

Nussbaum, E. (2007, 06/07/07). Say everything. *New York Magazine*. Retrieved from http://nymag.com/news/features/27341/

Nyboe, L. and Drotner, K. (2008). Identity, aesthetics and digital narration. In K. Lundby (ed.), *Mediatized Stories*. New York: Peter Lang.

O'Connell, R. and Bryce, J. (2006). *Young People, Well-Being and Risk On-Line*. Strasbourg: Media Division, Directorate General of Human Rights, Council of Europe.

Ofcom (2004a). *The Communications Market 2004*. London: Office of Communications.

—— (2004b). *Ofcom's Strategy and Priorities for the Promotion of Media Literacy: A Statement*. London: Office of Communications.

—— (2006a). *Media Literacy Audit: Report on Children's Media Literacy*. London: Office of Communications.

—— (2006b). *Ofcom Response to European Commission Consultation on Media Literacy*. Retrieved from http://ec.europa.eu/avpolicy/media_literacy/docs/contributions/68_88_lmnopqr/81_51_ofcom.pdf

—— (2007a). *The Future of Children's Television Programming: Research Report*. London: Office of Communications.

—— (2007b). *Ofcom's Submission to the Byron Review. Annex 5: The Evidence Base – The Views of Children, Young People and Parents*. London: Office of Communications.

—— (2008a). *Media Literacy Audit: Report on UK Children's Media Literacy*. London: Office of Communications.

—— (2008b). *Social Networking: A Quantitative and Qualitative Research Report into Attitudes, Behaviours and Use*. London: Office of Communications.

—— (2008c). *The Communications Market 2008*. London: Ofcom.

Office of the e-Envoy. (2004). *UK Online Annual Report*. London: Office of the e-Envoy.

OfSTED (2004). *ICT in Schools – The Impact of Government Initiatives Five Years on*: OfSTED. Retrieved 16 Dec 2008 from http://www.ofsted. gov.uk/content/download/1355/9827/file/The%20impact%20of%20government%20initiatives%20five%20years%20on%20(PDF%20format). pdf

ONS (2007). *Social Trends 37, 2007 Edition* (A publication of the Government Statistical Service No. 37). London: Office for National Statistics.

Orgad, S. (2007). The interrelations between 'online' and 'offline': questions, issues and implications. In R. Mansell, C. Avgerou, D. Quah and R. Silverstone (eds), *The Oxford Handbook of Information and Communication Technologies*. Oxford: Oxford University Press.

Osgerby, B. (1998). *Youth in Britain Since 1945*. Oxford: Blackwell.

Oswell, D. (1998). The place of childhood in Internet content regulation: A case study of policy in the UK. *International Journal of Cultural Studies*, *1*(1), 131–51.

—— (1999). The dark side of cyberspace: Internet content regulation and child protection. *Convergence: The Journal of Research into New Media Technologies*, *5*(4), 42–62.

—— (2008). Media and communications regulation and child protection: An overview of the field In K. Drotner and S. Livingstone (eds), *International Handbook of Children, Media and Culture* (pp. 475–92). London: Sage.

Oudshoorn, N. and Pinch, T. (2003). Introduction: How users and non-users matter. In N. Oudshoorn (ed.), *How Users Matter: The Co-Construction of Users and Technology* (pp. 4–22). Cambridge, MA: MIT Press.

Outhwaite, W. (ed.). (1996). *The Habermas Reader*. Cambridge: Polity.

Palfrey, J. and Gasser, U. (2008). *Born Digital: Understanding the First Generation of Digital Natives*. New York: Basic Books.

Palmer, S. (2007). *Toxic Childhood: How The Modern World is Damaging Our Children and what we can do About it*. London: Orion.

Palmer, T. and Stacey, L. (2004). *Just One Click: Sexual Abuse of Children and Young People Through the Internet and Mobile Telephone Technology*. Ilford: Barnardo's.

Papacharissi, Z. (2004). Democracy online: Civility, politeness, and the democratic potential of online political discussion groups. *New Media and Society*, *6*(2), 259–83.

Papert, S. (1980). *Mindstorms: Children, Computers and Powerful Ideas*. New York: Basic Books.

Passey, D., Rogers, C., Machell, J. and McHugh, G. (2004). *The motivational effect of ICT on pupils – research report RR523*: DfES. Retrieved 17 Dec 2008 from http://www.dfes.gov.uk/research/data/uploadfiles/rr523new.pdf

Patchin, J. W. and Hinduja, S. (2006). Bullies Move Beyond the Schoolyard: A Preliminary Look at Cyberbullying. *Youth Violence and Juvenile Justice*, *4*(2), 148–69.

282 References

Pattie, C. J., Seyd, P. and Whiteley, P. (2004). *Citizenship in Britain: Values, Participation and Democracy.* Cambridge: Cambridge University Press.

Pearson, G. (1983). *Hooligan: A History of Respectable Fears.* London: Macmillan.

Perkel, D. (2008). Copy and paste literacy? Literacy practices in the production of a MySpace profile. In K. Drotner, H. S. Jensen and K. Schroeder (eds), *Informal Learning and Digital Media: Constructions, Contexts, Consequences* (pp. 203–44). Newcastle, UK: Cambridge Scholars Press.

Peter, J. and Valkenburg, P. M. (2006a). Adolescents' Exposure to Sexually Explicit Material on the Internet. *Communication Research, 33*(2), 178–204.

—— (2006b). Adolescents' internet use: Testing the 'disappearing digital divide' versus the 'emerging differentiation' approach. *Poetics, 34,* 293–305.

Peter, J., Valkenburg, P. M. and Fluckiger, C. (in press). Adolescents' and social network sites: What do we know about identity construction, friendships, and privacy? In S. Livingstone and L. Haddon (eds), *Kids Online: Opportunities and Risks for Children.* London: Policy.

Peter, J., Valkenburg, P. M. and Schouten, A. P. (2006). Characteristics and Motives of Adolescents Talking with Strangers on the Internet. *CyberPsychology and Behavior, 9*(5), 526–30.

Petty, R. E. and Cacioppo, J. T. (1986). *Communication and Persuasion: Central and Peripheral Routes to Attitude Change.* New York: Springer-Verlag.

Pew Internet and American Life Project. (2008, Aug 2008). Demographics of Internet Users. Retrieved 17 December, 2008, from http://www.pewinternet.org/trends/User_Demo_10%2020%2008.htm

Pharr, S. and Putnam, R. (eds). (2000). *Disaffected Democracies.* Cambridge, MA: Harvard University Press.

Phipps, L. (2000). New communications technologies: A conduit for social inclusion. *Information, Communication and Society, 3*(1), 39–68.

Piaget, J. and Inhelder, B. (1969). *The Psychology of the Child.* London: Routledge and Paul Kegan Ltd.

Poster, M. (1997). Cyberdemocracy: Internet and the public sphere. In D. Porter (ed.), *Internet Culture* (pp. 210–18). New York: Routledge.

—— (2001). *What's the Matter with the Internet?* Minneapolis: University of Minnesota.

Postman, N. (1983). *The Disappearance of Childhood.* London: W. H. Allen.

Potter, W. J. (2004). *Theory of Media Literacy: A Cognitive Approach.* Thousand Oaks: Sage.

Prensky, M. (2001). Digital natives, digital immigrants. *On the Horizon, 9*(5), 1–2.

Prout, A. (2000). Children's participation: Control and self-realisation in British late modernity. *Children and Society, 14*(4), 304–15.

Putnam, R. (2000). *Bowling Alone: The Collapse and Revival of American Community.* New York: Simon and Schuster.

Quayle, E. and Taylor, M. (2005). *Viewing Child Pornography on the Internet : Understanding the Offence, Managing the Offender, Helping the Victims.* Lyme Regis: Russell House.

Quinn, V. (1997). *Critical Thinking in Young Minds*. London: David Fulton Publishers.

Qvortrup, J. (1994). *Childhood Matters: Social Theory, Practice and Politics.* Avebury: Aldershot.

—— (1995). Childhood and modern society: A paradoxical relationship. In J. Brannen and M. O'Brien (eds), *Childhood and Parenthood* (pp. 189–98). London: Institute of Education, University of London.

RIS (2006) *RIS 2006 – Gospodinjs tva (RIS-DCO-2006)*. Report available at: http://www.ris.org/uploadi/editor/1171361207InternetInSlovenskaDrz ava2006.pdf

Rajagopal, S. (2004). Suicide pacts and the internet. *British Medical Journal, 329*(7478), 1298–9.

Raynes-Goldie, K. and Walker, L. (2008). Our space: Online civic engagement tools for youth. In W. L. Bennett (ed.), *Civic Life Online: Learning How Digital Media Can Engage Youth* (vol. 1, pp. 161–88). Cambridge: MIT Press.

Reid-Walsh, J. (2008). Harlequin meets the SIMS: A history of interactive narrative media for children and youth from early flap books to contemporary multi media. In K. Drotner and S. Livingstone (eds), *International Handbook of Children, Media and Culture* (pp. 71–86). London: Sage.

Ribak, R. (2001). 'Like immigrants': Negotiating power in the face of the home computer. *New Media and Society, 3*(2), 220–38.

Rice, R. and Haythornthwaite, C. (2006). Perspectives on internet use: Access, involvement and interaction. In L. Lievrouw and S. Livingstone (eds), *Handbook of New Media: Social Shaping and Social Consequences* (Updated Student Edition) (pp. 92–113). London: Sage.

Rideout, V. (2007). *Parents, Children and Media: A Kaiser Family Foundation Survey*. Menlo Park, CA: Kaiser Family Foundation.

Roberts, D., Foehr, U. and Rideout, V. (2005). *Generation M: Media in the Lives of 8–18 Year Olds*. Menlo Park, Cal.: Kaiser Family Foundation.

Rogers, E. M. (1995). *Diffusion of Innovations* (vol. 4). New York: Free Press.

Roker, D., Player, K. and Coleman, J. (1997). *Challenging the Image: Young People as Volunteers and Ccampaigners*. Brighton: Trust for the Study of Adolescence.

Rose, N. (1990). *Governing the Soul: The Shaping of the Private Self*. London: Routledge.

—— (1996). Governing 'advanced' liberal democracies. In A. Barry, T. Osborne and N. Rose (eds), *Foucault and Political Reason: Liberalism, Neo-Liberalism and Rationalities of Government* (pp. 37–64). London: UCL Press.

Rosen, L. D. (2006). Adolescents in MySpace: Identity formation, friendship and sexual predators. Retrieved from http://www.csudh.edu/psych/lrosen. htm

Rowland, W. R. (1983). *The Politics of TV Violence: Policy Uses of Communication Research*. Beverley Hills: Sage.

Rudd, T., Morrison, J., Facer, K. and Gifford, C. (2006). *What if...? Re-imagining learning spaces*. Bristol: Futurelab.

Russell, D. (1980). The incidence and prevalence of intrafamilial and extrafamilial sexual abuse for female children. *Child Abuse and Neglect, 7*, 133–46.

284 References

Safer Social Networking Principles for the EU (2009). Available at http://
ec.europa.eu/information_society/activities/social_networking/docs/sn_
principles.pdf (accessed 24/2/09).

Samarajiva, R. (1996). Surveillance by design: Public networks and the control of consumption. In R. E. Mansell and R. Silverstone (eds), *Communication by Design: The Politics of Information and Communication Technologies* (pp. 129–56). Oxford: Oxford University Press.

Scannell, P. (1988). Radio times: The temporal arrangements of broadcasting in the modern world. In P. Drummond and R. Paterson (eds), *Television and its Audience: International Research Perspectives*. London: British Film Institute.

Schifferes, S. (2008). Internet key to Obama victories [Electronic Version]. *BBC News*. Retrieved 15/09/08 from http://news.bbc.co.uk/1/hi/technology/7412045.stm.

Schor, J. B. (2004). *Born to Buy: The Commercialized Child and the New Consumer Culture*. New York: Scribner.

Scribner, S. and Cole, M. (1973). Cognitive Consequences of Formal and Informal Education. *Science*, *182*(4112), 553–9.

Sefton-Green, J. (2004). *Literature Review in Informal Learning with Technology Outside School*. Bristol: Futurelab.

—— (ed.). (1999). *Young People, Creativity and New Technologies: The Challenge of Digital Arts*. London: Routledge.

Seiter, E. (1993). *Sold Separately: Children and Parents in Consumer Culture*. New Brunswick: Rutgers University Press.

—— (2005). *The Internet Playground: Children's Access, Entertainment, and Mis-Education*. New York: Peter Lang.

—— (2008). Practicing at home: Computers, pianos, and cultural capital. In T. McPherson (ed.), *Digital Youth, Innovations, and the Unexpected* (vol. 4, pp. 27–52). Cambridge: MIT Press.

Selwyn, N. (2003). Apart from technology: Understanding people's non-use of information and communication technologies in everyday life. *Technology in Society*, *25*(1), 99–116.

—— (2004). Reconsidering Political and Popular Understandings of the Digital Divide. *New Media and Society*, *6*(3), 341–62(322).

—— (2008). *Developing the Technological Imagination: Theorising the Social Shaping and Consequences of New Technologies*. Paper presented at the ESRC Seminar Series: The educational and social impact of new technologies on young people in Britain, Oxford.

Selwyn, N. and Facer, K. (2007). *Beyond the Digital Divide: Rethinking Digital Inclusion for the 21st Century*. Bristol: Futurelab.

Shaffer, D., Squire, K., Halverson, R. and Gee, J. (2005). Video games and the future of learning. *Phi Delta Kappan*, *87*(2), 104–111.

Sheard, M. and Ahmed, J. (2007). *Engaging the 'Xbox Generation of Learners' in Higher Education*: University of Huddersfield, School of Education and Professional Development.

Sheehan, K. B. (2002). Toward a typology of internet users and online privacy concerns. *The Information Society*, *18*(1), 21–32.

Shim, J. W., Lee, S. and Paul, B. (2007). Who responds to unsolicited sexually explicit materials on the Internet?: The role of individual differences. *Cyberpsychology and Behavior*, *10*(1), 71–79.

Sillence, E., Briggs, P., Harris, P. R. and Fishwick, L. (2007). How do patients evaluate and make use of online health information? *Social Science and Medicine*, *64*(9), 1853–62.

Silverstone, R. (1994). *Television and Everyday Life*. London: Routledge.

—— (2005). The sociology of mediation and communication. In C. J. Calhoun, C. Rojek and B. S. Turner (eds), *The SAGE handbook of sociology* (pp. 188–207). London: SAGE Publications.

—— (2006). Domesticating domestication: Reflections on the life of a concept. In T. Berker, M. Hartmann, Y. Punie and K. J. Ward (eds), *The Domestication of Media and Technology* (pp. 229–48). Maidenhead: Open University Press.

Silverstone, R. and Hirsch, E. (eds). (1992). *Consuming Technologies: Media and Information in Domestic Spaces*. London: Routledge.

Silverstone, R. and Mansell, R. (1996). The Politics of Information and Communication Technologies. In R. E. Mansell and R. Silverstone (eds), *Communication by Design: The Politics of Information and Communication Technologies* (pp. 213–28). Oxford: Oxford University Press.

Six, P., Lasky, K. and Fletcher, A. (1998). *The Future of Privacy. Volume 1: Private Llife and Public Policy*. London: Demos.

Slater, D. (2002). Social relationships and identity online and offline. In L. Lievrouw and S. Livingstone (eds), *The Handbook of New Media* (pp. 534–47). London: Sage.

Smith, A. and Rainie, L. (2008). *The Internet and the 2008 Election*. Washington, DC: Pew Internet & American Life Project.

Smith, N., Lister, R., Middleton, S. and Cox, L. (2005). Young people as real citizens: Towards an inclusionary understanding of citizenship. *Journal of Youth Studies*, *8*(4), 425–43.

Smith, R. and Curtin, P. (1998). Children, computers and life online: Education in a cyber-world. In I. Snyder (ed.), *Page to Screen: Taking Literacy into the Electronic Era* (pp. 211–33). London: Routledge.

Smith, R. and Fletcher, D. (2007). How the politicians are out to get youth their sites [Electronic Version]. *The Daily Mirror*. Retrieved 15/07/08 from http://www.mirror.co.uk/news/top-stories/2007/04/16/how-the-politicians-are-out-to-get-youth-their-sites-89520-18910951/.

Smythe, D. (1981). *Dependency Road: Communications, capitalism, consciousness, and Canada*. Norwood, NJ: Ablex.

Snyder, I. (2007). Literacy, learning and technology studies. In R. Andrews and C. Haythornthwaite (eds), *The SAGE Handbook of E-learning Research* (pp. 394–415). London: Sage.

—— (ed.). (1998). *Page to Screen: Taking Literacy into the Electronic Era*. London: Routledge.

286 References

Snyder, I., Angus, L. and Sutherland-Smith, W. (2004). 'They're the future and they're going to take over everywhere': ICTs, literacy and disadvantage. In *Doing Literacy Online: Teaching, Learning, and Playing in an Electronic World* (pp. 225–44). Cresskill, NJ: Hampton Press.

Somekh, B., Lewin, C., Mavers, D., Fisher, T., Harrison, C., Haw, K., *et al.* (2002). *ImpaCT2: Pupils' and Teachers' Perceptions of ICT in the Home, School and Community.* Coventry: Becta.

Sparkes, J. (1999). *Schools, Education and Social Exclusion.* London: Centre for Analysis of Social Exclusion, London School of Economics and Political Science.

Spigel, L. (1992). *Make Room for TV: Television and the Family Ideal in Postwar America.* Chicago: University of Chicago Press.

Squire, K. (2005). Changing the game: What happens when video games enter the classroom? *Innovate, 1*(6).

Staksrud, E. (2005). *SAFT Project Final Report.* Safety, Awareness, Facts and Tools. Retrieved from http://ec.europa.eu/information_society/activities/sip/archived/docs/pdf/projects/saft_final_report.pdf

Staksrud, E. and Livingstone, S. (in press). Children and online risk: Powerless victims or resourceful participants? *Information, Communication and Society.*

Star, L. and Bowker, G. (2006). How to infrastructure. In L. Lievrouw and S. Livingstone (eds), *The Handbook of New Media* (Updated Student Edition) (pp. 230–45). London: Sage.

State Agency for Child Protection. (2003) National Center for Studying the Public Opinion *First National Representative Study on the issues related with children's safety in internet.* SACP, Program 2003 'Internet and children's rights'. Bulgaria.

Stead, G., Sharpe, B., Anderson, P., Cych, L. and Philpott, M. (2006). *Emerging Technologies for Learning.* Coventry: Becta

Steele, J. R. and Brown, J. D. (1994). Studying media in the context of everyday life. *Journal of Youth Adolescence, 24*(5), 551–76.

Stein, L. and Sinha, N. (2006). New global media and the role of the state. In L. Lievrouw and S. Livingstone (eds), *The Handbook of New Media* (Updated Student Edition)(pp. 415–42). London: Sage.

Stern, S. (2002). Sexual selves on the world wide web: Adolescent girls' home pages as sites for sexual self-expression. In J. Brown, J. Steele and K. Walsh-Childers (eds), *Sexual Teens, Sexual Media: Investigating Media's Influence on Adolescent Sexuality* (pp. 265–85). Mahwah, NJ: Lawrence Erlbaum Associates.

—— (2008). Producing sites, exploring identities: Youth online authorship. In D. Buckingham (ed.), *Youth, Identity, and Digital Media* (vol. 6, pp. 95–117). Cambridge: MIT Press.

Street, B. (1995). *Social Literacies: Critical Approaches to Literacy in Development, Ethnography and Education.* London: Longman.

Suleiman, S. and Crosman, I. (eds). (1980). *The Reader in the Text.* Princeton: Princeton University Press.

Sundén, J. (2003). *Material Virtualities: Approaching Online Textual Embodiment.* New York: Peter Lang.

Suss, D. (2001). Computers and the internet in school: Closing the knowledge gap? In S. Livingstone and M. Bovill (eds), *Children and Their Changing Media Environment: A European Comparative Study* (pp. 221–42). Mahwah, NJ: Erlbaum.

Suzuki, L. and Calzo, J. (2004). The search for peer advice in cyberspace: An examination of online teen bulletin boards about health and sexuality. *Applied Developmental Psychology, 25*, 685–98.

Takahashi, T. (2008). Japanese young people, media and everyday life: Towards the de-westernising of media studies In K. Drotner and S. Livingstone (eds), *International Handbook of Children, Media and Culture* (pp. 413–30). London: Sage.

Tapscott, D. (1997). *Growing Up Digital: The Rise of the Net Generation.* New York: Mc-Graw Hill.

—— (2008). *Grown up Digital : How the Net Generation is Changing the World.* New York: McGraw-Hill.

Taylor, A. S. and Harper, R. (2002). *Age-Old Practices in the 'New World': A Study of Gift-Giving Between Teenage Mobile Phone Users.* Paper presented at the SIGCHI Conference on Human Factors in Computing Systems, Minneapolis, MN, USA.

Thiessen, V. and Looker, E. D. (2007). Digital divides and capital conversion: The optimal use of information and communication technology for youth reading achievement. *Information, Communication and Society, 10*(2), 159–80.

Thomas, A. (2000). Textual Constructions of Children's Online Identities. *CyberPsychology and Behavior, 3*(4), 665–72.

Thomas, F. and Ludger, W. (2004). *Computers and Student Learning: Bivariate and Multivariate Evidence on the Availability and Use of Computers at Home and at School.* Munich: IFO Institute for Economic Research.

Thompson, J. B. (1995). *The Media and Modernity: A Social Theory of the Media.* Cambridge: Polity.

Thornburgh, D. and Lin, H. S. (2002). *Youth, Pornography, and the Internet.* Washington, DC: National Academy Press.

Thumim, N. (2008). 'It's good for them to know my story': Cultural mediation as tension. In K. Lundby (ed.), *Digital Storytelling, Mediatized Stories: Self-representations in New Media* (pp. 85–104). New York: Peter Lang.

Tomlinson, J. (1991). *Cultural Imperialism: A Critical Introduction.* London: Continuum.

Tsagarousianou, R., Tambini, D. and Bryan, C. (eds) (1998). *Cyberdemocracy: Technology, Cities, and Civic Networks.* London: Routledge.

Turkle, S. (1995). *Life on the Screen: Identity in the Age of the Internet.* New York: Simon and Schuster.

Turow, J. (2000). *Privacy Policies on Children's Websites: Do They Play by the Rules?* Philadelphia, PA: Annenberg Public Policy Center.

—— (2001). Family boundaries, commercialism, and the Internet: A framework for research. *Journal of Applied Developmental Psychology, 22*(1), 73–86.

Turow, J. and Tsui, L. (2008). *The Hyperlinked Society: Questioning Connections in the Digital Age.* Ann Arbor: University of Michigan Press.

288 References

Twining, P., Broadie, R., Cook, D., Ford, K., Morris, D., Twiner, A., *et al.* (2006). *Educational Change and ICT: An Exploration of Priorities 2 and 3 of the DfES e-Strategy in Schools and Colleges – The Current Landscape and Implementation Issues.* Coventry: Becta.

Tyner, K. (1998). *Literacy in a Digital World: Teaching and Learning in the Age of Information.* Mahwah, NJ: Lawrence Erlbaum Associates.

UNESCO (n.d.). Information and Media Literacy. Retrieved 29/8/08, from http://portal.unesco.org/ci/en/ev.php-URL_ID=15886andURL_DO=DO_TOPICandURL_SECTION=201.html

UNICEF (1999). The Oslo Challenge. Retrieved 28/3/07, from http://www.unicef.org/magic/briefing/oslo.html

—— (2007). *Child Poverty in Perspective: An Overview of Child Well-Being in Rich Countries, Innocenti Report Card 7.* Florence: UNICEF Innocenti Research Centre.

United Nations (1989). Convention on the Rights of the Child. Retrieved 29 January, 2008, from http://www2.ohchr.org/english/law/crc.htm

USC (2004). *The Digital Future Report: Surveying the Digital Future Year Four – Ten Years, Ten Trends*: USC Annenberg School, Centre for the Digital Future (www.digitalcenter.org).

Valentine, G., Marsh, J. and Pattie, C. (2005). *Children and Young People's Home Use of ICT for Educational Purposes: The Impact on Attainment at Key Stages 1 – 4.* London: Department for Education and Skills.

Valkenburg, P. M. (2004). *Children's Responses to the Screen: A Media Psychological Approach.* Mahwah, NJ: Lawrence Erlbaum.

Valkenburg, P. M., Krcmar, M., Peeters, A. L. and Marseille, N. M. (1999). Developing a scale to assess three different styles of television mediation: 'Instructive mediation', 'restrictive mediation', and 'social coviewing'. *Journal of Broadcasting and Electronic Media, 43*(1), 52–66.

Valkenburg, P. M. and Peter, J. (2007). Internet communication and its relation to well-being: Identifying some underlying mechanisms. *Media Psychology, 9*(1), 43–58.

Van-Rompaey, V. and Roe, K. (2001). The Home as a multimedia environment: Families' conception of space and the introduction of information and communication technologies in the home. *Communications, 26*(4), 351–69.

Van-Rompaey, V., Roe, K. and Struys, K. (2002). Children and the internet: Adoption in the family context. *Communication and Society, 5*(2), 189–206.

Van Dijk, J. (2005). *The Deepening Divide, Inequality in the Information Society.* London: Sage.

Vandewater, E. A., Park, S. E., Huang, X. and Wartella, E. A. (2005). 'No – You can't watch that' – Parental rules and young children's media use. *American Behavioral Scientist, 48*(5), 608–23.

Vasudevan, L. (2006). Making known differently: Engaging visual modalities as spaces to author new selves. *E-Learning, 3*(2), 207–16.

Vazire, S. and Gosling, S. D. (2004). E-Perceptions: Personality impressions based on personal websites. *Journal of Personality and Social Psychology, 87*(1), 123–32.

Vygotsky, L. S. (1978). *Mind in Society: The Development of Higher Psychological Processes*. Cambridge: Harvard University Press.

Walkerdine, V., Lucey, H. and Melody, J. (2001). *Growing Up Girl*. Basingstoke: Palgrave.

Walton, M. and Archer, A. (2004). The Web and information literacy: Scaffolding the use of web sources in a project-based curriculum. *British Journal of Educational Technology*, 35(2), 173–86.

Warnick, B. (2002). *Critical Literacy in a Digital Era: Technology, Rhetoric and the Public Interest*. Mahway, NJ: Lawrence Erlbaum Associates.

Warschauer, M. (2003). *Technology and Social Inclusion: Rethinking the Digital Divide*. Cambridge, MA: MIT Press.

Wartella, E. and Jennings, N. (2000). Children and computers: New technology – old concerns. *Children and Computer Technology*, 10(2), 31–43.

Wasko, J. (2008). The commodification of youth culture. In K. Drotner and S. Livingstone (eds), *International Handbook of Children, Media and Culture* (pp. 460–74). London: Sage.

Waskul, D. D. (2004). *Net.seXXX: Readings on Sex, Pornography, and the Internet*. New York: Peter Lang.

Webwise. (2006). *Survey of Children's Use of the Internet: Investigating Online Risk Behaviour*. Ireland: Webwise.

Wellman, B. (2004). The three ages of internet studies: Ten, five and zero years ago. *New Media and Society*, 6(1), 123–9.

Wellman, B. and Haythornthwaite, C. (2002). *The Internet in Everyday Life*. Oxford: Blackwell.

Wertsch, J. (1985). *Vygotsky and the Social Formation of Mind*. Cambridge, MA: Harvard University Press.

White House Office of the Press Secretary (2002). President Bush Signs Child Internet Safety Legislation [Electronic Version]. Retrieved 15/9/08 from http://www.whitehouse.gov/news/releases/2002/12/20021204-1.html.

Whitlock, J. L., Powers, J. L. and Eckenrode, J. (2006). The virtual cutting edge: the Internet and adolescent self-injury. *Developmental Psychology*, 42(3), 407–17.

Willard, N. (2003). Off-campus, harmful online student speech. *Journal of School Violence*, 2(1), 65–93.

Willett, R. (2005). New Models of Learning for New Media: Observations of Young People Learning Digital Design. In B. Bachmair, P. Diepold and C. de Witt (eds), *Jahrbuch Medienpädagogik* (vol. 4, pp. 127–44). Opladen: VS Verlag für Sozialwissenschaften.

—— (2008). Consumer Citizens online: Structure, agency, and gender in online participation. In D. Buckingham (ed.), *Youth, Identity, and Digital Media* (vol. 6, pp. 49–69). Cambridge: MIT Press.

Willett, R. and Burn, A. (2005). 'What exactly is a paedophile?': Children talking about Internet risk. *Jahrbuch Medienpädagogik*, 5, 237–254.

Williams, R. (1974). The Technology and Society. In *Television: Technology and Cultural Form* (pp. 9–31). London: Fontana.

290   References

—— (1983). *Keywords: A Vocabulary of Culture and Society.* London: Fontana.

Winston, B. (1996). *Media Technology and Society: A History – From the Telegraph to the Internet.* London: Routledge.

Wojtasik, L. (2003). *Pedophilia and Pornography on the Internet: Threats to Children.* Warsaw: Nobody's Children Foundation

Wolak, J., Finkelhor, D., Mitchell, K. J. and Ybarra, M. L. (2008). Online 'predators' and their victims. *American Psychologist, 63*(2), 111–28.

Wolak, J., Mitchell, K. and Finkelhor, D. (2003). Escaping or connecting? Characteristics of youth who form close online relationships. *Journal of Adolescence, 26*, 105–19.

—— (2007). Unwanted and wanted exposure to online pornography in a national sample of youth internet users. *Pediatrics, 119*(2), 247–57.

—— (2006). *Online Victimization of Youth: Five Years on.* Durham, NH: Crimes against Children Research Centre. Retrieved from http://www. missingkids.com/

Woolgar, S. (1996). Technologies as cultural artifacts. In W. H. Dutton (ed.), *Information and Communication Technologies: Visions and Realities* (pp. 87–102). Oxford: Oxford University Press.

—— (2002). Five rules of virtuality. In S. Woolgar (ed.), *Virtual Society? Technology, Cyberbole, Reality* (pp. 1–22). Oxford: Oxford University Press.

World Internet Project. (2009). *International Report 2009.* www.worldinternetproject.net

Wyatt, S. (2005). Living in a network society: The imperative to connect. In O. Coutard., R. Hanley. and R. Zimmerman. (eds), *Sustaining Urban Networks, The Social Diffusion of Large Technical Systems* (pp. 135–48). New York: Routledge.

Xenos, M. and Bennett, W. L. (2007). The disconnection in online politics: The youth political web sphere and US election sites, 2002–2004. *Information, Communication and Society, 10*(4), 443–64.

Yates, J. and Orlikowski, W. (1992). Genres of organizational communication: A structurational approach to studying communication and media. *Academy of Management Review, 17*(2), 299–326.

Ybarra, M. L. and Mitchell, K. J. (2004a). Online aggressor/targets, aggressors, and targets: A comparison of associated youth characteristics. *Journal of Child Psychology and Psychiatry, 45*(7), 1308.

—— (2004b). Youth engaging in online harassment: Associations with caregiver–child relationships, Internet use, and personal characteristics. *Journal of Adolescence, 27*, 319–36.

—— (2008). How risky are social networking sites? A comparison of places online where youth sexual solicitation and harassment occurs. *Pediatrics, 121*, e350–e357.

Ybarra, M. L., Mitchell, K. J., Finkelhor, D. and Wolak, J. (2007). Internet prevention messages: Targeting the right online behaviors. *Archives of Pediatrics and Adolescent Medicine, 161*(2), 138–45.

Ziehe, T. (1994). From living standard to life style. *Young: Nordic Journal of Youth Research, 2*(2), 2–16.

Index